English
Seventeenth-Century
Verse

VOLUME 1

EDITED WITH AN
INTRODUCTION AND NOTES BY
LOUIS L. MARTZ

W · W · NORTON & COMPANY
New York · London

First published in the Norton Library 1973
by arrangement with Doubleday & Company, Inc.

Published simultaneously in Canada by Stoddart,
a subsidiary of General Publishing Co. Ltd,
Don Mills. Ontario.

W. W. Norton & Company, Inc., also publishes *The Norton Anthology of English Literature,* edited by M. H. Abrams et al; *The Norton Anthology of Poetry,* edited by Arthur M. Eastman et al; *World Masterpieces,* edited by Maynard Mack et al; *The Norton Reader,* edited by Arthur M. Eastman et al; *The Norton Facsimile of the First Folio of Shakespeare,* prepared by Charlton Hinman; *The Norton Anthology of Modern Poetry,* edited by Richard Ellmann and Robert O'Clair; *The Norton Anthology of Short Fiction,* edited by R. V. Cassill; *The Norton Anthology of American Literature,* edited by Ronald Gottesman et al; and the *Norton Critical Editions.*

Material from *The Poems of John Donne,* edited by Sir Herbert Grierson, and *Thomas Traherne: Centuries, Poems, and Thanksgivings,* edited by H. M. Margoliouth, used by the permission of the Clarendon Press, Oxford. Portions of the Introduction have appeared previously in *Master Poems of the English Language,* edited by Oscar Williams, Trident Press, New York, 1966, and in *The Poem of the Mind, by* Louis L. Martz, Oxford University Press, New York, 1966, and are here reproduced by permission of the original publishers.

This is a revised edition of *The Meditative Poem,* published by Anchor Books in 1963 under the title *The Anchor Anthology of Seventeenth-Century Verse,* Volume I.

Library of Congress Cataloging in Publication Data

Martz, Louis Lohr, comp.
English seventeenth-century verse.

PR
1209
.M26
1973
v. 1

(The Norton library)
Reprint of the rev. ed. of The meditative poem
(first published in 1963), which was published in
1969 as v. 1 of The Anchor anthology of seventeenth-
century verse.
Includes bibliographical references.
1. English poetry—Early modern (to 1700)
I. Title.
[PR1209.M26   1973]   821'4'08   72-12674

ISBN 0-393-00675-1
W. W. Norton & Company, Inc., 500 Fifth Avenue, New York, N.Y. 10110
W. W. Norton & Company Ltd., 37 Great Russell Street, London WC1B 3NU

CONTENTS

JOHN DONNE (1572–1631)

GEORGE HERBERT (1593–1633)

FRANCIS QUARLES (1592–1644)

RICHARD CRASHAW (1612?–1649)

CONTENTS

LIST OF ILLUSTRATIONS

PREFACE

The present volume is a revision of the anthology entitled *The Meditative Poem*, which appeared in 1963 in the Anchor Seventeenth-Century Series and, clothbound, in the New York University Press Stuart Editions. In this revision many secular poems by Donne and Marvell have been added, the Introduction has been greatly expanded, the Commentary has been extensively revised, with bibliographies brought up to date, and some materials have been omitted or rearranged. The aim has been to provide an ample and representative selection from the poets concerned, in order to form part of a general collection of seventeenth-century poetry, in two volumes. Selections from Milton have not been included in either of these volumes, because it was felt that most readers would prefer to have a separate volume of Milton's poetry. Although Robert Southwell died in 1595, a brief selection from his poetry has been retained, because of his interest as a precursor of the seventeenth-century line of religious poets.

INTRODUCTION

The poetry included in the present volume has been described by a remarkable variety of terms: it has been called "metaphysical," "devotional," "meditative," "mystical," or, in terms drawn from the world of visual art, "mannerist" and "baroque." The complexity and range of the poems deserve such a wealth of terminology, and every one of these terms may be found helpful in illuminating certain aspects of the poetry. This Introduction will concentrate upon two of these terms, "metaphysical" and "meditative," in order to explore the inner working of the poetry and to suggest some of its relationships to the age in which it was composed.

I

The term "metaphysical poetry," as used by literary critics over the past fifty or sixty years, has come to include poetry, notably that of Herbert or Donne, which possesses the following characteristics. First, abrupt and dramatic openings, often with a vivid image or exclamation: "For Godsake hold your tongue, and let me love." Secondly, a colloquial, familiar manner of speech, used in the most adored and sanctified presences, whether it be the presence of a Lady, or the presence of the Lord. Thirdly, a firm argumentative construction, which makes the last line of the poem implicit in the first and gives to the whole poem a peculiar tautness and concentration. Fourthly, an introspective quality, an element of self-analysis, particularly when the poet is dealing with the nature of love, whether sacred or profane. And finally, most distinctively, the quality that Samuel Johnson described when he found in this poetry "a combination of dissimilar images, or discovery of occult resemblances in things apparently unlike." "The most heterogeneous ideas are yoked by violence together; nature and art are ransacked for illustrations, comparisons, and allusions; their learning instructs, and their subtilty surprises; but the reader commonly thinks his improvement dearly bought, and, though he sometimes admires, is seldom pleased."[1] Modern readers, more often pleased by this daring use of metaphor, have come to accept the "metaphysical conceit" as a valid and significant mode of poetical action.

Metaphysical poems tend to begin in the midst of an occasion; and the meaning of the occasion is explored and grasped through this peculiar use of metaphor. The old Renaissance conceit, the ingenious comparison, is developed into a device by which the extremes of abstraction and concreteness, the extremes of unlikeness, may be woven together into a fabric of argument unified by the prevailing force of "wit." *Wit,* in all the rich and varied senses that the word held in this era: intellect, reason, powerful mental capacity, cleverness, ingenuity, intellectual quickness, inventive and constructive ability, a talent for uttering brilliant things, the power of amusing surprise.

One way of using this metaphysical, "conceited" style may be represented by Thomas Carew's poem, "To my inconstant Mistris," a poem that shows the strong influence of Donne:

> When thou, poore excommunicate
>   From all the joyes of love, shalt see
> The full reward, and glorious fate,
>   Which my strong faith shall purchase me,
>   Then curse thine owne inconstancy.
>
> A fayrer hand than thine, shall cure
>   That heart, which thy false oathes did wound;
> And to my soul, a soul more pure
>   Than thine, shall by Loves hand be bound,
>   And both with equall glory crown'd.
>
> Then shalt thou weepe, entreat, complain
>   To Love, as I did once to thee;

---

[1] Samuel Johnson, "Life of Cowley," in *Lives of the English Poets,* 2 vols., Oxford University Press ("World's Classics"), 1952; see I, 12–16, for Johnson's account of the metaphysical poets.

> When all thy teares shall be as vain
>   As mine were then, for thou shalt bee
>   Damn'd for thy false Apostasie.

The poem is built upon an original use of the familiar conceit by which the experience of human love is rendered in religious terms. Here the faithless lady is excommunicated as an apostate from the religion of love, while her lover will receive the reward of his "strong faith" by being crowned in glory, like the saints in heaven. But, paradoxically, his faith will be demonstrated, his constancy in love rewarded, by the act of turning to another lady, with a "fayrer hand" and "a soul more pure." Inconstancy is thus met with the threat of counter-inconstancy; and all the rich religious terms take on in the end a swagger of bravado. The poem thus presents a brief episode in erotic frustration, a vignette in which the backlash of the lover's bitterness is conveyed by the immediacy of his language, by the conversational flexibility of actual speech working within a strict stanza-form.

One should, however, note that this poem contains certain elements that are not peculiar to "metaphysical poetry," but are discernible throughout the poetry of the English Renaissance. Abrupt openings and the use of conversational speech are also found, for example, in Wyatt, Sidney, and Ben Jonson, the last of whom, as a practicing dramatist, knew all about the use of colloquial idiom in poetry. The voice of living speech is everywhere in the poetry of Donne's time; it is not a distinguishing quality of metaphysical poetry, but rather a part of the whole Elizabethan heritage of song and sonnet and drama. Conversely, the quality of introspection and self-analysis, so characteristic of Donne and Herbert, plays no significant part in Carew's love-song. It seems clear that this quality does not form an indispensable part of a definition of metaphysical poetry, since certain poems by Suckling, Carew, Lovelace, Waller, and Davenant are often included under this term. Consider, for example, the following poem by Thomas Carew, "Boldnesse in Love":

> Marke how the bashfull morne, in vaine
> Courts the amorous Marigold,
> With sighing blasts, and weeping raine;
> Yet she refuses to unfold.

But when the Planet of the day,
Approacheth with his powerfull ray,
Then she spreads, then she receives
His warmer beames into her virgin leaves.
So shalt thou thrive in love, fond Boy;
If thy teares, and sighes discover
Thy griefe, thou never shalt enjoy
The just reward of a bold lover:
But when with moving accents, thou
Shalt constant faith, and service vow,
Thy *Celia* shall receive those charmes
With open eares, and with unfolded armes.

Such a poem as this is clearly not metaphysical by any definition that would include an introspective quality; this and many other poems like it have been called metaphysical because of their intricate manipulation of imagery and their employment of the argued metaphor, the metaphysical conceit. This use of metaphor is a common quality in nearly all the poems usually included under the term metaphysical poetry; it is, I think, the prime distinguishing quality of this poetry.

In many poems, though not perhaps in Carew's, this peculiar use of metaphor may be called "metaphysical" in a sense approaching the philosophical use of that word. This point has been made clear by the recent studies of Mazzeo and Bethell, which have had the effect of extending, enriching, and giving a positive emphasis to Samuel Johnson's view of the metaphysical use of imagery, through a careful examination of the theories of poetic wit developed on the Continent during the seventeenth century by critical writers such as Gracián and Tesauro.[2] From the standpoint of these

[2] See Joseph Anthony Mazzeo, "A Seventeenth-Century Theory of Metaphysical Poetry," and "Metaphysical Poetry and the Poetic of Correspondence," originally published in 1951 and 1953 and now collected in Mazzeo's *Renaissance and Seventeenth-Century Studies* (Columbia University Press, 1964), pp. 29–59. Much the same view has been independently presented by S. L. Bethell, "The Nature of Metaphysical Wit," *Northern Miscellany of Literary Criticism*, 1 (1953), 19–40; more easily available in Frank Kermode's collection, *Discussions of John Donne* (Boston, Heath, 1962), pp. 136–49.

seventeenth-century critics, the witty use of the conceit, when properly developed, had a truly metaphysical significance, for it arose from the philosophic doctrine of correspondences. As Mazzeo sums up the view: "Thus God created a world full of metaphors, analogies and conceits, and so far from being ornamentation, they are the law by which creation was effected. God wrote the book of nature in metaphor, and so it should be read. . . . The universe is a vast net of correspondences which unites the whole multiplicity of being. The poet approaches and creates his reality by a series of more or less elaborate correspondences." "God created such a world for the purpose of arousing the wonder of men, and man himself made conceits because he alone of all the creatures of God needed to seek out the variety of the universe and express it."[3] In short, the metaphysical use of metaphor derives from a belief in the existence of a universal harmony of being, based upon the Renaissance doctrine of hierarchies, wherein all created things, from angels down to minerals, are arranged in classes, with each class having its corresponding items in a class above or below. The result is that from this point of view all classes or planes of being, all links in the chain, were seen as being connected by what Tillyard calls a "network of correspondences."[4] Renaissance man lived in a universe of analogy which was for him not a fiction but a scientific fact. The primary function of the intellect of man was to discover these analogies, for they were the clues to a unity created by the greatest intellect of all, the mind of God. Thus the use of man's intellect corresponds to the divine power of creation.

One example from the poetry of Henry Vaughan may serve to illustrate the search for correspondences: "The Showre":

> 'Twas so, I saw thy birth: That drowsie Lake
> From her faint bosome breath'd thee, the disease
> Of her sick waters, and Infectious Ease.
> >> But, now at Even
> >> Too grosse for heaven,
> Thou fall'st in teares, and weep'st for thy mistake.

[3] Mazzeo, *Renaissance and Seventeenth-Century Studies*, pp. 54–56.

[4] E. M. W. Tillyard, *The Elizabethan World Picture* (New York, Macmillan, 1944), p. 77.

Ah! it is so with me; oft have I prest
Heaven with a lazie breath, but fruitles this
Peirc'd not; Love only can with quick accesse
    Unlock the way,
    When all else stray
The smoke, and Exhalations of the breast.

Yet, if as thou doest melt, and with thy traine
Of drops make soft the Earth, my eyes could weepe
O're my hard heart, that's bound up, and asleepe,
    Perhaps at last
    (Some such showres past,)
My God would give a Sun-shine after raine.

Vaughan has trained himself to see analogies between himself and the outer universe. He has trained himself to find the moral and spiritual application of outer images to his inner being. "I see the use," he cries in another poem, as he watches a raging storm; that is, he sees the correspondence between the storm and his own turbulent state of mind. In such poems the chosen image is thoroughly explored to bear out the principle of the network of analogies. Such poems then are deservedly called metaphysical through their use of metaphor: they seek through images drawn from the *many* to discover the *One*. By unifying man's inner being, such a quest becomes metaphysical in the true and basic sense of the word "metaphysics": "That branch of speculative inquiry which treats of the first principles of things, including such concepts as being, substance, essence, time, space, cause, identity, etc.; theoretical philosophy as the ultimate science of Being and Knowing" (OED).

This is the sense in which John Dryden used the word when he wrote that Donne "affects the metaphysics" (that is to say, inclines toward the metaphysics) "not only in his satires, but in his amorous verses, where nature only should reign; and perplexes the minds of the fair sex with nice speculations of philosophy, when he should engage their hearts, and entertain them with the softnesses of love."[5] Dryden there expresses the difference between a social poet, who

[5] *Essays of John Dryden,* ed. W. P. Ker, 2 vols. (Oxford, Clarendon Press, 1926), II, 19.

sees nature in terms of the human community,[6] and the metaphysical poet, who sees nature as the key to a transcendent truth alive in the entire universe. Samuel Johnson, evidently picking up the term metaphysical from Dryden, then went on to give his own classic definition of the method of the metaphysical poets: "Their attempts were always analytick; they broke every image into fragments: and could no more represent, by their slender conceits and laboured particularities, the prospects of nature, or the scenes of life, than he, who dissects a sun-beam with a prism, can exhibit the wide effulgence of a summer noon." But the wide effulgence of a summer noon had for Donne and Herbert and Vaughan its major interest as a field of imagery where analytic attempts could discover some hint of a higher principle, the principle of universal analogy, by which all created things are bound together in the mind of God, and secondarily, within the mind of man.

Poetry is metaphysical, then, when it seeks by complex analogies to find a central principle of being, within the bounds of a given situation. That situation may involve the relationship between a man and a woman, at various levels of seriousness, or it may involve the relationship between man and the Deity. One may find a metaphysical correspondence presented by Richard Lovelace in his poem, "Gratiana dauncing and singing":

> See! with what constant Motion
> Even, and glorious, as the Sunne,
>   Gratiana steers that Noble Frame,
> Soft as her breast, sweet as her voyce
> That gave each winding Law and poyze,
>   And swifter than the wings of Fame.
>
> She beat the happy Pavement
> By such a Starre made Firmament,
>   Which now no more the Roofe envies;
> But swells up high with Atlas ev'n,
> Bearing the brighter, nobler Heav'n,
>   And in her, all the Deities.

[6] For the tradition of social poetry in the seventeenth century, see Sylvester's Introduction to Volume 2 of this collection.

Different as they are, Lovelace and Vaughan are both using the universe of correspondences to seek their central principle of being, whether it lies in a Lady or in God. The basic quality of metaphysical poetry, then, is that long ago described by James Smith in an essay too often neglected, where he argues that the central impulse of such poetry "is given by an overwhelming concern with metaphysical problems; with problems either deriving from, or closely resembling in the nature of their difficulty, the problem of the Many and the One."[7]

II

In his interesting anthology, *European Metaphysical Poetry,* Frank Warnke has made an important distinction between the terms meditative and metaphysical. He suggests that "the meditation is a genre—one which recurs at intervals in our history and which, in the sixteenth and seventeenth centuries, assumed a special importance." "Metaphysical poetry is a particular style, an historically limited manner of writing in various genres. At the same time, one must recognize the important relationship which this genre and this style bear to one another."[8] I would agree with Warnke that the roots of this relationship lie in the spirit of the age; meditative action and the metaphysical style reflect a kindred response to the same basic conditions.

The metaphysical style of writing arose, it seems, in response to a widespread reaction against the efflorescent, expansive, highly melodious mode of the earlier Renaissance, as found in Edmund Spenser; it arose also, I believe, in response to a widespread feeling that the manifold expansions of human outlook were rapidly moving out of control: expansions through recovery of the classics, through access to the Bible in vernacular languages, through a new emphasis upon the early fathers of the Church, through the fierce religious controversies that rocked the age, through the advance of science in

[7] James Smith, "On Metaphysical Poetry," in *Determinations,* ed. F. R. Leavis (London, Chatto, 1934), p. 24.

[8] *European Metaphysical Poetry,* tr. and ed. by Frank J. Warnke (Yale University Press, 1961), p. 56, n. 72.

all areas, and through the vigorous exploration of the earth by seamen, traders, and conquistadors. As a result, in the latter part of the sixteenth century poetry showed a tendency to coalesce and concentrate its powers toward the sharp illumination and control of carefully selected moments in experience.

The widespread practice of methodical religious meditation during the same era may be traced, I believe, to the same causes: religious meditation was a way of finding order within the self, a way of controlling the chaos of worldly experience, by concentrating the mind's powers upon a single image, event, or problem. Since the process of meditation, as practiced in this era, was an intensely imaginative action of the mind, it inevitably bears a close relationship to the writing of poetry. The relationship is shown by the poem's own internal action, as the mind engages in acts of interior dramatization. The speaker accuses himself; he talks to God within the self; he approaches the love of God through memory, understanding, and will; he sees, hears, smells, tastes, touches by imagination the scenes of Christ's life as they are represented on a mental stage. Essentially, the meditative action consists of an interior drama, in which a man projects a self upon an inner stage, and there comes to know that self in the light of a divine presence.

To understand the "art of meditation" as it was taught and practiced in Donne's time, one may turn to the compact treatise printed as an appendix in this volume: "The Practical Methode of Meditation," written by the Jesuit Edward Dawson for an English audience, and published on the Continent in 1614.[9] Dawson's treatise, written at the peak of the period's intense concern with the "method" of meditation, sums up the principles that had gradually come to dominate the meditative life of the Continent, primarily through the influence of the *Spiritual Exercises* of Ignatius Loyola. Dawson's handbook is in fact a paraphrase of the *Spiritual Exercises,* with adaptations and extensions prompted, as he says, by "approved Authors and experience." He gives the essence of the advice for meditation that was being offered by spiritual counselors throughout Europe, as well as by the numerous underground priests in England.

[9] Unless otherwise noted, all the subsequent quotations concerning the practice of meditation are taken from this treatise.

At the same time this advice was being offered in dozens of popular treatises on meditation that were circulating in thousands of copies throughout Europe, and in England as well.

Dawson shows by his blunt, simple, "practical" manner the way in which the art of meditation might become part of the everyday life of everyman. The matter-of-fact tone of the treatise, indeed, helps to convey its central and pervasive assumptions: that man, whether he will or not, lives in the intimate presence of God, and that his first duty in life is to cultivate an awareness of that presence. Thus arises the whole elaborate ceremony of meditation: the careful preparation of materials the night before; the "practice of the presence of God," as it was called, before actual meditation; the preparatory prayers; the preludes; the deliberate, orderly operation of the "three powers of the soul"—memory, understanding, will; and the conclusion in "some affectionate speach" or colloquy with God or the saints, in which "wee may talke with God as a servant with his Maister, as a sonne with his Father, as one friend with another, as a spouse with her beloved bridgrome, or as a guilty prisoner with his Judge, or in any other manner which the holy Ghost shall teach us." The aim of meditation is to apprehend the reality and the meaning of the presence of God with every faculty at man's command. The body must first learn its proper behavior during the ceremony: hence we have detailed advice on whether to kneel, or walk, or sit, or stand. The five senses must learn how to bend their best efforts toward this end: hence the elaborately detailed explanation of the Jesuit "application of the senses" to the art of meditation. Everyday life must come to play its part, for the meditative man must feel that the presence of God is here, now, on his own hearth, in his own stable, and in the deep center of the mind: thus "we may help our selves much to the framing of spirituall conceites [thoughts], if we apply unto our matter familiar similitudes, drawne from our ordinary actions, and this as well in historicall, as spirituall meditations." That is to say, analogies from the world of daily actions must be brought to bear upon the history of the life of Christ, as well as upon such matters as the problem of sin and the excellence of the virtues.

Among all the varied ways of using the senses and physical life in meditation, the most important, most effective, and most famous is the prelude known as the "composition of place." This brilliant Ignatian invention, to which the Jesuit *Exercises* owe a large part of their power, is given its full and proper emphasis by Dawson: "for on the well making of this *Preludium* depends both the understanding of the mystery, and attention in our meditation." Whatever the subject may be, the imagination, the image-making power of man, must endeavor to represent it "so lively, as though we saw [it] indeed, with our corporall eyes." For historical matters, such as events in the life of Christ or a saint, we must visualize the scene in the most vivid and exact detail, "by imagining our selves to be really present at those places." In treating spiritual subjects we must gain the same end by creating "some similitude, answerable to the matter." Thus, for the Last Things, Death, Judgment, Hell, and Heaven, the similitude may be created by imagining the scene in detail, by creating, for example, a likeness of one's self on the deathbed, "forsaken of the Physitians, compassed about with our weeping friends, and expecting our last agony." But the similitude may also be much more figurative: the word "similitude," in seventeenth-century usage, could refer to any kind of parable, allegory, simile, or metaphor. Dawson, discussing the preparation for meditation, suggests that we should "begin to take some tast of our meditation" before the actual performance begins, by stirring up the "affections," the emotions, appropriate to each meditation: "Which we may performe more easily," he adds, "yf we keep in our mind some similitude answering to the affection we would have." And later he suggests that, among several dramatic ways of strengthening these affections, we may sometimes proceed by "faygning [imagining] the very vertues in some venerable shape bewayling their neglect." Thus too he notes that, in the opening similitude for the meditation on sins, "we may imagine our soule to be cast out of Paradise, and to be held prisoner in this body of ours, fettered with the chaines of disordinate Passions, and affections, and clogged with the burden of our owne flesh." In short, this insistence upon "seeing the place" and upon the frequent use of "similitudes" in meditation invites every man to use his image-making faculty with the utmost vigor, in order to ensure a concrete, dramatic setting within which the meditative action may develop. Upon the inward stage of that scene or similitude, the memory, the understanding, and the will may then proceed to explore and understand and feel the proper role of the self in relation to the divine omnipotence and charity. Thus heaven and earth are brought together in the mind; and human action is placed in a responsive, intimate relation with the supernatural.

An important qualification, however, needs to be added to the advice of Dawson. In the Ignatian way, he insists that every meditation must begin with some vivid "composition," but we should not be led to expect that every meditative poem will begin with some vivid scene or symbol. Many do so, directly or implicitly, with the speaker present, for example, at some scene in the life of Christ; but many meditative poems also begin simply with a brief, terse statement of the problem or theme to be explored:

> Why are wee by all creatures waited on?

> Why do I languish thus, drooping and dull . . .

> Come, come, what doe I here?

> I Sing the *Name* which none can say,
> But touch't with an interiour *Ray,*
> The *Name* of our *New Peace,* our *Good,*
> Our *Blisse,* and supernaturall *Blood,*
> The *Name* of all our Lives, and Loves.

Such openings, though not mentioned by Dawson, are advised by other writers for abstract topics, particularly by St. François de Sales, who notes, "It is true that we may use some similitude or comparison to assist us in the consideration of these subjects," but he fears that the making of "such devices" may prove burdensome, and thus for the meditation of "invisible things" he advises one to begin with "a simple proposal" of the theme.[10] A meditative poem, then, will tend to open in any one of three ways: (1) with a vivid participation in some scene in the life of Christ or a saint; (2) with a "similitude, answerable to the matter," that is, with some imaginary setting or

---

[10] See St. Francis de Sales, *Introduction to the Devout Life* (1609), tr. and ed. by John K. Ryan (Image Books, 1955), pp. 83–84. The whole treatise, especially the second part, is of the utmost interest to anyone concerned with studying the details of meditative practice in this era.

metaphorical representation; (3) with a "simple proposal" of the issue to be considered.

With the event or theme thus firmly presented within a "recollected" mind fully aware of the presence of God, the meditative action of the three powers of the soul begins to develop each "point" (usually three) into which the long process of meditation (usually lasting an hour) has been divided during the period of preparation. It is evident from Dawson's account that the operation of the memory is inseparable from and continuous with the opening composition or proposal; for the role of memory is to set forth the subject with all its necessary "persons, wordes, and workes." The understanding then proceeds to analyze ("discourse" upon) the meaning of the topic, in relation to the individual self, until gradually the will takes fire and the appropriate personal affections arise. It is clear too from Dawson's account that these affections of the will inevitably lead into the colloquy, where the speaker utters his fears and hopes, his sorrows and joys, in "affectionate speach" before God. The full process of meditation always ends with such a colloquy, but, as Dawson points out, "We may make such manner of speaches in other places of our meditation, and it will be best, and almost needfull so to do."

At the same time, the interior drama will tend to have a firm construction, for the process of meditation, in treating each "point," will tend to display a threefold movement, according with the action of that interior trinity, memory, understanding, and will. Now and then we may find this threefold process echoed or epitomized within the borders of a short poem; or we may find the process suggested at length in a long poem such as Southwell's "Saint Peters Complaint" or Crashaw's "On the name of Jesus"; or we may find it suggested by a sequence of short poems, as in the poems of Traherne in the Dobell manuscript.[11] But what one should expect to find, more often, is some part of the whole meditative action, set down as particularly memorable, perhaps in accordance with the kind of self-examination advised by Dawson under the heading: "What is to be done after Meditation." One is urged here to scrutinize carefully the

[11] See John Malcolm Wallace, "Thomas Traherne and the Structure of Meditation," *A Journal of English Literary History*, 25 (1958), 79–89.

manner in which one has performed every part of the meditative process, from preparation through colloquy; to examine closely the distractions, consolations, or desolations that one may have experienced; and finally, to "note in some little booke those thinges which have passed in our Meditation, or some part of them, if we think them worth the paynes." Meditative poems present such memorable moments of self-knowledge, affections of sorrow and love, colloquies with the divine presence, recollected and preserved through the aid of the kindred art of poetry.

Meditation points toward poetry in its use of images, in its technique of arousing the passionate affections of the will, in its suggestion that the ultimate reach of meditation is found in the advice of Paul to the Ephesians: "Be filled with the Spirit; speaking to yourselves in psalms and hymns and spiritual songs, singing and making melody in your heart to the Lord." A meditative poem, then, represents the convergence of two arts upon a single object: in English poetry of the late Renaissance the art of meditation entered into and transformed its kindred art of poetry. To express its highest reaches, the art of meditation drew upon all the poetical resources available in the culture of its day. Southwell, writing in an era dominated by the uninspired verse of the poetical miscellanies—with their heavy-footed, alliterative style and their doggerel ballad-stanzas—could use his meditative techniques, along with his knowledge of Italian poetry, to impart a new and startling vigor even to a moribund poetical mode. Alabaster, writing near the end of the 1590's, at the close of the great era of English sonneteering, could use his meditative art to transform the Elizabethan sonnet. Donne, knowing all the devices of current poetry—whether in satire, love song, sonnet, Ovidian elegy, funeral elegy, courtly compliment, or religious hymn—attained many of his greatest creations in those poems where his mastery of the meditative art could add a new dimension to these modes of poetic art. Herbert, master of music, adept in every form of Elizabethan song or sonnet, could turn all these varied forms into a temple of praise for his Master's presence. And Crashaw, drawn to the extravagant modes of the Continental baroque, could nevertheless, at his best, tame and control his extravaganzas by the firm structure of a meditation.

To illustrate this convergence of the arts, let us look closely at one great poem that may be said to represent an epitome of the art of meditation, as Dawson has explained the process. It is Donne's "Hymn to God my God, in my sicknesse," written in 1623 (or perhaps in 1631), when Donne was in his fifties: it is thus a poem that may be regarded as the culmination of a lifetime's practice in the arts of poetry and meditation.

Its opening stanza recalls the careful preparation that preceded meditation: preparation in which the end and aim of the process was fully plotted and foreseen, and in which the speaker placed himself securely in the presence of God:

> Since I am comming to that Holy roome,
>> Where, with thy quire of Saints for evermore,
> I shall be made thy Musique; As I come
>> I tune the Instrument here at the dore,
> And what I must doe then, thinke here before.

The emphasis falls upon the deliberate process of *thinking:* the meditation will proceed by rational, articulated stages. First comes the "composition of place," in which the speaker, lying upon what he believes will be his deathbed, works out a careful "similitude" that will enable him to understand himself:

> Whilst my Physitians by their love are growne
>> Cosmographers, and I their Mapp, who lie
> Flat on this bed, that by them may be showne
>> That this is my Southwest discoverie
>> *Per fretum febris,* by these streights to die . . .

The doctors are charting forth upon his outstretched body a "discoverie" such as Magellan made; but the "streights" through which this passage will be made are the straits, the difficulties and pains, of death: *Per fretum febris,* "through the straits of fever." The witty play on words shows a remarkable equanimity, that striking ability of Donne to view his own situation from a distance, to hold his own body and soul off at arm's length and study his situation in objective detail, as the art of meditation encouraged one to do.

So Donne sees that he is now upon his westward passage, toward sundown, but as he questions himself, he finds joy in the prospect, for he knows that a flat map is only an illusory diagram. At the far edge, West becomes East, sundown becomes sunrise:

> I joy, that in these straits, I see my West;
>   For, though theire currants yeeld returne to none,
> What shall my West hurt me? As West and East
>   In all flatt Maps (and I am one) are one,
>   So death doth touch the Resurrection.

Donne's questioning in the middle stanzas of the poem indicates a process of analysis bent upon understanding the goal of his passage, and indeed the very questions imply the goal:

> Is the Pacifique Sea my home? Or are
>   The Easterne riches? Is *Jerusalem?*
> *Anyan,* and *Magellan,* and *Gibraltare,*
>   All streights, and none but streights, are wayes to them,
>   Whether where *Japhet* dwelt, or *Cham,* or *Sem.*

The traveler to the peaceful ocean, or to the wealth of the Orient, or to that holy city whose name means "Vision of Peace," may move through the "Straits of Anyan" (supposed to separate Asia and America), or the Straits of Magellan, or the Straits of Gibraltar. But however one goes, the voyage is full of pain and difficulty. And this is true whatever regions of the earth he may sail from or sail between, "Whether where *Japhet* dwelt, or *Cham,* or *Sem.*" In thus recalling the ancient division of the earth into the inheritance given to the three sons of Noah, Donne suggests the universality and the inevitability of those straits which face every man who seeks his ultimate home.

In the geography of Donne's present moment there is only one goal, the heavenly Paradise made possible by Calvary, redemption by the sacrifice of Christ. In the outer world this singleness of aim is suggested by the fact that the Paradise of Eden (usually set in Mesopotamia) and Calvary have both been located in the same region of the earth, the Near East. In the same way Adam and Christ now meet in the sick man on his bed. The sweat of his fever fulfills the curse laid upon the first Adam, but the blood of Christ will, the speaker hopes, redeem his soul:

> We thinke that *Paradise* and *Calvarie,*
> *Christs* Crosse, and *Adams* tree, stood in one place;
> Looke Lord, and finde both *Adams* met in me;
> As the first *Adams* sweat surrounds my face,
> May the last *Adams* blood my soule embrace.

He prays in familiar colloquy that, for his funeral shroud, he may be wrapped in the blood of Christ, a royal garment of purple, and that thus he may be granted the Crown of Glory in Heaven. So the poem ends with a recapitulation of the central paradox: death is the passage to life, West and East are one, flatness leads to rising:

> So, in his purple wrapp'd receive mee Lord,
> By these his thornes give me his other Crowne;
> And as to others soules I preach'd thy word,
> Be this my Text, my Sermon to mine owne,
> Therfore that he may raise the Lord throws down.

The closing colloquy reminds us that the whole poem has been spoken in the presence of God: it is all a testimony of faith presented as a hymn of gratitude to the Creator.

The poem, then, reveals in miniature all the essential components of a full religious meditation: preparation, composition, discourse (in the old sense of analytic reasoning), and colloquy; or, to use other terms of the time, memory, understanding, and will, the three powers of the soul which are unified in the process of meditation, forming an interior trinity that represents an image, although defaced, of the greater Trinity. The poem thus becomes the ultimate tuning of that "Instrument" which was John Donne himself: poet, theologian, voyager, preacher, meditative man. If one wonders to find such wit and ingenuity manifested even on the deathbed, the answer is clear: here is the instrument that God has made, and at the last, it is proper that the unique timbre and tone of the instrument should be heard.

IV

At the same time, this meditative poem is also a work in the metaphysical style, since it displays the characteristic use of the conceit, as described by Dame Helen Gardner: "In a metaphysical poem the conceits are instruments of definition in an argument or instruments to persuade."[12] In secular love-poetry the conceits form part of an argument or a process of persuasion addressed to a lady. In religious poetry the conceits are used by a voice that is speaking inwardly, to the self, or to God, or to the self in the presence of God, for the purpose of defining the relation of the self to God, persuading the self to accept and love that relationship and its creator, or persuading God to accept that human self, with all its faults.

There is thus a natural affinity between the meditative action and the metaphysical style, an affinity that may be seen quite clearly in a sonnet written, it seems, about ten years before John Donne's Holy Sonnets: one of William Alabaster's poems dealing with "the ensignes of Christes Crucifyinge." The sonnet begins with a direct address to the symbols of the Crucifixion, which the speaker appears to have directly before his eyes; crying out to them, fully aware of the paradoxes that they represent, he proposes the question of his own proper response:

> O sweete and bitter monuments of paine,
> bitter to Christ who all the paine endured,
> butt sweete to mee, whose Death my life procured,
> how shall I full express such loss, such gaine?

Turning to consider the faculties that lie within himself, his tongue, his eyes, his soul, he proceeds to explain to himself how these may be led toward their proper end, by writing in the book of his soul the record of his sin:

> My tonge shall bee my penne, mine eyes shall raine
> teares for my inke, the place where I was cured
> shall bee my booke, where haveing all abjured

[12] The Metaphysical Poets, ed. Helen Gardner, Penguin (rev. ed., 1966), p. 21.

> and calling heavens to record in that plaine,
> thus plainely will I write, noe sinne like mine;

And finally, holding fast with tenacious logic to his previous images, he closes in colloquy with the Lord, whose presence has been implicit throughout:

> when I have done, doe thou, Jesue divine,
> take upp the tarte spunge of thy passione
> and blott itt forth: then bee thy spiritt the Quill,
> thy bloode the Inke, and with compassione
> write thus uppon my soule: thy Jesue still.

Abrupt opening, condensed and compact phrasing, with touches of colloquial speech, witty development of central conceits, coalescing the abstract and the concrete, logic, paradox—all the qualities of the European metaphysical style are there—yet something more creates the poem's modest success. The speaker has learned how to make himself present before the "monuments" of the Passion, how to concentrate memory, understanding, and will upon these symbols of Christ's suffering, how to develop the personal meaning of the Passion through the use of appropriate similitudes, how to drive home the meaning for the self in affectionate colloquy with God. The art of meditation has provided the techniques by which Alabaster could create a brief interior drama. It is, I believe, in these techniques of self-dramatization that we find the peculiar contribution of the art of meditation to poetry. They are techniques which find a most congenial alliance with the metaphysical style, but which may also combine with a variety of other styles: early Elizabethan, Jonsonian, baroque, or Miltonic.

This effort to distinguish between the meditative and the metaphysical may help to solve the problem of Donne's relation to later poets of the seventeenth century. Specific debts to Donne are obvious in some of the secular poetry of the period, such as Carew's, but in the religious poetry of Herbert, Crashaw, or Vaughan, where one somehow feels a more essential kinship, such debts are much more elusive, indeed almost nonexistent. To some it has seemed possible to argue that in general Herbert descends from Donne, and that since Herbert influenced Crashaw and Vaughan, the two latter poets are thus at least the grandsons of Donne. But recent studies have shown Herbert's deep-rooted independence of Donne: his use of medieval forms and symbols, his mastery of all varieties of Elizabethan poetry and song, his mastery of the meditative techniques. What Herbert passed on to Vaughan was his own great and original creation, which Vaughan proceeded to use in his own highly original way, combining Herbert's example with the example of the Sons of Ben Jonson, to whose line he displays his allegiance in his early secular poems. The few echoes of Donne that we meet in Vaughan's first volume (1646) are overwhelmed by his dominant experiments in the Jonsonian mode of couplet-rhetoric, as the opening poem of the volume clearly testifies, a poem addressed to a certain friend, R.W.:

> When we are dead, and now, no more
> Our harmles mirth, our wit, and score
> Distracts the Towne; when all is spent
> That the base niggard world hath lent
> Thy purse, or mine; when the loath'd noise
> Of Drawers, Prentises, and boyes
> Hath left us, and the clam'rous barre
> Items no pints i'th'Moone, or Starre . . .
> When all these Mulcts are paid, and I
> From thee, deare wit, must part, and dye;
> Wee'le beg the world would be so kinde,
> To give's one grave, as wee'de one minde;
> There (as the wiser few suspect,
> That spirits after death affect)
> Our soules shall meet, and thence will they
> (Freed from the tyranny of clay)
> With equall wings, and ancient love
> Into the Elysian fields remove,
> Where in those blessed walkes they'le find,
> More of thy Genius, and my mind:
> First, in the shade of his owne bayes,
> Great *BEN* they'le see, whose sacred Layes,
> The learned Ghosts admire, and throng,
> To catch the subject of his Song.

Then *Randolph* in those holy Meades,
His Lovers, and *Amyntas* reads,[13]
Whilst his Nightingall close by,
Sings his, and her owne Elegie;
From thence dismiss'd by subtill roades,
Through airie paths, and sad aboads;
They'le come into the drowsie fields
Of Lethe, which such vertue yeelds,
That (if what Poets sing be true)
The streames all sorrow can subdue.

This steady, terse, and easy handling of the tetrameter couplet
is a hallmark of the Jonsonian mode, and it is a form into which
many of Vaughan's finest poems in *Silex Scintillans* are cast. Yet po-
ems in the tetrameter couplet are not at all characteristic of Donne
or Herbert. It is worth noting, too, in passing, that this Jonsonian
use of the tetrameter couplet is found in Crashaw's poems on St.
Teresa (along with variations into the pentameter); and it is also
one of Andrew Marvell's favorite forms. This does not mean that we
should substitute Jonson for Donne as the prime poetical model for
these writers; in fact, the influence of Jonson and that of Donne are
almost inseparably intermingled throughout the seventeenth cen-
tury, and particularly in Marvell, the most eclectic of poets. But the
appearance of a Jonsonian style in these poets will provide striking
evidence of the way in which the art of meditation could and did
combine with any available mode in poetry.

v

At the same time, in dealing with Vaughan, Marvell, or Traherne,
one should remember that the strict Ignatian method of meditation,
as outlined by Dawson, was itself an outgrowth of ancient ways of
meditation that had been developing since the days of Augustine,
and earlier. In fact, the Augustinian mode of meditation was still

---

[13] Thomas Randolph (1605–1635), a follower of Ben Jonson; his pastoral
drama *Amyntas* was published in 1638; the next two lines refer to Randolph's
poem "On the Death of a Nightingale." See the selection from Randolph in
Volume 2 of this collection.

highly influential in the seventeenth century, through the wide-spread circulation of the works of Augustine and his followers. The Augustinian way of meditation was less formal and less logical in its procedures, since it consisted in a roving quest for the traces, the vestiges of God, first in external nature and then, most importantly, within the mind of man. As Augustine explains the quest in the tenth book of his *Confessions* (chapters 6 through 27), it consists of a search for the image of God within the mind of man, an image defaced by sin, but nevertheless restored in its essential powers through the sacrifice of Christ. It is man's duty, according to Augustinian thought, to advance as far as he can toward a renewal of this image, with the help of divine grace.

A superb account of the entire process is given in Henry Vaughan's poem, "Vanity of Spirit." Here the meditative man has apparently been studying in his room, which has come to seem oppressive to him, and so the poem begins:

> Quite spent with thoughts I left my Cell, and lay
> Where a shrill spring tun'd to the early day.

In the presence of this active, vital aspect of nature the speaker begins his quest for the divine light:

> I beg'd here long, and gron'd to know
> Who gave the Clouds so brave a bow,
> Who bent the spheres, and circled in
> Corruption with this glorious Ring,
> What is his name, and how I might
> Descry some part of his great light.

First he turns to external nature in the effort to find the vestiges of divinity:

> I summon'd nature: peirc'd through all her store,
> Broke up some seales, which none had touch'd before,
>   Her wombe, her bosome, and her head
>   Where all her secrets lay a bed
>   I rifled quite, and having past
>   Through all the Creatures, came at last
>   To search my selfe, where I did find
>   Traces, and sounds of a strange kind.

The word "traces" is simply a translation of the Augustinian term *vestigia*, vestiges of divinity. As he finds those traces of the divine within himself, he discovers that they are in fact closely related to external nature, as he goes on to say: "Here of this mighty spring, I found some drills," that is, some trickles or small streams of the spring with which the poem has opened. The same forces appear to be working within himself as are at work in outer nature, with an implication perhaps that one "mighty spring" lies behind all:

> Here of this mighty spring, I found some drills,
> With Ecchoes beaten from th' eternall hills;
>> Weake beames, and fires flash'd to my sight,
>> Like a young East, or Moone-shine night,
>> Wich shew'd me in a nook cast by
>> A peece of much antiquity,
>> With Hyerogliphicks quite dismembred,
>> And broken letters scarce remembred.

This is a symbol of the image of God within man, the defaced image which the speaker wishes to restore:

> I tooke them up, and (much Joy'd,) went about
> T' unite those peeces, hoping to find out
>> The mystery; but this neer done,
>> That little light I had was gone:
>> It griev'd me much. At last, said I,
>> *Since in these veyls my Ecclips'd Eye*
>> *May not approach thee, (for at night*
>> *Who can have commerce with the light?)*
>> *I'le disapparell, and to buy*
>> *But one half glaunce, most gladly dye.*

One should note that the mysterious, roving action represented in this poem is an action different from the method of meditation set forth by Dawson's treatise. This Ignatian method shows the powerful impact of medieval thought, with its emphasis upon analysis by the human understanding, and also upon the principle central to the philosophy of Thomas Aquinas: that all human knowledge must be drawn from sensory experience. The method of meditation set forth by Dawson is, as we have seen, a precise, carefully designed process, moving from the composition of place into the threefold movement of the memory, understanding, and will. But in what may be called the Augustinian mode of meditation, we can find no exact method; it consists rather of a groping movement into areas of the mind that lie beyond the knowledge gained through the senses, areas which contain a knowledge deriving from the vestiges of the image of God, which has never been totally destroyed in man. This is the view of the soul's interior action represented in a passage of Andrew Marvell's "On a Drop of Dew," where the word "recollecting" is used in its basic sense, to indicate an act of "collecting together again" the divine light within the mind or soul of man:

> So the Soul, that Drop, that Ray
> Of the clear Fountain of Eternal Day,
> Could it within the humane flow'r be seen,
>   Remembring still its former height,
>   Shuns the sweat leaves and blossoms green;
>   And, recollecting its own Light,
> Does, in its pure and circling thoughts, express
> The greater Heaven in an Heaven less.

Such a view of the sources of human knowledge is of course strongly influenced by platonic and neoplatonic thought, which enjoyed a powerful revival during the Renaissance, first among the platonists of Florence, and later among the group of seventeenth-century English philosophers known as the Cambridge Platonists. Vaughan and Traherne were both deeply influenced by these currents of platonism, including the strange, occult variant of neoplatonism associated with alchemy and known as the "Hermetic Philosophy," from its attribution to the mythical writer, Hermes Trismegistus. As the last selection in this volume we have included some passages from the prose meditations of Traherne which illustrate these tendencies toward Christian platonism that flourished in England in the middle of the seventeenth century.

Thus the ways in which a meditative action may be found in poetry are manifold: the meditative art is as changing, resourceful, and elusive as the mind in which the meditation is enacted. Now and then, as in the case of Donne's Hymn, one may say that the poem is a meditation: Donne himself uses the term to describe his fifteenth Holy Sonnet:

> Wilt thou love God, as he thee! then digest,
> My Soule, this wholsome meditation . . .

But, for the most part, it is better to speak of meditative poems, that is to say, poems in which some aspects of the meditative art may be discerned. From this standpoint, a poem such as Marvell's "Dialogue, between the Resolved Soul, and Created Pleasure" might be called meditative, since it enacts an interior drama; but it is not, of course, a meditation of the kind that Dawson describes. One may also, in poets such as Donne or Marvell, find some reflection of meditative habits in poems that are secular ("The Garden") or in poems that are cleverly profane ("The Funerall"). If, as Wallace Stevens suggests, meditation is the mind's "essential exercise," one would expect the results to ramify throughout a poet's career.

Finally, whatever terms we may prefer to use in discussing this poetry, it is wise to remember the advice of Kenneth Burke: "As, in musical theory, one chord is capable of various analyses, so in literature the appeal of one event may be explained by various principles. The important thing is not to confine the explanation to *one* principle, but to formulate sufficient principles to make an explanation possible."[14]

LOUIS L. MARTZ

Saybrook College
Yale University

[14] Kenneth Burke, *Counter-Statement,* 2nd ed. (Phoenix Books, 1957), p. 129.

ACKNOWLEDGMENTS

I wish to thank Mr. Robert Hayes, Mrs. Susan Holahan, and Mrs. Sara VandenBerg for valuable assistance in the preparation of some parts of this volume, and also to thank Professor Max Patrick, Mr. Eugene Eoyang, Mr. Carl Morse, Miss Susan Burchardt, and Miss Susanna Lesan for valuable advice during the planning of the volume and its preparation for the press. I am indebted to the Pierpont Morgan Library for providing a photograph of the title page of Herbert's *Temple;* to the Bodleian Library for providing photographs of the original engravings for Quarles's *Emblemes;* and to the Yale University Library (especially to Miss Marjorie Wynne) for providing photographs for the other illustrations in this volume.

ROBERT SOUTHWELL
1561–1595

The Author to his loving Cosen

Poets by abusing their talent, and making the follies and fayninges
of love, the customary subject of their base endevours, have so dis-
credited this facultie, that a Poet, a Lover, and a Liar, are by many
reckoned but three wordes of one signification. But the vanity of
men, cannot counterpoyse the authority of God, who delivering
many partes of Scripture in verse, and by his Apostle willing us to
exercise our devotion in Himnes and Spirituall Sonnets,[1] warrant-
eth the Arte to bee good, and the use allowable. And therefore not
onely among the Heathens, whose Gods were chiefely canonized
by their Poets, and their Painim Divinitie Oracled in verse: But
even in the Old and New Testament it hath bene used by men of
greatest Pietie, in matters of most devotion. Christ himselfe by mak-
ing a Himne,[2] the conclusion of his last Supper, and the Prologue
to the first Pageant of his Passion, gave his Spouse a methode to
immitate, as in the office of the Church it appeareth, and all men a
paterne to know the true use of this measured and footed stile. But
the Divell as hee affecteth Deitie, and seeketh to have all the com-
plements of Divine honor applied to his service, so hath he among
the rest possessed also most Poets with his idle fansies. For in lieu
of solemne and devout matter, to which in duety they owe their
abilities, they now busy themselves in expressing such passions, as
onely serve for testimonies to how unwoorthy affections[3] they have
wedded their wils. And because the best course to let them see the
errour of their workes, is to weave a new webbe in their owne loome;
I have heere layd a few course threds together, to invite some skill-
fuller wits to goe forward in the same, or to begin some finer peece,
wherein it may be seene, how well verse and vertue sute together.
Blame me not (good Cosen) though I send you a blamewoorthy
present, in which the most that can commend it, is the good will of
the writer, neither Arte nor invention, giving it any credite. If in

THE AUTHOR TO HIS LOVING COSEN.

[1] See Ephesians 5:19; Colossians 3:16.

[2] See Matthew 26:30; Mark 14:26 (cf. Alabaster, Sonnet 2).

[3] emotions, inclinations.

mee this be a fault, you cannot be faultlesse that did importune mee to committe it, and therefore you must beare parte of the pennance, when it shall please sharpe censures to impose it. In the meane time with many good wishes I send you these few ditties,[4] add you the Tunes, and let the Meane,[5] I pray you, be still a part in all your Musicke.

Looke home

Retyred thoughts enjoy their owne delights,
As beawtie doth in selfe beholding eye:
Mans mind a myrrour is of heavenly sights,
A breefe wherein all marvailes summed lye.
Of fayrest formes, and sweetest shapes the store,   5
Most gracefull all, yet thought may grace them more.

The mind a creature is, yet can create,
To natures paterns adding higher skill:
Of finest workes wit better could the state,
If force of wit had equall power of will.   10
Devise of man in working hath no end,
What thought can thinke an other thought can mend.

Mans soule of endles beauties image is,
Drawne by the worke of endlesse skill and might:
This skilfull might gave many sparkes of blisse,   15
And to discerne this blisse a native light.
To frame Gods image as his worthes requirde:
His might, his skill, his word, and will conspirde.

[4] words to be set to music.

[5] a middle part in any musical composition; also, moderation, "the golden mean."

LOOKE HOME.

9, 10 *wit:* intellect, mental capacity.

All that he had his image should present,
All that it should present he could afford: 20
To that he could afford his will was bent,
His will was followed with performing word.
Let this suffice, by this conceive the rest
He should, he could, he would he did the best.

At home in Heaven

Faire soule, how long shall veyles thy graces shroud?
    How long shall this exile with-hold thy right,
When will thy sunne disperse this mortall cloud?
    And give thy gloryes scope to blaze their light?
O that a Starre more fit for Angels eyes,   5
Should pyne in earth, not shine above the skyes.

Thy ghostly beautie offred force to God,
    It cheyn'd him in the lynckes of tender love.
It woon his will with man to make abode:
    It stai'd his Sword, and did his wrath remove.   10
It made the rigor of his Justice yeeld,
And Crowned mercye Empresse of the feelde.

This lull'd our heavenly *Sampson* fast a sleepe,
    And laid him in our feeble natures lapp.
This made him under mortall load to creepe: 15
    And in our flesh his god head to enwrap.
This made him sojourne with us in exile:
And not disdayne our tytles in his style.

This brought him from theranckes of heaven'ly quires,
    Into this vale of teares, and cursed soyle: 20
From flow'rs of grace, into a world of bryers:

AT HOME IN HEAVEN.
  7 *ghostly:* spiritual.

[5]

From life to death, from blisse to balefull toyle.
This made him wander in our Pilgrim weede,
And tast our tormentes, to relieve our neede.

O soule do not thy noble thoughtes abase,   25
    To lose thy loves in any mortall weight:
Content thyne eye at home with native grace,
    Sith God him selfe is ravisht with thy sight.
If on thy beautie God enamored bee:
Base is thy love of any lesse then hee.   30

Give not assent to muddy minded skill,
    That deemes the feature of a pleasing face,
To be the sweetest baite to lure the will:
    Not valewing right the worth of Ghostly grace:
Let Gods and Angels censure winne beliefe,   35
That of all bewties judge our soules the chiefe.

Queene *Hester* was of rare and pearelesse hew,
    And *Judeth* once for beauty bare the vaunt,
But he that could our soules endowments vew,
    Would soone to soules the Crowne of beautie graunt, 40
O soule out of thy selfe seeke God alone:
Grace more then thine, but Gods, the world hath none.

Sinnes heavie loade

O Lord my sinne doth over-charge thy brest,
    The poyse thereof doth force thy knees to bow;

23 *weede:* garment.
26 *weight:* wight, person, being.
28 *sith:* since.
35 *censure:* judgment, opinion.
38 *bare the vaunt:* bore the boast.
SINNES HEAVIE LOADE: a meditation (like the next poem) on the scene in Gethsemane: Matthew 26:36 f.; Mark 14:32 f.; Luke 22:39 f.
2 *poyse:* poise, weight.

Yea flat thou fallest with my faults opprest,
    And bloody sweat runs trickling from thy brow:
But had they not to earth thus pressed thee,   5
Much more they would in hell have pestred mee.

This Globe of earth doth thy one finger prop,
    The world thou doo'st within thy hand embrace;
Yet all this waight of sweat drew not a drop,
    Ne made thee bow, much lesse fall on thy face: 10
But now thou hast a loade so heavy found,
That makes thee bow, yea flat fall to the ground.

O sinne, how huge and heavie is thy waight,
    Thou wayest more then all the world beside.
Of which when Christ had taken in his fraight   15
    The poyse thereof his flesh could not abide;
Alas, if God himselfe sinke under sinne,
What will become of man that dies therein.

First, flat thou fel'st, when earth did thee receave,
    In closet pure of Maries virgin brest;   20
And now thou fall'st of earth to take thy leave,
    Thou kissest it as cause of thy unrest:
O loving Lord that so doost love thy foe,
As thus to kisse the ground where he doth goe.

Thou minded in thy heaven our earth to weare,   25
    Doo'st prostrate now thy heaven our earth to blisse;
As God, to earth thou often wert severe,
    As man, thou seal'st a peace with bleeding kisse:
For as of soules thou common Father art,
So is she Mother of mans other part.   30

She shortly was to drink thy dearest blood,
    And yeeld thy soule a way to sathans cave;
She shortly was thy corse in tombe to shrowd,

26 *blisse:* variant spelling of *bless,* with connotations of the verb *to bliss:* to
make glad.

And with them all thy deitie to have:
Now then in one thou joyntly yeeldest all,   35
That severally to earth should shortly fall.

O prostrate Christ, erect my crooked minde,
    Lord let thy fall my flight from earth obtaine;
Or if I still in earth must needes be shrinde,
    Then Lord on earth come fall yet once againe: 40
And eyther yeeld with me in earth to lie,
Or else with thee to take me to the skie.

Christs sleeping friends

When Christ with care and pangs of death opprest
From frighted flesh a bloody sweate did raine,
And full of feare without repose or rest
In agony did pray and watch in paine
Three sundrie times he his disciples findes   5
With heavy eies, but farre more heavy mindes;

With milde rebuke he warned them to wake:
Yet sleepe did still their drousie sences hold:
As when the sunne the brightest shew doth make
In darkest shrouds the night birdes them infolde,   10
His foes did watch to worke their cruell spight,
His drousie friendes slept in his hardest plight.

As *Jonas* sayled once from *Joppaes* shoare
A boystrous tempest in the aire did broile,
The waves did rage, the thundring heavens did roare,   15
The stormes, the rockes, the lightnings threatned spoile,
The shippe was billowes game, and chaunces pray,
Yet carelesse *Jonas* mute and sleeping lay:

CHRISTS SLEEPING FRIENDS.
  14 *broile:* struggle in confusion.

[8]

So now though *Judas* like a blustring gust,
Doe stirre the furious sea of Jewish ire,   20
Though storming troopes in quarrels most unjust
Against the barke of all our blisse conspire,
Yet these disciples sleeping lie secure,
As though their wonted calme did still endure.

So *Jonas* once his weary limmes to rest,   25
Did shrowd himselfe in pleasant ivy shade,
But lo, while him a heavy sleep opprest,
His shadowy bowre, to withered stalke did fade,
A cankered worme had gnawen the root away,
And brought the glorious branches to decay.   30

O gratious plant, O tree of heavenly spring,
The paragon for leafe, for fruit and flower,
How sweete a shadow did thy braunches bring
To shrowd these soules that chose thee for their bower,
But now while they with *Jonas* fall a sleepe,   35
To spoile their plant an envious worme doth creepe.

Awake ye slumbring wightes lift up your eies,
Marke *Judas* how to teare your roote he strives,
Alas the glorie of your arbor dies,
Arise and guarde the comforte of your lives.   40
No *Jonas* ivy, no *Zacheus* tree,
Were to the world so great a losse as he.

41 *Zacheus:* see Luke 19:2–6.

New Prince, new pompe

Behold a silly tender Babe,
    In freesing Winter night;
In homely manger trembling lies,
    Alas a pitteous sight:

The Innes are full, no man will yeeld   5
    This little Pilgrime bed;
But forc'd he is with silly beasts,
    In Crib to shrowd his head.

Despise not him for lying there,
    First what he is enquire: 10
An orient pearle is often found,
    In depth of dirty mire,

Waigh not his Crib, his wooden dish,
    Nor beasts that by him feede:
Waigh not his Mothers poore attire,   15
    Nor Josephs simple weede.

This stable is a Princes Court,
    The Crib his chaire of state:
The beasts are parcell of his pompe,
    The wooden dish his plate.   20

The persons in that poore attire,
    His royall livories weare,
The Prince himselfe is come from heaven,
    This pompe is prized there.

NEW PRINCE, NEW POMPE.

1 *silly*: innocent, helpless, deserving of pity; also, poor, simple; with connotations of the related word *seely*: fortunate, blessed.

22 *livories*: liveries, uniforms.

With joy approach o Christian wight,   25
    Doe homage to thy King;
And highly prise this humble pompe,
    Which he from heaven dooth bring.

The burning Babe

As I in hoarie Winters night
    Stoode shivering in the snow,
Surpris'd I was with sodaine heate,
    Which made my hart to glow;

And lifting up a fearefull eye,   5
    To view what fire was neare,
A pretty Babe all burning bright
    Did in the ayre appeare;

Who scorched with excessive heate,
    Such floods of teares did shed,   10
As though his floods should quench his flames,
    Which with his teares were fed:

Alas (quoth he) but newly borne,
    In fierie heates I frie,
Yet none approach to warme their harts   15
    Or feele my fire, but I;

My faultlesse breast the furnace is,
    The fuell wounding thornes:
Love is the fire, and sighs the smoake,
    The ashes, shame and scornes;   20

The fewell Justice layeth on,
    And Mercie blowes the coales,

THE BURNING BABE.
  1 *hoarie:* white, with associations of *hoarfrost.*

The mettall in this furnace wrought,
    Are mens defiled soules:

For which, as now on fire I am   25
    To worke them to their good,
So will I melt into a bath,
    To wash them in my blood.

With this he vanisht out of sight,
    And swiftly shrunk away,   30
And straight I called unto minde,
    That it was Christmasse day.

New heaven, new warre

Come to your heaven you heavenly quires,
  Earth hath the heaven of your desires;
Remove your dwelling to your God,
A stall is now his best abode;
Sith men their homage doe denie,   5
Come Angels all their fault supplie.

His chilling cold doth heate require,
Come Seraphins in liew of fire;
This little Arke no cover hath,
  Let Cherubs wings his body swath: 10
Come Raphaell, this Babe must eate,
Provide our little Tobie meate.

Let Gabriell be now his groome,
  That first took up his earthly roome;
Let Michaell stand in his defence,   15

NEW HEAVEN, NEW WARRE.
  9–10 See Exodus 25:10–22.
  11–12 See the apocryphal book of Tobit 5–6.

Whom love hath linck'd to feeble sence,
Let Graces rock when he doth crie,
And Angels sing his lullabie.

The same you saw in heavenly seate,
Is he that now sucks Maries teate;   20
Agnize your King a mortall wight,
His borrowed weede lets not your sight:
Come kisse the maunger where he lies,
That is your blisse above the skies.

This little Babe so few dayes olde,   25
Is come to ryfle sathans folde;
All hell doth at his presence quake,
Though he himselfe for cold doe shake:
For in this weake unarmed wise,
The gates of hell he will suprise.   30

With teares he fights and winnes the field,
His naked breast stands for a shield;
His battering shot are babish cryes,
His Arrowes lookes of weeping eyes,
His Martiall ensignes cold and neede,   35
And feeble flesh his warriers steede.

His Campe is pitched in a stall,
His bulwarke but a broken wall:
The Crib his trench, hay stalks his stakes,
Of Sheepheards he his Muster makes;   40
And thus as sure his foe to wound,
The Angells trumps alarum sound.

My soule with Christ joyne thou in fight,
Sticke to the tents that he hath pight;

21 *Agnize:* acknowledge.
22 *weede:* clothing (flesh); *lets:* hinders.
29 *in this . . . wise:* in this manner.
44 *pight:* pitched.

Within his Crib is surest ward,   45
This little Babe will be thy guard:
If thou wilt foyle thy foes with joy,
Then flit not from this heavenly boy.

Marie Magdalens complaint at Christs death

Sith my life from life is parted:
    Death come take thy portion.
Who survives, when life is murdred,
    Lives by meere extortion.
All that live, and not in God: 5
Couch their life in deaths abod.

Seely starres must needes leave shining,
    When the sunne is shaddowed.
Borrowed streames refraine their running,
    When head springs are hindered.   10
One that lives by others breath,
Dieth also by his death.

O true life, sith thou hast left me,
    Mortall life is tedious.
Death it is to live without thee,   15
    Death, of all most odious.
Turne againe or take me to thee,
Let me die or live thou in mee.

45 *ward:* defence, protection.
48 *flit:* depart.
MARIE MAGDALENS COMPLAINT.
  4 *meere:* absolute, nothing less than.
  7 *seely:* see fn. above on *silly* ("New Prince, new pompe").

Where the truth once was, and is not,
    Shaddowes are but vanitie: 20
Shewing want, that helpe they cannot:
    Signes, not salves of miserie.
Paynted meate no hunger feedes,
Dying life each death exceedes.

With my love, my life was nestled   25
    In the sonne of happinesse:
From my love, my life is wrested
    To a world of heavinesse.
O, let love my life remove,
Sith I live not where I love.   30

O my soule, what did unloose thee
    From thy sweete captivitie?
God, not I, did still possesse thee:
    His, not mine, thy libertie.
O, too happie thrall thou wart,   35
When thy prison, was his hart.

Spitefull speare, that breakst this prison,
    Seate of all felicitie,
Working thus, with double treason,
    Loves and lifes deliverie: 40
Though my life thou drav'st away,
Maugre thee my love shall stay.

28 *heavinesse:* sadness, grief, affliction.
41 *drav'st:* drovest, drove.
42 *maugre:* in spite of.

.

WILLIAM ALABASTER
1568–1640

1

The night, the starlesse night of passion,
from heaven begann on heaven beneath to fall
when Christ did sound the onsett mertiall,
a sacred hymne, uppon his foes to runn,
that with the fierie Contemplacion   5
of love and joy, his soule and sences all
surchardged, might not dread the bitter thrall
of paine and greife, and torments all in one.
Then since my holie vowes have undertooke
to take the portract of Christs death in mee,   10
then lett my love with sonnetts fill this booke,
with hymnes to give the onsett as did hee,
that thoughts enflamed with such heavenlie muse
the coldest ice of feare may not refuse. (1J)

2

What meaneth this, that Christ an hymne did singe,
an hymne triumphantt, for an happie fight,
as if his enemies weare putt to flight
when yett hee was not com'd within the ringe?
soe gyaunt-like did this victorious Kinge   5
exult to runn the race he had in sight,
that he anticipated with delight

SONNET 1.
    4 See Matthew 26:30; Mark 14:26.
    7 *thrall:* thralldom.
    10 *portract:* portrait, image, likeness (spelling indicates derivation from Latin *protractus*).
SONNET 2.
    4 *com'd:* archaic use of past participle.

the present paines which should such glories bringe.
O what a previledge of favoure tis
to suffer for god's cause, when Christ doth give   10
a grace of thankes for haveinge gotten this;
and wheare for other guifts, wheareby wee live,
when theis bee had, the rent of thankes we render,
for sufferinges beforehand wee must tender. (2J)

15

My soule a world is by Contraccion,
the heavens therein is my internall sence,
moved by my will as an intelligence,
my hart the element, my love the sonne;
and as the sonne about the earth doth run   5
and with his beames doth drawe thin vapours thence
which after in the aire doe condence
and power downe raine uppon the earth anon,
soe moves my love about the heavenlie spheare
and draweth thence with an attractive fire   10
the purest argument witt can desire,
whereby devotion after may arise,
and theis conceiptes, digest by thoughts retire,
are turned into aprill showers of teares. (15J)

12–14 "for other gifts we render thanks after receiving them, but for sufferings we must tender (offer) thanks beforehand."
SONNET 15: see NOTE.
  1 *world:* universe (the Ptolemaic system).
  2 *internall sence:* general perceptive faculty of the mind or soul.
  3 *intelligence:* angel or spirit supposed to move each sphere in the Ptolemaic system.
  4 *element:* sky.
  8 *power:* pour.
  11 *argument:* subject matter, theme; *witt:* understanding, intellect, reason.
  13 *conceiptes:* thoughts, conceptions; *digest:* digested; *thoughts retire:* thought's retirement, withdrawal from distractions.

16

Three sortes of teares doe from myne eies distraine:
the first are bitter, of Compunction,
the seacond brynish, of Compassion,
the third are sweete, which from devoutnes raine,
and theis deversities they doe obteine   5
by difference of place, from which they runn;
the first come from the meditacion
of all my sinnes, which made a bitter vaine,
the next passe through the sea of others teares,
and soe that saltnesse in the tast appeares,   10
the third doth issue from Christs wounded side,
and thence such sweetenes in them doth abide.
Never did Contraries soe well agree,
for th'one without th'other will not bee. (16J)

19

Jesu, thie love within mee is soe maine
and my poore hart soe narrow of Content
that with thie love my hart well-nie is rent,
and yett, I love to beare such loveinge paine.
O take thie Crosse and nailes, and therewith straine   5
my harts desire unto his full extent,
that thie deare love may not therein bee pent,
but thoughts may have free scope, thie love to explaine.

SONNET 16.
   1 *distraine:* strain or press (themselves) forth.
   8 *vaine:* vein.
SONNET 19.
   1 *maine:* powerful.

O now my hart more paineth then before,
because it can receive and hath noe more.   10
Oh fill this emptines or ells I dye,
now stretch my hart againe and now supply,
now I want space, now grace, to end this smart,
since my hart holdes not thee, hold thou my hart. (20J)

24

O sweete and bitter monuments of paine,
bitter to Christ who all the paine endured,
butt sweete to mee, whose Death my life procured,
how shall I full express such loss, such gaine?
My tonge shall bee my penne, mine eyes shall raine   5
teares for my inke, the place where I was cured
shall bee my booke, where haveing all abjured
and calling heavens to record in that plaine,
thus plainely will I write, noe sinne like mine;
when I have done, doe thou, Jesue divine,   10
take upp the tarte spunge of thy passione
and blott itt forth: then bee thy spiritt the Quill,
thy bloode the Inke, and with compassione
write thus uppon my soule: thy Jesue still. (1B)

37

Haile gracefull morning of eternall Daye,
the periode of Judaes throned righte
and latest minute of the Legall nighte,

SONNET 24.
  6 *place:* see NOTE.
SONNET 37: ms. B has heading: "to the blessed virgine."
  3 *Legall nighte:* era of the Law of the Old Testament.

whome wakefull Prophetts spied, farre awaye,
chasinge the night from the worldes Easterne bay;   5
within whose pudent lapp and rosall plighte
conceived was the Sonne of unborne lighte
whose light gave beeing to the worldes arraye,
unspotted morninge whome noe mist of Sinne
nor cloude of humane mixtuer did obscuer,   10
strange morninge that, since day hath entred inne,
before and after doth alike enduer;
and well it seemes a Day that never wasteth
should have a morning that for ever lasteth. (4B)

32

Beehould a cluster to itt selfe a vine,
behould a vine extended in one cluster
whose grapes doe swell with grace and heavenly luster
clyming uppon a crosse with lovely twine,
sent downe to earth from Canaan divine   5
to styrr us upp unto our warlike muster
to take that garden where this Cluster grew
whose nectar sweete the Angells doth bedewe;
see how the purple bloode doth from it draine
with thornes, and whippes, and nailes, and speare diffus'd;   10
drinke, drinke apace, my Soule, that Soveraigne raine
by which heaven is into my spiritt infusd.
O drinke to thirst, and thirst to drinke that treasuer,
where the onely danger is to keepe a measuer. (5B)

6 *pudent:* modest; *rosall plighte:* roseate fold or pleat (womb).
SONNET 32: see NOTE.

33

Now that the midd day heate doth scorch my shame
with lightning of fonde lust, I will retyer
under this vine whose armes with wandring spyer
doe clyme uppon the cross, and on the same
devise a coole repose from lawless flame,   5
whose leaves are intertwist with love entyer
that enveyes eye cannot transfuse her fyer,
but is rebated on the shadye frame,
and youthfull vigor from the leaved tyer
doth streame uppon my soule a new desyer.   10
List, list! the dittyes of sublimed fame
which in the Closett of those leaves the Quire
of heavenly birds doe warble to his name.
O where was I, that was not where I am? (8B)

34

Now I have found thee, I will ever more
embrace this standerd where thou sitest above:
feed greedy eyes, and from hence never rove,
sucke hungrye Soule of this eternall store.
Issue my hearte from thy two leaved dore   5
and lett my lipps from kissinge not remove.
O that I were transformed into Love

SONNET 33: see NOTE.

   2 *fonde:* foolish, infatuated.

   3 *spyer:* spiral; also with ref. to *spire* in the old meaning of *stem* or *shoot* of a plant.

   9 *tyer:* tier.

SONNET 34: see NOTE.

and as a plante might springe upp in his flowre,
like wandring ivy, or sweete hony suckle,
how would I with my twine aboute it buckle!   10
and kiss his feete with my ambitiouse bowes
and clime alonge uppon his sacred brest
and make a garland for his wounded browes!
Lord, soe I am if here my thoughtes might rest. (13B)

44

O starry Temple of unvalted space
and flooer unbounded, built of just desier,
not reared upp by pillares straighning spyer,
for whether should it rise withoute a base
or whether should it fall, whose tearme and space   5
is God him selfe? when shall my soule aspyer
to heare the musick of thy heavenly quire
and beare a part of that melodiouse grace
wheras Apostles, Martyres, and Confessores,
Archangles, Angles, Virgines, and Professores   10
doe make a consorte of combined voices
with due breath'd aire of Love, that heaven doth ringe
and pay againe theyr unconfused noises
with interest ever: list, I heare them singe. (16B)

11 *bowes:* boughs.
SONNET 44.

   4, 5 *whether:* whither.

   5 *tearme:* term, end, boundary.

   9 *wheras:* where; *Confessores:* those who have maintained their faith under persecution, but have not suffered martyrdom.

   10 *Professores:* those who have openly professed their belief or vows.

   11 *consorte:* harmony, band of musicians.

   12 *due breath'd:* properly breathed, with a play on *aire,* song.

   14 See NOTE.

46

A way feare with thy projectes, noe false fyre
which thou doest make, can ought my courage quaile,
or cause mee leward come, or strike my sayle;
what if the world doe frowne att my retyre,
what if denyall dash my wish'd desire   5
and purblind pitty doe my state bewaile
and wonder cross it selfe, and free speech raile
and greatnes take it not, and death shew nigher?
Tell him, my Soule, the feares that make mee quake:
the smothering brimstone, and the burninge lake,   10
life feeding Death, Death ever life devowring,
tormentes not moved, unheard, yett still roaring,
God lost, hell fownd: ever, never begune:
now bidd mee into flame from smoake to runne. (18B)

70

The sunne begins uppon my heart to shine:
now lett a cloude of thoughts in order traine
as dewy spangles wonte, and entertaine
in many drops his Passione Divine,
that on them, as a rainbow, may recline   5
the white of innocence, the black of paine,

SONNET 46.

  1 *projectes:* notions, speculations.

  3 *leward:* see NOTE.

  12 *not moved:* not removed, eternal.

SONNET 70: see NOTE.

  2 *traine:* lengthen out, spin out (one after another).

  3 *wonte:* are accustomed (to do); *entertaine:* receive, admit to consideration.

the blew of stripes, the yellow of disdaine,
and purple which his blood doth weell designe,
and lett those thousand thoughts powre on mine eyes
a thousand tears, as glasses to beehould him,   10
and thousand tears, thousand sweete words devise
uppon my lipps, as pictures to unfold him.
Soe shall reflect three rainbowes from one sunne:
thoughts, tears, and words, all end in Actione. (40B)

71

When without tears I looke on Christ, I see
only a story of some passion
which any common eye may wonder on,
butt if I look through tears Christ smiles on mee,
yea there I see my selfe: and from that tree   5
he bendeth downe to my devotione
and from his side the blood doth spinn, wheron
my hart, my mouth, mine eyes still sucking bee.
Like as in optick workes, one thing appears
in open gaze, in closer other wise: 10
then since tears see the best I aske in tears,
Lord either thaw mine eyes to tears, or freeze
my tears to eyes, or lett my hart tears bleede,
or bringe where eyes, nor tears, nor blood shall neede. (41B)

8 "And purple which well signifies his blood."

14 *all end in Actione:* the aim of meditation is to produce "good acts"; see NOTE.

SONNET 71: see NOTE.

2 *passion:* suffering; see NOTE.

9 *optick workes:* drawings or constructions designed according to the rules of optics or perspective.

14 *shall neede:* shall be necessary.

JOHN DONNE
1572–1631

ELEGY 1

Jealosie

Fond woman, which would'st have thy husband die,
And yet complain'st of his great jealousie;
If swolne with poyson, hee lay in'his last bed,
His body with a sere-barke covered,
Drawing his breath, as thick and short, as can   5
The nimblest crocheting Musitian,
Ready with loathsome vomiting to spue
His Soule out of one hell, into a new,
Made deafe with his poore kindreds howling cries,
Begging with few feign'd teares, great legacies,   10
Thou would'st not weepe, but jolly,'and frolicke bee,
As a slave, which to morrow should be free;
Yet weep'st thou, when thou seest him hungerly
Swallow his owne death, hearts-bane jealousie.
O give him many thanks, he'is courteous,   15
That in suspecting kindly warneth us.
Wee must not, as wee us'd, flout openly,
In scoffing ridles, his deformitie;
Nor at his boord together being satt,
With words, nor touch, scarce lookes adulterate.   20
Nor when he swolne, and pamper'd with great fare,
Sits downe, and snorts, cag'd in his basket chaire,

ELEGY 1.

1 *Fond:* foolish.

3 *in'his:* the apostrophe, when thus used, indicates elision.

4 *sere-barke:* suggesting a "cerecloth", a waxed cloth used for wrapping a dead body; *barke* implies perhaps a covering of scabs.

6 *crocheting:* playing quarter-notes, or thus embellishing a musical score.

14 *hearts-bane:* destroyer of the heart, poison.

19 *boord:* table.

20 *scarce lookes:* scarcely (with) looks; *adulterate:* commit adultery.

22 *snorts:* snores.

Must wee usurpe his owne bed any more,
Nor kisse and play in his house, as before.
Now I see many dangers; for that is   25
His realme, his castle, and his diocesse.
But if, as envious men, which would revile
Their Prince, or coyne his gold, themselves exile
Into another countrie,'and doe it there,
Wee play'in another house, what should we feare?   30
There we will scorne his houshold policies,
His seely plots, and pensionary spies,
As the inhabitants of Thames right side
Do Londons Mayor; or Germans, the Popes pride.

ELEGY 4

The Perfume

Once, and but once found in thy company,
All thy suppos'd escapes are laid on mee;
And as a thiefe at barre, is question'd there
By all the men, that have beene rob'd that yeare,
So am I, (by this traiterous meanes surpriz'd)   5
By thy Hydroptique father catechiz'd.
Though he had wont to search with glazed eyes,
As though he came to kill a Cockatrice,
Though hee hath oft sworne, that hee would remove
Thy beauties beautie, and food of our love,   10
Hope of his goods, if I with thee were seene,

32 *seely:* weak, silly.

33 *Thames right side:* the South Bank, except for Southwark, lay outside the Lord Mayor's jurisdiction and was notorious for its lawlessness.

ELEGY 4.

2 *escapes:* sexual escapades.

6 *Hydroptique:* dropsical.

8 *Cockatrice:* a fabled serpent who kills by its glance, but could be similarly killed if it is seen first.

Yet close and secret, as our soules, we'have beene.
Though thy immortall mother which doth lye
Still buried in her bed, yet will not dye,
Takes this advantage to sleepe out day-light,   15
And watch thy entries, and returnes all night,
And, when she takes thy hand, and would seeme kind,
Doth search what rings, and armelets she can finde,
And kissing notes the colour of thy face,
And fearing least thou'art swolne, doth thee embrace;   20
To trie if thou long, doth name strange meates,
And notes thy palenesse, blushing, sighs, and sweats;
And politiquely will to thee confesse
The sinnes of her owne youths ranke lustinesse;
Yet love these Sorceries did remove, and move   25
Thee to gull thine owne mother for my love.
Thy little brethren, which like Faiery Sprights
Oft skipt into our chamber, those sweet nights,
And kist, and ingled on thy fathers knee,
Were brib'd next day, to tell what they did see: 30
The grim eight-foot-high iron-bound serving-man,
That oft names God in oathes, and onely than,
He that to barre the first gate, doth as wide
As the great Rhodian Colossus stride,
Which, if in hell no other paines there were,   35
Makes mee feare hell, because he must be there:
Though by thy father he were hir'd to this,
Could never witnesse any touch or kisse.
But Oh, too common ill, I brought with mee
That, which betray'd mee to my enemie: 40
A loud perfume, which at my entrance cryed
Even at thy fathers nose, so were wee spied.

21 "To test whether you have desires (for them), doth name strange foods";
traditional symptoms of pregnancy.

26 *gull:* deceive.

29 *ingled:* fondled.

34 *Colossus:* the statue of Apollo, about 120 feet high, which was said to
have stood astride the entrance to the harbor at Rhodes, and was one of the
seven wonders of the ancient world.

When, like a tyran King, that in his bed
Smelt gunpowder, the pale wretch shivered.
Had it beene some bad smell, he would have thought   45
That his owne feet, or breath, that smell had wrought.
But as wee in our Ile emprisoned,
Where cattell onely,'and diverse dogs are bred,
The pretious Unicornes, strange monsters call,
So thought he good, strange, that had none at all.   50
I taught my silkes, their whistling to forbeare,
Even my opprest shoes, dumbe and speechlesse were,
Onely, thou bitter sweet, whom I had laid
Next mee, mee traiterously hast betraid,
And unsuspected hast invisibly   55
At once fled unto him, and staid with mee.
Base excrement of earth, which dost confound
Sense, from distinguishing the sicke from sound;
By thee the seely Amorous sucks his death
By drawing in a leprous harlots breath;   60
By thee, the greatest staine to mans estate
Falls on us, to be call'd effeminate;
Though you be much lov'd in the Princes hall,
There, things that seeme, exceed substantiall;
Gods, when yee fum'd on altars, were pleas'd well,   65
Because you'were burnt, not that they lik'd your smell;
You'are loathsome all, being taken simply alone,
Shall wee love ill things joyn'd, and hate each one?
If you were good, your good doth soone decay;
And you are rare, that takes the good away.   70
All my perfumes, I give most willingly
To'embalme thy fathers corse; What? will hee die?

48 *cattell:* live-stock in general, not only cattle in the modern sense.
53 *sweet:* fragrance.
72 *corse:* corpse.

ELEGY 16

On his Mistris

By our first strange and fatall interview,
By all desires which thereof did ensue,
By our long starving hopes, by that remorse
Which my words masculine perswasive force
Begot in thee, and by the memory   5
Of hurts, which spies and rivals threatned me,
I calmly beg: But by thy fathers wrath,
By all paines, which want and divorcement hath,
I conjure thee, and all the oathes which I
And thou have sworne to seale joynt constancy,   10
Here I unsweare, and overswear them thus,
Thou shalt not love by wayes so dangerous.
Temper, ô faire Love, loves impetuous rage,
Be my true Mistris still, not my faign'd Page;
I'll goe, and, by thy kinde leave, leave behinde   15
Thee, onely worthy to nurse in my minde,
Thirst to come backe; ô if thou die before,
My soule from other lands to thee shall soare.
Thy (else Almighty) beautie cannot move
Rage from the Seas, nor thy love teach them love,   20
Nor tame wilde Boreas harshnesse; Thou hast reade

ELEGY 16: *Mistris:* "a woman who has command over a man's heart" (OED).

1 *fatall:* fated, controlling one's destiny; fraught with implications for the future; *interview:* sight of each other, meeting.

3 *remorse:* pity.

14 *faign'd Page:* a common disguise in Renaissance literature, as with Viola in *Twelfth Night.*

21 *Boreas:* the North Wind took Orithea from Athens to Thrace, where she bore twin sons by him; Donne seems to have fused or confused this legend with some other story.

How roughly hee in peeces shivered
Faire Orithea, whom he swore he lov'd.
Fall ill or good, 'tis madnesse to have prov'd
 Dangers unurg'd; Feed on this flattery,   25
That absent Lovers one in th'other be.
Dissemble nothing, not a boy, nor change
Thy bodies habite, nor mindes; bee not strange
To thy selfe onely; All will spie in thy face
A blushing womanly discovering grace;   30
 Richly cloath'd Apes, are call'd Apes, and as soone
Ecclips'd as bright we call the Moone the Moone.
Men of France, changeable Camelions,
Spittles of diseases, shops of fashions,
Loves fuellers, and the rightest company   35
Of Players, which upon the worlds stage be,
 Will quickly knowe thee, and knowe thee; and alas
Th'indifferent Italian, as we passe
His warme land, well content to thinke thee Page,
Will hunt thee with such lust, and hideous rage,   40
As *Lots* faire guests were vext. But none of these
Nor spungy hydroptique Dutch shall thee displease,
If thou stay here. O stay here, for, for thee
England is onely a worthy Gallerie,

24 *prov'd:* experienced, endured.

25 *unurg'd:* not forced on oneself.

27 *Dissemble:* (1) disguise; (2) pretend to be.

28 *habite:* (1) clothing; (2) mental constitution.

34 *Spittles:* a *spittle* was a house for receiving the poor or the diseased, especially "one chiefly occupied by persons of a low class or afflicted with foul diseases" (OED).

37 Grierson and Miss Gardner agree that this is the "original reading," as preserved in good manuscripts; but Grierson, for reasons of delicacy, keeps the weak reading of 1635: "Will quickly know thee, and no lesse, alas!" The repetition of "know" carries of course the sexual meaning.

38 *indifferent:* not inclined one way or another.

41 *Lots faire guests:* the angels in Sodom; see Genesis 19.

42 *hydroptique:* dropsical; with insatiable thirst; *Dutch:* refers to Germans as well as to Hollanders.

44 *Gallerie:* a long, narrow room used as a waiting room before entering the presence of a noble or king.

To walke in expectation, till from thence 45
Our greatest King call thee to his presence.
When I am gone, dreame me some happinesse,
Nor let thy lookes our long hid love confesse,
Nor praise, nor dispraise me, nor blesse nor curse
Openly loves force, nor in bed fright thy Nurse 50
With midnights startings, crying out, oh, oh
Nurse, ô my love is slaine, I saw him goe
O'r the white Alpes alone; I saw him I,
Assail'd, fight, taken, stabb'd, bleed, fall, and die.
Augure me better chance, except dread *Jove* 55
Thinke it enough for me to'have had thy love.

ELEGY 19

Going to Bed

Come, Madam, come, all rest my powers defie,
Until I labour, I in labour lie.
The foe oft-times having the foe in sight,
Is tir'd with standing though he never fight.
Off with that girdle, like heavens Zone glittering, 5
But a far fairer world incompassing.
Unpin that spangled breastplate which you wear,
That th'eyes of busie fooles may be stopt there.
Unlace your self, for that harmonious chyme,
Tells me from you, that now it is bed time. 10
Off with that happy busk, which I envie,

55 *Augure me:* predict for me.
ELEGY 19.
   5 *Zone:* referring to the constellation of Orion or to the outermost sphere of the universe, that of the fixed stars.
   9 *chyme:* perhaps referring to the sound of unlacing, or to some kind of striking watch.
   11 *busk:* corset.

That still can be, and still can stand so nigh.
Your gown going off, such beautious state reveals,
As when from flowry meads th'hills shadow steales.
Off with that wyerie Coronet and shew   15
The haiery Diademe which on you doth grow:
Now off with those shooes, and then safely tread
In this loves hallow'd temple, this soft bed.
In such white robes, heaven's Angels us'd to be
Receavd by men; Thou Angel bringst with thee   20
A heaven like Mahomets Paradise; and though
Ill spirits walk in white, we easly know,
By this these Angels from an evil sprite,
Those set our hairs, but these our flesh upright.
  Licence my roaving hands, and let them go,   25
Before, behind, between, above, below.
O my America! my new-found-land,
My kingdome, safeliest when with one man man'd,
My Myne of precious stones, My Emperie,
How blest am I in this discovering thee!   30
To enter in these bonds, is to be free;
Then where my hand is set, my seal shall be.
  Full nakedness! All joyes are due to thee,
As souls unbodied, bodies uncloth'd must be,
To taste whole joyes. Gems which you women use   35
Are like Atlanta's balls, cast in mens views,
That when a fools eye lighteth on a Gem,
His earthly soul may covet theirs, not them.
Like pictures, or like books gay coverings made
For lay-men, are all women thus array'd;   40
Themselves are mystick books, which only wee
(Whom their imputed grace will dignifie)

21 *Mahomets Paradise:* supposed to be filled with physical pleasures.

29 *Emperie:* territory ruled by an emperor.

30 *discovering:* with play on the meaning, "uncovering."

36 With ref. to the legend in which Hippomenes defeated Atalanta in the foot race by throwing three golden apples in her path.

42 *imputed grace:* with a play upon the theological doctrine that the merit or righteousness of Christ is *imputed* (attributed) by divine grace to those who

Must see reveal'd. Then since that I may know;
As liberally, as to a Midwife, shew
Thy self: cast all, yea, this white lynnen hence,　　　　45
There is no pennance due to innocence.
　　To teach thee, I am naked first; why than
What needst thou have more covering then a man.

Satire 3

Kinde pitty chokes my spleene; brave scorn forbids
Those teares to issue which swell my eye-lids;
I must not laugh, nor weepe sinnes, and be wise,
Can railing then cure these worne maladies?
Is not our Mistresse faire Religion,　　　　5
As worthy of all our Soules devotion,
As vertue was to the first blinded age?
Are not heavens joyes as valiant to asswage
Lusts, as earths honour was to them? Alas,
As wee do them in meanes, shall they surpasse　　　　10
Us in the end, and shall thy fathers spirit
Meete blinde Philosophers in heaven, whose merit
Of strict life may be imputed faith, and heare
Thee, whom hee taught so easie wayes and neare
To follow, damn'd? O if thou dar'st, feare this;　　　　15
This feare great courage, and high valour is.
Dar'st thou ayd mutinous Dutch, and dar'st thou lay
Thee in ships woodden Sepulchers, a prey
To leaders rage, to stormes, to shot, to dearth?
Dar'st thou dive seas, and dungeons of the earth?　　　　20

---

have faith; believers are thus made worthy (*dignified,* in the basic sense) of salvation.

46 Miss Gardner, with good reason, prefers the reading: "Here is no pennance, much less innocence." In either case the point is that *white,* the sign of penitence and innocence, is hardly appropriate.

SATIRE 3.

13 *imputed faith:* see fn. on Elegy 19, line 42.

Hast thou couragious fire to thaw the ice
Of frozen North discoveries? and thrise
Colder then Salamanders, like divine
Children in th'oven, fires of Spaine, and the line,
Whose countries limbecks to our bodies bee,   25
Canst thou for gaine beare? and must every hee
Which cryes not, Goddesse, to thy Mistresse, draw,
Or eate thy poysonous words? courage of straw!
O desperate coward, wilt thou seeme bold, and
To thy foes and his (who made thee to stand   30
Sentinell in his worlds garrison) thus yeeld,
And for forbidden warres, leave th'appointed field?
Know thy foes: The foule Devill (whom thou
Strivest to please,) for hate, not love, would allow
Thee faine, his whole Realme to be quit; and as   35
The worlds all parts wither away and passe,
So the worlds selfe, thy other lov'd foe, is
In her decrepit wayne, and thou loving this,
Dost love a withered and worne strumpet; last,
Flesh (it selfes death) and joyes which flesh can taste,   40
Thou lovest; and thy faire goodly soule, which doth
Give this flesh power to taste joy, thou dost loath.
Seeke true religion. O where? Mirreus
Thinking her unhous'd here, and fled from us,
Seekes her at Rome, there, because hee doth know   45
That shee was there a thousand yeares agoe,
He loves her ragges so, as wee here obey
The statecloth where the Prince sate yesterday.
Crantz to such brave Loves will not be inthrall'd,
But loves her onely, who at Geneva is call'd   50

23–24 *divine Children:* see Daniel 3, and the Song of the Three Holy Children, in the Apocrypha.
24 *the line:* the equator.
25 *limbecks:* alembics, apparatuses for distilling.
35 *faine:* willingly, gladly; *quit:* rid of (you).
38 *wayne:* waning.
48 *statecloth:* a canopy over a throne.
49 *brave:* finely dressed, showy.

Religion, plaine, simple, sullen, yong,
Contemptuous, yet unhansome; As among
Lecherous humors, there is one that judges
No wenches wholsome, but course country drudges.
Graius stayes still at home here, and because   55
Some Preachers, vile ambitious bauds, and lawes
Still new like fashions, bid him thinke that shee
Which dwels with us, is onely perfect, hee
Imbraceth her, whom his Godfathers will
Tender to him, being tender, as Wards still   60
Take such wives as their Guardians offer, or
Pay valewes. Carelesse Phrygius doth abhorre
All, because all cannot be good, as one
Knowing some women whores, dares marry none.
Graccus loves all as one, and thinkes that so   65
As women do in divers countries goe
In divers habits, yet are still one kinde,
So doth, so is Religion; and this blind-
nesse too much light breeds; but unmoved thou
Of force must one, and forc'd but one allow;   70
And the right; aske thy father which is shee,
Let him aske his; though truth and falshood bee
Neare twins, yet truth a little elder is;
Be busie to seeke her, beleeve mee this,
Hee's not of none, nor worst, that seekes the best.   75
To adore, or scorne an image, or protest,
May all be bad; doubt wisely; in strange way
To stand inquiring right, is not to stray;
To sleepe, or runne wrong, is. On a huge hill,
Cragged, and steep, Truth stands, and hee that will   80
Reach her, about must, and about must goe;
And what the hills suddennes resists, winne so;
Yet strive so, that before age, deaths twilight,

53 *humors:* dispositions.
62 *Pay valewes:* pay a sum of money for refusing the marriage.
67 *habits:* clothing.
71 See Deuteronomy 32:7.
82 *suddennes:* steepness.

Thy Soule rest, for none can worke in that night.
To will, implyes delay, therefore now doe: 85
Hard deeds, the bodies paines; hard knowledge too
The mindes indeavours reach, and mysteries
Are like the Sunne, dazling, yet plaine to all eyes.
Keepe the truth which thou hast found; men do not stand
In so ill case here, that God hath with his hand   90
Sign'd Kings blanck-charters to kill whom they hate,
Nor are they Vicars, but hangmen to Fate.
Foole and wretch, wilt thou let thy Soule be tyed
To mans lawes, by which she shall not be tryed
At the last day? Oh, will it then boot thee   95
To say a Philip, or a Gregory,
A Harry, or a Martin taught thee this?
Is not this excuse for mere contraries,
Equally strong? cannot both sides say so?
That thou mayest rightly obey power, her bounds know;   100
Those past, her nature, and name is chang'd; to be
Then humble to her is idolatrie.
As streames are, Power is; those blest flowers that dwell
At the rough streames calme head, thrive and do well,
But having left their roots, and themselves given   105
To the streames tyrannous rage, alas, are driven
Through mills, and rockes, and woods, and at last, almost
Consum'd in going, in the sea are lost:
So perish Soules, which more chuse mens unjust
Power from God claym'd, then God himselfe to trust.   110

95 *boot thee:* do you good, be of profit to you.
96, 97 Philip II of Spain; Pope Gregory XIII or XIV; Henry VIII of England;
Martin Luther.
98 *mere:* absolute.

The good-morrow

I wonder by my troth, what thou, and I
Did, till we lov'd? were we not wean'd till then?
But suck'd on countrey pleasures, childishly?
Or snorted we in the seaven sleepers den?
T'was so; But this, all pleasures fancies bee.   5
If ever any beauty I did see,
Which I desir'd, and got, t'was but a dreame of thee.

And now good morrow to our waking soules,
Which watch not one another out of feare;
For love, all love of other sights controules,   10
And makes one little roome, an every where.
Let sea-discoverers to new worlds have gone,
Let Maps to other, worlds on worlds have showne,
Let us possesse one world, each hath one, and is one.

My face in thine eye, thine in mine appeares,   15
And true plain hearts doe in the faces rest,
Where can we finde two better hemispheares
Without sharpe North, without declining West?
What ever dyes, was not mixt equally;
If our two loves be one, or, thou and I   20
Love so alike, that none doe slacken, none can die.

THE GOOD-MORROW: good-morning.

3 *countrey:* rustic (wholly physical).

4 *seaven sleepers den:* according to legend, seven Christian youths of Ephesus were sealed in a cave and left for dead by their persecutors; they slept for nearly 200 years and emerged to find that Christianity had triumphed.

5 *But:* except for.

13 *Maps:* astronomical charts; *other:* other people.

18 *sharpe:* severely cold (also with ref. to point of the compass).

19 With ref. to the medieval doctrine that mixtures containing contrary elements must decay.

Song

Goe, and catche a falling starre,
   Get with child a mandrake roote,
Tell me, where all past yeares are,
   Or who cleft the Divels foot,
Teach me to heare Mermaides singing,   5
Or to keep off envies stinging,
        And finde
        What winde
Serves to advance an honest minde.

If thou beest borne to strange sights,   10
   Things invisible to see,
Ride ten thousand daies and nights,
   Till age snow white haires on thee,
Thou, when thou retorn'st, wilt tell mee
All strange wonders that befell thee,   15
        And sweare
        No where
Lives a woman true, and faire.

If thou findst one, let mee know,
   Such a Pilgrimage were sweet;   20
Yet doe not, I would not goe,
   Though at next doore wee might meet,
Though shee were true, when you met her,
And last, till you write your letter,
        Yet shee   25
        Will bee
False, ere I come, to two, or three.

SONG.

  2 *mandrake:* the forked root of the mandrake plant was thought to resemble the human form.

Womans constancy

Now thou hast lov'd me one whole day,
To morrow when thou leav'st, what wilt thou say?
Wilt thou then Antedate some new made vow?
      Or say that now
We are not just those persons, which we were?   5
Or, that oathes made in reverentiall feare
Of Love, and his wrath, any may forsweare?
Or, as true deaths, true maryages untie,
So lovers contracts, images of those,
Binde but till sleep, deaths image, them unloose?   10
      Or, your owne end to Justifie,
For having purpos'd change, and falsehood; you
Can have no way but falsehood to be true?
Vaine lunatique, against these scapes I could
      Dispute, and conquer, if I would,   15
      Which I abstaine to doe,
For by to morrow, I may thinke so too.

The Sunne Rising

     Busie old foole, unruly Sunne,
     Why dost thou thus,
Through windowes, and through curtaines call on us?
Must to thy motions lovers seasons run?
     Sawcy pedantique wretch, goe chide   5
     Late schoole boyes, and sowre prentices,

WOMANS CONSTANCY.
  14 *scapes:* breaches of proper conduct; fickle behavior.

[45]

Goe tell Court-huntsmen, that the King will ride,
  Call countrey ants to harvest offices;
Love, all alike, no season knowes, nor clyme,
Nor houres, dayes, moneths, which are the rags of time.

    Thy beames, so reverend, and strong   11
      Why shouldst thou thinke?
I could eclipse and cloud them with a winke,
But that I would not lose her sight so long:
    If her eyes have not blinded thine,   15
      Looke, and to morrow late, tell mee,
  Whether both the'India's of spice and Myne
  Be where thou leftst them, or lie here with mee.
Aske for those Kings whom thou saw'st yesterday,
And thou shalt heare, All here in one bed lay.   20

    She'is all States, and all Princes, I,
      Nothing else is.
Princes doe but play us; compar'd to this,
All honor's mimique; All wealth alchimie.
    Thou sunne art halfe as happy'as wee,   25
      In that the world's contracted thus;
  Thine age askes ease, and since thy duties bee
  To warme the world, that's done in warming us.
Shine here to us, and thou art every where;
This bed thy center is, these walls, thy spheare.   30

THE SUNNE RISING.

7 Probably with ref. to King James's fondness for hunting in the early morning.

8 "Call the farm-workers to their duties (*offices*) of harvesting."

9 *Love, all alike:* love, which never changes.

17 *India's:* the East Indies and the West Indies, respectively.

24 *alchimie:* "a metallic composition imitating gold" (OED).

30 *center:* the earth, around which the sun orbits in its *spheare,* according to the Ptolemaic astronomy.

The Indifferent

I can love both faire and browne,
Her whom abundance melts, and her whom want betraies,
Her who loves lonenesse best, and her who maskes and plaies,
Her whom the country form'd, and whom the town,
Her who beleeves, and her who tries,   5
Her who still weepes with spungie eyes,
And her who is dry corke, and never cries;
I can love her, and her, and you and you,
I can love any, so she be not true.

Will no other vice content you?   10
Wil it not serve your turn to do, as did your mothers?
Or have you all old vices spent, and now would finde out others?
Or doth a feare, that men are true, torment you?
Oh we are not, be not you so,
Let mee, and doe you, twenty know.   15
Rob mee, but binde me not, and let me goe.
Must I, who came to travaile thorow you,
Grow your fixt subject, because you are true?

Venus heard me sigh this song,
And by Loves sweetest Part, Variety, she swore,   20
She heard not this till now; and that it should be so no more.
She went, examin'd, and return'd ere long,

THE INDIFFERENT: one who has no inclination toward one thing more than toward another.

1 *faire and browne:* blonde and brunette; the conventional Elizabethan beauty was fair.

2 *want:* poverty.

5 *tries:* tests her lover, because she is skeptical.

6 *still:* always.

17 *travaile:* (as a verb) to labor, or to travel; (as a noun) trouble, suffering; *thorow:* through (in several senses: including "on account of").

And said, alas, Some two or three
Poore Heretiques in love there bee,
Which thinke to stablish dangerous constancie.   25
But I have told them, since you will be true,
You shall be true to them, who'are false to you.

The Canonization

For Godsake hold your tongue, and let me love,
   Or chide my palsie, or my gout,
My five gray haires, or ruin'd fortune flout,
    With wealth your state, your minde with Arts improve,
     Take you a course, get you a place,   5
     Observe his honour, or his grace,
Or the Kings reall, or his stamped face
   Contemplate, what you will, approve,
   So you will let me love.

Alas, alas, who's injur'd by my love?   10
   What merchants ships have my sighs drown'd?
Who saies my teares have overflow'd his ground?
    When did my colds a forward spring remove?
     When did the heats which my veines fill
     Adde one more to the plaguie Bill?   15
Soldiers finde warres, and Lawyers finde out still
   Litigious men, which quarrels move,
   Though she and I do love.

26 *will be:* insist on being.
THE CANONIZATION.

   5 *course:* a course of action; *place:* a position, a job.
   6 *his honour:* a title given to any person of rank; *his grace:* a title given to people of very high rank, such as a duke, an archbishop, or a monarch.
   7 *stamped face:* on a coin.
   8 *approve:* try.
   13 *forward:* early.
   15 *plaguie Bill:* list of deaths caused by the plague.

Call us what you will, wee are made such by love;
  Call her one, mee another flye,   20
We'are Tapers too, and at our owne cost die,
  And wee in us finde the'Eagle and the Dove.
    The Phœnix ridle hath more wit
    By us, we two being one, are it.
So to one neutrall thing both sexes fit,   25
  Wee dye and rise the same, and prove
  Mysterious by this love.

Wee can dye by it, if not live by love,
  And if unfit for tombes and hearse
Our legend bee, it will be fit for verse;   30
  And if no peece of Chronicle wee prove,
    We'll build in sonnets pretty roomes;
    As well a well wrought urne becomes
The greatest ashes, as halfe-acre tombes,
  And by these hymnes, all shall approve   35
  Us *Canoniz'd* for Love:

And thus invoke us; You whom reverend love
  Made one anothers hermitage;
You, to whom love was peace, that now is rage;
  Who did the whole worlds soule extract, and drove   40

20 *flye:* any winged insect, esp. a moth or butterfly (the phrase "taper-fly" was in current usage: see next line).

21 *Tapers:* candles.

22 *Eagle . . . Dove:* symbols of masculine strength and feminine gentleness.

23 *Phœnix:* symbol of immortality; there was only one phoenix, a bird who lived for 500 or 600 years, consumed itself in fire, and rose again from its own ashes; *wit:* sense, meaning.

29 *hearse:* a wooden framework built over the bier or coffin for funerals; "it was customary for friends to pin short poems or epitaphs upon it" (OED).

30 *legend:* a saint's life; a history; also, an inscription.

32 *sonnets:* short love-songs; *roomes:* with perhaps a play on the Italian word, "stanza," meaning "room."

35 *approve:* confirm.

40 *extract:* Grierson reads "contract," but Miss Gardner has shown that the reading of the manuscripts in right: "The 'soul' of the world is extracted and

Into the glasses of your eyes
So made such mirrors, and such spies,
That they did all to you epitomize,
Countries, Townes, Courts: Beg from above
A patterne of your love!   45

Lovers infinitenesse

If yet I have not all thy love,
Deare, I shall never have it all,
I cannot breath one other sigh, to move;
Nor can intreat one other teare to fall.
And all my treasure, which should purchase thee,   5
Sighs, teares, and oathes, and letters I have spent,
Yet no more can be due to mee,
Then at the bargaine made was ment,
If then thy gift of love were partiall,
That some to mee, some should to others fall,   10
    Deare, I shall never have Thee All.

Or if then thou gavest mee all,
All was but All, which thou hadst then,
But if in thy heart, since, there be or shall,
New love created bee, by other men,   15
Which have their stocks intire, and can in teares,
In sighs, in oathes, and letters outbid mee,
This new love may beget new feares,
For, this love was not vowed by thee.
And yet it was, thy gift being generall,   20
The ground, thy heart is mine, what ever shall
    Grow there, deare, I should have it all.

---

driven into their eyes as an alchemist makes an extract by sublimation and
distillation, driving it through the pipes of the still into the 'glasses', or vessels,
in which it is stored" (see her ed. of *Songs and Sonets*, pp. lxxxvi, 204).

Yet I would not have all yet,
Hee that hath all can have no more,
And since my love doth every day admit   25
New growth, thou shouldst have new rewards in store;
Thou canst not every day give me thy heart,
If thou canst give it, then thou never gavest it:
Loves riddles are, that though thy heart depart,
It stayes at home, and thou with losing savest it: 30
But wee will have a way more liberall,
Then changing hearts, to joyne them, so wee shall
 Be one, and one anothers All.

Song

 Sweetest love, I do not goe,
  For wearinesse of thee,
 Nor in hope the world can show
  A fitter Love for mee;
   But since that I   5
 Must dye at last, 'tis best,
 To use my selfe in jest
  Thus by fain'd deaths to dye;

 Yesternight the Sunne went hence,
  And yet is here to day,   10
 He hath no desire nor sense,
  Nor halfe so short a way:
   Then feare not mee,
 But beleeve that I shall make
 Speedier journeyes, since I take   15
  More wings and spurres then hee.

LOVERS INFINITENESSE.
 30 *with losing savest it:* see Mark 8:35.
SONG.
 7 *use:* accustom.

[51]

O how feeble is mans power,
    That if good fortune fall,
Cannot adde another houre,
    Nor a lost houre recall!   20
      But come bad chance,
And wee joyne to'it our strength,
And wee teach it art and length,
    It selfe o'r us to'advance.

When thou sigh'st, thou sigh'st not winde,   25
    But sigh'st my soule away,
When thou weep'st, unkindly kinde,
    My lifes blood doth decay.
      It cannot bee
That thou lov'st mee, as thou say'st,   30
If in thine my life thou waste,
    Thou art the best of mee.

Let not thy divining heart
    Forethinke me any ill,
Destiny may take thy part,   35
    And may thy feares fulfill;
      But thinke that wee
Are but turn'd aside to sleepe;
They who one another keepe
    Alive, ne'r parted bee.   40

Aire and Angels

Twice or thrice had I loved thee,
Before I knew thy face or name,
So in a voice, so in a shapelesse flame,
Angells affect us oft, and worship'd bee;

33 *divining:* prophetic.

Still when, to where thou wert, I came,   5
Some lovely glorious nothing I did see.
　　But since my soule, whose child love is,
Takes limmes of flesh, and else could nothing doe,
　　More subtile then the parent is,
Love must not be, but take a body too,   10
　　And therefore what thou wert, and who,
　　　　I bid Love aske, and now
That it assume thy body, I allow,
And fixe it selfe in thy lip, eye, and brow.

Whilst thus to ballast love, I thought,   15
And so more steddily to have gone,
With wares which would sinke admiration,
I saw, I had loves pinnace overfraught,
　　Ev'ry thy haire for love to worke upon
Is much too much, some fitter must be sought;   20
　　For, nor in nothing, nor in things
Extreme, and scatt'ring bright, can love inhere;
　　Then as an Angell, face, and wings
Of aire, not pure as it, yet pure doth weare,
　　So thy love may be my loves spheare;   25
　　　　Just such disparitie
As is twixt Aire and Angells puritie,
'Twixt womens love, and mens will ever bee.

AIRE AND ANGELS.

5 *Still:* always.

9 *subtile:* delicate, rarefied.

15 *ballast:* stabilize, by adding sufficient weight.

18 *pinnace:* a small ship; *overfraught:* overweighted.

22–23 According to medieval thought, angels assumed bodies of air or mist; *pure:* in a scientific sense: not mixed with anything that defiles or impairs.

25 "Your love for me will be the sphere in which my love for you can move."

26–28 These lines reflect the assumption of Donne's time that masculine love is superior to feminine love; but with a witty turn Donne pays a compliment to the lady: her love is less pure because it is directed toward him; his love is more pure because it is directed toward a being of angelic purity, as in the tradition of Petrarchan compliment.

The Anniversarie

All Kings, and all their favorites,
   All glory of honors, beauties, wits,
The Sun it selfe, which makes times, as they passe,
Is elder by a yeare, now, then it was
When thou and I first one another saw: 5
All other things, to their destruction draw,
   Only our love hath no decay;
This, no to morrow hath, nor yesterday,
Running it never runs from us away,
But truly keepes his first, last, everlasting day.   10

Two graves must hide thine and my coarse,
   If one might, death were no divorce.
Alas, as well as other Princes, wee,
(Who Prince enough in one another bee,)
Must leave at last in death, these eyes, and eares,   15
Oft fed with true oathes, and with sweet salt teares;
   But soules where nothing dwells but love
(All other thoughts being inmates) then shall prove
This, or a love increased there above,
When bodies to their graves, soules from their graves remove.   20

And then wee shall be throughly blest,
   But wee no more, then all the rest;
Here upon earth, we'are Kings, and none but wee
Can be such Kings, nor of such subjects bee;
Who is so safe as wee? where none can doe   25
Treason to us, except one of us two.

THE ANNIVERSARIE.
   11 *coarse:* corpse.
   18 *inmates:* lodgers, subtenants.
   21 *throughly:* thoroughly.

True and false feares let us refraine,
Let us love nobly, and live, and adde againe
Yeares and yeares unto yeares, till we attaine
To write threescore: this is the second of our raigne.   30

Twicknam garden

Blasted with sighs, and surrounded with teares,
    Hither I come to seeke the spring,
    And at mine eyes, and at mine eares,
Receive such balmes, as else cure every thing;
    But O, selfe traytor, I do bring   5
The spider love, which transubstantiates all,
    And can convert Manna to gall,
And that this place may thoroughly be thought
    True Paradise, I have the serpent brought.

'Twere wholsomer for mee, that winter did   10
    Benight the glory of this place,
    And that a grave frost did forbid
These trees to laugh, and mocke mee to my face;
    But that I may not this disgrace
Indure, nor yet leave loving, Love let mee   15
    Some senslesse peece of this place bee;

27 *refraine:* restrain.

TWICKNAM GARDEN: From 1608 to 1617, Twickenham Park was the home of the Countess of Bedford, Donne's patroness and friend.

1 *surrounded:* flooded.

6 *spider:* said to convert all it consumed into poison.

7 *Manna:* (1) food miraculously provided for the Israelites in the wilderness; (2) a prefiguration of the Eucharist. Love inverts the Eucharistic transubstantiation (the Mass) by turning wholesomeness into a poisonous bitterness (*gall*).

14 *disgrace:* disfavor, reproach, and humiliation.

15 *Indure, nor yet leave loving:* so 1633 text (Grierson). Manuscripts read: "Indure, nor leave this garden" (Gardner).

Make me a mandrake, so I may groane here,
   Or a stone fountaine weeping out my yeare.

Hither with christall vyals, lovers come,
   And take my teares, which are loves wine,   20
   And try your mistresse Teares at home,
 For all are false, that tast not just like mine;
   Alas, hearts do not in eyes shine,
Nor can you more judge womans thoughts by teares,
   Then by her shadow, what she weares.   25
O perverse sexe, where none is true but shee,
   Who's therefore true, because her truth kills mee.

Loves growth

I scarce beleeve my love to be so pure
     As I had thought it was,
     Because it doth endure
Vicissitude, and season, as the grasse;
Me thinkes I lyed all winter, when I swore,   5
My love was infinite, if spring make'it more.

But if this medicine, love, which cures all sorrow
With more, not onely bee no quintessence,
But mixt of all stuffes, paining soule, or sense,
And of the Sunne his working vigour borrow,   10
Love's not so pure, and abstract, as they use
To say, which have no Mistresse but their Muse,

17 *groane:* the mandrake plant "was fabled to utter a deadly shriek when plucked up from the ground" (OED).

21 *try:* test.

26–27 The lady is true to someone else; or perhaps the lover here is suffering from remorse over his infidelity to a lady who remains true to him?

LOVES GROWTH.

1 *pure:* in a scientific sense, unmixed: a "pure essence."

8 *quintessence:* an essence extracted from all things, with curative power.

But as all else, being elemented too,
Love sometimes would contemplate, sometimes do.

And yet no greater, but more eminent,   15
　　Love by the spring is growne;
　　As, in the firmament,
Starres by the Sunne are not inlarg'd, but showne.
Gentle love deeds, as blossomes on a bough,
From loves awakened root do bud out now.   20

If, as in water stir'd more circles bee
Produc'd by one, love such additions take,
Those like so many spheares, but one heaven make,
For, they are all concentrique unto thee;
And though each spring doe adde to love new heate,   25
As princes doe in times of action get
New taxes, and remit them not in peace,
No winter shall abate the springs encrease.

The Dreame

Deare love, for nothing lesse then thee
Would I have broke this happy dreame,
　　　　It was a theame
For reason, much too strong for phantasie,
Therefore thou wakd'st me wisely; yet   5
My Dreame thou brok'st not, but continued'st it,
Thou art so truth, that thoughts of thee suffice,
To make dreames truths; and fables histories;
Enter these armes, for since thou thoughtst it best,
Not to dreame all my dreame, let's act the rest.   10

As lightning, or a Tapers light,
Thine eyes, and not thy noise wak'd mee;
　　　　Yet I thought thee
(For thou lovest truth) an Angell, at first sight,

But when I saw thou sawest my heart,   15
And knew'st my thoughts, beyond an Angels art,
When thou knew'st what I dreamt, when thou knew'st when
Excesse of joy would wake me, and cam'st then,
I must confesse, it could not chuse but bee
Prophane, to thinke thee any thing but thee.   20

Comming and staying show'd thee, thee,
But rising makes me doubt, that now,
       Thou art not thou.
That love is weake, where feare's as strong as hee;
'Tis not all spirit, pure, and brave,   25
If mixture it of *Feare, Shame, Honor,* have.
Perchance as torches which must ready bee,
Men light and put out, so thou deal'st with mee,
Thou cam'st to kindle, goest to come; Then I
Will dreame that hope againe, but else would die.   30

A Valediction: of weeping

      Let me powre forth
My teares before thy face, whil'st I stay here,
For thy face coines them, and thy stampe they beare,
And by this Mintage they are something worth,
        For thus they bee   5
        Pregnant of thee;
Fruits of much griefe they are, emblemes of more,
When a teare falls, that thou falst which it bore,
So thou and I are nothing then, when on a divers shore.

THE DREAME.

   16 Angels cannot know human thoughts; only God can know these things.
   20 The lady is equated with Deity: see Exodus 3:14:"I am that I am."
   27–28 A torch that has been used is easier to light than a new one.

On a round ball   10
A workeman that hath copies by, can lay
An Europe, Afrique, and an Asia,
And quickly make that, which was nothing, *All*,
    So doth each teare,
    Which thee doth weare,   15
A globe, yea world by that impression grow,
Till thy teares mixt with mine doe overflow
This world, by waters sent from thee, my heaven dissolved so.

    O more then Moone,
Draw not up seas to drowne me in thy spheare,   20
Weepe me not dead, in thine armes, but forbeare
To teach the sea, what it may doe too soone;
    Let not the winde
    Example finde,
To doe me more harme, then it purposeth;   25
Since thou and I sigh one anothers breath,
Who e'r sighes most, is cruellest, and hasts the others death.

Loves Alchymie

Some that have deeper digg'd loves Myne then I,
Say, where his centrique happinesse doth lie:
    I have lov'd, and got, and told,
But should I love, get, tell, till I were old,
I should not finde that hidden mysterie;   5
    Oh, 'tis imposture all:
And as no chymique yet th'Elixar got,
    But glorifies his pregnant pot,

LOVES ALCHYMIE.

  3 *told:* counted, calculated.

  7 *chymique:* alchemist; *Elixar:* a preparation sought by alchemists for the purpose of changing base metals into gold; a hypothetical substance able to prolong human life, a universal remedy for disease.

If by the way to him befall
Some odoriferous thing, or medicinall,   10
  So, lovers dreame a rich and long delight,
  But get a winter-seeming summers night.

Our ease, our thrift, our honor, and our day,
Shall we, for this vaine Bubles shadow pay?
    Ends love in this, that my man,   15
Can be as happy'as I can; If he can
Endure the short scorne of a Bridegroomes play?
    That loving wretch that sweares,
'Tis not the bodies marry, but the mindes,
    Which he in her Angelique findes,   20
    Would sweare as justly, that he heares,
In that dayes rude hoarse minstralsey, the spheares.
  Hope not for minde in women; at their best
  Sweetnesse and wit, they'are but *Mummy*, possest.

The Flea

Marke but this flea, and marke in this,
How little that which thou deny'st me is;
It suck'd me first, and now sucks thee,
And in this flea, our two bloods mingled bee;
Thou know'st that this cannot be said   5
A sinne, nor shame, nor losse of maidenhead,
  Yet this enjoyes before it wooe,
  And pamper'd swells with one blood made of two,
  And this, alas, is more then wee would doe.

17 "Endure the short mockery of the marriage ceremony, with its attendant festivities."

22 With ref. to the raucous music of the wedding day, as contrasted with the alleged music of the spheres.

24 *Mummy:* a substance, used as medicine, derived from embalmed bodies such as the Egyptian mummies.

Oh stay, three lives in one flea spare, 10
Where wee almost, yea more then maryed are,
This flea is you and I, and this
Our mariage bed, and mariage temple is;
Though parents grudge, and you, w'are met,
And cloysterd in these living walls of Jet. 15
   Though use make you apt to kill mee,
   Let not to that, selfe murder added bee,
   And sacrilege, three sinnes in killing three.

Cruell and sodaine, hast thou since
Purpled thy naile, in blood of innocence? 20
Wherein could this flea guilty bee,
Except in that drop which it suckt from thee?
Yet thou triumph'st, and saist that thou
Find'st not thy selfe, nor mee the weaker now;
   'Tis true, then learne how false, feares bee; 25
   Just so much honor, when thou yeeld'st to mee,
   Will wast, as this flea's death tooke life from thee.

The Apparition

When by thy scorne, O murdresse, I am dead,
   And that thou thinkst thee free
From all solicitation from mee,
Then shall my ghost come to thy bed,
And thee, fain'd vestall, in worse armes shall see; 5

THE FLEA: Miss Gardner has shown that fleas were popular topics for erotic poetry throughout Europe; she notes one volume of 1582 that contained more than fifty poems on this topic in five languages. She points out: "Donne's originality transforms this well-worn subject by making the flea bite both him and his mistress, thus making it a symbol not of the lover's desire but of the desired union" (see her ed. of *Songs and Sonets*, p. 174).

THE APPARITION.

   5 *vestall:* Vestal virgin.

Then thy sicke taper will begin to winke,
And he, whose thou art then, being tyr'd before,
Will, if thou stirre, or pinch to wake him, thinke
     Thou call'st for more,
And in false sleepe will from thee shrinke,   10
And then poore Aspen wretch, neglected thou
Bath'd in a cold quicksilver sweat wilt lye
     A veryer ghost then I;
What I will say, I will not tell thee now,
Lest that preserve thee'; and since my love is spent,   15
I'had rather thou shouldst painfully repent,
Then by my threatnings rest still innocent.

The Extasie

Where, like a pillow on a bed,
  A Pregnant banke swel'd up, to rest
The violets reclining head,
  Sat we two, one anothers best.
Our hands were firmely cimented   5
  With a fast balme, which thence did spring,
Our eye-beames twisted, and did thred
  Our eyes, upon one double string;
So to'entergraft our hands, as yet
  Was all the meanes to make us one,   10
And pictures in our eyes to get
  Was all our propagation.
As 'twixt two equal Armies, Fate
  Suspends uncertaine victorie,

6 *winke:* flicker.
11 *Aspen:* trembling, quaking.
13 *veryer:* truer.
17 *innocent:* without a sense of guilt.
THE EXTASIE: a mystical state; see NOTE.

Our soules, (which to advance their state,   15
    Were gone out,) hung 'twixt her, and mee.
And whil'st our soules negotiate there,
    Wee like sepulchrall statues lay;
All day, the same our postures were,
    And wee said nothing, all the day.   20
If any, so by love refin'd,
    That he soules language understood,
And by good love were growen all minde,
    Within convenient distance stood,
He (though he knew not which soule spake,   25
    Because both meant, both spake the same)
Might thence a new concoction take,
    And part farre purer then he came.
This Extasie doth unperplex
    (We said) and tell us what we love,   30
Wee see by this, it was not sexe,
    Wee see, we saw not what did move:
But as all severall soules containe
    Mixture of things, they know not what,
Love, these mixt soules doth mixe againe,   35
    And makes both one, each this and that.
A single violet transplant,
    The strength, the colour, and the size,
(All which before was poore, and scant,)
    Redoubles still, and multiplies.   40
When love, with one another so
    Interinanimates two soules,
That abler soule, which thence doth flow,
    Defects of lonelinesse controules.
Wee then, who are this new soule, know,   45
    Of what we are compos'd, and made,
For, th'Atomies of which we grow,

27 *concoction:* a process of purification or maturing by heat.
33 *severall:* separate, individual.
47 *Atomies:* atoms.

[63]

Are soules, whom no change can invade.
But O alas, so long, so farre
  Our bodies why doe wee forbeare? 50
They'are ours, though they'are not wee, Wee are
  The intelligences, they the spheare.
We owe them thankes, because they thus,
  Did us, to us, at first convay,
Yeelded their forces, sense, to us, 55
  Nor are drosse to us, but allay.
On man heavens influence workes not so,
  But that it first imprints the ayre,
Soe soule into the soule may flow,
  Though it to body first repaire. 60
As our blood labours to beget
  Spirits, as like soules as it can,
Because such fingers need to knit
  That subtile knot, which makes us man:
So must pure lovers soules descend 65
  T'affections, and to faculties,
Which sense may reach and apprehend,
  Else a great Prince in prison lies.
To'our bodies turne wee then, that so
  Weake men on love reveal'd may looke; 70
Loves mysteries in soules doe grow,
  But yet the body is his booke.
And if some lover, such as wee,
  Have heard this dialogue of one,
Let him still marke us, he shall see 75
  Small change, when we'are to bodies gone.

---

52 *intelligences:* angels or spirits supposed to move the spheres in the Ptolemaic system; *spheare:* "one or other of the concentric, transparent, hollow globes imagined by the older astronomers as revolving round the earth and respectively carrying with them the several heavenly bodies" (OED). Here used collectively for the "heavens."

56 *allay:* alloy.

62 *Spirits:* vapors arising from the blood, thought to link soul and body.

Loves Deitie

I long to talke with some old lovers ghost,
  Who dyed before the god of Love was borne:
I cannot thinke that hee, who then lov'd most,
  Sunke so low, as to love one which did scorne.
But since this god produc'd a destinie,   5
And that vice-nature, custome, lets it be;
  I must love her, that loves not mee.

Sure, they which made him god, meant not so much,
  Nor he, in his young godhead practis'd it;
But when an even flame two hearts did touch,   10
  His office was indulgently to fit
Actives to passives. Correspondencie
Only his subject was; It cannot bee
  Love, till I love her, that loves mee.

But every moderne god will now extend   15
  His vast prerogative, as far as Jove.
To rage, to lust, to write to, to commend,
  All is the purlewe of the God of Love.
Oh were wee wak'ned by this Tyrannie
To ungod this child againe, it could not bee   20
  I should love her, who loves not mee.

Rebell and Atheist too, why murmure I,
  As though I felt the worst that love could doe?

LOVES DEITIE.
  10 *even:* equal.
  12 *Correspondencie:* agreement, sympathetic response.
  13 *subject:* business; person or thing under the dominion of another.
  18 *purlewe:* "a place where one has the right to range at large" (OED);
with allusion to the questionable assertion of royal authority over lands ("pur-
lieus") formerly forested, and thus coming under special law.

Love might make me leave loving, or might trie
    A deeper plague, to make her love me too,   25
Which, since she loves before, I'am loth to see;
Falshood is worse then hate; and that must bee,
    If shee whom I love, should love mee.

The Funerall

Who ever comes to shroud me, do not harme
    Nor question much
That subtile wreath of haire, which crowns my arme;
The mystery, the signe you must not touch,
    For 'tis my outward Soule,   5
Viceroy to that, which then to heaven being gone,
    Will leave this to controule,
And keepe these limbes, her Provinces, from dissolution.

For if the sinewie thread my braine lets fall
    Through every part,   10
Can tye those parts, and make mee one of all;
These haires which upward grew, and strength and art
    Have from a better braine,
Can better do'it; Except she meant that I
    By this should know my pain,   15
As prisoners then are manacled, when they'are condemn'd to die.

What ere shee meant by'it, bury it with me,
    For since I am
Loves martyr, it might breed idolatrie,
If into others hands these Reliques came;
    As 'twas humility   20
To afford to it all that a Soule can doe,

26 *loves before:* loves someone else.
THE FUNERALL.
    3 *subtile:* of fine texture; also, cleverly devised.

So,'tis some bravery,
That since you would save none of mee, I bury some of you.

The Blossome

Little think'st thou, poore flower,
    Whom I have watch'd sixe or seaven dayes,
And seene thy birth, and seene what every houre
Gave to thy growth, thee to this height to raise,
And now dost laugh and triumph on this bough,   5
        Little think'st thou
That it will freeze anon, and that I shall
To morrow finde thee falne, or not at all.

Little think'st thou poore heart
    That labour'st yet to nestle thee,   10
And think'st by hovering here to get a part
In a forbidden or forbidding tree,
And hop'st her stiffenesse by long siege to bow:
        Little think'st thou,
That thou to morrow, ere that Sunne doth wake,   15
Must with this Sunne, and mee a journey take.

But thou which lov'st to bee
    Subtile to plague thy selfe, wilt say,
Alas, if you must goe, what's that to mee?
Here lyes my businesse, and here I will stay: 20
You goe to friends, whose love and meanes present
        Various content

23 *bravery:* a proud or defiant action: bravado.
THE BLOSSOME.
    12 The Petrarchan lady traditionally is either married or disdainful.
    15 *that Sunne:* his lady.
    17 *thou:* his heart.

To your eyes, eares, and tongue, and every part.
If then your body goe, what need you a heart?

    Well then, stay here; but know,   25
      When thou hast stayd and done thy most;
A naked thinking heart, that makes no show,
Is to a woman, but a kinde of Ghost;
How shall shee know my heart; or having none,
           Know thee for one?   30
Practise may make her know some other part,
But take my word, shee doth not know a Heart.

    Meet mee at London, then,
      Twenty dayes hence, and thou shalt see
Mee fresher, and more fat, by being with men,   35
Then if I had staid still with her and thee.
For Gods sake, if you can, be you so too:
           I would give you
There, to another friend, whom wee shall finde
As glad to have my body, as my minde.   40

The Relique

    When my grave is broke up againe
    Some second ghest to entertaine,
    (For graves have learn'd that woman-head
    To be to more then one a Bed)
        And he that digs it, spies   5
A bracelet of bright haire about the bone,
        Will he not let'us alone,
And thinke that there a loving couple lies,

THE RELIQUE: object venerated as memorial of a saint.
3 *woman-head:* quality natural to a woman.

[68]

Who thought that this device might be some way
To make their soules, at the last busie day,   10
Meet at this grave, and make a little stay?

    If this fall in a time, or land,
    Where mis-devotion doth command,
      Then, he that digges us up, will bring
      Us, to the Bishop, and the King,   15
        To make us Reliques; then
Thou shalt be a Mary Magdalen, and I
        A something else thereby;
All women shall adore us, and some men;
And since at such time, miracles are sought,   20
I would have that age by this paper taught
What miracles wee harmelesse lovers wrought.

    First, we lov'd well and faithfully,
    Yet knew not what wee lov'd, nor why,
      Difference of sex no more wee knew,   25
      Then our Guardian Angells doe;
        Comming and going, wee
Perchance might kisse, but not between those meales;
        Our hands ne'r toucht the seales,
Which nature, injur'd by late law, sets free: 30
These miracles wee did; but now alas,
All measure, and all language, I should passe,
Should I tell what a miracle shee was.

10 *last busie day:* the Day of Judgment.

17 *Mary Magdalen:* traditionally regarded as a repentant harlot; represented in Renaissance paintings with "bright haire".

18 *A something else:* "some other kind of saint—equally mistaken".

20 *at such time:* miracles are required for the canonization of a saint, and to prove the authenticity of a relic.

A Lecture upon the Shadow

Stand still, and I will read to thee
A Lecture, Love, in loves philosophy.
    These three houres that we have spent,
    Walking here, Two shadowes went
Along with us, which we our selves produc'd;   5
But, now the Sunne is just above our head,
    We doe those shadowes tread;
    And to brave clearnesse all things are reduc'd.
So whilst our infant loves did grow,
Disguises did, and shadowes, flow,   10
From us, and our cares; but, now 'tis not so.

That love hath not attain'd the high'st degree,
Which is still diligent lest others see.

Except our loves at this noone stay,
We shall new shadowes make the other way.   15
    As the first were made to blinde
    Others; these which come behinde
Will worke upon our selves, and blind our eyes.
If our loves faint, and westwardly decline;
    To me thou, falsly, thine,   20
    And I to thee mine actions shall disguise.
The morning shadowes weare away,
But these grow longer all the day,
But oh, loves day is short, if love decay.

Love is a growing, or full constant light;   25
And his first minute, after noone, is night.

A LECTURE UPON THE SHADOW.
  10 *shadowes:* disguises; also, touches of worry and anxiety.
  17 *behinde:* later.

To Mr C.B.

Thy friend, whom thy deserts to thee enchaine,
  Urg'd by this unexcusable occasion,
  Thee and the Saint of his affection
Leaving behinde, doth of both wants complaine;
And let the love I beare to both sustaine   5
  No blott nor maime by this division,
  Strong is this love which ties our hearts in one,
And strong that love pursu'd with amorous paine;
But though besides thy selfe I leave behind
  Heavens liberall, and earths thrice-fairer Sunne,   10
  Going to where sterne winter aye doth wonne,
Yet, loves hot fires, which martyr my sad minde,
  Doe send forth scalding sighes, which have the Art
  To melt all Ice, but that which walls her heart.

To Mr R.W.

Kindly I envy thy songs perfection
  Built of all th'elements as our bodyes are:
  That Litle of earth that is in it, is a faire

TO MR C.B.: presumably Christopher Brooke (c. 1570–1628), Donne's close friend, who gave away the bride at Donne's secret marriage. Note the use of traditional sonnet-form and Petrarchan imagery.

  10 The sun, and the poet's lady.

  11 *wonne:* dwell.

TO MR R.W.: presumably Rowland Woodward (1573–1637), another close friend, who has here sent Donne a poem to read. Again Donne uses traditional sonnet-form for a verse-letter.

  1 *Kindly:* affectionately; and also naturally, considering that both are poets.

  2 *all th'elements:* earth, water, fire, and air, all of which are involved in the following images.

Delicious garden where all sweetes are sowne.
In it is cherishing fyer which dryes in mee 5
   Griefe which did drowne me: and halfe quench'd by it
   Are satirique fyres which urg'd me to have writt
In skorne of all: for now I admyre thee.
   And as Ayre doth fullfill the hollownes
   Of rotten walls; so it myne emptines, 10
Where tost and mov'd it did beget this sound
Which as a lame Eccho of thyne doth rebound.
   Oh, I was dead; but since thy song new Life did give,
   I recreated, even by thy creature, live.

To Mr Rowland Woodward

Like one who'in her third widdowhood doth professe
Her selfe a Nunne, tyed to retirednesse,
So'affects my muse now, a chast fallownesse;

Since shee to few, yet to too many'hath showne
How love-song weeds, and Satyrique thornes are growne 5
Where seeds of better Arts, were early sown.

Though to use, and love Poëtrie, to mee,
Betroth'd to no'one Art, be no'adulterie;
Omissions of good, ill, as ill deeds bee.

For though to us it seeme,'and be light and thinne, 10
Yet in those faithfull scales, where God throwes in
Mens workes, vanity weighs as much as sinne.

If our Soules have stain'd their first white, yet wee
May cloth them with faith, and deare honestie,
Which God imputes, as native puritie. 15

4 *sweetes:* fragrant flowers.
10 *so it:* so your poem (fills).

There is no Vertue, but Religion:
Wise, valiant, sober, just, are names, which none
Want, which want not Vice-covering discretion.

Seeke wee then our selves in our selves; for as
Men force the Sunne with much more force to passe,   20
By gathering his beames with a christall glasse;

So wee, If wee into our selves will turne,
Blowing our sparkes of vertue, may outburne
The straw, which doth about our hearts sojourne.

You know, Physitians, when they would infuse   25
Into any'oyle, the Soules of Simples, use
Places, where they may lie still warme, to chuse.

So workes retirednesse in us; To rome
Giddily, and be every where, but at home,
Such freedome doth a banishment become.   30

Wee are but farmers of our selves, yet may,
If we can stocke our selves, and thrive, uplay
Much, much deare treasure for the great rent day.

Manure thy selfe then, to thy selfe be'approv'd,
And with vaine outward things be no more mov'd,   35
But to know, that I love thee'and would be lov'd.

TO MR ROWLAND WOODWARD.
   18 *want:* lack.
   23 *outburne:* burn longer than, burn more brightly than; perhaps also, burn away.
   26 *Soules of Simples:* essences of medicinal plants.
   31 *farmers:* those who cultivate land not owned by themselves.
   34 *manure:* cultivate.

La Corona

1. Deigne at my hands this crown of prayer and praise,
Weav'd in my low devout melancholie,
Thou which of good, hast, yea art treasury,
All changing unchang'd Antient of dayes;
But doe not, with a vile crowne of fraile bayes,   5
Reward my muses white sincerity,
But what thy thorny crowne gain'd, that give mee,
A crowne of Glory, which doth flower alwayes;
The ends crowne our workes, but thou crown'st our ends,
For, at our end begins our endlesse rest;   10
The first last end, now zealously possest,
With a strong sober thirst, my soule attends.
'Tis time that heart and voice be lifted high,
Salvation to all that will is nigh.

Annunciation

2. Salvation to all that will is nigh;
That All, which alwayes is All every where,
Which cannot sinne, and yet all sinnes must beare,
Which cannot die, yet cannot chuse but die,
Loe, faithfull Virgin, yeelds himselfe to lye   5
In prison, in thy wombe; and though he there

LA CORONA: see NOTE.
1.1 *Deigne:* think worthy of acceptance.
  4 *Antient of dayes:* see Daniel 7:9.
  5 *bayes:* laurels, the crown of poetic achievement.
  6 *sincerity:* with ref. to Latin *sincerus:* clean, pure.
 12 *attends:* awaits.

ANNO DNI. 1591
ÆTATIS SVÆ 18

ANTES MVDADO
MVERTO QVE...

This was for youth, Strength, Mirth, and wit that Time
Most count their golden Age; but t'was not thine.
Thine was thy later yeares, so much refind
From youths Drosse, Mirth, & wit; as thy pure mind
Thought (like the Angels) nothing but the Praise
Of thy Creator, in those last, best Dayes.
     Witnes this Booke, (thy Embleme) which begins
     With Love; but endes, with Sighes, & Teares for sins.

Will: Marshall sculpsit.   IZ: WA:

PLATE I Portrait of John Donne at the age of eighteen, from the second
edition of Donne's *Poems*, 1635.

Can take no sinne, nor thou give, yet he'will weare
Taken from thence, flesh, which deaths force may trie.
Ere by the spheares time was created, thou
Wast in his minde, who is thy Sonne, and Brother;   10
Whom thou conceiv'st, conceiv'd; yea thou art now
Thy Makers maker, and thy Fathers mother;
Thou'hast light in darke; and shutst in little roome,
Immensity cloysterd in thy deare wombe.

Nativitie

   3. *Immensitie cloysterd in thy deare wombe,*
Now leaves his welbelov'd imprisonment,
There he hath made himselfe to his intent
Weake enough, now into our world to come;
But Oh, for thee, for him, hath th'Inne no roome?   5
Yet lay him in this stall, and from the Orient,
Starres, and wisemen will travell to prevent
Th'effect of *Herods* jealous generall doome.
Seest thou, my Soule, with thy faiths eyes, how he
Which fils all place, yet none holds him, doth lye?   10
Was not his pity towards thee wondrous high,
That would have need to be pittied by thee?
Kisse him, and with him into Egypt goe,
With his kinde mother, who partakes thy woe.

Temple

   4. *With his kinde mother who partakes thy woe,*
Joseph turne backe; see where your child doth sit,
Blowing, yea blowing out those sparks of wit,
Which himselfe on the Doctors did bestow;

3.7 *prevent:* anticipate, come before.

The Word but lately could not speake, and loe,   5
It sodenly speakes wonders, whence comes it,
That all which was, and all which should be writ,
A shallow seeming child, should deeply know?
His Godhead was not soule to his manhood,
Nor had time mellowed him to this ripenesse,   10
But as for one which hath a long taske, 'tis good,
With the Sunne to beginne his businesse,
He in his ages morning thus began
By miracles exceeding power of man.

Crucifying

5. *By miracles exceeding power of man,*
Hee faith in some, envie in some begat,
For, what weake spirits admire, ambitious, hate;
In both affections many to him ran,
But Oh! the worst are most, they will and can,   5
Alas, and do, unto the immaculate,
Whose creature Fate is, now prescribe a Fate,
Measuring selfe-lifes infinity to'a span,
Nay to an inch. Loe, where condemned hee
Beares his owne crosse, with paine, yet by and by   10
When it beares him, he must beare more and die.
Now thou art lifted up, draw mee to thee,
And at thy death giving such liberall dole,
Moyst, with one drop of thy blood, my dry soule.

5.4 *affections:* emotions.
  8 *span:* the extent of a hand: nine inches.

Resurrection

6. *Moyst with one drop of thy blood, my dry soule*
Shall (though she now be in extreme degree
Too stony hard, and yet too fleshly,) bee
Freed by that drop, from being starv'd, hard, or foule,
And life, by this death abled, shall controule   5
Death, whom thy death slue; nor shall to mee
Feare of first or last death, bring miserie,
If in thy little booke my name thou enroule,
Flesh in that long sleep is not putrified,
But made that there, of which, and for which 'twas;   10
Nor can by other meanes be glorified.
May then sinnes sleep, and deaths soone from me passe,
That wak't from both, I againe risen may
Salute the last, and everlasting day.

Ascention

7. *Salute the last and everlasting day,*
Joy at the uprising of this Sunne, and Sonne,
Yee whose just teares, or tribulation
Have purely washt, or burnt your drossie clay;
Behold the Highest, parting hence away,   5
Lightens the darke clouds, which hee treads upon,
Nor doth hee by ascending, show alone,
But first hee, and hee first enters the way.
O strong Ramme, which hast batter'd heaven for mee,
Mild Lambe, which with thy blood, hast mark'd the path;   10
Bright Torch, which shin'st, that I the way may see,

6.4 *starv'd:* probably in the sense of withered.
  5 *abled:* given strength or power.

[77]

Oh, with thy owne blood quench thy owne just wrath,
And if thy holy Spirit, my Muse did raise,
Deigne at my hands this crowne of prayer and praise.

HOLY SONNETS

1.

Thou hast made me, And shall thy worke decay?
Repaire me now, for now mine end doth haste,
I runne to death, and death meets me as fast,
And all my pleasures are like yesterday;
I dare not move my dimme eyes any way,   5
Despaire behind, and death before doth cast
Such terrour, and my feeble flesh doth waste
By sinne in it, which it t'wards hell doth weigh;
Onely thou art above, and when towards thee
By thy leave I can looke, I rise againe;   10
But our old subtle foe so tempteth me,
That not one houre my selfe I can sustaine;
Thy Grace may wing me to prevent his art,
And thou like Adamant draw mine iron heart.

2.

As due by many titles I resigne
My selfe to thee, O God, first I was made
By thee, and for thee, and when I was decay'd
Thy blood bought that, the which before was thine;

HOLY SONNETS: see NOTE.
1.13 *prevent:* anticipate, forestall, balk.
   14 *Adamant:* a stone of extreme hardness; also, of magnetic power.
2.1 *titles:* in legal usage, the proofs of ownership; *resigne:* give up, hand over.

I am thy sonne, made with thy selfe to shine,   5
Thy servant, whose paines thou hast still repaid,
Thy sheepe, thine Image, and, till I betray'd
My selfe, a temple of thy Spirit divine;
Why doth the devill then usurpe on mee?
Why doth he steale, nay ravish that's thy right?   10
Except thou rise and for thine owne worke fight,
Oh I shall soone despaire, when I doe see
That thou lov'st mankind well, yet wilt'not chuse me,
And Satan hates mee, yet is loth to lose mee.

3.

O might those sighes and teares returne againe
Into my breast and eyes, which I have spent,
That I might in this holy discontent
    Mourne with some fruit, as I have mourn'd in vaine;
In mine Idolatry what showres of raine   5
Mine eyes did waste? what griefs my heart did rent?
That sufferance was my sinne; now I repent;
'Cause I did suffer I must suffer paine.
Th'hydroptique drunkard, and night-scouting thiefe,
The itchy Lecher, and selfe tickling proud   10
Have the remembrance of past joyes, for reliefe
Of comming ills. To (poore) me is allow'd
    No ease; for, long, yet vehement griefe hath beene
Th'effect and cause, the punishment and sinne.

10 *that's:* that which is.
3.6 *rent:* rend, tear.
    7 *sufferance:* suffering pain; also, permission, consent (to engage in such follies).
    8 *suffer:* suffer grief (in love); also, allow, permit.
    9 *night-scouting:* lurking in the night.
    10 *selfe tickling proud:* the proud man who finds pleasure in admiring himself.

4.

Oh my blacke Soule! now thou art summoned
By sicknesse, deaths herald, and champion;
Thou art like a pilgrim, which abroad hath done
Treason, and durst not turne to whence hee is fled,
Or like a thiefe, which till deaths doome be read,   5
Wisheth himselfe delivered from prison;
But damn'd and hal'd to execution,
Wisheth that still he might be imprisoned.
Yet grace, if thou repent, thou canst not lacke;
But who shall give thee that grace to beginne?   10
Oh make thy selfe with holy mourning blacke,
And red with blushing, as thou art with sinne;
Or wash thee in Christs blood, which hath this might
That being red, it dyes red soules to white.

5.

I am a little world made cunningly
Of Elements, and an Angelike spright,
But black sinne hath betraid to endlesse night
My worlds both parts, and (oh) both parts must die.
You which beyond that heaven which was most high   5
Have found new sphears, and of new lands can write,
Powre new seas in mine eyes, that so I might
Drowne my world with my weeping earnestly,

4.1–2 The image is that of being *summoned* in the legal sense to undergo a trial by combat, in which sickness is the *champion* or official representative of death.

  7 *damn'd:* condemned.

5.1 *cunningly:* skillfully.

  2 *spright:* spirit.

  5–6 With ref. to the astronomical controversies of Donne's time, when the theory of the Ptolemaic universe, with its concentric spheres, was being questioned, altered, and rejected.

Or wash it, if it must be drown'd no more:
But oh it must be burnt! alas the fire   10
Of lust and envie have burnt it heretofore,
And made it fouler; Let their flames retire,
And burne me ô Lord, with a fiery zeale
Of thee and thy house, which doth in eating heale.

6.

This is my playes last scene, here heavens appoint
My pilgrimages last mile; and my race
Idly, yet quickly runne, hath this last pace,
My spans last inch, my minutes latest point,
And gluttonous death, will instantly unjoynt   5
My body, and soule, and I shall sleepe a space,
But my'ever-waking part shall see that face,
Whose feare already shakes my every joynt:
Then, as my soule, to'heaven her first seate, takes flight
And earth-borne body, in the earth shall dwell,   10
So, fall my sinnes, that all may have their right,
To where they'are bred, and would presse me, to hell.
Impute me righteous, thus purg'd of evill,
For thus I leave the world, the flesh, the devill.

7.

At the round earths imagin'd corners, blow
Your trumpets, Angells, and arise, arise
From death, you numberlesse infinities
Of soules, and to your scattred bodies goe,
All whom the flood did, and fire shall o'erthrow,   5
All whom warre, dearth, age, agues, tyrannies,

9–10 See Genesis 9:11 and 2 Peter 3:10.
13–14 See Psalm 69:9.
6.9 *seate:* place of residence.
7.1–2 See Revelation 7:1.

Despaire, law, chance, hath slaine, and you whose eyes,
Shall behold God, and never tast deaths woe.
But let them sleepe, Lord, and mee mourne a space,
For, if above all these, my sinnes abound,   10
'Tis late to aske abundance of thy grace,
When wee are there; here on this lowly ground,
Teach mee how to repent; for that's as good
As if thou'hadst seal'd my pardon, with thy blood.

8.

If faithfull soules be alike glorifi'd
As Angels, then my fathers soule doth see,
And adds this even to full felicitie,
That valiantly I hels wide mouth o'rstride:
But if our mindes to these soules be descry'd   5
By circumstances, and by signes that be
Apparent in us, not immediately,
How shall my mindes white truth by them be try'd?
They see idolatrous lovers weepe and mourne,
And vile blasphemous Conjurers to call   10
On Jesus name, and Pharisaicall
Dissemblers feigne devotion. Then turne
O pensive soule, to God, for he knowes best
Thy true griefe, for he put it in my breast.

9.

If poysonous mineralls, and if that tree,
Whose fruit threw death on else immortall us,
If lecherous goats, if serpents envious
Cannot be damn'd; Alas; why should I bee?

8 See Luke 9:27.
8.1–2 "If faithfull souls in heaven are, like Angels, endowed with the power
of intuitive knowledge" (as opposed to human modes of perception on earth).
  8 *try'd:* proven, tested.

Why should intent or reason, borne in mee,   5
  Make sinnes, else equall, in mee more heinous?
And mercy being easie, and glorious
To God; in his sterne wrath, why threatens hee?
But who am I, that dare dispute with thee
O God? Oh! of thine onely worthy blood,   10
And my teares, make a heavenly Lethean flood,
And drowne in it my sinnes blacke memorie;
That thou remember them, some claime as debt,
I thinke it mercy, if thou wilt forget.

10.

Death be not proud, though some have called thee
Mighty and dreadfull, for, thou art not soe,
For, those, whom thou think'st, thou dost overthrow,
Die not, poore death, nor yet canst thou kill mee.
From rest and sleepe, which but thy pictures bee,   5
Much pleasure, then from thee, much more must flow,
And soonest our best men with thee doe goe,
Rest of their bones, and soules deliverie.
Thou art slave to Fate, Chance, kings, and desperate men,
And dost with poyson, warre, and sicknesse dwell,   10
And poppie, or charmes can make us sleepe as well,
And better then thy stroake; why swell'st thou then?
One short sleepe past, wee wake eternally,
And death shall be no more; death, thou shalt die.

11.

Spit in my face you Jewes, and pierce my side,
Buffet, and scoffe, scourge, and crucifie mee,
For I have sinn'd, and sinn'd, and onely hee,
Who could do no iniquitie, hath dyed:

10.8 *deliverie:* release, liberation.

But by my death can not be satisfied   5
My sinnes, which passe the Jewes impiety:
They kill'd once an inglorious man, but I
Crucifie him daily, being now glorified.
Oh let mee then, his strange love still admire:
Kings pardon, but he bore our punishment.   10
And *Jacob* came cloth'd in vile harsh attire
But to supplant, and with gainfull intent:
God cloth'd himselfe in vile mans flesh, that so
Hee might be weake enough to suffer woe.

12.

Why are wee by all creatures waited on?
Why doe the prodigall elements supply
Life and food to mee, being more pure then I,
Simple, and further from corruption?
Why brook'st thou, ignorant horse, subjection?   5
Why dost thou bull, and bore so seelily
Dissemble weaknesse, and by'one mans stroke die,
Whose whole kinde, you might swallow and feed upon?
Weaker I am, woe is mee, and worse then you,
You have not sinn'd, nor need be timorous.   10
But wonder at a greater wonder, for to us
Created nature doth these things subdue,
But their Creator, whom sin, nor nature tyed,
For us, his Creatures, and his foes, hath dyed.

13.

What if this present were the worlds last night?
Marke in my heart, O Soule, where thou dost dwell,

11.5 *satisfied:* atoned for.
  11–12 See Genesis 27.
12.4 *Simple:* of a single substance, not mixed.
  6 *seelily:* sillily, foolishly.

The picture of Christ crucified, and tell
Whether that countenance can thee affright,
Teares in his eyes quench the amasing light, 5
Blood fills his frownes, which from his pierc'd head fell.
And can that tongue adjudge thee unto hell,
Which pray'd forgivenesse for his foes fierce spight?
No, no; but as in my idolatrie
I said to all my profane mistresses, 10
Beauty, of pitty, foulnesse onely is
A signe of rigour: so I say to thee,
To wicked spirits are horrid shapes assign'd,
This beauteous forme assures a pitious minde.

14.

Batter my heart, three person'd God; for, you
As yet but knocke, breathe, shine, and seeke to mend;
That I may rise, and stand, o'erthrow mee,'and bend
Your force, to breake, blowe, burn and make me new.
I, like an usurpt towne, to'another due, 5
Labour to'admit you, but Oh, to no end,
Reason your viceroy in mee, mee should defend,
But is captiv'd, and proves weake or untrue.
Yet dearely'I love you,'and would be loved faine,
But am betroth'd unto your enemie: 10
Divorce mee,'untie, or breake that knot againe,
Take mee to you, imprison mee, for I
Except you'enthrall mee, never shall be free,
Nor ever chast, except you ravish mee.

13.5 *amasing:* terrifying, stupefying.
14.1–4 Note the precise allusions to the three persons of the Trinity: God the
Father *knocks,* but should *break;* the Holy Spirit *breathes,* but should *blow;*
and the Son (sun) *shines,* but should *burn.*

15.

Wilt thou love God, as he thee! then digest,
My Soule, this wholsome meditation,
How God the Spirit, by Angels waited on
In heaven, doth make his Temple in thy brest.
The Father having begot a Sonne most blest,   5
And still begetting, (for he ne'r begonne)
Hath deign'd to chuse thee by adoption,
Coheire to'his glory,'and Sabbaths endlesse rest.
And as a robb'd man, which by search doth finde
His stolne stuffe sold, must lose or buy'it againe: 10
The Sonne of glory came downe, and was slaine,
Us whom he'had made, and Satan stolne, to unbinde.
'Twas much, that man was made like God before,
But, that God should be made like man, much more.

16.

Father, part of his double interest
Unto thy kingdome, thy Sonne gives to mee,
His joynture in the knottie Trinitie
Hee keepes, and gives to me his deaths conquest.
This Lambe, whose death, with life the world hath blest,   5
Was from the worlds beginning slaine, and he
Hath made two Wills, which with the Legacie
Of his and thy kingdome, doe thy Sonnes invest.
Yet such are thy laws, that men argue yet
Whether a man those statutes can fulfill;   10
None doth; but all-healing grace and spirit

16.1 *interest:* legal claim to or participation in ownership.
  3 *joynture:* right to an estate held in joint tenancy.
  6 See Revelation 13:8.
  7 *two Wills:* the Old and the New Testaments.
  8 *invest:* place in possession of.

Revive againe what law and letter kill.
Thy lawes abridgement, and thy last command
Is all but love; Oh let this last Will stand!

A Valediction: forbidding mourning

As virtuous men passe mildly away,
    And whisper to their soules, to goe,
Whilst some of their sad friends doe say,
    The breath goes now, and some say, no:

So let us melt, and make no noise,   5
    No teare-floods, nor sigh-tempests move,
T'were prophanation of our joyes
    To tell the layetie our love.

Moving of th'earth brings harmes and feares,
    Men reckon what it did and meant,   10
But trepidation of the spheares,
    Though greater farre, is innocent.

Dull sublunary lovers love
    (Whose soule is sense) cannot admit
Absence, because it doth remove   15
    Those things which elemented it.

But we by a love, so much refin'd,
    That our selves know not what it is,
Inter-assured of the mind,
    Care lesse, eyes, lips, and hands to misse.   20

14 *all but love: but* in the sense of *only:* "nothing but love"; see John 13:34.
A VALEDICTION: FORBIDDING MOURNING.

11 *trepidation:* a technical term from Ptolemaic astronomy, describing the movement attributed to the ninth sphere in order to explain the "precession of the equinoxes." Here contrasted with the earthquakes of line 9.

12 *innocent:* harmless.

14 *admit:* permit, allow.

Our two soules therefore, which are one,
   Though I must goe, endure not yet
A breach, but an expansion,
   Like gold to ayery thinnesse beate.

If they be two, they are two so   25
   As stiffe twin compasses are two,
Thy soule the fixt foot, makes no show
   To move, but doth, if the'other doe.

And though it in the center sit,
   Yet when the other far doth rome,   30
It leanes, and hearkens after it,
   And growes erect, as that comes home.

Such wilt thou be to mee, who must
   Like th'other foot, obliquely runne;
Thy firmnes makes my circle just,   35
   And makes me end, where I begunne.

The First Anniuersarie.

AN ANATOMIE

of the VVorld.

Wherein,

BY OCCASION OF

the vntimely death of Mistris

ELIZABETH DRVRY,

the frailtie and the decay of
this whole World is
represented.

LONDON,

Printed by *M. Bradwood* for *S. Macham*, and are
to be sold at his shop in Pauls Church-yard at the
signe of the Bull-head. 1612.

Figure 1. Title page of the second edition of Donne's *An Anatomie of the World*, 1612.

The First Anniversary.
An Anatomie of the World

When that rich Soule which to her heaven is gone,
Whom all they celebrate, who know they have one,
(For who is sure he hath a Soule, unlesse
It see, and judge, and follow worthinesse,
And by Deedes praise it? hee who doth not this,   5
May lodge an In-mate soule, but 'tis not his.)
When that Queene ended here her progresse time,
And, as t'her standing house to heaven did climbe,
Where loath to make the Saints attend her long,
She's now a part both of the Quire, and Song,   10
This World, in that great earthquake languished;
For in a common bath of teares it bled,
Which drew the strongest vitall spirits out:
But succour'd then with a perplexed doubt,
Whether the world did lose, or gaine in this,   15
(Because since now no other way there is,
But goodnesse, to see her, whom all would see,
All must endeavour to be good as shee,)
This great consumption to a fever turn'd,
And so the world had fits; it joy'd, it mourn'd;   20
And, as men thinke, that Agues physick are,
And th'Ague being spent, give over care,
So thou sicke World, mistak'st thy selfe to bee
Well, when alas, thou'rt in a Lethargie.
Her death did wound and tame thee than, and than   25
Thou might'st have better spar'd the Sunne, or Man.

THE FIRST ANNIVERSARY: *Anatomie:* a dissection; see NOTE.
1 f. Marginal gloss: *The entrie into the worke.*
7 *progresse:* the formal journey of a monarch.
8 *standing house:* permanent dwelling place.
13 *vitall:* life-giving.
21 *physick:* curative treatment.

That wound was deep, but 'tis more misery,
That thou hast lost thy sense and memory.
'Twas heavy then to heare thy voyce of mone,
But this is worse, that thou art speechlesse growne. 30
Thou hast forgot thy name, thou hadst; thou wast
Nothing but shee, and her thou hast o'rpast.
For as a child kept from the Font, untill
A prince, expected long, come to fulfill
The ceremonies, thou unnam'd had'st laid, 35
Had not her comming, thee her Palace made:
Her name defin'd thee, gave thee forme, and frame,
And thou forgett'st to celebrate thy name.
Some moneths she hath beene dead (but being dead,
Measures of times are all determined) 40
But long she'ath beene away, long, long, yet none
Offers to tell us who it is that's gone.
But as in states doubtfull of future heires,
When sicknesse without remedie empaires
The present Prince, they're loth it should be said, 45
The Prince doth languish, or the Prince is dead:
So mankinde feeling now a generall thaw,
A strong example gone, equall to law,
The Cyment which did faithfully compact,
And glue all vertues, now resolv'd, and slack'd, 50
Thought it some blasphemy to say sh'was dead,
Or that our weaknesse was discovered
In that confession; therefore spoke no more
Then tongues, the Soule being gone, the losse deplore.
But though it be too late to succour thee, 55
Sicke World, yea, dead, yea putrified, since shee
Thy'intrinsique balme, and thy preservative,

29 *heavy:* sad, melancholy.
32 *o'rpast:* passed over, neglected.
37 *frame:* construction, order.
40 *determined:* ended.
50 *resolv'd:* loosened, dissolved.
52 *discovered:* revealed.
57 *intrinsique balme:* inward or inherent preservative essence (alchemical conception).

Can never be renew'd, thou never live,
I (since no man can make thee live) will try,
What wee may gaine by thy Anatomy.   60
Her death hath taught us dearely, that thou art
Corrupt and mortall in thy purest part.
Let no man say, the world it selfe being dead,
'Tis labour lost to have discovered
The worlds infirmities, since there is none   65
Alive to study this dissection;
For there's a kinde of World remaining still,
Though shee which did inanimate and fill
The world, be gone, yet in this last long night,
Her Ghost doth walke; that is, a glimmering light,   70
A faint weake love of vertue, and of good,
Reflects from her, on them which understood
Her worth; and though she have shut in all day,
The twilight of her memory doth stay;
Which, from the carcasse of the old world, free,   75
Creates a new world, and new creatures bee
Produc'd: the matter and the stuffe of this,
Her vertue, and the forme our practice is:
And though to be thus elemented, arme
These creatures, from home-borne intrinsique harme,   80
(For all assum'd unto this dignitie,
So many weedlesse Paradises bee,
Which of themselves produce no venemous sinne,
Except some forraine Serpent bring it in)
Yet, because outward stormes the strongest breake,   85
And strength it selfe by confidence growes weake,
This new world may be safer, being told
The dangers and diseases of the old:
For with due temper men doe then forgoe,
Or covet things, when they their true worth know.   90
There is no health; Physitians say that wee,

67 f. Marginal gloss: *What life the world hath stil.*
81 *assum'd:* raised up, received.
88 f. Marginal gloss: *The sicknesses of the World.*
89 *temper:* disposition, mental composure.
91 f. Marginal gloss: *Impossibility of health.*

At best, enjoy but a neutralitie.
And can there bee worse sicknesse, then to know
That we are never well, nor can be so?
Wee are borne ruinous: poore mothers cry,   95
That children come not right, nor orderly;
Except they headlong come and fall upon
An ominous precipitation.
How witty's ruine! how importunate
Upon mankinde! it labour'd to frustrate   100
Even Gods purpose; and made woman, sent
For mans reliefe, cause of his languishment.
They were to good ends, and they are so still,
But accessory, and principall in ill;
For that first marriage was our funerall: 105
One woman at one blow, then kill'd us all,
And singly, one by one, they kill us now.
We doe delightfully our selves allow
To that consumption; and profusely blinde,
Wee kill our selves to propagate our kinde.   110
And yet we do not that; we are not men:
There is not now that mankinde, which was then,
When as the Sunne and man did seeme to strive,
(Joynt tenants of the world) who should survive;
When, Stagge, and Raven, and the long-liv'd tree,   115
Compar'd with man, dy'd in minoritie;
When, if a slow pac'd starre had stolne away
From the observers marking, he might stay
Two or three hundred yeares to see't againe,
And then make up his observation plaine;   120
When, as the age was long, the sise was great;
Mans growth confess'd, and recompenc'd the meat;
So spacious and large, that every Soule
Did a faire Kingdome, and large Realme controule:
And when the very stature, thus erect,   125

99 *witty:* ingenious, clever.
114 f. Marginal gloss: *Shortnesse of life.*
116 *minoritie:* childhood.
122 *confess'd:* manifested, made known; *meat:* food.

Did that soule a good way towards heaven direct.
Where is this mankinde now? who lives to age,
Fit to be made *Methusalem* his page?
Alas, we scarce live long enough to try
Whether a new made clocke run right, or lie.   130
Old Grandsires talke of yesterday with sorrow,
And for our children wee reserve to morrow.
So short is life, that every peasant strives,
In a torne house, or field, to have three lives.
And as in lasting, so in length is man   135
Contracted to an inch, who was a spanne;
For had a man at first in forrests stray'd,
Or shipwrack'd in the Sea, one would have laid
A wager, that an Elephant, or Whale,
That met him, would not hastily assaile   140
A thing so equall to him: now alas,
The Fairies, and the Pigmies well may passe
As credible; mankinde decayes so soone,
We'are scarce our Fathers shadowes cast at noone:
Onely death addes t'our length: nor are wee growne   145
In stature to be men, till we are none.
But this were light, did our lesse volume hold
All the old Text; or had wee chang'd to gold
Their silver; or dispos'd into lesse glasse
Spirits of vertue, which then scatter'd was.   150
But 'tis not so: w'are not retir'd, but dampt;
And as our bodies, so our mindes are crampt:
'Tis shrinking, not close weaving that hath thus,
In minde, and body both bedwarfed us.
Wee seeme ambitious, Gods whole worke t'undoe;   155
Of nothing hee made us, and we strive too,
To bring our selves to nothing backe; and wee
Doe what wee can, to do't so soone as hee.

134 *three lives:* past, present, and future, by owning some small property.
Also, the duration of a lease.
136 f. Marginal gloss: *Smalnesse of stature.*
147 *light:* trivial, of no importance.
151 *retir'd:* condensed, contracted; *dampt:* extinguished, stifled.

With new diseases on our selves we warre,
And with new Physicke, a worse Engin farre.   160
Thus man, this worlds Vice-Emperour, in whom
All faculties, all graces are at home;
And if in other creatures they appeare,
They're but mans Ministers, and Legats there,
To worke on their rebellions, and reduce   165
Them to Civility, and to mans use:
This man, whom God did wooe, and loth t'attend
Till man came up, did downe to man descend,
This man, so great, that all that is, is his,
Oh what a trifle, and poore thing he is!   170
If man were any thing, he's nothing now:
Helpe, or at least some time to wast, allow
T'his other wants, yet when he did depart
With her whom we lament, hee lost his heart.
She, of whom th'Ancients seem'd to prophesie,   175
When they call'd vertues by the name of shee;
Shee in whom vertue was so much refin'd,
That for Allay unto so pure a minde
Shee tooke the weaker Sex; shee that could drive
The poysonous tincture, and the staine of *Eve*,   180
Out of her thoughts, and deeds; and purifie
All, by a true religious Alchymie;
Shee, shee is dead; shee's dead: when thou knowest this,
Thou knowest how poore a trifling thing man is.
And learn'st thus much by our Anatomie,   185
The heart being perish'd, no part can be free.
And that except thou feed (not banquet) on
The supernaturall food, Religion,
Thy better Growth growes withered, and scant;

160 *Engin:* device.
166 *Civility:* a civilized condition.
167 *attend:* wait.
173 *depart:* part.
187 *banquet:* eat lightly: in old usage a *banquet* could indicate a "snack" between meals, or a "course of sweetmeats, fruit, and wine, served either as a separate entertainment, or as a continuation of the principal meal" (OED).

Be more then man, or thou'rt lesse then an Ant.   190
Then, as mankinde, so is the worlds whole frame
Quite out of joynt, almost created lame:
For, before God had made up all the rest,
Corruption entred, and deprav'd the best:
It seis'd the Angels, and then first of all   195
The world did in her cradle take a fall,
And turn'd her braines, and tooke a generall maime,
Wronging each joynt of th'universall frame.
The noblest part, man, felt it first; and than
Both beasts and plants, curst in the curse of man.   200
So did the world from the first houre decay,
That evening was beginning of the day,
And now the Springs and Sommers which we see,
Like sonnes of women after fiftie bee.
And new Philosophy calls all in doubt,   205
The Element of fire is quite put out;
The Sun is lost, and th'earth, and no mans wit
Can well direct him where to looke for it.
And freely men confesse that this world's spent,
When in the Planets, and the Firmament   210
They seeke so many new; they see that this
Is crumbled out againe to his Atomis.
'Tis all in peeces, all cohaerence gone;
All just supply, and all Relation:
Prince, Subject, Father, Sonne, are things forgot,   215
For every man alone thinkes he hath got
To be a Phœnix, and that there can bee
None of that kinde, of which he is, but hee.
This is the worlds condition now, and now
She that should all parts to reunion bow,   220
She that had all Magnetique force alone,
To draw, and fasten sundred parts in one;

200 f. Marginal gloss: *Decay of nature in other parts.*
205 *Philosophy:* natural philosophy, science.
207 *wit:* intellect, mental capacity.
214 *just supply:* proper support or fulfilling of needs.
220 *bow:* incline, direct.

She whom wise nature had invented then
When she observ'd that every sort of men
Did in their voyage in this worlds Sea stray,   225
And needed a new compasse for their way;
She that was best, and first originall
Of all faire copies, and the generall
Steward to Fate; she whose rich eyes, and brest
Guilt the West Indies, and perfum'd the East;   230
Whose having breath'd in this world, did bestow
Spice on those Iles, and bad them still smell so,
And that rich Indie which doth gold interre,
Is but as single money, coyn'd from her:
She to whom this world must it selfe refer,   235
As Suburbs, or the Microcosme of her,
Shee, shee is dead; shee's dead: when thou knowst this,
Thou knowst how lame a cripple this world is.
And learn'st thus much by our Anatomy,
That this worlds generall sickenesse doth not lie   240
In any humour, or one certaine part;
But as thou sawest it rotten at the heart,
Thou seest a Hectique feaver hath got hold
Of the whole substance, not to be contrould,
And that thou hast but one way, not t'admit   245
The worlds infection, to be none of it.
For the worlds subtilst immateriall parts
Feele this consuming wound, and ages darts.
For the worlds beauty is decai'd, or gone,
Beauty, that's colour, and proportion.   250
We thinke the heavens enjoy their Sphericall,
Their round proportion embracing all.
But yet their various and perplexed course,
Observ'd in divers ages, doth enforce
Men to finde out so many Eccentrique parts,   255

241 *humour:* one of the four chief fluids of the body, according to the old
physiology.
247 *subtilst:* most rarefied, thinnest.
250 f. Marginal gloss: *Disformity of parts.*
253 *perplexed:* involved, tangled.

Such divers downe-right lines, such overthwarts,
As disproportion that pure forme: It teares
The Firmament in eight and forty sheeres,
And in those Constellations there arise
New starres, and old doe vanish from our eyes: 260
As though heav'n suffered earthquakes, peace or war,
When new Townes rise, and old demolish't are.
They have impal'd within a Zodiake
The free-borne Sun, and keepe twelve Signes awake
To watch his steps; the Goat and Crab controule,   265
And fright him backe, who else to either Pole
(Did not these Tropiques fetter him) might runne:
For his course is not round; nor can the Sunne
Perfit a Circle, or maintaine his way
One inch direct; but where he rose to-day   270
He comes no more, but with a couzening line,
Steales by that point, and so is Serpentine:
And seeming weary with his reeling thus,
He meanes to sleepe, being now falne nearer us.
So, of the Starres which boast that they doe runne   275
In Circle still, none ends where he begun.
All their proportion's lame, it sinkes, it swels.
For of Meridians, and Parallels,
Man hath weav'd out a net, and this net throwne
Upon the Heavens, and now they are his owne.   280
Loth to goe up the hill, or labour thus
To goe to heaven, we make heaven come to us.
We spur, we reine the starres, and in their race

256 *downe-right:* vertical; *overthwarts:* transverse lines (with ref. to the increasing complications made in the Ptolemaic system in an effort to account for new astronomical observations).

258 *sheeres:* shares, parts; with reference to the forty-eight constellations of the old astronomy (perhaps also with allusion to or confusion with the word *shires?*).

263 *impal'd:* fenced in, as with a paling.

265 *Goat and Crab:* the zodiacal signs of Capricorn and Cancer.

269 *Perfit:* perfect.

271 *couzening:* cozening, cheating, deceiving.

They're diversly content t'obey our pace.
But keepes the earth her round proportion still?   285
Doth not a Tenarif, or higher Hill
Rise so high like a Rocke, that one might thinke
The floating Moone would shipwracke there, and sinke?
Seas are so deepe, that Whales being strooke to day,
Perchance to morrow, scarce at middle way   290
Of their wish'd journies end, the bottome, die.
And men, to sound depths, so much line untie,
As one might justly thinke, that there would rise
At end thereof, one of th'Antipodies:
If under all, a Vault infernall bee,   295
(Which sure is spacious, except that we
Invent another torment, that there must
Millions into a strait hot roome be thrust)
Then solidnesse, and roundnesse have no place.
Are these but warts, and pock-holes in the face   300
Of th'earth? Thinke so: but yet confesse, in this
The worlds proportion disfigured is;
That those two legges whereon it doth rely,
Reward and punishment are bent awry.
And, Oh, it can no more be questioned,   305
That beauties best, proportion, is dead,
Since even griefe it selfe, which now alone
Is left us, is without proportion.
Shee by whose lines proportion should bee
Examin'd, measure of all Symmetree,   310
Whom had that Ancient seen, who thought soules made
Of Harmony, he would at next have said
That Harmony was shee, and thence infer,

286 *Tenarif:* the peak of Tenerife, highest (c. 12,200 ft.) in the Canary Islands.

289 *Strooke:* struck.

298 *strait:* narrow, small.

303 f. Marginal gloss: *Disorder in the world.*

311 *that Ancient:* probably a reference to Pythagoras, or perhaps to Aristoxenus.

312 *at next:* directly after.

That soules were but Resultances from her,
And did from her into our bodies goe,   315
As to our eyes, the formes from objects flow:
Shee, who if those great Doctors truly said
That the Arke to mans proportions was made,
Had been a type for that, as that might be
A type of her in this, that contrary   320
Both Elements, and Passions liv'd at peace
In her, who caus'd all Civill war to cease.
Shee, after whom, what forme so'er we see,
Is discord, and rude incongruitie;
Shee, shee is dead, shee's dead; when thou knowst this   325
Thou knowst how ugly a monster this world is:
And learn'st thus much by our Anatomie,
That here is nothing to enamour thee:
And that, not only faults in inward parts,
Corruptions in our braines, or in our hearts,   330
Poysoning the fountaines, whence our actions spring,
Endanger us: but that if every thing
Be not done fitly'and in proportion,
To satisfie wise, and good lookers on,
(Since most men be such as most thinke they bee)   335
They're lothsome too, by this Deformitee.
For good, and well, must in our actions meete;
Wicked is not much worse than indiscreet.
But beauties other second Element,
Colour, and lustre now, is as neere spent.   340
And had the world his just proportion,
Were it a ring still, yet the stone is gone.
As a compassionate Turcoyse which doth tell
By looking pale, the wearer is not well,
As gold falls sicke being stung with Mercury,   345
All the worlds parts of such complexion bee.

314 *Resultances:* products, emanations.
338 *indiscreet:* lacking sound judgment.
343 *Turcoyse:* a turquoise gem.
346 *complexion:* disposition, constitution.

When nature was most busie, the first weeke,
Swadling the new borne earth, God seem'd to like
That she should sport her selfe sometimes, and play,
To mingle, and vary colours every day: 350
And then, as though shee could not make inow,
Himselfe his various Rainbow did allow.
Sight is the noblest sense of any one,
Yet sight hath only colour to feed on,
And colour is decai'd: summers robe growes   355
Duskie, and like an oft dyed garment showes.
Our blushing red, which us'd in cheekes to spred,
Is inward sunke, and only our soules are red.
Perchance the world might have recovered,
If she whom we lament had not beene dead: 360
But shee, in whom all white, and red, and blew
(Beauties ingredients) voluntary grew,
As in an unvext Paradise; from whom
Did all things verdure, and their lustre come,
Whose composition was miraculous,   365
Being all colour, all Diaphanous,
(For Ayre, and Fire but thick grosse bodies were,
And liveliest stones but drowsie, and pale to her,)
Shee, shee, is dead: shee's dead: when thou know'st this,
Thou knowst how wan a Ghost this our world is: 370
And learn'st thus much by our Anatomie,
That it should more affright, then pleasure thee.
And that, since all faire colour then did sinke,
'Tis now but wicked vanitie, to thinke
To colour vicious deeds with good pretence,   375
Or with bought colors to illude mens sense.
Nor in ought more this worlds decay appeares,

351 *inow:* enough.
352 See Genesis 9:13.
368 *to her:* compared to her.
375 f. Marginal gloss: *Weaknesse in the want of correspondence of heaven
and earth.*
376 *illude:* deceive.
377 *ought:* aught, anything.

Then that her influence the heav'n forbeares,
Or that the Elements doe not feele this,
The father, or the mother barren is. 380
The cloudes conceive not raine, or doe not powre,
In the due birth time, downe the balmy showre;
Th'Ayre doth not motherly sit on the earth,
To hatch her seasons, and give all things birth;
Spring-times were common cradles, but are tombes; 385
And false-conceptions fill the generall wombes;
Th'Ayre showes such Meteors, as none can see,
Not only what they meane, but what they bee;
Earth such new wormes, as would have troubled much
Th'Ægyptian Mages to have made more such. 390
What Artist now dares boast that he can bring
Heaven hither, or constellate any thing,
So as the influence of those starres may bee
Imprison'd in an Hearbe, or Charme, or Tree,
And doe by touch, all which those stars could doe? 395
The art is lost, and correspondence too.
For heaven gives little, and the earth takes lesse,
And man least knowes their trade and purposes.
If this commerce twixt heaven and earth were not
Embarr'd, and all this traffique quite forgot, 400
She, for whose losse we have lamented thus,
Would worke more fully'and pow'rfully on us:
Since herbes, and roots, by dying lose not all,
But they, yea Ashes too, are medicinall,
Death could not quench her vertue so, but that 405

378–80 With reference to the supposed influence of the stars upon the growth of things on earth: either the influence is no longer exerted, or the elements no longer feel it: *heav'n* being the *father, earth,* the *mother.*

390 *Mages:* magicians, wizards.

391 *Artist:* astrologer, one expert in occult "sciences."

392 *constellate:* to construct a magical charm or talisman under the power of a particular constellation or star.

394 *Charme:* talisman.

396 *correspondence:* relationship (between the stars and the earth).

398 *trade:* mutual communication, interchange: cf. *commerce, traffique,* lines 399–400.

It would be (if not follow'd) wondred at:
And all the world would be one dying Swan,
To sing her funerall praise, and vanish than.
But as some Serpents poyson hurteth not,
Except it be from the live Serpent shot,   410
So doth her vertue need her here, to fit
That unto us; shee working more then it.
But shee, in whom to such maturity
Vertue was growne, past growth, that it must die;
She, from whose influence all Impressions came,   415
But, by Receivers impotencies, lame,
Who, though she could not transubstantiate
All states to gold, yet guilded every state,
So that some Princes have some temperance;
Some Counsellers some purpose to advance   420
The common profit; and some people have
Some stay, no more then Kings should give, to crave;
Some women have some taciturnity,
Some nunneries some graines of chastitie.
She that did thus much, and much more could doe,   425
But that our age was Iron, and rustie too,
Shee, shee is dead; shee's dead; when thou knowst this,
Thou knowst how drie a Cinder this world is.
And learn'st thus much by our Anatomy,
That 'tis in vaine to dew, or mollifie   430
It with thy teares, or sweat, or blood: no thing
Is worth our travaile, griefe, or perishing,
But those rich joyes, which did possesse her heart,
Of which she's now partaker, and a part.
But as in cutting up a man that's dead,   435
The body will not last out, to have read
On every part, and therefore men direct
Their speech to parts, that are of most effect;
So the worlds carcasse would not last, if I

422 *stay*: restraint.
426 *Iron*: the last of the four mythological ages of the world, which has de-
clined from golden, silver, and bronze to iron.
435 Marginal gloss: *Conclusion.*
436–37 *to have read On*: to have instruction (lectures) given on.

Were punctuall in this Anatomy;   440
Nor smels it well to hearers, if one tell
Them their disease, who faine would think they're well.
Here therefore be the end: And, blessed maid,
Of whom is meant what ever hath been said,
Or shall be spoken well by any tongue,   445
Whose name refines course lines, and makes prose song,
Accept this tribute, and his first yeares rent,
Who till his darke short tapers end be spent,
As oft as thy feast sees this widowed earth,
Will yearely celebrate thy second birth,   450
That is, thy death; for though the soule of man
Be got when man is made, 'tis borne but than
When man doth die; our body's as the wombe,
And, as a Mid-wife, death directs it home.
And you her creatures, whom she workes upon,   455
And have your last, and best concoction
From her example, and her vertue, if you
In reverence to her, do thinke it due,
That no one should her praises thus rehearse,
As matter fit for Chronicle, not verse;   460
Vouchsafe to call to minde that God did make
A last, and lasting'st peece, a song. He spake
To *Moses* to deliver unto all,
That song, because hee knew they would let fall
The Law, the Prophets, and the History,   465
But keepe the song still in their memory:
Such an opinion (in due measure) made
Me this great Office boldly to invade:
Nor could incomprehensiblenesse deterre
Mee, from thus trying to emprison her,   470
Which when I saw that a strict grave could doe,
I saw not why verse might not do so too.
Verse hath a middle nature: heaven keepes Soules,
The Grave keepes bodies, Verse the Fame enroules.

440 *punctuall:* detailed, dealing with small points.
449 *feast:* saint's day.
461–64 See Deuteronomy 31:19–30 and 32.

The Second Anniuersarie.

OF
THE PROGRES
of the Soule.

Wherein:

BY OCCASION OF THE
Religious Death of Miftris
ELIZABETH DRVRY,
the incommodities of the Soule
in this life and her exaltation in
the next, are Contem-
*pla*ted.

LONDON,
Printed by *M. Bradwood* for *S. Macham*, and are
to be fould at his fhop in Pauls Church-yard at
the figne of the Bull-head.
1612.

Figure 2. Title page of the first edition of Donne's *Progres of the Soule*, 1612.

The Second Anniversarie.
Of the Progres of the Soule

Nothing could make me sooner to confesse
That this world had an everlastingnesse,
Then to consider, that a yeare is runne,
Since both this lower world's, and the Sunnes Sunne,
The Lustre, and the vigor of this All,⁣   5
Did set; 'twere blasphemie to say, did fall.
But as a ship which hath strooke saile, doth runne
By force of that force which before, it wonne:
Or as sometimes in a beheaded man,
Though at those two Red seas, which freely ranne,⁣   10
One from the Trunke, another from the Head,
His soule be sail'd, to her eternall bed,
His eyes will twinckle, and his tongue will roll,
As though he beckned, and cal'd backe his soule,
He graspes his hands, and he pulls up his feet,⁣   15
And seemes to reach, and to step forth to meet
His soule; when all these motions which we saw,
Are but as Ice, which crackles at a thaw:
Or as a Lute, which in moist weather, rings
Her knell alone, by cracking of her strings:⁣   20
So struggles this dead world, now shee is gone;
For there is motion in corruption.
As some daies are at the Creation nam'd,
Before the Sunne, the which fram'd daies, was fram'd,
So after this Sunne's set, some show appeares,⁣   25
And orderly vicissitude of yeares.
Yet a new Deluge, and of Lethe flood,

THE SECOND ANNIVERSARIE: title page: *Progres:* a journey, along with the abstract meaning of "advancement"; *incommodities:* troubles, disadvantages.
  1 f. Marginal gloss: *The entrance.*
  13 *twinckle:* wink, blink.
  24 *fram'd:* created.

Hath drown'd us all, All have forgot all good,
Forgetting her, the maine reserve of all.
Yet in this deluge, grosse and generall,   30
Thou seest me strive for life; my life shall bee,
To be hereafter prais'd, for praysing thee;
Immortall Maid, who though thou would'st refuse
The name of Mother, be unto my Muse
A Father, since her chast Ambition is,   35
Yearely to bring forth such a child as this.
These Hymnes may worke on future wits, and so
May great Grand children of thy prayses grow.
And so, though not revive, embalme and spice
The world, which else would putrifie with vice.   40
For thus, Man may extend thy progeny,
Untill man doe but vanish, and not die.
These Hymnes thy issue, may encrease so long,
As till Gods great Venite change the song.
Thirst for that time, O my insatiate soule,   45
And serve thy thirst, with Gods safe-sealing Bowle.
Be thirstie still, and drinke still till thou goe;
'Tis th'only Health, to be Hydropique so.
Forget this rotten world; And unto thee
Let thine owne times as an old storie bee,   50
Be not concern'd: studie not why, nor when;
Doe not so much as not beleeve a man.
For though to erre, be worst, to try truths forth,
Is far more businesse, then this world is worth.
The world is but a carkasse; thou art fed   55
By it, but as a worme, that carkasse bred;
And why should'st thou, poore worme, consider more,
When this world will grow better then before,
Then those thy fellow wormes doe thinke upon
That carkasses last resurrection.   60

45 f. Marginal gloss: *A just disestimation of this world. disestimation*: action
of disesteeming, despising.
46 *safe-sealing*: see Revelation 7:2–3; *Bowle*: the Eucharist.
48 *Hydropique*: having an insatiable thirst, dropsical.

Forget this world, and scarce thinke of it so,
As of old clothes, cast off a yeare agoe.
To be thus stupid is Alacritie;
Men thus Lethargique have best Memory.
Look upward; that's towards her, whose happy state   65
We now lament not, but congratulate.
Shee, to whom all this world was but a stage,
Where all sat harkning how her youthfull age
Should be emploi'd, because in all shee did,
Some Figure of the Golden times was hid.   70
Who could not lacke, what e'r this world could give,
Because shee was the forme, that made it live;
Nor could complaine, that this world was unfit
To be staid in, then when shee was in it;
Shee that first tried indifferent desires   75
By vertue, and vertue by religious fires,
Shee to whose person Paradise adher'd,
As Courts to Princes, shee whose eyes ensphear'd
Star-light enough, t'have made the South controule,
(Had shee beene there) the Star-full Northerne Pole,   80
Shee, shee is gone; she is gone; when thou knowest this,
What fragmentary rubbidge this world is
Thou knowest, and that it is not worth a thought;
He honors it too much that thinkes it nought.
Thinke then, My soule, that death is but a Groome,   85
Which brings a Taper to the outward roome,
Whence thou spiest first a little glimmering light,
And after brings it nearer to thy sight:
For such approaches doth heaven make in death.
Thinke thy selfe labouring now with broken breath,   90
And thinke those broken and soft Notes to bee
Division, and thy happyest Harmonie.
Thinke thee laid on thy death-bed, loose and slacke;

66 *congratulate:* rejoice at.
72 *forme:* in Scholastic philosophy, the essential, creative principle of a thing.
75 *indifferent:* neutral, midway between excess and defect.
85 f. Marginal gloss: *Contemplation of our state in our death-bed.*
92 *Division:* a musical term indicating a rapid passage of melody, a run.

And thinke that, but unbinding of a packe,
To take one precious thing, thy soule from thence.   95
Thinke thy selfe parch'd with fevers violence,
Anger thine ague more, by calling it
Thy Physicke; chide the slacknesse of the fit.
Thinke that thou hear'st thy knell, and think no more,
But that, as Bels cal'd thee to Church before,   100
So this, to the Triumphant Church, calls thee.
Thinke Satans Sergeants round about thee bee,
And thinke that but for Legacies they thrust;
Give one thy Pride, to'another give thy Lust:
Give them those sinnes which they gave thee before,   105
And trust th'immaculate blood to wash thy score.
Thinke thy friends weeping round, and thinke that they
Weepe but because they goe not yet thy way.
Thinke that they close thine eyes, and thinke in this,
That they confesse much in the world, amisse,   110
Who dare not trust a dead mans eye with that,
Which they from God, and Angels cover not.
Thinke that they shroud thee up, and think from thence
They reinvest thee in white innocence.
Thinke that thy body rots, and (if so low,   115
Thy soule exalted so, thy thoughts can goe,)
Think thee a Prince, who of themselves create
Wormes which insensibly devoure their State.
Thinke that they bury thee, and thinke that rite
Laies thee to sleepe but a Saint Lucies night.   120
Thinke these things cheerefully: and if thou bee
Drowsie or slacke, remember then that shee,
Shee whose Complexion was so even made,

102 *Sergeants:* minor officials who perform arrests or otherwise carry out judgments and official commands.

114 *reinvest:* reclothe.

120 See NOTE on Donne's "Nocturnall."

123 *Complexion:* in the old physiology, the combination in the body of the four qualities, cold, hot, moist, dry, associated with the four elements; or the combination of the four "humors": blood, phlegm, choler (yellow bile), and melancholy (black bile).

That which of her Ingredients should invade
The other three, no Feare, no Art could guesse: 125
So far were all remov'd from more or lesse.
But as in Mithridate, or just perfumes,
Where all good things being met, no one presumes
To governe, or to triumph on the rest,
Only because all were, no part was best.   130
And as, though all doe know, that quantities
Are made of lines, and lines from Points arise,
None can these lines or quantities unjoynt,
And say this is a line, or this a point,
So though the Elements and Humors were   135
In her, one could not say, this governes there.
Whose even constitution might have wonne
Any disease to venter on the Sunne,
Rather then her: and make a spirit feare,
That hee to disuniting subject were.   140
To whose proportions if we would compare
Cubes, th'are unstable; Circles, Angular;
She who was such a chaine as Fate employes
To bring mankinde all Fortunes it enjoyes;
So fast, so even wrought, as one would thinke,   145
No Accident could threaten any linke;
Shee, shee embrac'd a sicknesse, gave it meat,
The purest blood, and breath, that e'r it eate;
And hath taught us, that though a good man hath
Title to heaven, and plead it by his Faith,   150
And though he may pretend a conquest, since
Heaven was content to suffer violence,
Yea though hee plead a long possession too,
(For they're in heaven on earth who heavens workes do)
Though hee had right and power and place, before,   155

127 *Mithridate:* an old medicine with many ingredients, regarded as a universal antidote.
138 *venter:* venture.
147 *meat:* food.
151 *pretend:* put forward a claim to.
152 See Matthew 11:12.

Yet Death must usher, and unlocke the doore.
Thinke further on thy selfe, my Soule, and thinke
How thou at first wast made but in a sinke;
Thinke that it argued some infirmitie,
That those two soules, which then thou foundst in me,   160
Thou fedst upon, and drewst into thee, both
My second soule of sense, and first of growth.
Thinke but how poore thou wast, how obnoxious;
Whom a small lumpe of flesh could poyson thus.
This curded milke, this poore unlittered whelpe   165
My body, could, beyond escape or helpe,
Infect thee with Originall sinne, and thou
Couldst neither then refuse, nor leave it now.
Thinke that no stubborne sullen Anchorit,
Which fixt to'a pillar, or a grave, doth sit   170
Bedded, and bath'd in all his ordures, dwels
So fowly as our Soules in their first-built Cels.
Thinke in how poore a prison thou didst lie
After, enabled but to suck, and crie.
Thinke, when'twas growne to most,'twas a poore Inne,   175
A Province pack'd up in two yards of skinne,
And that usurp'd or threatned with the rage
Of sicknesses, or their true mother, Age.
But thinke that Death hath now enfranchis'd thee,
Thou hast thy'expansion now, and libertie;   180
Thinke that a rustie Peece, discharg'd, is flowne
In peeces, and the bullet is his owne,
And freely flies: This to thy Soule allow,
Thinke thy shell broke, thinke thy Soule hatch'd but now.

157 f. Marginal gloss: *Incommodities of the Soule in the Body.*
158 *sinke:* cesspool, sewer.
160–62 With ref. to the old conception of the "vegetative" soul in plants, the "sensible" or "sensitive" soul in animals, and the "rational" soul in man, which includes the other two kinds of "soul."
163 *obnoxious:* exposed to harm.
165 *unlittered:* unborn, as of animals.
179 *enfranchis'd:* set free.
180 f. Marginal gloss: *Her liberty by death.*

And think this slow-pac'd soule, which late did cleave   185
To'a body, and went but by the bodies leave,
Twenty, perchance, or thirty mile a day,
Dispatches in a minute all the way
Twixt heaven, and earth; she stayes not in the ayre,
To looke what Meteors there themselves prepare;   190
She carries no desire to know, nor sense,
Whether th'ayres middle region be intense;
For th'Element of fire, she doth not know,
Whether she past by such a place or no;
She baits not at the Moone, nor cares to trie   195
Whether in that new world, men live, and die.
Venus retards her not, to'enquire, how shee
Can, (being one starre) Hesper, and Vesper bee;
Hee that charm'd Argus eyes, sweet Mercury,
Workes not on her, who now is growne all eye;   200
Who, if she meet the body of the Sunne,
Goes through, not staying till his course be runne;
Who findes in Mars his Campe no corps of Guard;
Nor is by Jove, nor by his father barr'd;
But ere she can consider how she went,   205
At once is at, and through the Firmament.
And as these starres were but so many beads
Strung on one string, speed undistinguish'd leads
Her through those Spheares, as through the beads, a string,
Whose quick succession makes it still one thing: 210
As doth the pith, which, lest our bodies slacke,
Strings fast the little bones of necke, and backe;
So by the Soule doth death string Heaven and Earth;
For when our Soule enjoyes this her third birth,

189–206 A summation of the old Ptolemaic view of a concentric universe: first, the regions of earth, water, air, and fire; then on to the spheres of the Moon, Venus, Mercury (Donne reverses the traditional order of Mercury and Venus), Sun, Mars, Jupiter, Saturn, and the Firmament of fixed stars.

192 *intense:* violent, turbulent.

195 *baits:* pauses for rest and refreshment, as at an inn.

208 *undistinguish'd:* without any distinct parts: that is, without pause or variation.

(Creation gave her one, a second, grace,)   215
Heaven is as neare, and present to her face,
As colours are, and objects, in a roome
Where darknesse was before, when Tapers come.
This must, my Soule, thy long-short Progresse bee;
To'advance these thoughts, remember then, that shee,   220
Shee, whose faire body no such prison was,
But that a Soule might well be pleas'd to passe
An age in her; she whose rich beauty lent
Mintage to others beauties, for they went
But for so much as they were like to her;   225
Shee, in whose body (if we dare preferre
This low world, to so high a marke as shee,)
The Westerne treasure, Easterne spicerie,
Europe, and Afrique, and the unknowne rest
Were easily found, or what in them was best;   230
And when w'have made this large discoverie
Of all, in her some one part there will bee
Twenty such parts, whose plenty and riches is
Enough to make twenty such worlds as this;
Shee, whom had they knowne who did first betroth   235
The Tutelar Angels, and assign'd one, both
To Nations, Cities, and to Companies,
To Functions, Offices, and Dignities,
And to each severall man, to him, and him,
They would have given her one for every limbe;   240
She, of whose soule, if wee may say, 'twas Gold,
Her body was th'Electrum, and did hold
Many degrees of that; wee understood
Her by her sight; her pure, and eloquent blood
Spoke in her cheekes, and so distinctly wrought,   245
That one might almost say, her body thought;
Shee, shee, thus richly and largely hous'd, is gone:
And chides us slow-pac'd snailes who crawle upon

226 *preferre*: advance, promote.
236 *Tutelar*: tutelary, guardian.
238 *Dignities*: high offices or ranks.
242 *Electrum*: an alloy of gold and silver.

Our prisons prison, earth, nor thinke us well,
Longer, then whil'st wee beare our brittle shell.   250
But 'twere but little to have chang'd our roome,
If, as we were in this our living Tombe
Oppress'd with ignorance, wee still were so.
Poore soule, in this thy flesh what dost thou know?
Thou know'st thy selfe so little, as thou know'st not,   255
How thou didst die, nor how thou wast begot.
Thou neither know'st, how thou at first cam'st in,
Nor how thou took'st the poyson of mans sinne.
Nor dost thou, (though thou know'st, that thou art so)
By what way thou art made immortall, know.   260
Thou art too narrow, wretch, to comprehend
Even thy selfe: yea though thou wouldst but bend
To know thy body. Have not all soules thought
For many ages, that our body'is wrought
Of Ayre, and Fire, and other Elements?   265
And now they thinke of new ingredients,
And one Soule thinkes one, and another way
Another thinkes, and 'tis an even lay.
Knowst thou but how the stone doth enter in
The bladders cave, and never breake the skinne?   270
Know'st thou how blood, which to the heart doth flow,
Doth from one ventricle to th'other goe?
And for the putrid stuffe, which thou dost spit,
Know'st thou how thy lungs have attracted it?
There are no passages, so that there is   275
(For ought thou know'st) piercing of substances.
And of those many opinions which men raise
Of Nailes and Haires, dost thou know which to praise?
What hope have wee to know our selves, when wee
Know not the least things, which for our use be?   280
Wee see in Authors, too stiffe to recant,
A hundred controversies of an Ant;
And yet one watches, starves, freeses, and sweats,

251 f. Marginal gloss: *Her ignorance in this life and knowledge in the next.*
283 *watches:* stays awake.

To know but Catechismes and Alphabets
Of unconcerning things, matters of fact;   285
How others on our stage their parts did Act;
What Cæsar did, yea, and what Cicero said.
Why grasse is greene, or why our blood is red,
Are mysteries which none have reach'd unto.
In this low forme, poore soule, what wilt thou doe?   290
When wilt thou shake off this Pedantery,
Of being taught by sense, and Fantasie?
Thou look'st through spectacles; small things seeme great
Below; But up unto the watch-towre get,
And see all things despoyl'd of fallacies: 295
Thou shalt not peepe through lattices of eyes,
Nor heare through Labyrinths of eares, nor learne
By circuit, or collections to discerne.
In heaven thou straight know'st all, concerning it,
And what concernes it not, shall straight forget.   300
There thou (but in no other schoole) maist bee
Perchance, as learned, and as full, as shee,
Shee who all libraries had throughly read
At home in her owne thoughts, and practised
So much good as would make as many more: 305
Shee whose example they must all implore,
Who would or doe, or thinke well, and confesse
That all the vertuous Actions they expresse,
Are but a new, and worse edition
Of her some one thought, or one action: 310
She who in th'art of knowing Heaven, was growne
Here upon earth, to such perfection,
That she hath, ever since to Heaven she came,
(In a far fairer print,) but read the same:
Shee, shee not satisfied with all this waight,   315
(For so much knowledge, as would over-fraight
Another, did but ballast her) is gone

292 *Fantasie:* the mental faculty that apprehends the objects of sensory perception.

299 *straight:* straightway, immediately.

As well t'enjoy, as get perfection.
And cals us after her, in that shee tooke,
(Taking her selfe) our best, and worthiest booke.   320
Returne not, my Soule, from this extasie,
And meditation of what thou shalt bee,
To earthly thoughts, till it to thee appeare,
With whom thy conversation must be there.
With whom wilt thou converse? what station   325
Canst thou choose out, free from infection,
That will nor give thee theirs, nor drinke in thine?
Shalt thou not finde a spungie slacke Divine
Drinke and sucke in th'instructions of Great men,
And for the word of God, vent them agen?   330
Are there not some Courts (and then, no things bee
So like as Courts) which, in this let us see,
That wits and tongues of Libellers are weake,
Because they do more ill, then these can speake?
The poyson's gone through all, poysons affect   335
Chiefly the chiefest parts, but some effect
In nailes, and haires, yea excrements, will show;
So will the poyson of sinne in the most low.
Up, up, my drowsie Soule, where thy new eare
Shall in the Angels songs no discord heare;   340
Where thou shalt see the blessed Mother-maid
Joy in not being that, which men have said.
Where she is exalted more for being good,
Then for her interest of Mother-hood.
Up to those Patriarchs, which did longer sit   345
Expecting Christ, then they'have enjoy'd him yet.
Up to those Prophets, which now gladly see
Their Prophesies growne to be Historie.

320 f. Marginal gloss: *Of our company in this life, and in the next.*
324 *conversation:* action of living among people: society.
325 *converse:* associate with.
331 *Courts:* referring to the body of courtiers surrounding a sovereign.
342 "Men have said" that Mary was conceived without sin, but Donne here implies the Protestant denial of the doctrine of Immaculate Conception.
346 *Expecting:* awaiting (along with modern sense).

Up to th'Apostles, who did bravely runne
All the Suns course, with more light then the Sunne.   350
Up to those Martyrs, who did calmly bleed
Oyle to th'Apostles Lamps, dew to their seed.
Up to those Virgins, who thought, that almost
They made joyntenants with the Holy Ghost,
If they to any should his Temple give.   355
 Up, up, for in that squadron there doth live
She, who hath carried thither new degrees
(As to their number) to their dignities.
Shee, who being to her selfe a State, injoy'd
All royalties which any State employ'd;   360
For shee made warres, and triumph'd; reason still
Did not o'rthrow, but rectifie her will:
And she made peace, for no peace is like this,
That beauty, and chastity together kisse:
She did high justice, for she crucified   365
Every first motion of rebellious pride:
And she gave pardons, and was liberall,
For, onely her selfe except, she pardon'd all:
Shee coy'nd, in this, that her impressions gave
To all our actions all the worth they have: 370
She gave protections; the thoughts of her brest
Satans rude Officers could ne'r arrest.
As these prerogatives being met in one,
Made her a soveraigne State; religion
Made her a Church; and these two made her all.   375
She who was all this All, and could not fall
To worse, by company, (for she was still
More Antidote, then all the world was ill,)
Shee, shee doth leave it, and by Death, survive
All this, in Heaven; whither who doth not strive   380
The more, because shees there, he doth not know
That accidentall joyes in Heaven doe grow.
But pause, my soule; And study, ere thou fall

382 *accidentall:* non-essential, incidental.

[118]

On accidentall joyes, th'essentiall.
Still before Accessories doe abide   385
A triall, must the principall be tride.
And what essentiall joy can'st thou expect
Here upon earth? what permanent effect
Of transitory causes? Dost thou love
Beauty? (And beauty worthy'st is to move)   390
Poore cousened cousenor, that she, and that thou,
Which did begin to love, are neither now;
You are both fluid, chang'd since yesterday;
Next day repaires, (but ill) last dayes decay.
Nor are, (although the river keepe the name)   395
Yesterdaies waters, and to daies the same.
So flowes her face, and thine eyes, neither now
That Saint, nor Pilgrime, which your loving vow
Concern'd, remaines; but whil'st you thinke you bee
Constant, you'are hourely in inconstancie.   400
Honour may have pretence unto our love,
Because that God did live so long above
Without this Honour, and then lov'd it so,
That he at last made Creatures to bestow
Honour on him; not that he needed it,   405
But that, to his hands, man might grow more fit.
But since all Honours from inferiours flow,
(For they doe give it; Princes doe but show
Whom they would have so honor'd) and that this
On such opinions, and capacities   410
Is built, as rise and fall, to more and lesse:
Alas, 'tis but a casuall happinesse.
Hath ever any man to'himselfe assign'd
This or that happinesse to'arrest his minde,
But that another man which takes a worse,   415
Thinks him a foole for having tane that course?

384 f. Marginal gloss: *Of essentiall joy in this life and in the next.*
391 *cousenor:* cozener, deceiver.
401 *pretence:* claim.
412 *casuall:* subject to chance, uncertain; also, non-essential, "accidental."
416 *tane:* taken.

They who did labour Babels tower to'erect,
Might have considered, that for that effect,
All this whole solid Earth could not allow
Nor furnish forth materialls enow;   420
And that this Center, to raise such a place,
Was farre too little, to have beene the Base;
No more affords this world, foundation
To erect true joy, were all the meanes in one.
But as the Heathen made them severall gods,   425
Of all Gods Benefits, and all his Rods,
(For as the Wine, and Corne, and Onions are
Gods unto them, so Agues bee, and Warre)
And as by changing that whole precious Gold
To such small Copper coynes, they lost the old,   430
And lost their only God, who ever must
Be sought alone, and not in such a thrust:
So much mankinde true happinesse mistakes;
No Joy enjoyes that man, that many makes.
Then, Soule, to thy first pitch worke up againe;   435
Know that all lines which circles doe containe,
For once that they the Center touch, doe touch
Twice the circumference; and be thou such;
Double on heaven thy thoughts on earth emploid;
All will not serve; Only who have enjoy'd   440
The sight of God, in fulnesse, can thinke it;
For it is both the object, and the wit.
This is essentiall joy, where neither hee
Can suffer diminution, nor wee;
'Tis such a full, and such a filling good,   445
Had th'Angels once look'd on him, they had stood.
To fill the place of one of them, or more,
Shee whom wee celebrate, is gone before.
She, who had Here so much essentiall joy,

420 *enow:* enough.
421 *Center:* the earth, as center of the old universe.
426 *Rods:* punishments.
427 *Corne:* grain.
432 *thrust:* crowd.

As no chance could distract, much lesse destroy;   450
Who with Gods presence was acquainted so,
(Hearing, and speaking to him) as to know
His face in any naturall Stone, or Tree,
Better then when in Images they bee:
Who kept by diligent devotion,   455
Gods Image, in such reparation,
Within her heart, that what decay was growne,
Was her first Parents fault, and not her owne:
Who being solicited to any act,
Still heard God pleading his safe precontract;   460
Who by a faithfull confidence, was here
Betroth'd to God, and now is married there;
Whose twilights were more cleare, then our mid-day;
Who dreamt devoutlier, then most use to pray;
Who being here fil'd with grace, yet strove to bee,   465
Both where more grace, and more capacitie
At once is given: she to Heaven is gone,
Who made this world in some proportion
A heaven, and here, became unto us all,
Joy, (as our joyes admit) essentiall.   470
But could this low world joyes essentiall touch,
Heavens accidentall joyes would passe them much.
How poore and lame, must then our casuall bee?
If thy Prince will his subjects to call thee
My Lord, and this doe swell thee, thou art than,   475
By being a greater, growne to bee lesse Man.
When no Physitian of redresse can speake,
A joyfull casuall violence may breake
A dangerous Apostem in thy breast;
And whil'st thou joyest in this, the dangerous rest,   480
The bag may rise up, and so strangle thee.
What e'r was casuall, may ever bee.

464 *use to:* are accustomed to.
470 *admit:* permit, allow.
471 f. Marginal gloss: *Of accidentall joys in both places.*
479 *Apostem:* a large abscess.

What should the nature change? Or make the same
Certaine, which was but casuall, when it came?
All casuall joy doth loud and plainly say,   485
Only by comming, that it can away.
Only in Heaven joyes strength is never spent;
And accidentall things are permanent.
Joy of a soules arrivall ne'r decaies;
For that soule ever joyes and ever staies.   490
Joy that their last great Consummation
Approaches in the resurrection;
When earthly bodies more celestiall
Shall be, then Angels were, for they could fall;
This kinde of joy doth every day admit   495
Degrees of growth, but none of losing it.
In this fresh joy, 'tis no small part, that shee,
Shee, in whose goodnesse, he that names degree,
Doth injure her; ('Tis losse to be cal'd best,
There where the stuffe is not such as the rest)   500
Shee, who left such a bodie, as even shee
Only in Heaven could learne, how it can bee
Made better; for shee rather was two soules,
Or like to full, on both sides written Rols,
Where eyes might reade upon the outward skin,   505
As strong Records for God, as mindes within;
Shee, who by making full perfection grow,
Peeces a Circle, and still keepes it so,
Long'd for, and longing for it, to heaven is gone,
Where shee receives, and gives addition.   510
Here in a place, where mis-devotion frames
A thousand Prayers to Saints, whose very names
The ancient Church knew not, Heaven knows not yet:
And where, what lawes of Poetry admit,
Lawes of Religion have at least the same,   515
Immortall Maide, I might invoke thy name.

511 The poem is being composed in France, in December 1611 or early in
1612. Marginal gloss: *Conclusion.*

PLATE II Portrait of John Donne in his shroud, at the age of fifty-nine, from the first edition of his final sermon, *Deaths Duell*, 1632.

Could any Saint provoke that appetite,
Thou here should'st make me a French convertite.
But thou would'st not; nor would'st thou be content,
To take this, for my second yeares true Rent,   520
Did this Coine beare any other stampe, then his,
That gave thee power to doe, me, to say this.
Since his will is, that to posteritie,
Thou should'st for life, and death, a patterne bee,
And that the world should notice have of this,   525
The purpose, and th'Authoritie is his;
Thou art the Proclamation; and I am
The Trumpet, at whose voyce the people came.

Goodfriday, 1613. Riding Westward

Let mans Soule be a Spheare, and then, in this,
The intelligence that moves, devotion is,
And as the other Spheares, by being growne
Subject to forraigne motions, lose their owne,
And being by others hurried every day,   5
Scarce in a yeare their naturall forme obey:
Pleasure or businesse, so, our Soules admit
For their first mover, and are whirld by it.
Hence is't, that I am carryed towards the West
This day, when my Soules forme bends toward the East.   10
There I should see a Sunne, by rising set,
And by that setting endlesse day beget;
But that Christ on this Crosse, did rise and fall,
Sinne had eternally benighted all.
Yet dare I'almost be glad, I do not see   15

518 *convertite:* convert.

528 *Trumpet . . . people:* among numerous biblical references, see Joshua 6:5, 20; I Kings 1:39–40; Isaiah 27:13; Ezekiel 33:3–6.

GOODFRIDAY, 1613: For the opening imagery see Alabaster's Sonnet 15 and Donne's "Extasie," line 52.

6, 10 *forme:* essential creative principle.

That spectacle of too much weight for mee.
Who sees Gods face, that is selfe life, must dye;
What a death were it then to see God dye?
It made his owne Lieutenant Nature shrinke,
It made his footstoole crack, and the Sunne winke. 20
Could I behold those hands which span the Poles,
And turne all spheares at once, peirc'd with those holes?
Could I behold that endlesse height which is
Zenith to us, and our Antipodes,
Humbled below us? or that blood which is 25
The seat of all our Soules, if not of his,
Made durt of dust, or that flesh which was worne
By God, for his apparell, rag'd, and torne?
If on these things I durst not looke, durst I
Upon his miserable mother cast mine eye, 30
Who was Gods partner here, and furnish'd thus
Halfe of that Sacrifice, which ransom'd us?
Though these things, as I ride, be from mine eye,
They'are present yet unto my memory,
For that looks towards them; and thou look'st towards mee,
O Saviour, as thou hang'st upon the tree; 36
I turne my backe to thee, but to receive
Corrections, till thy mercies bid thee leave.
O thinke mee worth thine anger, punish mee,
Burne off my rusts, and my deformity, 40
Restore thine Image, so much, by thy grace,
That thou may'st know mee, and I'll turne my face.

20 *footstoole:* the earth: see Isaiah 66:1.
26 *seat:* residence, abode.
38 *leave:* "leave off," cease.

A nocturnall upon S. *Lucies* day, Being the shortest day

Tis the yeares midnight, and it is the dayes,
Lucies, who scarce seaven houres herself unmaskes,
   The Sunne is spent, and now his flasks
   Send forth light squibs, no constant rayes;
     The worlds whole sap is sunke: 5
The generall balme th'hydroptique earth hath drunk,
Whither, as to the beds-feet, life is shrunke,
Dead and enterr'd; yet all these seeme to laugh,
Compar'd with mee, who am their Epitaph.

Study me then, you who shall lovers bee   10
 At the next world, that is, at the next Spring:
   For I am every dead thing,
   In whom love wrought new Alchimie.
     For his art did expresse
A quintessence even from nothingnesse,   15
 From dull privations, and leane emptinesse:
He ruin'd mee, and I am re-begot
Of absence, darknesse, death; things which are not.

All others, from all things, draw all that's good,
Life, soule, forme, spirit, whence they beeing have;   20
   I, by loves limbecke, am the grave
   Of all, that's nothing. Oft a flood
     Have wee two wept, and so

A NOCTURNALL UPON S. LUCIES DAY: see NOTE.

  3 *flasks:* cases to hold gunpowder.

  4 *squibs:* fireworks.

  6 *balme:* balsam: in alchemical usage, a preservative essence supposed to exist in all organic bodies.

  14 *expresse:* press out.

Drownd the whole world, us two; oft did we grow
To be two Chaosses, when we did show   25
Care to ought else; and often absences
Withdrew our soules, and made us carcasses.

But I am by her death, (which word wrongs her)
Of the first nothing, the Elixer grown;
   Were I a man, that I were one,   30
  I needs must know; I should preferre,
     If I were any beast,
Some ends, some means; Yea plants, yea stones detest,
And love; All, all some properties invest;
If I an ordinary nothing were,   35
As shadow, a light, and body must be here.

But I am None; nor will my Sunne renew.
You lovers, for whose sake, the lesser Sunne
   At this time to the Goat is runne
  To fetch new lust, and give it you,   40
     Enjoy your summer all;
Since shee enjoyes her long nights festivall,
Let mee prepare towards her, and let mee call
This houre her Vigill, and her Eve, since this
Both the yeares, and the dayes deep midnight is.   45

29 *Elixer:* the quintessence, the essential principle (of the original "nothing" that preceded Creation).

34 *properties:* distinctive qualities or attributes; *invest:* envelop: that is, "*some* qualities belong to all things."

39 *Goat:* the Tropic of Capricorn, or the zodiacal sign of Capricorn.

42 *festivall:* feast: the feast day of a saint.

43 *prepare:* place oneself in a state of mental readiness; *towards* implies a metaphor of preparing oneself for a journey: "get ready to go to."

44 *Vigill, Eve:* the evening before a saint's day: see OED, *Vigil,* 1, b: "A devotional watching, esp. the watch kept on the eve of a festival or holy day; a nocturnal service or devotional exercise." The definition aptly sums up the total impact of the poem.

HOLY SONNETS

17.

Since she whom I lov'd hath payd her last debt
To Nature, and to hers, and my good is dead,
And her Soule early into heaven ravished,
Wholly on heavenly things my mind is sett.
Here the admyring her my mind did whett   5
To seeke thee God; so streames do shew their head;
But though I have found thee, and thou my thirst hast fed,
A holy thirsty dropsy melts mee yett.
But why should I begg more Love, when as thou
Dost wooe my soule for hers; offring all thine: 10
And dost not only feare least I allow
My Love to Saints and Angels, things divine,
But in thy tender jealosy dost doubt
Least the World, Fleshe, yea Devill putt thee out.

18.

Show me deare Christ, thy spouse, so bright and clear.
What! is it She, which on the other shore
Goes richly painted? or which rob'd and tore
Laments and mournes in Germany and here?
Sleepes she a thousand, then peepes up one yeare?   5
Is she selfe truth and errs? now new, now outwore?

HOLY SONNETS.
17.1 Donne's wife, Anne, died on August 15, 1617, in her thirty-third year.
  13 *doubt:* fear.
18.1 *spouse:* the Church.
  6 *selfe truth:* truth itself.

Doth she, and did she, and shall she evermore
On one, on seaven, or on no hill appeare?
Dwells she with us, or like adventuring knights
First travaile we to seeke and then make Love?   10
Betray kind husband thy spouse to our sights,
And let myne amorous soule court thy mild Dove,
Who is most trew, and pleasing to thee, then
When she'is embrac'd and open to most men.

19.

Oh, to vex me, contraryes meet in one:
Inconstancy unnaturally hath begott
A constant habit; that when I would not
I change in vowes, and in devotione.
As humorous is my contritione   5
As my prophane Love, and as soone forgott:
As ridlingly distemper'd, cold and hott,
As praying, as mute; as infinite, as none.
I durst not view heaven yesterday; and to day
In prayers, and flattering speaches I court God: 10
To morrow I quake with true feare of his rod.
So my devout fitts come and go away
Like a fantastique Ague: save that here
Those are my best dayes, when I shake with feare.

10 *travaile:* work hard; also, travel.
19.5 *humorous:* capricious.
    7 *ridlingly distemper'd:* bewilderingly, perplexingly disordered.

A Hymne to Christ, at the Authors last going into Germany

In what torne ship soever I embarke,
That ship shall be my embleme of thy Arke;
What sea soever swallow mee, that flood
Shall be to mee an embleme of thy blood;
Though thou with clouds of anger do disguise   5
Thy face; yet through that maske I know those eyes,
   Which, though they turne away sometimes,
     They never will despise.

I sacrifice this Iland unto thee,
And all whom I lov'd there, and who lov'd mee;   10
When I have put our seas twixt them and mee,
Put thou thy sea betwixt my sinnes and thee.
As the trees sap doth seeke the root below
In winter, in my winter now I goe,
   Where none but thee, th'Eternall root   15
     Of true Love I may know.

Nor thou nor thy religion dost controule,
The amorousnesse of an harmonious Soule,
But thou would'st have that love thy selfe: As thou
Art jealous, Lord, so I am jealous now,   20
Thou lov'st not, till from loving more, thou free
My soule: Who ever gives, takes libertie:
   O, if thou car'st not whom I love
     Alas, thou lov'st not mee.

Seale then this bill of my Divorce to All,   25
On whom those fainter beames of love did fall;

A HYMNE TO CHRIST: Donne left England for Germany in May 1619, as chaplain
to Lord Doncaster on a diplomatic mission; he returned in January 1620.

Marry those loves, which in youth scattered bee
On Fame, Wit, Hopes (false mistresses) to thee.
Churches are best for Prayer, that have least light:
To see God only, I goe out of sight: 30
    And to scape stormy dayes, I chuse
      An Everlasting night.

Hymne to God my God, in my sicknesse

Since I am comming to that Holy roome,
    Where, with thy Quire of Saints for evermore,
I shall be made thy Musique; As I come
    I tune the Instrument here at the dore,
    And what I must doe then, thinke here before.   5

Whilst my physitians by their love are growne
    Cosmographers, and I their Mapp, who lie
Flat on this bed, that by them may be showne
    That this is my South-west discoverie
    Per fretum febris, by these streights to die,   10

I joy, that in these straits, I see my West;
    For, though theire currants yeeld returne to none,
What shall my West hurt me? As West and East
    In all flatt Maps (and I am one) are one,
    So death doth touch the Resurrection.   15

Is the Pacifique Sea my home? Or are
    The Easterne riches? Is *Jerusalem?*
Anyan, and *Magellan,* and *Gibraltare,*

HYMNE TO GOD MY GOD.

  10 *Per fretum febris: fretum* means both *strait* and *raging heat* (of fever);
streights: straits, difficult circumstances.

  12 *currants:* there may be a play here on the *current* or circulation of money
(currency).

  18 the "Straits of Anyan" were supposed to separate America and Asia, ac-
cording to old geographers.

All streights, and none but streights, are wayes to them,
Whether where *Japhet* dwelt, or *Cham*, or *Sem*.   20

We thinke that *Paradise* and *Calvarie*,
    Christs Crosse, and *Adams* tree, stood in one place;
Looke Lord, and finde both *Adams* met in me;
    As the first *Adams* sweat surrounds my face,
    May the last *Adams* blood my soule embrace.   25

So, in his purple wrapp'd receive mee Lord,
    By these his thornes give me his other Crowne;
And as to others soules I preach'd thy word,
    Be this my Text, my Sermon to mine owne,
    Therfore that he may raise the Lord throws down.   30

To Christ

Wilt thou forgive that sinn, where I begunn,
    Which is my sinn, though it were done before?
Wilt thou forgive those sinns through which I runn
    And doe them still, though still I doe deplore?
        When thou hast done, thou hast not done,   5
            for I have more.

Wilt thou forgive that sinn, by which I'have wonne
    Others to sinn, & made my sinn their dore?
Wilt thou forgive that sinn which I did shunne
    A yeare or twoe, but wallowed in a score?   10
        When thou hast done, thou hast not done,
            for I have more.

---

20 The three sons of Noah, who, according to tradition, inherited the world
as follows: Europe (Japhet); Africa (Ham); and Asia (Shem).

22 *place:* region: see Miss Gardner's discussion, *Divine Poems,* pp. 135–37.
TO CHRIST: see NOTE.

I have a sinn of feare that when I have spunn
  My last thred, I shall perish on the shore;
Sweare by thy self that at my Death, thy Sunn   15
  Shall shine as it shines nowe, & heretofore;
    And having done that, thou hast done,
        I have noe more.

GEORGE HERBERT
1593–1633

Figure 3. Title page of the first edition of Herbert's *Temple*, 1633.

From *THE TEMPLE* (1633)

The Dedication

Lord, my first fruits present themselves to thee;
Yet not mine neither: for from thee they came,
And must return. Accept of them and me,
And make us strive, who shall sing best thy name.
  Turn their eyes hither, who shall make a gain: 5
  Theirs, who shall hurt themselves or me, refrain.

THE DEDICATION.
  6 *refrain:* prevent, stop.

The Church-porch

Perirrhanterium

Thou, whose sweet youth and early hopes inhance
Thy rate and price, and mark thee for a treasure;
Hearken unto a Verser, who may chance
Ryme thee to good, and make a bait of pleasure.
  A verse may finde him, who a sermon flies,   5
  And turn delight into a sacrifice.

Beware of lust: it doth pollute and foul
Whom God in Baptisme washt with his own blood.
It blots thy lesson written in thy soul;
The holy lines cannot be understood.   10
  How dare those eyes upon a Bible look,
  Much lesse towards God, whose lust is all their book?

Abstain wholly, or wed. Thy bounteous Lord
Allows thee choise of paths: take no by-wayes;
But gladly welcome what he doth afford;   15
Not grudging, that thy lust hath bounds and staies.
  Continence hath his joy: weigh both; and so
  If rottennesse have more, let Heaven go.

If God had laid all common, certainly
Man would have been th'incloser: but since now   20
God hath impal'd us, on the contrarie

THE CHURCH-PORCH: *Perirrhanterium:* a brush (*aspergillum*) used for sprinkling holy water.

  2 *rate:* valuation.

  16 *staies:* stays, restraints.

  21 *impal'd us:* fenced us in (with ref. to practice of enclosing, for private use, lands that were formerly common).

Man breaks the fence, and every ground will plough.
  O what were man, might he himself misplace!
  Sure to be crosse he would shift feet and face.

Drink not the third glasse, which thou canst not tame,   25
When once it is within thee; but before
Mayst rule it, as thou list; and poure the shame,
Which it would poure on thee, upon the floore.
  It is most just to throw that on the ground,
  Which would throw me there, if I keep the round.   30

He that is drunken, may his mother kill
Bigge with his sister: he hath lost the reins,
Is outlawd by himself: all kinde of ill
Did with his liquour slide into his veins.
  The drunkard forfets Man, and doth devest   35
  All worldly right, save what he hath by beast.

       ✿   ✿   ✿   ✿   ✿

Slight those who say amidst their sickly healths,
Thou liv'st by rule. What doth not so, but man?
Houses are built by rule, and common-wealths.   135
Entice the trusty sunne, if that thou can,
  From his Ecliptick line: becken the skie.
  Who lives by rule then, keeps good companie.

Who keeps no guard upon himself, is slack,
And rots to nothing at the next great thaw.   140
Man is a shop of rules, a well truss'd pack,
Whose every parcell under-writes a law.
  Lose not thy self, nor give thy humours way:
  God gave them to thee under lock and key.

24 *crosse:* perverse.
27 *list:* wish, choose.
30 *keep the round:* keep on drinking each round of liquor.
35 *devest:* a legal term: take away, annul.
142 *parcell:* part; *under-writes:* agrees to, confirms by signature.

By all means use sometimes to be alone. 145
Salute thy self: see what thy soul doth wear.
Dare to look in thy chest; for 'tis thine own:
And tumble up and down what thou find'st there.
    Who cannot rest till hee good fellows finde,
    He breaks up house, turns out of doores his minde. 150

        ✿   ✿   ✿   ✿   ✿

When once thy foot enters the church, be bare.
God is more there, then thou: for thou art there
Onely by his permission. Then beware, 405
And make thy self all reverence and fear.
    Kneeling ne're spoil'd silk stocking: quit thy state.
    All equall are within the churches gate.

Resort to sermons, but to prayers most:
Praying 's the end of preaching. O be drest; 410
Stay not for th' other pin: why thou hast lost
A joy for it worth worlds. Thus hell doth jest
    Away thy blessings, and extreamly flout thee,
    Thy clothes being fast, but thy soul loose about thee.

In time of service seal up both thine eies, 415
And send them to thine heart; that spying sinne,
They may weep out the stains by them did rise:
Those doores being shut, all by the eare comes in.
    Who marks in church-time others symmetrie,
    Makes all their beautie his deformitie. 420

Let vain or busie thoughts have there no part:
Bring not thy plough, thy plots, thy pleasures thither.
Christ purg'd his temple; so must thou thy heart.

145 *use:* observe as custom or practice.
146 *Salute:* greet.
148 *tumble:* search through by turning over (with a play on the word *chest*).
407 *quit thy state:* give up your formal dignity.
409 *resort to:* attend, go to.

All worldly thoughts are but theeves met together
    To couzin thee. Look to thy actions well: 425
    For churches are either our heav'n or hell.

Judge not the preacher; for he is thy Judge:
If thou mislike him, thou conceiv'st him not.
God calleth preaching folly. Do not grudge
To pick out treasures from an earthen pot.   430
    The worst speak something good: if all want sense,
    God takes a text, and preacheth patience.

He that gets patience, and the blessing which
Preachers conclude with, hath not lost his pains.
He that by being at church escapes the ditch,   435
Which he might fall in by companions, gains.
    He that loves Gods abode, and to combine
    With saints on earth, shall one day with them shine.

Jest not at preachers language, or expression:
How know'st thou, but thy sinnes made him miscarrie?
Then turn thy faults and his into confession: 440
God sent him, whatsoe're he be: O tarry,
    And love him for his Master: his condition,
    Though it be ill, makes him no ill Physician.

None shall in hell such bitter pangs endure,   445
As those, who mock at Gods way of salvation.
Whom oil and balsames kill, what salve can cure?
They drink with greedinesse a full damnation.
    The Jews refused thunder; and we, folly.
    Though God do hedge us in, yet who is holy?   450

425 *couzin:* cozen.
428 *conceiv'st him not:* do not understand him.
429 See 1 Corinthians 1:21.
447 *balsames:* balms, medicinal salves.
449 See Exodus 19:16 and 1 Corinthians 1:18.

Summe up at night, what thou hast done by day;
And in the morning, what thou hast to do.
Dresse and undresse thy soul: mark the decay
And growth of it: if with thy watch, that too
    Be down, then winde up both; since we shall be   455
    Most surely judg'd, make thy accounts agree.

In brief, acquit thee bravely; play the man.
Look not on pleasures as they come, but go.
Deferre not the least vertue: lifes poore span
Make not an ell, by trifling in thy wo.   460
    If thou do ill; the joy fades, not the pains:
    If well; the pain doth fade, the joy remains.

Superliminare

Thou, whom the former precepts have
Sprinkled and taught, how to behave
Thy self in church; approach, and taste
The churches mysticall repast.

Avoid profanenesse; come not here: 5
Nothing but holy, pure, and cleare,
Or that which groneth to be so,
May at his perill further go.

SUPERLIMINARE: a lintel (i.e., the inscription on the lintel over the church door).
  5 *Avoid:* probably in sense of "go away": a direct address to "profanenesse" as a personified quality.

The Altar

A broken A L T A R, Lord, thy servant reares,
Made of a heart, and cemented with teares:
  Whose parts are as thy hand did frame;
  No workmans tool hath touch'd the same.

      A H E A R T alone   5
      Is   such a   stone,
      As   nothing   but
      Thy pow'r doth cut.
      Wherefore each part
      Of my hard heart   10
      Meets in this frame,
      To praise thy name.
  That if I chance to hold my peace,
  These stones to praise thee may not cease.
O let thy blessed S A C R I F I C E be mine,   15
And sanctifie this A L T A R to be thine.

The Thanksgiving

Oh King of grief! (a title strange, yet true,
  To thee of all kings onely due)
Oh King of wounds! how shall I grieve for thee,
  Who in all grief preventest me?

THE ALTAR.

  3 *frame:* construct, create.

  11 *frame:* structure.

THE THANKSGIVING.

  1 *grief:* suffering, injury (along with modern sense).

  4 *preventest:* anticipates.

Shall I weep bloud? why thou hast wept such store   5
    That all thy body was one doore.
Shall I be scourged, flouted, boxed, sold?
    'Tis but to tell the tale is told.
My God, my God, why dost thou part from me?
    Was such a grief as cannot be.   10
Shall I then sing, skipping thy dolefull storie,
    And side with thy triumphant glorie?
Shall thy strokes be my stroking? thorns, my flower?
    Thy rod, my posie? crosse, my bower?
But how then shall I imitate thee, and   15
    Copie thy fair, though bloudie hand?
Surely I will revenge me on thy love,
    And trie who shall victorious prove.
If thou dost give me wealth; I will restore
    All back unto thee by the poore.   20
If thou dost give me honour; men shall see,
    The honour doth belong to thee.
I will not marry; or, if she be mine,
    She and her children shall be thine.
My bosome friend, if he blaspheme thy name,   25
    I will tear thence his love and fame.
One half of me being gone, the rest I give
    Unto some Chappell, die or live.
As for thy passion—But of that anon,
    When with the other I have done.   30
For thy predestination I'le contrive,
    That three yeares hence, if I survive,
I'le build a spittle, or mend common wayes,
    But mend mine own without delayes.
Then I will use the works of thy creation,   35
    As if I us'd them but for fashion.

5 *store:* abundance.
14 *posie:* bouquet.
17 *revenge me:* the expression is deliberately extravagant, implying a fervent desire to "pay back."
33 *spittle:* hospital, poorhouse; *common wayes:* public highways.

The world and I will quarrell; and the yeare
　　Shall not perceive, that I am here.
My musick shall finde thee, and ev'ry string
　　Shall have his attribute to sing;　　　　　　　　40
That all together may accord in thee,
　　And prove one God, one harmonie.
If thou shalt give me wit, it shall appeare,
　　If thou hast giv'n it me, 'tis here.
Nay, I will reade thy book, and never move　　　　45
　　Till I have found therein thy love;
Thy art of love, which I'le turn back on thee,
　　O my deare Saviour, Victorie!
Then for thy passion—I will do for that—
　　Alas, my God, I know not what.　　　　　　　50

The Reprisall

　　I have consider'd it, and finde
There is no dealing with thy mighty passion:
For though I die for thee, I am behinde;
　　My sinnes deserve the condemnation.

　　O make me innocent, that I　　　　　　　　　5
May give a disentangled state and free:
And yet thy wounds still my attempts defie,
　　For by thy death I die for thee.

　　Ah! was it not enough that thou
By thy eternall glorie didst outgo me?　　　　　10
Couldst thou not griefs sad conquests me allow,
　　But in all vict'ries overthrow me?

43 *wit:* intellectual power, mental creativity.
THE REPRISALL.
　　6 *disentangled state:* an estate free of debts.

Yet by confession will I come
Into the conquest. Though I can do nought
Against thee, in thee I will overcome   15
    The man, who once against thee fought.

The Agonie

Philosophers have measur'd mountains,
Fathom'd the depths of seas, of states, and kings,
Walk'd with a staffe to heav'n, and traced fountains:
    But there are two vast, spacious things,
The which to measure it doth more behove: 5
Yet few there are that sound them; Sinne and Love.

Who would know Sinne, let him repair
Unto mount Olivet; there shall he see
A man so wrung with pains, that all his hair,
    His skinne, his garments bloudie be.   10
Sinne is that presse and vice, which forceth pain
To hunt his cruell food through ev'ry vein.

Who knows not Love, let him assay
And taste that juice, which on the crosse a pike
Did set again abroach; then let him say   15
    If ever he did taste the like.
Love is that liquour sweet and most divine,
Which my God feels as bloud; but I, as wine.

THE AGONIE.

1 *Philosophers:* students in all branches of "philosophy," esp. science, "natural philosophy."

3 *staffe:* a measuring rod, with a play on the divining rod, used to discover water.

5 *it doth more behove:* it is more necessary.

7 *repair:* go.

13 *assay:* test the quality of.

Redemption

Having been tenant long to a rich Lord,
    Not thriving, I resolved to be bold,
    And make a suit unto him, to afford
A new small-rented lease, and cancell th' old.

In heaven at his manour I him sought:
    They told me there, that he was lately gone
    About some land, which he had dearly bought
Long since on earth, to take possession.

I straight return'd, and knowing his great birth,
    Sought him accordingly in great resorts;
    In cities, theatres, gardens, parks, and courts:
At length I heard a ragged noise and mirth

    Of theeves and murderers: there I him espied,
    Who straight, *Your suit is granted*, said, & died.

Sepulchre

O blessed bodie! Whither art thou thrown?
No lodging for thee, but a cold hard stone?
So many hearts on earth, and yet not one
            Receive thee?

Sure there is room within our hearts good store;   5
For they can lodge transgressions by the score:

SEPULCHRE.
   5 *good store:* used adverbially: in good quantity or measure.

Thousands of toyes dwell there, yet out of doore
           They leave thee.

But that which shews them large, shews them unfit.
What ever sinne did this pure rock commit,   10
Which holds thee now? Who hath indited it
           Of murder?

Where our hard hearts have took up stones to brain thee,
And missing this, most falsly did arraigne thee;
Onely these stones in quiet entertain thee,   15
           And order.

And as of old, the law by heav'nly art
Was writ in stone; so thou, which also art
The letter of the word, find'st no fit heart
           To hold thee.   20

Yet do we still persist as we began,
And so should perish, but that nothing can,
Though it be cold, hard, foul, from loving man
           Withold thee.

Easter

Rise heart; thy Lord is risen. Sing his praise
           Without delayes,
Who takes thee by the hand, that thou likewise
           With him mayst rise:
That, as his death calcined thee to dust,   5
His life may make thee gold, and much more just.

7 *toyes:* trivial things.
17–20 See 2 Corinthians 3:2–8.

Awake, my lute, and struggle for thy part
                     With all thy art.
The crosse taught all wood to resound his name,
                     Who bore the same.   10
His stretched sinews taught all strings, what key
Is best to celebrate this most high day.

Consort both heart and lute, and twist a song
                     Pleasant and long:
Or since all musick is but three parts vied   15
                     And multiplied;
O let thy blessed Spirit bear a part,
And make up our defects with his sweet art.

I got me flowers to straw thy way;
I got me boughs off many a tree: 20
But thou wast up by break of day,
And brought'st thy sweets along with thee.

The Sunne arising in the East,
Though he give light, & th' East perfume;
If they should offer to contest   25
With thy arising, they presume.

Can there be any day but this,
Though many sunnes to shine endeavour?
We count three hundred, but we misse:
There is but one, and that one ever.   30

EASTER.

13 *Consort:* sing together, harmonize.

15 *three parts:* with ref. to the musical term, "triad"; *vied:* placed in competition; see NOTE.

19 *straw:* strew.

22 *sweets:* perfumes.

Easter wings

Lord, who createdst man in wealth and store,
  Though foolishly he lost the same,
    Decaying more and more,
      Till he became
        Most poore: 5
        With thee
      O let me rise
    As larks, harmoniously,
  And sing this day thy victories:
Then shall the fall further the flight in me.   10

My tender age in sorrow did beginne:
  And still with sicknesses and shame
    Thou didst so punish sinne,
      That I became
        Most thinne.   15
        With thee
      Let me combine,
    And feel this day thy victorie:
  For, if I imp my wing on thine,
Affliction shall advance the flight in me.   20

Affliction (I)

When first thou didst entice to thee my heart,
        I thought the service brave:
So many joyes I writ down for my part,
        Besides what I might have

EASTER WINGS: see NOTE.
  19 *imp:* see NOTE.
AFFLICTION (1).
  2 *brave:* fine, elegant.

[148]

Out of my stock of naturall delights,   5
Augmented with thy gracious benefits.

I looked on thy furniture so fine,
        And made it fine to me:
Thy glorious houshold-stuffe did me entwine,
        And 'tice me unto thee.   10
Such starres I counted mine: both heav'n and earth
Payd me my wages in a world of mirth.

What pleasures could I want, whose King I served?
        Where joyes my fellows were.
Thus argu'd into hopes, my thoughts reserved   15
        No place for grief or fear.
Therefore my sudden soul caught at the place,
And made her youth and fiercenesse seek thy face.

At first thou gav'st me milk and sweetnesses;
        I had my wish and way: 20
My dayes were straw'd with flow'rs and happinesse;
        There was no moneth but May.
But with my yeares sorrow did twist and grow,
And made a partie unawares for wo.

My flesh began unto my soul in pain,   25
        Sicknesses cleave my bones;
Consuming agues dwell in ev'ry vein,
        And tune my breath to grones.
Sorrow was all my soul; I scarce beleeved,
Till grief did tell me roundly, that I lived.   30

---

7 *furniture:* furnishings, equipment; the physical aspects of the church building and services.

12 *mirth:* joy, happiness.

24 *partie:* a side in a dispute.

25 *began:* began to complain; as Hutchinson suggests, the next three lines seem to be the direct complaint of the flesh.

30 *roundly:* bluntly, plainly.

When I got health, thou took'st away my life,
    And more; for my friends die:
My mirth and edge was lost; a blunted knife
    Was of more use then I.
Thus thinne and lean without a fence or friend,   35
I was blown through with ev'ry storm and winde.

Whereas my birth and spirit rather took
    The way that takes the town;
Thou didst betray me to a lingring book,
    And wrap me in a gown.   40
I was entangled in the world of strife,
Before I had the power to change my life.

Yet, for I threatned oft the siege to raise,
    Not simpring all mine age,
Thou often didst with Academick praise   45
    Melt and dissolve my rage.
I took thy sweetned pill, till I came neare;
I could not go away, nor persevere.

Yet lest perchance I should too happie be
    In my unhappinesse,   50
Turning my purge to food, thou throwest me
    Into more sicknesses.
Thus doth thy power crosse-bias me, not making
Thine own gift good, yet me from my wayes taking.

Now I am here, what thou wilt do with me   55
    None of my books will show:
I reade, and sigh, and wish I were a tree;
    For sure then I should grow
To fruit or shade: at least some bird would trust
Her houshold to me, and I should be just.   60

53 *crosse-bias:* give a bias or inclination counter to my own.

Yet, though thou troublest me, I must be meek;
   In weaknesse must be stout.
Well, I will change the service, and go seek
   Some other master out.
Ah my deare God! though I am clean forgot,   65
Let me not love thee, if I love thee not.

Prayer

Prayer the Churches banquet, Angels age,
  Gods breath in man returning to his birth,
  The soul in paraphrase, heart in pilgrimage,
The Christian plummet sounding heav'n and earth;

Engine against th' Almightie, sinners towre,   5
  Reversed thunder, Christ-side-piercing spear,
  The six-daies world transposing in an houre,
A kinde of tune, which all things heare and fear;

Softnesse, and peace, and joy, and love, and blisse,
  Exalted Manna, gladnesse of the best,   10
  Heaven in ordinarie, man well drest,
The milkie way, the bird of Paradise,

  Church-bels beyond the starres heard, the souls bloud,
  The land of spices; something understood.

65–66 See NOTE.

PRAYER.

1 *Angels age:* "prayer acquaints man with the blessed timeless existence of the angels" (Hutchinson).

3 *soul in paraphrase:* "in prayer the soul opens out and more fully discovers itself" (Hutchinson).

5 *Engine against:* device for overcoming or reaching.

The H. Communion

Not in rich furniture, or fine aray,
    Nor in a wedge of gold,
    Thou, who from me wast sold,
    To me dost now thy self convey;
For so thou should'st without me still have been,   5
    Leaving within me sinne:

But by the way of nourishment and strength
    Thou creep'st into my breast;
    Making thy way my rest,
    And thy small quantities my length;   10
Which spread their forces into every part,
    Meeting sinnes force and art.

Yet can these not get over to my soul,
    Leaping the wall that parts
    Our souls and fleshly hearts;   15
    But as th' outworks, they may controll
My rebel-flesh, and carrying thy name,
    Affright both sinne and shame.

Onely thy grace, which with these elements comes,
    Knoweth the ready way,   20
    And hath the privie key,
    Op'ning the souls most subtile rooms;

THE H. COMMUNION: see NOTE.
  2 See Joshua 7:20–21.
  5 *without:* outside.
 13 *these:* the physical elements of the Communion.
 19 *elements:* the bread and wine of the Communion.
 20 *ready:* easy, quick, direct.
 21 *privie:* private.
 22 *subtile:* delicate, intangible.

While those to spirits refin'd, at doore attend
    Dispatches from their friend.

Give me my captive soul, or take   25
    My bodie also thither.
Another lift like this will make
    Them both to be together.

Before that sinne turn'd flesh to stone,
    And all our lump to leaven;   30
A fervent sigh might well have blown
    Our innocent earth to heaven.

For sure when Adam did not know
    To sinne, or sinne to smother;
He might to heav'n from Paradise go,   35
    As from one room t'another.

Thou hast restor'd us to this ease
    By this thy heav'nly bloud;
Which I can go to, when I please,
    And leave th' earth to their food.   40

Love

I.

Immortall Love, authour of this great frame,
    Sprung from that beautie which can never fade;
    How hath man parcel'd out thy glorious name,
And thrown it on that dust which thou hast made,

23 *those:* the bread and wine, transformed into "spirits" or vapors arising from the blood.
24 *friend:* Christ, speaking within the soul to the body of man.
LOVE I.
1 *this great frame:* the universe.

While mortall love doth all the title gain!   5
   Which siding with invention, they together
   Bear all the sway, possessing heart and brain,
(Thy workmanship) and give thee share in neither.

Wit fancies beautie, beautie raiseth wit:
   The world is theirs; they two play out the game,   10
   Thou standing by: and though thy glorious name
Wrought our deliverance from th' infernall pit,

   Who sings thy praise? onely a skarf or glove
   Doth warm our hands, and make them write of love.

II.

Immortall Heat, O let thy greater flame
   Attract the lesser to it: let those fires,
   Which shall consume the world, first make it tame;
And kindle in our hearts such true desires,

As may consume our lusts, and make thee way.   5
   Then shall our hearts pant thee; then shall our brain
   All her invention on thine Altar lay,
And there in hymnes send back thy fire again:

Our eies shall see thee, which before saw dust;
   Dust blown by wit, till that they both were blinde: 10
   Thou shalt recover all thy goods in kinde,
Who wert disseized by usurping lust:

   All knees shall bow to thee; all wits shall rise,
   And praise him who did make and mend our eies.

6 *invention:* creative, imaginative power.
LOVE II.
  12 *disseized:* dispossessed (a legal term).
  13 *wits:* mental powers.

GEORGE HERBERT

Sonnets from Walton's
LIFE OF HERBERT, 1670

My God, where is that ancient heat towards thee,
  Wherewith whole showls of *Martyrs* once did burn,
  Besides their other flames. Doth Poetry
Wear *Venus* Livery? only serve her turn?
Why are not *Sonnets* made of thee? and layes   5
  Upon thine Altar burnt? Cannot thy love
  Heighten a spirit to sound out thy praise
As well as any she? Cannot thy *Dove*
Out-strip their *Cupid* easily in flight?
  Or, since thy wayes are deep, and still the same,   10
  Will not a verse run smooth that bears thy name!
Why doth that fire, which by thy power and might
  Each breast does feel, no braver fuel choose
  Than that, which one day, Worms, may chance refuse.

Sure Lord, there is enough in thee to dry
  Oceans of *Ink;* for, as the Deluge did
  Cover the Earth, so doth thy Majesty:
Each Cloud distills thy praise, and doth forbid
Poets to turn it to another use.   5
  Roses and *Lillies* speak thee; and to make
  A pair of Cheeks of them, is thy abuse.
Why should I *Womens eyes* for Chrystal take?
Such poor invention burns in their low mind

SONNETS FROM WALTON'S *Life:* see NOTE.
  2 *showls:* shoals, crowds.

[155]

Whose fire is wild, and doth not upward go   10
   To praise, and on thee Lord, some *Ink* bestow.
Open the bones, and you shall nothing find
   In the best *face* but *filth*, when Lord, in thee
   The *beauty* lies, in the *discovery*.

The Temper

How should I praise thee, Lord! how should my rymes
   Gladly engrave thy love in steel,
   If what my soul doth feel sometimes,
      My soul might ever feel!

Although there were some fourtie heav'ns, or more,   5
   Sometimes I peere above them all;
   Sometimes I hardly reach a score,
      Sometimes to hell I fall.

O rack me not to such a vast extent;
   Those distances belong to thee: 10
   The world's too little for thy tent,
      A grave too big for me.

Wilt thou meet arms with man, that thou dost stretch
   A crumme of dust from heav'n to hell?
   Will great God measure with a wretch?   15
      Shall he thy stature spell?

O let me, when thy roof my soul hath hid,
   O let me roost and nestle there:
   Then of a sinner thou art rid,
      And I of hope and fear.   20

THE TEMPER: proper disposition: see NOTE.
13 *meet*: with a play on *mete* (measure).

Yet take thy way; for sure thy way is best:
    Stretch or contract me, thy poore debter:
    This is but tuning of my breast,
        To make the musick better.

Whether I flie with angels, fall with dust,   25
    Thy hands made both, and I am there:
    Thy power and love, my love and trust
        Make one place ev'ry where.

The H. Scriptures. I

Oh Book! infinite sweetnesse! let my heart
    Suck ev'ry letter, and a hony gain,
    Precious for any grief in any part;
To cleare the breast, to mollifie all pain.

Thou art all health, health thriving, till it make   5
    A full eternitie: thou art a masse
    Of strange delights, where we may wish & take.
Ladies, look here; this is the thankfull glasse,

That mends the lookers eyes: this is the well
    That washes what it shows. Who can indeare   10
    Thy praise too much? thou art heav'ns Lidger here,
Working against the states of death and hell.

    Thou art joyes handsell: heav'n lies flat in thee,
    Subject to ev'ry mounters bended knee.

THE H. SCRIPTURES. I.
  11 *Lidger:* resident ambassador.
  13 *handsell:* token of good to come.

Mattens

I cannot ope mine eyes,
But thou art ready there to catch
My morning-soul and sacrifice:
Then we must needs for that day make a match.

My God, what is a heart?   5
Silver, or gold, or precious stone,
Or starre, or rainbow, or a part
Of all these things, or all of them in one?

My God, what is a heart,
That thou shouldst it so eye, and wooe,   10
Powring upon it all thy art,
As if that thou hadst nothing els to do?

Indeed mans whole estate
Amounts (and richly) to serve thee:
He did not heav'n and earth create,   15
Yet studies them, not him by whom they be.

Teach me thy love to know;
That this new light, which now I see,
May both the work and workman show:
Then by a sunne-beam I will climbe to thee.   20

MATTENS: matins, morning prayer.
   4 *match*: agreement, marriage.

Even-song

Blest be the God of love,
Who gave me eyes, and light, and power this day,
Both to be busie, and to play.
But much more blest be God above,

Who gave me sight alone,   5
Which to himself he did denie:
For when he sees my waies, I dy:
But I have got his sonne, and he hath none.

What have I brought thee home
For this thy love? have I discharg'd the debt,   10
Which this dayes favour did beget?
I ranne; but all I brought, was fome.

Thy diet, care, and cost
Do end in bubbles, balls of winde;
Of winde to thee whom I have crost,   15
But balls of wilde-fire to my troubled minde.

Yet still thou goest on,
And now with darknesse closest wearie eyes,
Saying to man, *It doth suffice:*
Henceforth repose; your work is done.   20

Thus in thy Ebony box
Thou dost inclose us, till the day
Put our amendment in our way,
And give new wheels to our disorder'd clocks.

I muse, which shows more love,   25
The day or night: that is the gale, this th' harbour;
That is the walk, and this the arbour;
Or that the garden, this the grove.

My God, thou art all love.
Not one poore minute scapes thy breast,   30
But brings a favour from above;
And in this love, more then in bed, I rest.

Church-monuments

While that my soul repairs to her devotion,
Here I intombe my flesh, that it betimes
May take acquaintance of this heap of dust;
To which the blast of deaths incessant motion,
Fed with the exhalation of our crimes,   5
Drives all at last. Therefore I gladly trust

My bodie to this school, that it may learn
To spell his elements, and finde his birth
Written in dustie heraldrie and lines;
Which dissolution sure doth best discern,   10
Comparing dust with dust, and earth with earth.
These laugh at Jeat, and Marble put for signes,

To sever the good fellowship of dust,
And spoil the meeting. What shall point out them,
When they shall bow, and kneel, and fall down flat   15
To kisse those heaps, which now they have in trust?
Deare flesh, while I do pray, learn here thy stemme
And true descent; that when thou shalt grow fat,

And wanton in thy cravings, thou mayst know,
That flesh is but the glasse, which holds the dust   20
That measures all our time; which also shall
Be crumbled into dust. Mark here below
How tame these ashes are, how free from lust,
That thou mayst fit thy self against thy fall.

CHURCH-MONUMENTS.
24 *fit thy self against:* prepare yourself for.

Church-musick

Sweetest of sweets, I thank you: when displeasure
    Did through my bodie wound my minde,
You took me thence, and in your house of pleasure
    A daintie lodging me assign'd.

Now I in you without a bodie move,   5
    Rising and falling with your wings:
We both together sweetly live and love,
    Yet say sometimes, *God help poore Kings.*

Comfort, I'le die; for if you poste from me,
    Sure I shall do so, and much more: 10
But if I travell in your companie,
    You know the way to heavens doore.

Church-lock and key

I know it is my sinne, which locks thine eares,
    And bindes thy hands,
Out-crying my requests, drowning my tears;
Or else the chilnesse of my faint demands.

But as cold hands are angrie with the fire,   5
    And mend it still;
So I do lay the want of my desire,
Not on my sinnes, or coldnesse, but thy will.

CHURCH-MUSICK.
  9 *poste:* hasten.

Yet heare, O God, onely for his blouds sake
                  Which pleads for me: 10
For though sinnes plead too, yet like stones they make
His blouds sweet current much more loud to be.

The Church-floore

Mark you the floore? that square & speckled stone,
           Which looks so firm and strong,
               Is *Patience:*

And th' other black and grave, wherewith each one
           Is checker'd all along,   5
               Humilitie:

The gentle rising, which on either hand
           Leads to the Quire above,
               Is *Confidence:*

But the sweet cement, which in one sure band   10
           Ties the whole frame, is *Love*
             And *Charitie.*

           Hither sometimes Sinne steals, and stains
           The marbles neat and curious veins:
But all is cleansed when the marble weeps.   15
           Sometimes Death, puffing at the doore,
           Blows all the dust about the floore:
But while he thinks to spoil the room, he sweeps.
           Blest be the *Architect,* whose art
           Could build so strong in a weak heart.   20

THE CHURCH-FLOORE.
  14 *curious:* delicately formed.

The Windows

Lord, how can man preach thy eternall word?
    He is a brittle crazie glasse:
Yet in thy temple thou dost him afford
    This glorious and transcendent place,
    To be a window, through thy grace.   5

But when thou dost anneal in glasse thy storie,
    Making thy life to shine within
The holy Preachers; then the light and glorie
    More rev'rend grows, & more doth win:
    Which else shows watrish, bleak, & thin.   10

Doctrine and life, colours and light, in one
    When they combine and mingle, bring
A strong regard and aw: but speech alone
    Doth vanish like a flaring thing,
    And in the eare, not conscience ring.   15

The Starre

Bright spark, shot from a brighter place,
    Where beams surround my Saviours face,
      Canst thou be any where
      So well as there?

THE WINDOWS.
  2 *crazie:* full of cracks.
  6 *anneal:* fix the colors by heating.

Yet, if thou wilt from thence depart,　　　　　　　5
　　Take a bad lodging in my heart;
　　　　For thou canst make a debter,
　　　　　And make it better.

First with thy fire-work burn to dust
　　Folly, and worse then folly, lust:　　　　　　10
　　　　Then with thy light refine,
　　　　　And make it shine:

So disengag'd from sinne and sicknesse,
　　Touch it with thy celestiall quicknesse,
　　　　That it may hang and move　　　　　　15
　　　　　After thy love.

Then with our trinitie of light,
　　Motion, and heat, let's take our flight
　　　　Unto the place where thou
　　　　　Before didst bow.　　　　　　　　20

Get me a standing there, and place
　　Among the beams, which crown the face
　　　　Of him, who dy'd to part
　　　　　Sinne and my heart:

That so among the rest I may　　　　　　　　25
　　Glitter, and curle, and winde as they:
　　　　That winding is their fashion
　　　　　Of adoration.

Sure thou wilt joy, by gaining me
　　To flie home like a laden bee　　　　　　　30
　　　　Unto that hive of beams
　　　　　And garland-streams.

THE STARRE.
　14 *quicknesse:* life, liveliness.

[164]

Deniall

When my devotions could not pierce
    Thy silent eares;
Then was my heart broken, as was my verse:
    My breast was full of fears
        And disorder: 5

My bent thoughts, like a brittle bow,
    Did flie asunder:
Each took his way; some would to pleasures go,
    Some to the warres and thunder
        Of alarms.   10

As good go any where, they say,
    As to benumme
Both knees and heart, in crying night and day,
    Come, come, my God, O come,
        But no hearing.   15

O that thou shouldst give dust a tongue
    To crie to thee,
And then not heare it crying! all day long
    My heart was in my knee,
        But no hearing.   20

Therefore my soul lay out of sight,
    Untun'd, unstrung:
My feeble spirit, unable to look right,
    Like a nipt blossome, hung
        Discontented.   25

DENIALL.
   10 *alarms:* calls to arms.

O cheer and tune my heartlesse breast,
  Deferre no time;
That so thy favours granting my request,
   They and my minde may chime,
    And mend my ryme.   30

Vertue

Sweet day, so cool, so calm, so bright,
The bridall of the earth and skie:
The dew shall weep thy fall to night;
   For thou must die.

Sweet rose, whose hue angrie and brave   5
Bids the rash gazer wipe his eye:
Thy root is ever in its grave,
   And thou must die.

Sweet spring, full of sweet dayes, and roses,
A box where sweets compacted lie;   10
My musick shows ye have your closes,
   And all must die.

Onely a sweet and vertuous soul,
Like season'd timber, never gives;
But though the whole world turn to coal,   15
   Then chiefly lives.

VERTUE.
 2 *bridall:* wedding.
 5 *angrie:* red.
 10 *sweets:* sweet odors, fragrances.
 11 *closes:* cadences, in music.
 15 *coal:* cinder, ashes.

The Pearl. *Matth. 13*

I know the wayes of Learning; both the head
And pipes that feed the presse, and make it runne;
What reason hath from nature borrowed,
Or of it self, like a good huswife, spunne
In laws and policie; what the starres conspire,   5
What willing nature speaks, what forc'd by fire;
Both th' old discoveries, and the new-found seas,
The stock and surplus, cause and historie:
All these stand open, or I have the keyes:
               Yet I love thee.   10

I know the wayes of Honour, what maintains
The quick returns of courtesie and wit:
In vies of favours whether partie gains,
When glorie swells the heart, and moldeth it
To all expressions both of hand and eye,   15
Which on the world a true-love-knot may tie,
And bear the bundle, wheresoe're it goes:
How many drammes of spirit there must be
To sell my life unto my friends or foes:
               Yet I love thee.   20

I know the wayes of Pleasure, the sweet strains,
The lullings and the relishes of it;
The propositions of hot bloud and brains;
What mirth and musick mean; what love and wit

THE PEARL: see Matthew 13:45–46.
  2 *presse:* with ref. to the olive or wine press and also to the printing press.
  5 *policie:* government; *conspire:* unite to produce.
 12 *wit:* clever repartee.
 13 *vies:* competitions; *whether partie:* which of two parties.
 18 *spirit:* intoxicating liquor.
 22 *relishes:* tastes, flavors; also, in musical sense, ornaments.

Have done these twentie hundred yeares, and more: 25
I know the projects of unbridled store:
My stuffe is flesh, not brasse; my senses live,
And grumble oft, that they have more in me
Then he that curbs them, being but one to five:
             Yet I love thee.   30

I know all these, and have them in my hand:
Therefore not seiled, but with open eyes
I flie to thee, and fully understand
Both the main sale, and the commodities;
And at what rate and price I have thy love;   35
With all the circumstances that may move:
Yet through these labyrinths, not my groveling wit,
But thy silk twist let down from heav'n to me,
Did both conduct and teach me, how by it
            To climbe to thee.   40

Affliction (IV)

Broken in pieces all asunder,
       Lord, hunt me not,
       A thing forgot,
Once a poore creature, now a wonder,
     A wonder tortur'd in the space   5
     Betwixt this world and that of grace.

My thoughts are all a case of knives,
       Wounding my heart
       With scatter'd smart,

26 *unbridled store:* uncontrolled wealth.

32 *seiled:* sealed, or seeled: in falconry *to seel* means to sew up the eyelids of a hawk for purposes of training.

34 *commodities:* advantages, benefits.

37 *wit:* mental capacity.

AFFLICTION (IV): see NOTE.

As watring pots give flowers their lives.   10
  Nothing their furie can controll,
  While they do wound and prick my soul.

All my attendants are at strife,
      Quitting their place
      Unto my face: 15
Nothing performs the task of life:
  The elements are let loose to fight,
  And while I live, trie out their right.

Oh help, my God! let not their plot
      Kill them and me,   20
      And also thee,
Who art my life: dissolve the knot,
  As the sunne scatters by his light
  All the rebellions of the night.

Then shall those powers, which work for grief,   25
      Enter thy pay,
      And day by day
Labour thy praise, and my relief;
  With care and courage building me,
  Till I reach heav'n, and much more thee.   30

Man

      My God, I heard this day,
That none doth build a stately habitation,
      But he that means to dwell therein.
      What house more stately hath there been,
Or can be, then is Man? to whose creation   5
      All things are in decay.

MAN.
  5 *to:* compared to.

           For Man is ev'ry thing,
And more: He is a tree, yet bears more fruit;
       A beast, yet is, or should be more:
       Reason and speech we onely bring.   10
Parrats may thank us, if they are not mute,
           They go upon the score.

           Man is all symmetrie,
Full of proportions, one limbe to another,
       And all to all the world besides: 15
       Each part may call the farthest, brother:
For head with foot hath private amitie,
           And both with moons and tides.

           Nothing hath got so farre,
But Man hath caught and kept it, as his prey.   20
       His eyes dismount the highest starre:
       He is in little all the sphere.
Herbs gladly cure our flesh; because that they
           Finde their acquaintance there.

           For us the windes do blow,   25
The earth doth rest, heav'n move, and fountains flow.
       Nothing we see, but means our good,
       As our *delight*, or as our *treasure*:
The whole is, either our cupboard of *food*,
           Or cabinet of *pleasure*.   30

           The starres have us to bed;
Night draws the curtain, which the sunne withdraws;
       Musick and light attend our head.
       All things unto our *flesh* are kinde

---

8 *more fruit:* see Note.
12 "are indebted to us": *score:* bill, account.
21 *dismount:* bring down.
22 *sphere:* universe.
34 *kinde:* kindred, related.

In their *descent* and *being;* to our *minde*   35
  In their *ascent* and *cause.*

  Each thing is full of dutie:
Waters united are our navigation;
  Distinguished, our habitation;
   Below, our drink; above, our meat;   40
Both are our cleanlinesse. Hath one such beautie?
  Then how are all things neat?

  More servants wait on Man,
Then he'l take notice of: in ev'ry path
  He treads down that which doth befriend him,   45
  When sicknesse makes him pale and wan.
Oh mightie love! Man is one world, and hath
  Another to attend him.

  Since then, my God, thou hast
So brave a Palace built; O dwell in it,   50
  That it may dwell with thee at last!
  Till then, afford us so much wit;
That, as the world serves us, we may serve thee,
  And both thy servants be.

Life

  I made a posie, while the day ran by:
Here will I smell my remnant out, and tie
   My life within this band.

39 *Distinguished:* separated.
40 *above, our meat:* as rain, water grows our food.
42 *neat:* skillfully made, well-proportioned.
LIFE.
1 *posie:* bouquet.
2–3 a parenthetical self-address, stating the aim of the meditation.
3 *band:* the string tying up the bouquet.

But time did becken to the flowers, and they
By noon most cunningly did steal away,   5
    And wither'd in my hand.

My hand was next to them, and then my heart:
I took, without more thinking, in good part
    Times gentle admonition:
Who did so sweetly deaths sad taste convey,   10
Making my minde to smell my fatall day;
    Yet sugring the suspicion.

Farewell deare flowers, sweetly your time ye spent,
Fit, while ye liv'd, for smell or ornament,
    And after death for cures.   15
I follow straight without complaints or grief,
Since if my sent be good, I care not, if
    It be as short as yours.

Mortification

  How soon doth man decay!
When clothes are taken from a chest of sweets
  To swaddle infants, whose young breath
    Scarce knows the way;
  Those clouts are little winding sheets,   5
Which do consigne and send them unto death.

  When boyes go first to bed,
They step into their voluntarie graves,
  Sleep bindes them fast; onely their breath
    Makes them not dead: 10

MORTIFICATION: the process of decay, as well as the discipline of "mortifying
the flesh" by meditation on its frailties.
   5 *clouts:* swaddling clothes; *winding sheets:* cloths in which the dead are
wrapped.

Successive nights, like rolling waves,
Convey them quickly, who are bound for death.

When youth is frank and free,
And calls for musick, while his veins do swell,
All day exchanging mirth and breath   15
                In companie;
That musick summons to the knell,
Which shall befriend him at the houre of death.

When man grows staid and wise,
Getting a house and home, where he may move   20
        Within the circle of his breath,
                Schooling his eyes;
That dumbe inclosure maketh love
Unto the coffin, that attends his death.

        When age grows low and weak,   25
Marking his grave, and thawing ev'ry yeare,
        Till all do melt, and drown his breath
                When he would speak;
A chair or litter shows the biere,
Which shall convey him to the house of death.   30

        Man, ere he is aware,
Hath put together a solemnitie,
        And drest his herse, while he has breath
                As yet to spare:
Yet Lord, instruct us so to die,   35
That all these dyings may be life in death.

17–18 *befriend him:* by summoning others to pray for the dying man.
24 *attends:* accompanies; also, awaits.
29 *shows:* foreshadows; *biere:* a stand for holding a coffin.
32 *solemnitie:* ceremony.
33 *drest:* prepared; *herse:* the framework over a coffin.

Decay

Sweet were the dayes, when thou didst lodge with Lot,
Struggle with Jacob, sit with Gideon,
Advise with Abraham, when thy power could not
Encounter Moses strong complaints and mone:
      Thy words were then, *Let me alone.*   5

One might have sought and found thee presently
At some fair oak, or bush, or cave, or well:
Is my God this way? No, they would reply:
He is to Sinai gone, as we heard tell:
      List, ye may heare great Aarons bell.   10

But now thou dost thy self immure and close
In some one corner of a feeble heart:
Where yet both Sinne and Satan, thy old foes,
Do pinch and straiten thee, and use much art
      To gain thy thirds and little part.   15

I see the world grows old, when as the heat
Of thy great love once spread, as in an urn
Doth closet up it self, and still retreat,
Cold sinne still forcing it, till it return,
      And calling Justice, all things burn.   20

DECAY.

    4 *encounter:* oppose.
    5 See Exodus 32:10.
    6 *presently:* immediately.
    10 See Exodus 28:33–35.
    14 *straiten:* confine.
    15 *thirds:* the third of a deceased husband's property to which a widow was entitled.

Jordan

When first my lines of heav'nly joyes made mention,
Such was their lustre, they did so excell,
That I sought out quaint words, and trim invention;
My thoughts began to burnish, sprout, and swell,
Curling with metaphors a plain intention,   5
Decking the sense, as if it were to sell.

Thousands of notions in my brain did runne,
Off'ring their service, if I were not sped:
I often blotted what I had begunne;
This was not quick enough, and that was dead.   10
Nothing could seem too rich to clothe the sunne,
Much lesse those joyes which trample on his head.

As flames do work and winde, when they ascend,
So did I weave my self into the sense.
But while I bustled, I might heare a friend   15
Whisper, *How wide is all this long pretence!*
There is in love a sweetnesse readie penn'd:
Copie out onely that, and save expense.

JORDAN: river of baptism: see NOTE.
  3 *quaint:* cleverly contrived, elegant.
  4 *burnish:* spread out.
  8 *were not sped:* were not successful.
 10 *quick:* alive, lively.
 16 *wide:* wide of the mark; *pretence:* pretentious effort.

Obedience

My God, if writings may
Convey a Lordship any way
Whither the buyer and the seller please;
    Let it not thee displease,
If this poore paper do as much as they.   5

On it my heart doth bleed
As many lines, as there doth need
To passe it self and all it hath to thee.
    To which I do agree,
And here present it as my speciall deed.   10

If that hereafter Pleasure
Cavill, and claim her part and measure,
As if this passed with a reservation,
    Or some such words in fashion;
I here exclude the wrangler from thy treasure.   15

O let thy sacred will
All thy delight in me fulfill!
Let me not think an action mine own way,
    But as thy love shall sway,
Resigning up the rudder to thy skill.   20

Lord, what is man to thee,
That thou shouldst minde a rotten tree?
Yet since thou canst not choose but see my actions;
    So great are thy perfections,
Thou mayst as well my actions guide, as see.   25

OBEDIENCE.
  2 *Convey a Lordship:* transfer title to a lord's domain.
  8 *passe:* convey legally (note the thread of legal terms throughout the poem).

Besides, thy death and bloud
Show'd a strange love to all our good:
Thy sorrows were in earnest; no faint proffer,
Or superficiall offer
Of what we might not take, or be withstood.   30

Wherefore I all forgo:
To one word onely I say, No:
Where in the deed there was an intimation
Of a *gift* or *donation,*
Lord, let it now by way of *purchase* go.   35

He that will passe his land,
As I have mine, may set his hand
And heart unto this deed, when he hath read;
And make the purchase spread
To both our goods, if he to it will stand.   40

How happie were my part,
If some kinde man would thrust his heart
Into these lines; till in heav'ns court of rolls
They were by winged souls
Entred for both, farre above their desert!   45

Conscience

Peace pratler, do not lowre:
Not a fair look, but thou dost call it foul:
Not a sweet dish, but thou dost call it sowre:
Musick to thee doth howl.
By listning to thy chatting fears   5
I have both lost mine eyes and eares.

42 *kinde:* of kindred spirit.
43 *court of rolls:* the English Court of the Master of the Rolls, which has custody of records.

Pratler, no more, I say:
My thoughts must work, but like a noiselesse sphere;
Harmonious peace must rock them all the day:
      No room for pratlers there.   10
    If thou persistest, I will tell thee,
    That I have physick to expell thee.

      And the receit shall be
My Saviours bloud: when ever at his board
I do but taste it, straight it cleanseth me,   15
      And leaves thee not a word;
    No, not a tooth or nail to scratch,
    And at my actions carp, or catch.

      Yet if thou talkest still,
Besides my physick, know there's some for thee: 20
Some wood and nails to make a staffe or bill
      For those that trouble me:
    The bloudie crosse of my deare Lord
    Is both my physick and my sword.

Sion

Lord, with what glorie wast thou serv'd of old,
When Solomons temple stood and flourished!
   Where most things were of purest gold;
   The wood was all embellished
With flowers and carvings, mysticall and rare: 5
All show'd the builders, crav'd the seers care.

CONSCIENCE.
   12 *physick:* medicine.
   13 *receit:* formula.
   14 *board:* table, "God's board," the Communion table.
   21 *bill:* halberd.
SION: the place of the Temple; see 1 Kings 5–7; Acts 7:47–48; 1 Corinthians 3:16–17.
   5 *mysticall:* having a secret significance.

Yet all this glorie, all this pomp and state
Did not affect thee much, was not thy aim;
   Something there was, that sow'd debate:
   Wherefore thou quitt'st thy ancient claim: 10
And now thy Architecture meets with sinne;
For all thy frame and fabrick is within.

There thou art struggling with a peevish heart,
Which sometimes crosseth thee, thou sometimes it:
   The fight is hard on either part.   15
   Great God doth fight, he doth submit.
All Solomons sea of brasse and world of stone
Is not so deare to thee as one good grone.

And truly brasse and stones are heavie things,
Tombes for the dead, not temples fit for thee: 20
   But grones are quick, and full of wings,
   And all their motions upward be;
And ever as they mount, like larks they sing;
The note is sad, yet musick for a king.

The British Church

   I joy, deare Mother, when I view
   Thy perfect lineaments, and hue
         Both sweet and bright.

   Beautie in thee takes up her place,
   And dates her letters from thy face,   5
         When she doth write.

   A fine aspect in fit aray,
   Neither too mean, nor yet too gay,
         Shows who is best.

THE BRITISH CHURCH.

  5 *dates her letters:* by giving dates according to holy days, and by beginning the year on Lady Day, March 25, the Feast of the Annunciation.

Outlandish looks may not compare: 10
For all they either painted are,
        Or else undrest.

She on the hills, which wantonly
Allureth all in hope to be
        By her preferr'd,   15

Hath kiss'd so long her painted shrines,
That ev'n her face by kissing shines,
        For her reward.

She in the valley is so shie
Of dressing, that her hair doth lie   20
        About her eares:

While she avoids her neighbours pride,
She wholly goes on th' other side,
        And nothing wears.

But dearest Mother, (what those misse)   25
The mean thy praise and glorie is,
        And long may be.

Blessed be God, whose love it was
To double-moat thee with his grace,
        And none but thee.   30

The Dawning

Awake sad heart, whom sorrow ever drowns;
   Take up thine eyes, which feed on earth;
Unfold thy forehead gather'd into frowns:

10 *outlandish:* foreign.
15 *preferr'd:* advanced (to heaven).

[180]

Thy Saviour comes, and with him mirth:
Awake, awake; 5
And with a thankfull heart his comforts take.
But thou dost still lament, and pine, and crie;
And feel his death, but not his victorie.

Arise sad heart; if thou dost not withstand,
Christs resurrection thine may be: 10
Do not by hanging down break from the hand,
Which as it riseth, raiseth thee:
Arise, arise;
And with his buriall-linen drie thine eyes:
Christ left his grave-clothes, that we might, when grief 15
Draws tears, or bloud, not want an handkerchief.

Dulnesse

Why do I languish thus, drooping and dull,
As if I were all earth?
O give me quicknesse, that I may with mirth
Praise thee brim-full!

The wanton lover in a curious strain 5
Can praise his fairest fair;
And with quaint metaphors her curled hair
Curl o're again.

Thou art my lovelinesse, my life, my light,
Beautie alone to me: 10
Thy bloudy death and undeserv'd, makes thee
Pure red and white.

DULNESSE.
5 curious: intricate, elegant, finely wrought.
7 quaint: elegant, skillfully made.

When all perfections as but one appeare,
    That those thy form doth show,
The very dust, where thou dost tread and go,   15
    Makes beauties here;

Where are my lines then? my approaches? views?
    Where are my window-songs?
Lovers are still pretending, & ev'n wrongs
    Sharpen their Muse: 20

But I am lost in flesh, whose sugred lyes
    Still mock me, and grow bold:
Sure thou didst put a minde there, if I could
    Finde where it lies.

Lord, cleare thy gift, that with a constant wit   25
    I may but look towards thee:
Look onely; for to *love* thee, who can be,
    What angel fit?

Peace

Sweet Peace, where dost thou dwell? I humbly crave,
    Let me once know.
I sought thee in a secret cave,
    And ask'd, if Peace were there.
A hollow winde did seem to answer, No: 5
    Go seek elsewhere.

I did; and going did a rainbow note:
    Surely, thought I,
This is the lace of Peaces coat:
    I will search out the matter.   10
But while I lookt, the clouds immediately
    Did break and scatter.

19 *pretending:* wooing, putting themselves forward.

Then went I to a garden, and did spy
      A gallant flower,
The crown Imperiall: Sure, said I,   15
      Peace at the root must dwell.
But when I digg'd, I saw a worm devoure
      What show'd so well.

At length I met a rev'rend good old man,
      Whom when for Peace   20
    I did demand; he thus began:
      There was a Prince of old
At Salem dwelt, who liv'd with good increase
      Of flock and fold.

He sweetly liv'd; yet sweetnesse did not save   25
      His life from foes.
    But after death out of his grave
      There sprang twelve stalks of wheat:
Which many wondring at, got some of those
      To plant, and set.   30

It prosper'd strangely, and did soon disperse
      Through all the earth:
    For they that taste it do rehearse,
      That vertue lies therein,
A secret vertue bringing peace and mirth   35
      By flight of sinne.

Take of this grain, which in my garden grows,
      And grows for you;
    Make bread of it: and that repose
      And peace which ev'ry where   40
With so much earnestnesse you do pursue,
      Is onely there.

PEACE.

    22–23 *Prince of Salem:* Melchizedek, King of Salem, regarded as a prefigura-
tion or "type" of Christ: see Genesis 14:18; Hebrews 7:1–2.

    33 *rehearse:* declare.

    34 *vertue:* healing power.

Confession

O what a cunning guest
Is this same grief! within my heart I made
　　Closets; and in them many a chest;
　　And like a master in my trade,
In those chests, boxes; in each box, a till:　　　　　5
Yet grief knows all, and enters when he will.

　　No scrue, no piercer can
Into a piece of timber work and winde,
　　As Gods afflictions into man,
　　When he a torture hath design'd.　　　　　10
They are too subtill for the subt'llest hearts;
And fall, like rheumes, upon the tendrest parts.

　　We are the earth; and they,
Like moles within us, heave, and cast about:
　　And till they foot and clutch their prey,　　　　15
　　They never cool, much lesse give out.
No smith can make such locks, but they have keyes:
Closets are halls to them; and hearts, high-wayes.

　　Onely an open breast
Doth shut them out, so that they cannot enter;　　　20
　　Or, if they enter, cannot rest,
　　But quickly seek some new adventure.
Smooth open hearts no fastning have; but fiction
Doth give a hold and handle to affliction.

　　Wherefore my faults and sinnes,　　　　25
Lord, I acknowledge; take thy plagues away:
　　For since confession pardon winnes,
　　I challenge here the brightest day,
The clearest diamond: let them do their best,
They shall be thick and cloudie to my breast.　　　30

The bunch of grapes

Joy, I did lock thee up: but some bad man
       Hath let thee out again:
And now, me thinks, I am where I began
       Sev'n yeares ago: one vogue and vein,
        One aire of thoughts usurps my brain.   5
I did toward Canaan draw; but now I am
Brought back to the Red sea, the sea of shame.

For as the Jews of old by Gods command
       Travell'd, and saw no town:
So now each Christian hath his journeys spann'd: 10
       Their storie pennes and sets us down.
       A single deed is small renown.
Gods works are wide, and let in future times;
His ancient justice overflows our crimes.

Then have we too our guardian fires and clouds;   15
       Our Scripture-dew drops fast:
We have our sands and serpents, tents and shrowds;
       Alas! our murmurings come not last.
       But where's the cluster? where's the taste
Of mine inheritance? Lord, if I must borrow,   20
Let me as well take up their joy, as sorrow.

But can he want the grape, who hath the wine?
       I have their fruit and more.
Blessed be God, who prosper'd *Noahs* vine,

THE BUNCH OF GRAPES: see Numbers 13:17–24; Exodus 13–17.
  4 *vogue:* general course.
  5 *aire:* manner.
 10 *spann'd:* measured out.
 17 *shrowds:* shelters.

And made it bring forth grapes good store.   25
But much more him I must adore,
Who of the laws sowre juice sweet wine did make,
Ev'n God himself, being pressed for my sake.

The Storm

If as the windes and waters here below
          Do flie and flow,
My sighs and tears as busie were above;
          Sure they would move
And much affect thee, as tempestuous times   5
Amaze poore mortals, and object their crimes.

Starres have their storms, ev'n in a high degree,
          As well as we.
A throbbing conscience spurred by remorse
          Hath a strange force: 10
It quits the earth, and mounting more and more,
Dares to assault thee, and besiege thy doore.

There it stands knocking, to thy musicks wrong,
          And drowns the song.
Glorie and honour are set by till it   15
          An answer get.
Poets have wrong'd poore storms: such dayes are best;
They purge the aire without, within the breast.

THE STORM.
  6 *object:* bring to mind.
  7 *Starres have their storms:* probably in the form of showers of meteors.

Ephes. 4. 30.
Grieve not the Holy Spirit, &c.

And art thou grieved, sweet and sacred Dove,
   When I am sowre,
   And crosse thy love?
Grieved for me? the God of strength and power
   Griev'd for a worm, which when I tread,   5
   I passe away and leave it dead?

Then weep mine eyes, the God of love doth grieve:
   Weep foolish heart,
   And weeping live:
For death is drie as dust. Yet if ye part,   10
   End as the night, whose sable hue
   Your sinnes expresse; melt into dew.

When sawcie mirth shall knock or call at doore,
   Cry out, Get hence,
   Or cry no more.   15
Almightie God doth grieve, he puts on sense:
   I sinne not to my grief alone,
   But to my Gods too; he doth grone.

Oh take thy lute, and tune it to a strain,
   Which may with thee   20
   All day complain.
There can no discord but in ceasing be.
   Marbles can weep; and surely strings
   More bowels have, then such hard things.

GRIEVE NOT THE HOLY SPIRIT, &C.

 16 *sense:* capability of feeling (pain).

 24 *bowels:* regarded in biblical usage as the source of emotions such as pity; here with a play on the use of gut strings in instruments.

Lord, I adjudge my self to tears and grief,   25
      Ev'n endlesse tears
      Without relief.
If a cleare spring for me no time forbears,
      But runnes, although I be not drie;
      I am no Crystall, what shall I?   30

Yet if I wail not still, since still to wail
      Nature denies;
      And flesh would fail,
If my deserts were masters of mine eyes:
      Lord, pardon, for thy sonne makes good   35
      My want of tears with store of bloud.

The Familie

What doth this noise of thoughts within my heart
      As if they had a part?
What do these loud complaints and puling fears,
      As if there were no rule or eares?

But, Lord, the house and familie are thine,   5
      Though some of them repine.
Turn out these wranglers, which defile thy seat:
      For where thou dwellest all is neat.

First Peace and Silence all disputes controll,
      Then Order plaies the soul;   10
And giving all things their set forms and houres,
      Makes of wilde woods sweet walks and bowres.

Humble Obedience neare the doore doth stand,
      Expecting a command:

THE FAMILIE.
  14 *expecting:* awaiting.

Then whom in waiting nothing seems more slow, 15
 Nothing more quick when she doth go.

Joyes oft are there, and griefs as oft as joyes;
  But griefs without a noise:
Yet speak they louder, then distemper'd fears.
  What is so shrill as silent tears? 20

This is thy house, with these it doth abound:
  And where these are not found,
Perhaps thou com'st sometimes, and for a day;
  But not to make a constant stay.

The Pilgrimage

I travell'd on, seeing the hill, where lay
  My expectation.
 A long it was and weary way.
 The gloomy cave of Desperation
I left on th' one, and on the other side 5
  The rock of Pride.

And so I came to phansies medow strow'd
  With many a flower:
 Fain would I here have made abode,
 But I was quicken'd by my houre. 10
So to cares cops I came, and there got through
  With much ado.

19 *distemper'd:* disordered, immoderate.
THE PILGRIMAGE.
 7 *phansies: fancy,* love; or *fantasy,* poetic imagination.
 9 *Fain:* gladly.
 11 *cops:* copse, grove.

That led me to the wilde of passion, which
        Some call the wold;
  A wasted place, but sometimes rich.   15
    Here I was robb'd of all my gold,
Save one good Angell, which a friend had ti'd
        Close to my side.

At length I got unto the gladsome hill,
        Where lay my hope,   20
    Where lay my heart; and climbing still,
    When I had gain'd the brow and top,
A lake of brackish waters on the ground
        Was all I found.

With that abash'd and struck with many a sting   25
        Of swarming fears,
    I fell, and cry'd, Alas my King;
      Can both the way and end be tears?
Yet taking heart I rose, and then perceiv'd
        I was deceiv'd: 30

My hill was further: so I flung away,
        Yet heard a crie
    Just as I went, *None goes that way*
    And lives: If that be all, said I,
After so foul a journey death is fair,   35
        And but a chair.

13 *passion:* suffering.
14 *wold:* deserted, hilly, open country.
17 *Angell:* a gold coin; also here, a guardian angel.
36 *chair:* a chair-litter.

Praise

King of Glorie, King of Peace,
      I will love thee:
And that love may never cease,
      I will move thee.

Thou hast granted my request,   5
      Thou hast heard me:
Thou didst note my working breast,
      Thou hast spar'd me.

Wherefore with my utmost art
      I will sing thee,   10
And the cream of all my heart
      I will bring thee.

Though my sinnes against me cried,
      Thou didst cleare me;
And alone, when they replied,   15
      Thou didst heare me.

Sev'n whole dayes, not one in seven,
      I will praise thee.
In my heart, though not in heaven,
      I can raise thee.   20

Thou grew'st soft and moist with tears,
      Thou relentedst:
And when Justice call'd for fears,
      Thou dissentedst.

Small it is, in this poore sort   25
      To enroll thee:
Ev'n eternitie is too short
      To extoll thee.

Longing

With sick and famisht eyes,
With doubling knees and weary bones,
    To thee my cries,
    To thee my grones,
To thee my sighs, my tears ascend: 5
      No end?

My throat, my soul is hoarse;
My heart is wither'd like a ground
      Which thou dost curse.
      My thoughts turn round,   10
And make me giddie; Lord, I fall,
      Yet call.

From thee all pitie flows.
Mothers are kinde, because thou art,
      And dost dispose   15
      To them a part:
Their infants, them; and they suck thee
      More free.

Bowels of pitie, heare!
Lord of my soul, love of my minde,   20
      Bow down thine eare!
      Let not the winde
Scatter my words, and in the same
      Thy name!

Look on my sorrows round!   25
Mark well my furnace! O what flames,

LONGING.
  26 *furnace:* the "furnace of affliction": Isaiah 48:10.

What heats abound!
What griefs, what shames!
Consider, Lord; Lord, bow thine eare,
  And heare!   30

Lord Jesu, thou didst bow
Thy dying head upon the tree:
    O be not now
    More dead to me!
Lord heare! *Shall he that made the eare,*   35
        Not heare?

Behold, thy dust doth stirre,
It moves, it creeps, it aims at thee:
    Wilt thou deferre
    To succour me,
Thy pile of dust, wherein each crumme   40
        Sayes, Come?

To thee help appertains.
Hast thou left all things to their course,
        And laid the reins   45
        Upon the horse?
Is all lockt? hath a sinners plea
        No key?

Indeed the world's thy book,
Where all things have their leafe assign'd: 50
    Yet a meek look
    Hath interlin'd.
Thy board is full, yet humble guests
        Finde nests.

Thou tarriest, while I die,   55
And fall to nothing: thou dost reigne,

And rule on high,
While I remain
In bitter grief: yet am I stil'd
    Thy childe.   60

   Lord, didst thou leave thy throne,
Not to relieve? how can it be,
   That thou art grown
   Thus hard to me?
Were sinne alive, good cause there were 65
    To bear.

   But now both sinne is dead,
And all thy promises live and bide.
   That wants his head;
   These speak and chide,   70
And in thy bosome poure my tears,
    As theirs.

   Lord J E S U , heare my heart,
Which hath been broken now so long,
   That ev'ry part   75
   Hath got a tongue!
Thy beggars grow; rid them away
    To day.

   My love, my sweetnesse, heare!
By these thy feet, at which my heart 80
   Lies all the yeare,
   Pluck out thy dart,
And heal my troubled breast which cryes,
    Which dyes.

The Bag

Away despair; my gracious Lord doth heare.
 Though windes and waves assault my keel,
 He doth preserve it: he doth steer,
 Ev'n when the boat seems most to reel.
 Storms are the triumph of his art: 5
Well may he close his eyes, but not his heart.

Hast thou not heard, that my Lord Jesus di'd?
 Then let me tell thee a strange storie.
 The God of power, as he did ride
 In his majestick robes of glorie,   10
 Resolv'd to light; and so one day
He did descend, undressing all the way.

The starres his tire of light and rings obtain'd,
 The cloud his bow, the fire his spear,
 The sky his azure mantle gain'd.   15
 And when they ask'd, what he would wear;
 He smil'd and said as he did go,
He had new clothes a making here below.

When he was come, as travellers are wont,
 He did repair unto an inne.   20
 Both then, and after, many a brunt
 He did endure to cancell sinne:
 And having giv'n the rest before,
Here he gave up his life to pay our score.

THE BAG: in *The Temple,* as here, this poem immediately follows "Longing," as
its answer; *Bag:* mailbag.
 6 *close his eyes:* see Matthew 8:24–26.
 13 *tire:* headdress.

But as he was returning, there came one   25
    That ran upon him with a spear.
    He, who came hither all alone,
    Bringing nor man, nor arms, nor fear,
    Receiv'd the blow upon his side,
And straight he turn'd, and to his brethren cry'd,   30

If ye have any thing to send or write,
    (I have no bag, but here is room)
    Unto my fathers hands and sight
    (Beleeve me) it shall safely come.
    That I shall minde, what you impart;   35
Look, you may put it very neare my heart.

Or if hereafter any of my friends
    Will use me in this kinde, the doore
    Shall still be open; what he sends
    I will present, and somewhat more,   40
    Not to his hurt. Sighs will convey
Any thing to me. Heark despair, away.

The Collar

I struck the board, and cry'd, No more.
    I will abroad.
What? shall I ever sigh and pine?
My lines and life are free; free as the rode,
    Loose as the winde, as large as store.   5
      Shall I be still in suit?
    Have I no harvest but a thorn
    To let me bloud, and not restore
What I have lost with cordiall fruit?

THE COLLAR.

  1 *board:* table, with overtones of "God's board," as in "Conscience," line 14, and "Longing," line 53.

Sure there was wine 10
Before my sighs did drie it: there was corn
Before my tears did drown it.
Is the yeare onely lost to me?
Have I no bayes to crown it?
No flowers, no garlands gay? all blasted? 15
All wasted?
Not so, my heart: but there is fruit,
And thou hast hands.
Recover all thy sigh-blown age
On double pleasures: leave thy cold dispute 20
Of what is fit, and not. Forsake thy cage,
Thy rope of sands,
Which pettie thoughts have made, and made to thee
Good cable, to enforce and draw,
And be thy law, 25
While thou didst wink and wouldst not see.
Away; take heed:
I will abroad.
Call in thy deaths head there: tie up thy fears.
He that forbears 30
To suit and serve his need,
Deserves his load.
But as I rav'd and grew more fierce and wilde
At every word,
Me thoughts I heard one calling, *Childe:* 35
And I reply'd, *My Lord.*

11 *corn:* grain.
14 *bayes:* laurels.
26 *wink:* close the eyes.

[197]

The Priesthood

Blest Order, which in power dost so excell,
That with th' one hand thou liftest to the sky,
And with the other throwest down to hell
In thy just censures; fain would I draw nigh,
Fain put thee on, exchanging my lay-sword   5
      For that of th' holy word.

But thou art fire, sacred and hallow'd fire;
And I but earth and clay: should I presume
To wear thy habit, the severe attire
My slender compositions might consume.   10
I am both foul and brittle; much unfit
      To deal in holy Writ.

Yet have I often seen, by cunning hand
And force of fire, what curious things are made
Of wretched earth. Where once I scorn'd to stand,   15
That earth is fitted by the fire and trade
Of skilfull artists, for the boards of those
      Who make the bravest shows.

But since those great ones, be they ne're so great,
Come from the earth, from whence those vessels come;   20
So that at once both feeder, dish, and meat
Have one beginning and one finall summe:
I do not greatly wonder at the sight,
      If earth in earth delight.

THE PRIESTHOOD.
  9 *habit:* clothing.
  14 *curious:* exquisite.
  18 *bravest:* most splendid.
  21 *meat:* food.

But th' holy men of God such vessels are,   25
As serve him up, who all the world commands:
When God vouchsafeth to become our fare,
Their hands convey him, who conveys their hands.
O what pure things, most pure must those things be,
    Who bring my God to me!   30

Wherefore I dare not, I, put forth my hand
To hold the Ark, although it seem to shake
Through th' old sinnes and new doctrines of our land.
Onely, since God doth often vessels make
Of lowly matter for high uses meet,   35
    I throw me at his feet.

There will I lie, untill my Maker seek
For some mean stuffe whereon to show his skill:
Then is my time. The distance of the meek
Doth flatter power. Lest good come short of ill   40
In praising might, the poore do by submission
    What pride by opposition.

The Search

   Whither, O, whither art thou fled,
     My Lord, my Love?
   My searches are my daily bread;
     Yet never prove.

   My knees pierce th' earth, mine eies the skie;   5
     And yet the sphere

32 *Ark:* See 2 Samuel 6:6; 1 Chronicles 13:9.
35 *meet:* suitable.
THE SEARCH.
 4 *prove:* succeed.
 6 *sphere:* heavens.

And centre both to me denie
      That thou art there.

Yet can I mark how herbs below
      Grow green and gay,   10
As if to meet thee they did know,
      While I decay.

Yet can I mark how starres above
      Simper and shine,
As having keyes unto thy love,   15
      While poore I pine.

I sent a sigh to seek thee out,
      Deep drawn in pain,
Wing'd like an arrow: but my scout
      Returns in vain.   20

I tun'd another (having store)
      Into a grone;
Because the search was dumbe before:
      But all was one.

Lord, dost thou some new fabrick mold   25
      Which favour winnes,
And keeps thee present, leaving th' old
      Unto their sinnes?

Where is my God? what hidden place
      Conceals thee still?   30
What covert dare eclipse thy face?
      Is it thy will?

7 *centre:* earth.
14 *Simper:* twinkle.
31 *covert:* covering.

O let not that of any thing;
        Let rather brasse,
Or steel, or mountains be thy ring,   35
        And I will passe.

Thy will such an intrenching is,
        As passeth thought:
To it all strength, all subtilties
        Are things of nought.   40

Thy will such a strange distance is,
        As that to it
East and West touch, the poles do kisse,
        And parallels meet.

Since then my grief must be as large,   45
        As is thy space,
Thy distance from me; see my charge,
        Lord, see my case.

O take these barres, these lengths away;
        Turn, and restore me: 50
Be not Almightie, let me say,
        Against, but for me.

When thou dost turn, and wilt be neare;
        What edge so keen,
What point so piercing can appeare   55
        To come between?

For as thy absence doth excell
        All distance known:
So doth thy nearenesse bear the bell,
        Making two one.   60

33 "Oh, of all things, do not permit that" (i.e., that your will should come between us).

35 *ring:* fence.

47 *charge:* burden.

59 *bear the bell:* take first place.

The Crosse

What is this strange and uncouth thing?
To make me sigh, and seek, and faint, and die,
Untill I had some place, where I might sing,
  And serve thee; and not onely I,
But all my wealth, and familie might combine   5
To set thy honour up, as our designe.

And then when after much delay,
Much wrastling, many a combate, this deare end,
So much desir'd, is giv'n, to take away
  My power to serve thee; to unbend   10
All my abilities, my designes confound,
And lay my threatnings bleeding on the ground.

One ague dwelleth in my bones,
Another in my soul (the memorie
What I would do for thee, if once my grones   15
  Could be allow'd for harmonie);
I am in all a weak disabled thing,
Save in the sight thereof, where strength doth sting.

Besides, things sort not to my will,
Ev'n when my will doth studie thy renown: 20
Thou turnest th' edge of all things on me still,
  Taking me up to throw me down:
So that, ev'n when my hopes seem to be sped,
I am to grief alive, to them as dead.

THE CROSSE.

 1 *uncouth:* unusual.

 12 *threatnings:* vows.

 18 "I am altogether weak except when I contemplate the cross; but its strength spurs me to action" (Hutchinson).

 19 *sort not to:* do not turn out in accord with.

To have my aim, and yet to be 25
Farther from it then when I bent my bow;
To make my hopes my torture, and the fee
    Of all my woes another wo,
Is in the midst of delicates to need,
And ev'n in Paradise to be a weed. 30

Ah my deare Father, ease my smart!
These contrarieties crush me: these crosse actions
Doe winde a rope about, and cut my heart:
    And yet since these thy contradictions
Are properly a crosse felt by thy sonne, 35
With but foure words, my words, *Thy will be done*.

The Flower

How fresh, O Lord, how sweet and clean
Are thy returns! ev'n as the flowers in spring;
    To which, besides their own demean,
The late-past frosts tributes of pleasure bring.
        Grief melts away 5
        Like snow in May,
    As if there were no such cold thing.

Who would have thought my shrivel'd heart
Could have recover'd greennesse? It was gone
    Quite under ground; as flowers depart 10
To see their mother-root, when they have blown;
        Where they together
        All the hard weather,
    Dead to the world, keep house unknown.

29 *delicates:* luxuries.
32 *crosse:* perverse.
THE FLOWER.
    3 *demean:* demeanor, appearance; also, demesne, estate.
    11 *blown:* bloomed.

These are thy wonders, Lord of power,   15
Killing and quickning, bringing down to hell
    And up to heaven in an houre;
Making a chiming of a passing-bell.
        We say amisse,
        This or that is: 20
Thy word is all, if we could spell.

O that I once past changing were,
Fast in thy Paradise, where no flower can wither!
    Many a spring I shoot up fair,
Offring at heav'n, growing and groning thither: 25
        Nor doth my flower
        Want a spring-showre,
My sinnes and I joining together:

But while I grow in a straight line,
Still upwards bent, as if heav'n were mine own,   30
    Thy anger comes, and I decline:
What frost to that? what pole is not the zone,
        Where all things burn,
        When thou dost turn,
And the least frown of thine is shown?   35

And now in age I bud again,
After so many deaths I live and write;
    I once more smell the dew and rain,
And relish versing: O my onely light,
        It cannot be   40
        That I am he
On whom thy tempests fell all night.

These are thy wonders, Lord of love,
To make us see we are but flowers that glide:
    Which when we once can finde and prove,   45
Thou hast a garden for us, where to bide.

18 "Making a harmony of bells, instead of the tolling of the death bell."

Who would be more,
Swelling through store,
Forfeit their Paradise by their pride.

The Glance

When first thy sweet and gracious eye
Vouchsaf'd ev'n in the midst of youth and night
To look upon me, who before did lie
    Weltring in sinne;
I felt a sugred strange delight,   5
Passing all cordials made by any art,
Bedew, embalme, and overrunne my heart,
    And take it in.

Since that time many a bitter storm
My soul hath felt, ev'n able to destroy,   10
Had the malicious and ill-meaning harm
    His swing and sway:
But still thy sweet originall joy
Sprung from thine eye, did work within my soul,
And surging griefs, when they grew bold, controll,   15
    And got the day.

If thy first glance so powerfull be,
A mirth but open'd and seal'd up again;
What wonders shall we feel, when we shall see
    Thy full-ey'd love!   20
When thou shalt look us out of pain,
And one aspect of thine spend in delight
More then a thousand sunnes disburse in light,
    In heav'n above.

THE GLANCE.
  7 *embalme:* anoint with balm.
  22 *aspect:* glance.

Marie Magdalene

When blessed Marie wip'd her Saviours feet,
(Whose precepts she had trampled on before)
And wore them for a jewell on her head,
   Shewing his steps should be the street,
   Wherein she thenceforth evermore   5
With pensive humblenesse would live and tread:

She being stain'd her self, why did she strive
To make him clean, who could not be defil'd?
Why kept she not her tears for her own faults,
   And not his feet? Though we could dive   10
   In tears like seas, our sinnes are pil'd
Deeper then they, in words, and works, and thoughts.

Deare soul, she knew who did vouchsafe and deigne
To bear her filth; and that her sinnes did dash
Ev'n God himself: wherefore she was not loth,   15
   As she had brought wherewith to stain,
   So to bring in wherewith to wash:
And yet in washing one, she washed both.

The Odour, 2. Cor. 2

How sweetly doth *My Master* sound! *My Master!*
    As Amber-greese leaves a rich sent
        Unto the taster:
    So do these words a sweet content,
An orientall fragrancie, *My Master*.   5

With these all day I do perfume my minde,
    My minde ev'n thrust into them both;
        That I might finde
    What cordials make this curious broth,
This broth of smells, that feeds and fats my minde.   10

My Master, shall I speak? O that to thee
    My servant were a little so,
        As flesh may be;
    That these two words might creep & grow
To some degree of spicinesse to thee!   15

Then should the Pomander, which was before
    A speaking sweet, mend by reflection,
        And tell me more:
    For pardon of my imperfection
Would warm and work it sweeter then before.   20

For when *My Master,* which alone is sweet,
    And ev'n in my unworthinesse pleasing,
        Shall call and meet,
    My servant, as thee not displeasing,
That call is but the breathing of the sweet.   25

This breathing would with gains by sweetning me
    (As sweet things traffick when they meet)
        Return to thee.
    And so this new commerce and sweet
Should all my life employ, and busie me.   30

THE ODOUR.
  16 *Pomander:* a ball or box of perfumed substances.
  27 *traffick:* carry on negotiations.

The Forerunners

The harbingers are come. See, see their mark;
White is their colour, and behold my head.
But must they have my brain? must they dispark
Those sparkling notions, which therein were bred?
     Must dulnesse turn me to a clod?   5
Yet have they left me, *Thou art still my God.*

Good men ye be, to leave me my best room,
Ev'n all my heart, and what is lodged there:
I passe not, I, what of the rest become,
So *Thou art still my God,* be out of fear.   10
     He will be pleased with that dittie;
And if I please him, I write fine and wittie.

Farewell sweet phrases, lovely metaphors.
But will ye leave me thus? when ye before
Of stews and brothels onely knew the doores,   15
Then did I wash you with my tears, and more,
     Brought you to Church well drest and clad:
My God must have my best, ev'n all I had.

Lovely enchanting language, sugar-cane,
Hony of roses, whither wilt thou flie?   20
Hath some fond lover tic'd thee to thy bane?
And wilt thou leave the Church, and love a stie?

THE FORERUNNERS.

1 *harbingers:* officials sent before a royal journey to requisition lodgings by marking doors with chalk.

3 *dispark:* dispossess of a park or country estate; with a play on "dis-spark."

6 See Psalm 31:14.

9 *passe:* care.

11 *dittie:* words for a song.

15 *stews:* houses of ill-fame.

21 *fond:* infatuated, foolish; *bane:* destruction.

   Fie, thou wilt soil thy broider'd coat,
And hurt thy self, and him that sings the note.

Let foolish lovers, if they will love dung,   25
 With canvas, not with arras clothe their shame:
Let follie speak in her own native tongue.
True beautie dwells on high: ours is a flame
   But borrow'd thence to light us thither.
Beautie and beauteous words should go together.   30

 Yet if you go, I passe not; take your way:
For, *Thou art still my God,* is all that ye
Perhaps with more embellishment can say,
Go birds of spring: let winter have his fee,
   Let a bleak palenesse chalk the doore,   35
So all within be livelier then before.

The Invitation

   Come ye hither all, whose taste
      Is your waste;
  Save your cost, and mend your fare.
  God is here prepar'd and drest,
      And the feast,   5
  God, in whom all dainties are.

   Come ye hither all, whom wine
      Doth define,
  Naming you not to your good:
  Weep what ye have drunk amisse,   10
      And drink this,
  Which before ye drink is bloud.

   Come ye hither all, whom pain
      Doth arraigne,

26 *arras:* fine tapestry.

Bringing all your sinnes to sight: 15
Taste and fear not: God is here
          In this cheer,
And on sinne doth cast the fright.

Come ye hither all, whom joy
          Doth destroy,   20
While ye graze without your bounds:
Here is joy that drowneth quite
          Your delight,
As a floud the lower grounds.

Come ye hither all, whose love   25
          Is your dove,
And exalts you to the skie:
Here is love, which having breath
          Ev'n in death,
After death can never die.   30

Lord I have invited all,
          And I shall
Still invite, still call to thee:
For it seems but just and right
          In my sight,   35
Where is all, there all should be.

The Banquet

Welcome sweet and sacred cheer,
          Welcome deare;
With me, in me, live and dwell:
For thy neatnesse passeth sight,
          Thy delight   5
Passeth tongue to taste or tell.

THE BANQUET.
  4 *neatnesse:* beauty in order and form.

O what sweetnesse from the bowl
      Fills my soul,
Such as is, and makes divine!
Is some starre (fled from the sphere)   10
      Melted there,
As we sugar melt in wine?

Or hath sweetnesse in the bread
      Made a head
To subdue the smell of sinne;   15
Flowers, and gummes, and powders giving
      All their living,
Lest the enemie should winne?

Doubtlesse, neither starre nor flower
      Hath the power   20
Such a sweetnesse to impart:
Onely God, who gives perfumes,
      Flesh assumes,
And with it perfumes my heart.

But as Pomanders and wood   25
      Still are good,
Yet being bruis'd are better sented:
God, to show how farre his love
      Could improve,
Here, as broken, is presented.   30

When I had forgot my birth,
      And on earth
In delights of earth was drown'd;
God took bloud, and needs would be
      Spilt with me,   35
And so found me on the ground.

Having rais'd me to look up,
      In a cup
Sweetly he doth meet my taste.

14 *Made a head:* created a force.

But I still being low and short,   40
    Farre from court,
Wine becomes a wing at last.

For with it alone I flie
    To the skie:
Where I wipe mine eyes, and see   45
What I seek, for what I sue;
    Him I view,
Who hath done so much for me.

Let the wonder of this pitie
    Be my dittie,   50
And take up my lines and life:
Hearken under pain of death,
    Hands and breath;
Strive in this, and love the strife.

A Parodie

Souls joy, when thou art gone,
   And I alone,
    Which cannot be,
Because thou dost abide with me,
  And I depend on thee;   5

Yet when thou dost suppresse
   The cheerfulnesse
    Of thy abode,
And in my powers not stirre abroad,
  But leave me to my load: 10

  O what a damp and shade
   Doth me invade!

A PARODIE: see NOTE.

[212]

No stormie night
Can so afflict or so affright,
As thy eclipsed light.   15

Ah Lord! do not withdraw,
Lest want of aw
Make Sinne appeare;
And when thou dost but shine lesse cleare,
Say, that thou art not here.   20

And then what life I have,
While Sinne doth rave,
And falsly boast,
That I may seek, but thou art lost;
Thou and alone thou know'st.   25

O what a deadly cold
Doth me infold!
I half beleeve,
That Sinne sayes true: but while I grieve,
Thou com'st and dost relieve.   30

Song
(Attributed to the Earl of Pembroke.)

Soules joy, now I am gone,
And you alone,
(Which cannot be,
Since I must leave my selfe with thee,
And carry thee with me)   5
Yet when unto our eyes
Absence denyes
Each others sight,

SONG: see NOTE on A PARODIE.

And makes to us a constant night,
  When others change to light;   10
   O give no way to griefe,
   But let beliefe
    Of mutuall love,
   This wonder to the vulgar prove
   Our Bodyes, not wee move.   15

Let not thy wit beweepe
   Wounds but sense-deepe,
   For when we misse
By distance our lipp-joyning blisse,
  Even then our soules shall kisse.   20
  Fooles have no meanes to meet,
   But by their feet.
   Why should our clay,
Over our spirits so much sway,
  To tie us to that way?   25
   O give no way to griefe, &c.

The Elixer

  Teach me, my God and King,
  In all things thee to see,
And what I do in any thing,
  To do it as for thee:

  Not rudely, as a beast,   5
  To runne into an action;
But still to make thee prepossest,
  And give it his perfection.

  A man that looks on glasse,
  On it may stay his eye;   10
Or if he pleaseth, through it passe,
  And then the heav'n espie.

All may of thee partake:
　　Nothing can be so mean,
Which with his tincture (for thy sake)　　　　15
　　Will not grow bright and clean.

A servant with this clause
　　Makes drudgerie divine:
Who sweeps a room, as for thy laws,
　　Makes that and th' action fine.　　　　20

This is the famous stone
　　That turneth all to gold:
For that which God doth touch and own
　　Cannot for lesse be told.

Death

Death, thou wast once an uncouth hideous thing,
　　　　Nothing but bones,
　　　　The sad effect of sadder grones:
Thy mouth was open, but thou couldst not sing.

For we consider'd thee as at some six　　　　5
　　　　Or ten yeares hence,
　　　　After the losse of life and sense,
Flesh being turn'd to dust, and bones to sticks.

We lookt on this side of thee, shooting short;
　　　　Where we did finde　　　　10

THE ELIXER: in alchemy, a preparation having the power to change metals into gold; identified with the "philosopher's stone."

15 *tincture:* in alchemy, an infused principle or substance; *for thy sake:* see Matthew 10:39.

23 *touch:* with a touchstone, used to test the purity of gold.

24 *told:* reckoned, counted.

The shells of fledge souls left behinde,
Dry dust, which sheds no tears, but may extort.

But since our Saviours death did put some bloud
      Into thy face;
    Thou art grown fair and full of grace,   15
Much in request, much sought for, as a good.

For we do now behold thee gay and glad,
      As at dooms-day;
    When souls shall wear their new aray,
And all thy bones with beautie shall be clad.   20

Therefore we can go die as sleep, and trust
      Half that we have
    Unto an honest faithfull grave;
Making our pillows either down, or dust.

Judgement

Almightie Judge, how shall poore wretches brook
      Thy dreadfull look,
Able a heart of iron to appall,
      When thou shalt call
    For ev'ry mans peculiar book?   5

What others mean to do, I know not well;
      Yet I heare tell,
That some will turn thee to some leaves therein
      So void of sinne,
    That they in merit shall excell.   10

DEATH.
    11 *fledge:* fledged, ready for flight.
JUDGEMENT.
    5 *peculiar book:* individual book of accounts.

But I resolve, when thou shalt call for mine,
   That to decline,
And thrust a Testament into thy hand:
   Let that be scann'd.
 There thou shalt finde my faults are thine.   15

Heaven

O who will show me those delights on high?
   Echo. *I.*
Thou Echo, thou art mortall, all men know.
   Echo. *No.*
Wert thou not born among the trees and leaves? 5
   Echo. *Leaves.*
And are there any leaves, that still abide?
   Echo. *Bide.*
What leaves are they? impart the matter wholly.
   Echo. *Holy.*   10
Are holy leaves the Echo then of blisse?
   Echo. *Yes.*
Then tell me, what is that supreme delight?
   Echo. *Light.*
Light to the minde: what shall the will enjoy? 15
   Echo. *Joy.*
But are there cares and businesse with the pleasure?
   Echo. *Leisure.*
Light, joy, and leisure; but shall they persever?
   Echo. *Ever.*   20

Love (III)

Love bade me welcome: yet my soul drew back,
      Guiltie of dust and sinne.
But quick-ey'd Love, observing me grow slack
      From my first entrance in,
Drew nearer to me, sweetly questioning,   5
      If I lack'd any thing.

A guest, I answer'd, worthy to be here:
      Love said, you shall be he.
I the unkinde, ungratefull? Ah my deare,
      I cannot look on thee.   10
Love took my hand, and smiling did reply,
      Who made the eyes but I?

Truth Lord, but I have marr'd them: let my shame
      Go where it doth deserve.
And know you not, sayes Love, who bore the blame?   15
      My deare, then I will serve.
You must sit down, sayes Love, and taste my meat:
      So I did sit and eat.

L'Envoy

King of glorie, King of peace,
With the one make warre to cease;
With the other blesse thy sheep,
Thee to love, in thee to sleep.
Let not Sinne devoure thy fold,   5

LOVE (III): see NOTE.

Bragging that thy bloud is cold,
That thy death is also dead,
While his conquests dayly spread;
That thy flesh hath lost his food,
And thy Crosse is common wood.   10
Choke him, let him say no more,
But reserve his breath in store,
Till thy conquests and his fall
Make his sighs to use it all,
And then bargain with the winde   15
To discharge what is behinde.

FRANCIS QUARLES
1592–1644

From EMBLEMES (1635)

To the Reader

An Embleme is but a silent Parable. Let not the tender Eye checke, to see the allusion to our blessed SAVIOUR figured, in these Types. In holy Scripture, He is sometimes called a Sower; sometimes, a Fisher; sometimes, a Physitian: And why not presented so, as well to the eye, as to the eare? Before the knowledge of letters, GOD was knowne by *Hierogliphicks;* And, indeed, what are the Heavens, the Earth, nay every Creature, but *Hierogliphicks* and *Emblemes* of His Glory? I have no more to say. I wish thee as much pleasure in the reading, as I had in the writing. Farewell Reader.

Hic peßima, Hic optima ſeruat.

Will: Marſhall ſculpſit.

Figure 4. Adapted from Quarles's *Emblemes*, Book 2, Emblem VII.

Book 2, Emblem VII

Deut. XXX.XIX.

*I have set before thee life and death, blessing
and cursing, therefore choose life, that thou
and thy seed may live.*

1

The world's a Floore, whose swelling heapes retaine
    The mingled wages of the Ploughmans toyle;
The world's a Heape, whose yet unwinnowed graine
    Is lodg'd with chaffe and buried in her soyle;
All things are mixt; the usefull with the vaine;   5
    The good with bad; the noble with the vile;
        The world's an Ark, wherein things pure and grosse
        Present their lossefull gaine, and gainfull losse,
Where ev'ry dram of Gold containes a pound of drosse.

2

This furnisht Ark presents the greedy view   10
    With all that earth can give, or heav'n can add;
Here, lasting joyes; here, pleasures hourely new,
    And hourely fading, may be wisht and had:
All points of Honour; counterfeit and true

BOOK 2, EMBLEM VII.
  1 *Floore:* threshing floor.
  4 *soyle:* dirty or waste matter.
  7 *Ark:* chest, coffer.
  10 *furnisht:* fully stocked.

Salute thy soule, and wealth both good and bad: 15
    Here maist thou open wide the two-leav'd doore
    Of all thy wishes, to receive that store
Which being emptied most; does overflow the more.

3

Come then, my soule, approach this royall Burse,
    And see what wares our great Exchange retaines;   20
Come, come; here's that shall make a firme divorse
    Betwixt thy Wants and thee, if want complaines;
No need to sit in councell with thy purse,
    Here's nothing, good, shall cost more price than paines;
        But O my soule, take heed; If thou relie   25
        Upon thy faithlesse Opticks, thou wilt buy
Too blind a bargaine: know; Fooles onely trade by th' Eye.

4

The worldly wisdome of the foolish man
    Is like a Sive, that does, alone, retaine
The grosser substance of the worthlesse Bran;   30
    But thou, my soule, let thy brave thoughts disdaine
So course a purchace; O, be thou a Fan
    To purge the Chaffe, and keep the winnow'd Graine;
        Make cleane thy thoughts, and dresse thy mixt desires;
        Thou art heav'ns Tasker; and thy GOD requires   35
The purest of thy Floore, as well as of thy fires.

15 *Salute:* greet.
19 *Burse:* Exchange.
26 *Opticks:* eyes.
31 *brave:* excellent, fine.
34 *dresse:* cleanse.
35 *Tasker:* one paid for work by the piece (task).

5

Let Grace conduct thee to the paths of peace,
    And wisdome blesse thy soule's unblemisht wayes,
No matter, then, how short or long's the Lease,
    Whose date determins thy selfe-numbred dayes;   40
No need to care for wealths or Fames increase,
    Nor *Mars* his Palme, nor high *Apollos* Bayes:
        LORD, If thy gracious bounty please to fill
        The floore of my desires, and teach me skill
To dresse and chuse the Corn, take those the Chaffe that will.   45

40 *determins:* ends.
45 *Corn:* grain.

O wretched Man that I am: who shall deliver me from the body of this Death.

Rom: 7. 24　　　　　　*Will·Simpson Sculp:*

Figure 5. Adapted from Quarles's *Emblemes*, Book 5, Emblem VIII.

Book 5, Emblem VIII

Rom. VII.XXIV.

*O wretched man that I am! who shall deliver
me from the body of this death?*

Behold thy darling, which thy lustfull care
Pampers; for which thy restlesse thoughts prepare
Such early Cares; For whom thy bubbling brow
So often sweats, and bankrupt eyes do owe
Such midnight scores to Nature, for whose sake   5
Base earth is Sainted, the Infernall Lake
Unfear'd; the Crowne of Glory poorely rated;
Thy GOD neglected, and thy brother hated:
Behold thy darling, whom thy soule affects
So dearely; whom thy fond Indulgence decks   10
And puppets up in soft, in silken weeds:
Behold thy darling, whom thy fondnesse feeds
With farre-fetch'd delicates, the deare-bought gaines
Of ill-spent Time, the price of halfe thy paines:
Behold thy darling, who, when clad by Thee,   15
Derides thy nakednesse; and, when most free,
Proclaimes her lover, slave; and, being fed
Most full, then strikes th' indulgent Feeder dead:
What meanst thou thus, my poore deluded soule,
To love so fondly? Can the burning Cole   20
Of thy Affection last without the fuell
Of counter-love? Is thy Compere so cruell,

BOOK 5, EMBLEM VIII.
  5 *scores:* debts.
  9 *affects:* loves.
  10 *fond:* foolishly affectionate.
  11 *puppets up:* dresses up like a doll or idol; *weeds:* garments.
  22 *Compere:* companion.

And thou so kind, to love unlov'd againe?
Canst thou sow favours, and thus reape disdaine?
Remember, O remember thou art borne   25
Of royall blood; remember, thou art sworne
A Maid of Honour in the Court of Heav'n;
Remember what a costly price was giv'n
To ransome thee from slav'ry thou wert in;
And wilt thou now, my soule, turne slave agin?   30
The Son and Heire to Heav'ns triune IEHOVE
Would faine become a Suitor for thy Love,
And offers for thy dow'r, his Fathers Throne,
To sit, for Seraphims to gaze upon;
Hee'l give thee Honour, Pleasure, Wealth, and Things   35
Transcending farre the Majesty of Kings:
And wilt thou prostrate to the odious charmes
Of this base Scullion? Shall his hollow Armes
Hugg thy soft sides? Shall these course hands untie
The sacred Zone of thy Virginitie?   40
For shame, degen'rous soule, let thy desire
Be quicknd up with more heroick fire;
Be wisely proud; let thy ambitious eye
Read nobler objects; let thy thoughts defie
Such am'rous basenesse; Let thy soule disdaine   45
Th' ignoble profers of so base a Swaine;
Or if thy vowes be past, and Himens bands
Have ceremonyed your unequall hands,
Annull, at least avoid thy lawlesse Act
With insufficience, or a Præcontract: 50
Or if the Act be good, yet maist thou plead
A second Freedome; for the flesh is dead.

32 *faine:* gladly, willingly.
40 *Zone:* girdle, belt.
47 *Himens bands:* bonds of marriage (Hymen: god of marriage).
49 *avoid:* make void; *Act:* decree.
50 *insufficience:* inability to fulfill requirements.
51 *good:* legally binding.

Bring my ſoule out of Priſon that I may praiſe thy Name. Ps: 142.7 williſimpſon. ſulpſir

Figure 6. Adapted from Quarles's *Emblemes*, Book 5, Emblem X.

Book 5, Emblem X

Psal. CXLII.VII
Bring my soule out of prison, that I may
praise thy Name.

My Soule is like a Bird; my Flesh, the Cage;
Wherein, she weares her weary Pilgrimage
Of houres as few as evill, daily fed
With sacred Wine, and Sacramentall Bread;
The keyes that locks her in, and lets her out,   5
Are Birth, and Death; 'twixt both, she hopps about
From perch to perch; from Sense to Reason; then,
From higher Reason, downe to Sense agen:
From Sense she climbes to Faith; where, for a season,
She sits and sings; then, down againe to Reason;   10
From Reason, back to Faith; and straight, from thence
She rudely flutters to the Perch of Sense;
From Sense, to Hope; then hopps from Hope to Doubt;
From Doubt, to dull Despaire; there, seeks about
For desp'rate Freedome; and at ev'ry Grate,   15
She wildly thrusts, and begs th'untimely date
Of unexpired thraldome, to release
Th'afflicted Captive, that can find no peace:
Thus am I coop'd within this fleshly Cage,
I weare my youth, and wast my weary Age,   20
Spending that breath which was ordain'd to chaunt
Heav'ns praises forth, in sighs and sad complaint:
Whilst happier birds can spread their nimble wing
From Shrubs to Cedars, and there chirp and sing,

BOOK 5, EMBLEM X.
2 *weares:* spends, wears away.
7 *Sense:* sensory perception.
16 *untimely:* before its due time.

[233]

In choice of raptures, the harmonious story   25
Of mans Redemption and his Makers Glory:
You glorious Martyrs; you illustrious Troopes,
That once were cloyster'd in your fleshly Coopes,
As fast as I, what Reth'rick had your tongues?
What dextrous Art had your Elegiak Songs?   30
What *Paul*-like pow'r had your admir'd devotion?
What shackle-breaking Faith infus'd such motion
To your strong Pray'rs, that could obtaine the boone
To be inlarg'd, to be uncag'd so soone?
When I (poore I) can sing my daily teares,   35
Growne old in Bondage, and can find no eares:
You great partakers of eternall Glory,
That with your heav'n-prevailing Oratory,
Releas'd your soules from your terrestriall Cage,
Permit the passion of my holy Rage   40
To recommend my sorrowes (dearely knowne
To you, in dayes of old; and, once, your owne)
To your best thoughts, (but oh 't does not befit ye
To moove our pray'rs; you love and joy; not pitie:
Great LORD of soules, to whom should prisners flie,   45
But Thee? Thou hadst thy Cage, as well as I:
And, for my sake, thy pleasure was to know
The sorrowes that it brought, and feltst them too;
O set me free, and I will spend those dayes,
Which now I wast in begging, in Thy praise.   50

30 *Elegiak Songs:* songs in elegiac meter, either of love or of sorrow.
34 *inlarg'd:* freed, set at large.
44 *moove:* plead, propose.

As the Hart panteth after the waterbrooks
So panteth my soule after thee O Lord.
Will: Simpson. Sculpsit

Figure 7. Adapted from Quarles's *Emblemes*, Book 5, Emblem XI.

Book 5, Emblem XI

Psal. XLII.I
As the Hart panteth after the water-brooks,
so panteth my soule after thee O God.

1

How shall my tongue expresse that hallow'd fire
    Which heav'n has kindled in my ravisht heart!
What Muse shall I invoke, that will inspire
    My lowly Quill to act a lofty part!
What Art shall I devise t'expresse desire,   5
    Too intricate to be exprest by Art!
        Let all the nine be silent; I refuse
        Their aid in this high task, for they abuse
The flames of Love too much: Assist me *Davids* Muse.

2

Not as the thirsty soyle desires soft showres,   10
    To quicken and refresh her Embrion graine;
Nor as the drooping Crests of fading flowres
    Request the bounty of a morning Raine,
Do I desire my GOD: These, in few houres,
    Re-wish, what late their wishes did obtaine,   15
        But as the swift-foot Hart does, wounded, flie
        To th' much desired streames, ev'n so do I
Pant after Thee, my GOD, whom I must find, or die.

BOOK 5, EMBLEM XI.
   11 *Embrion:* embryonic, immature.

3

Before a Pack of deep-mouth'd Lusts I flee;
  O, they have singled out my panting heart,   20
And wanton *Cupid,* sitting in a Tree,
   Hath pierc'd my bosome with a flaming dart;
My soule being spent, for refuge, seeks to Thee,
   But cannot find where Thou my refuge art:
    Like as the swift-foot Hart does, wounded, flie   25
    To the desired streames, ev'n so do I
Pant after Thee, my GOD, whom I must find, or die.

4

At length, by flight, I over-went the Pack;
  Thou drew'st the wanton dart from out my wound;
The blood, that follow'd, left a purple track,   30
   Which brought a Serpent, but in shape, a Hound;
We strove; He bit me; but thou brak'st his back,
   I left him grov'ling on th' envenom'd ground;
    But as the Serpent-bitten Hart does flie
    To the long-long'd for streames, ev'n so did I   35
Pant after Thee, my GOD, whom I must find or die.

5

If lust should chase my soule, made swift by fright,
  Thou art the streames whereto my soule is bound:
Or if a Iav'lin wound my sides, in flight,
   Thou art the Balsom that must cure my wound: 40
If poyson chance t'infest my soule, in fight,

28 *over-went:* left behind.

Thou art the Treacle that must make me sound;
Ev'n as the wounded Hart, embost, does flie
To th' streames extremely long'd for, so do I
Pant after Thee, my GOD, whom I must find, or die.   45

42 *Treacle:* a salve used to treat poisonous bites.
43 *embost:* driven to exhaustion.

RICHARD CRASHAW
1612?–1649

The Weeper

Loe where a wounded heart, with bleeding eyes conspire;
Is she a flaming fountaine, or a weeping fire?

    1 Haile, Sister Springs,
Parents of Silver-forded rills!
    Ever bubling things!
Thawing Chrystall! Snowy hills!
Still spending, never spent; I meane   5
Thy faire eyes, sweet *Magdalen.*

    2 Heavens thy faire eyes bee,
Heavens of ever falling starrs,
    'Tis seed-time still with thee
And stars thou sow'st, whose harvest dares   10
Promise the earth, to counter shine
What ever makes Heaven's forehead fine.

    3 But we are deceived all,
Stars indeed they are too true,
    For they but seeme to fall   15
As heav'ns other spangles doe:
It is not for our Earth and us,
To shine in things so pretious.

    4 Upwards thou do'st weepe,
Heav'ns bosome drinkes the gentle streame,   20
    Where th' milky Rivers creepe
Thine floates above, and is the creame.
Waters above the Heavens what they bee,
We' are taught best by thy Teares, and thee.

THE WEEPER.
  2 *Silver-forded:* see NOTE.
  9 *still:* always.
  11 *counter shine:* equal or surpass in shining.

5   Every Morne from hence,   25
A brisk Cherub something sips,
    Whose sacred influence
Adds sweetnes to his sweetest lips,
Then to his Musick, and his song
Tastes of this breakefast all day long.   30

6   Not in the Evening's eyes,
When they red with weeping are
    For the Sun that dyes,
Sits sorrow with a face so faire:
No where but here did ever meete,   35
Sweetnesse so sadd, sadnesse so sweete.

7   When sorrow would be seene,
In her brightest Majestie,
    (For she is a Queene)
Then is she drest by none but thee.   40
Then, and onely then, she weares,
Her proudest Pearls, I meane thy tears.

8   The dew no more will weepe,
The Primroses pale cheeke to decke,
    The deaw no more will sleepe,   45
Nuzzel'd in the Lyllies necke:
Much rather would it be thy teare,
And leave them both to tremble here.

9   There is no neede at all
That the Balsome-sweating bough   50
    So coylie should let fall
His med'cinable teares; for now
Nature hath learn't t' extract a dew,
More soveraigne, and sweet from you.

50 *Balsome:* balm, healing oil or resin.
51 *coylie:* in a reserved or reluctant manner.
54 *soveraigne:* of high curative power.

[244]

10   Yet let the poore drops weepe   55
(Weeping is the ease of woe)
   Softly let them creepe,
Sad that they are vanquisht so.
They though to others no reliefe
Balsom may be for their own griefe.   60

11   Such the maiden jemme
By the purpling Vine put on
   Peepes from her parent steme,
And blushes at the Bridegroome Sun:
This watrie Blossom of thy Eyne,   65
Ripe, will make the richer Wine.

12   When some new bright guest,
Takes up among the Stars a Roome,
   And Heav'n will make a feast
Angells with Crystall Voyalls come,   70
And draw from these full eyes of thine,
Their Masters Waters; Their own wine.

13   Golden though he be,
Golden *Tagus* murmures though;
   Were his way by thee,   75
Content and quiet he would goe:
So much more rich would he esteeme,
Thy silver, than his golden streame.

14   Well does the *May* that lyes
Smiling in thy cheekes, confesse   80
   The *Aprill* in thine eyes;
Mutuall sweetnesse they expresse:
No *Aprill* e're lent kinder showers,
Nor *May* return'd more faithfull flowers.

65 *Eyne:* eyes.
70 *Voyalls:* vials.
74 *Tagus:* the Spanish-Portuguese river.

15   O cheekes! Beds of chast loves,   85
By your own showers seasonably dash't,
   Eyes! nests of milkie Doves
In your owne wells decently washt.
O wit of love that thus could place,
Fountaine and Garden in one face!   90

16   O sweet contest of woes
With loves, and tears, and smiles disputing,
   O faire and friendly foes
Each other kissing and confuting,
While raine and Sun shine, cheeks and eyes,   95
Close in kind contrarieties.

17   But can these faire flouds bee
Friends with the bosom fires that fill thee?
   Can so great flames agree
Eternall teares should thus distill thee?   100
O flouds, ô fires, ô Suns, ô showers,
Mixt, and made friends by loves sweet powers.

18   'Twas his well pointed dart
That dig'd these wells, and drest this Vine,
   And taught that wounded heart,   105
The way into those weeping Eyne,
Vaine loves avant! Bold hands forbeare,
The Lamb hath dipt his white foote here.

19   And now where e're he strayes
Among the Galilæan mountains,   110
   Or more unwelcome wayes,
Hee's follow'd by two faithfull fountaines,
Two walking Bathes, two weeping motions;
Portable and compendious Oceans.

88 *decently:* appropriately, becomingly.
89 *wit:* ingenuity, quick intelligence.
104 *drest:* cultivated, pruned.
107 *avant:* begone.

20 O thou thy Lords faire store,   115
In thy so rich and large expences,
   Even when he show'd most poore,
He might provoke the wealth of Princes.
What Princes wanton'st pride e're could,
Wash with silver, wipe with gold?   120

   21 Who is that King, but he
Who calls't his crowne to be call'd thine,
   That thus can boast to be
Waited on by a wandring mine,
A voluntary mint, that strowes   125
Warme silver showers, where e're he goes?

   22 O pretious prodigall!
Faire spend-thrift of thy self! Thy measure
   (Mercilesse love!) is all
Even to thy last Pearle in thy treasure: 130
All places, times, and objects be,
Thy teares sweet opportunity.

   23 Does the day-star rise?
Still thy Stars doe fall, and fall;
   Does day close his eyes?   135
Still the fountaine weeps for all:
Let night or day doe what they will,
Thou hast thy taske, thou weepest still.

   24 Does thy song lull the aire?
Thy falling teares keep faithfull time;   140
   Does thy sweet breath'd praier
Up in clouds of incense climbe?
Still at each sigh, that is, each stop,
A bead, that is a teare doth drop.

115 *store:* accumulated wealth.
116 *expences:* expenditures.
117 *show'd:* appeared.
118 *provoke:* call forth.
125 *strowes:* strews.

25   At these thy weeping gates   145
  (Watching their watrie motion)
     Each winged moment waites,
  Takes his teare, and gets him gon.
By thine eyes tinct enobled thus
Time layes him up: Hee's precious.   150

26   Not so long she lived
  Shall thy tomb report of thee,
     But so long she grieved,
  Thus must we date thy memorie:
Others by moments, months, and years   155
Measure their ages, Thou by tears.

27   So doe perfumes expire,
  So sigh tormented sweets, opprest
     With proud unpittying fire;
  Such tears the suffering Rose that's vext   160
With ungentle flames does shed,
Sweating in a too warme bed.

28   Say ye bright Brothers,
  The fugitive sons of those faire eyes
     Your fruitfull Mothers,   165
  What make you here? what hopes can tice
You to be borne? what cause can borrow
You from those nests of noble sorrow?

29   Whither away so fast?
  For sure the sordid earth   170
     Your sweetnesse cannot taste,
  Nor does the dust deserve your Birth.
Sweet, whither haste you then? ô say
Why you trip so fast away?

149 *tinct:* tincture, with ref. to alchemy.
158 *sweets:* fragrant flowers.
166 *tice:* entice.

30   We goe not to seeke,   175
The darlings of *Aurora's* bed,
   The Roses modest cheeke,
Nor the Violets humble head:
Though the fields eyes too weepers bee,
Because they want such tears as wee.   180

31   Much lesse meane we to trace,
The fortune of inferior gems,
   Prefer'd to some proud face,
Or pearch't upon feard diadems:
Crown'd heads are Toyes; We goe to meete,   185
A worthy object; Our Lords Feet.

On the name of Jesus

I Sing the *Name* which none can say,
But touch't with an interiour *Ray:*
The *Name* of our *New Peace*, our *Good*,
Our *Blisse*, and supernaturall *Blood*,
The *Name* of all our Lives, and Loves.   5
Hearken, and Help ye holy Doves,
The high-borne brood of day, the bright
Candidates of blissefull light,
The *Heires* elect of Love, whose names belong
Unto the everlasting life of Song;   10
All yee wise *soules*, who in the wealthy brest,
Of this unbounded *name* build your warme nest.

180 *want:* lack.
181 *trace:* follow.
183 *Prefer'd:* advanced.
185 *Toyes:* trifles.
ON THE NAME OF JESUS: see NOTE.
   8 *Candidates:* aspirants; with ref. to Latin *candidatus* ("clothed in white")
and thus to the "white robes" of the saints in heaven: see Revelation 7:13–14,
19:8.

Awake my glory, *soule* (if such thou bee
And that fair *word* at all referre to thee)
     Awake and sing,   15
     And be all Wing,
Bring hither thy whole *selfe*, and let me see
What of thy parent Heaven yet speakes in thee;
     O thou art poore
     Of noble Powers I see,   20
And full of Nothing else but emptie Mee,
Narrow, and low, and infinitely lesse
Then this great *Morning's* mighty businesse;
     One little word or two
     (Alas) will never doe,   25
     We must have store,
Goe soule out of thy self, and seek for more,
     Goe and request
Great *nature* for the *key* of her huge chest
Of heav'ns, the self involving set of spheares, 30
Which dull mortality more feeles than heares,
     Then rouse the Nest
Of nimble *art*, and traverse round
The airie shop of soul-appeasing sound,
 And beat a summons in the same   35
     All soveraigne Name,
 To warn each severall kind
 And shape of sweetnesse, be they such
  As sigh with supple wind,
  Or answer artfull touch,   40
 That they convene and come away,
To waite at the love crowned doores of this illustrious day.
Shall we dare this, my soule? wee'l do't and bring
No other note for't but the *Name* we sing.

23 The poem may have been composed for the Feast of the Circumcision
(January 1), the occasion on which the name Jesus was formally given: see
Luke 2:21.

26 *store*: abundance.

30 *self involving*: self-containing; with ref. to the concentric arrangement of
spheres in the Ptolemaic universe.

37 *severall*: individual.

Wake *Lute*, and *Harpe*,   45
    And every sweet lipt thing
    That talkes with tunefull string,
  Start into life; and leap with me
Into a hasty fit of self tun'd Harmonie;
      Nor must you think it much   50
      T'obey my bolder touch,
I have authority in *Love's* name to take you
And to the worke of *Love* this morning wake you;
      Wake in the name
Of Him who never sleeps, All things that are,   55
      Or, what's the same,
      Are Musicall,
      Answer my call
      And come along,
Help me to meditate mine Immortall song.   60
Come ye soft Ministers of sweet sad mirth,
Bring all your Houshold-stuffe of Heav'n on earth;
    O you my soules most certaine wings,
    Complaining Pipes, and pratling strings,
      Bring all the store   65
Of sweets you have, And murmure that you have no more,
      Come ne're to part,
      Nature and Art,
      Come, and come strong
To the conspiracie of our spacious song,   70
      Bring all the *Powres* of Praise
Your Provinces of well united Worlds can raise,
  Bring al your *Lutes*, and *Harpes* of Heav'n and Earth,
What e're cooperates to the common mirth,
      Vessells of vocall joyes,   75
Or you more noble Architects of Intellectuall noyse,
    Cymballs of Heav'n or Humane spheares,
    Sollicitors of *Soules* or *Eares*,

49 *fit:* a strain of music, or portion of a song; see NOTE.
61 *mirth:* rejoicing, pleasure.
70 *conspiracie:* harmony, "breathing together" (with ref. to Latin *conspiro*).

And when you're come with all
That you can bring, or we can call,   80
O may you fixe
For ever here and mixe
Your selves into the long
And everlasting series of a deathlesse song;
Mix all your many *worlds* above   85
And lose them into *One* of *Love.*
Cheare thee my *Heart*
For thou too hast thy part
And place in the great throng
Of this *Unbounded,* all imbracing song.   90
Powres of my soule be proud
And speake aloud
To all the deare bought Nations, This redeeming *Name*
And in the wealth of one rich *word* proclaime
New similes to Nature.   95
May it be no wrong
Blest heav'ns to you, and your superiour song,
That we dark Sonnes of dust and sorrow
A while dare borrow
The *Name* of your *Delights,* and our *Desires*   100
And fit it to so far inferiour *Lyres;*
Our Murmers have their Musick too,
Yee mightie *Orbes,* as well as you,
Nor yield the Noblest nest
Of warbling *Seraphins,* to the eares of Love,   105
A choicer Lesson than the Loyall breast
Of a poore panting Turtle-Dove.
And we low Wormes, have leave to doe
The same bright businesse (ye third Heavns) with you.
Gentle spirits, doe not complaine,   110
We will have care
To keep it faire
And send it back to you againe.
Come lovely *Name* appeare forth from the bright
Regions of peacefull light,   115
Looke from thine owne Illustrious home,

Faire *King* of *Names,* and come,
Leave all thy Native Glories in their gorgious nest,
And give thy self a while the gracious guest
  Of humble soules, that seeke to find   120
    The hidden sweets,
    Which mans Heart meets,
  When thou art Master of the mind.
  Come lovely *Name,* life of our hope!
  Lo, we hold our Hearts wide ope!   125
  Unlock thy cabinet of day,
  Deerest sweet, and come away.
    Lo, how the thirsty lands
Gasp for thy golden showers, with long-stretcht hands!
    Lo how the labouring Earth   130
      That hopes to be
      All heavens by thee,
      Leapes at thy Birth.
The attending *world,* to wait thy Rise,
      First turn'd to eyes,   135
And then, not Knowing what to doe,
Turn'd them to *Teares,* and spent them too.
Come Royall name, and pay th' expence
Of all thy pretious Patience,
     O come away,   140
  And Kill the death of this delay.
O see so many *worlds* of barren yeares
Melted, and measur'd out in Seas of teares;
O see, the wearie lidds of wakefull hope
(Loves eastern windows) All wide ope,   145
    With curtains drawne,
To catch the day-breake of thy *Dawne.*
O dawne at last, long look't for day,
Take thine own wings and come away.

Lo, where aloft it comes! It comes among   150
The conduct of adoring *Spirits,* that throng
Like diligent Bees, And swarme about it;
    O they are wise,

And know what *sweets* are suckt from out it;
                    It is the Hive   155
                    By which they thrive,
          Where all their hoard of hony lyes,
Lo, where it comes, upon the snowy doves
Soft back, And brings a bosome big with loves;
Welcome to our dark world, Thou womb of day!   160
Unfold thy faire conceptions, and display
          The birth of our bright joyes;
                         O thou compacted
Body of blessings, spirit of soules extracted!
          O dissipate thy spicie Powers,   165
(Cloud of condensed sweets) and breake upon us
                    In balmy showers,
          O fill our sences, and take from us
All force of so prophane a fallacie
To think ought sweet but that which smells of thee.   170
          Faire flowry *name;* In none but thee,
          And thy Nectareal Fragrancie
                    Howerly there meetes
An universall *Synod* of all *Sweetes,*
          By whom it is defined thus,   175
                    That no perfume
                    For ever shall presume
                To passe for odoriferous,
But such alone whose sacred pedigree
Can prove it self some Kin (sweet Name) to thee.   180
     Sweet Name in thy each Sillabell
     A thousand blest *Arabias* dwell,
     A thousand Hills of Frankincense,
     Mountaines of Myrrh, and Bedds of spices,
     And ten thousand *Paradises,*   185
          The soule that tastes thee takes from thence.
     How many unknow'n *worlds* there are
          Of comforts which thou hast in keeping!
     How many thousand mercies there,
          In Pities soft lap, lye a sleeping!   190
     Happie he who has the Art

To awake them,
And to take them
Home and lodge them in his *Heart*.
O that it were as it was wont to bee!   195
When thy old friends of fire, all full of *thee*
Fought against frownes with smiles, gave glorious chase
To Persecutions, and against the face
Of *Death,* and fiercest dangers, durst with brave
And sober pace, march on to meet a *Grave*.   200
On their bold *Brests* about the world they bare thee,
And to the teeth of Hell stood up to teach thee;
In center of their inmost soules they ware thee
Where rackes and torments striv'd in vaine to reach thee;
                    Little alas thought they   205
             Who tore the faire *Brests* of thy friends,
                  Their fury but made way
For thee; And serv'd therin thy glorious ends.
What did their weapons but with wider Pores
        Inlarge thy flaming-brested *Lovers*   210
                  More freely to transpire
                  That impatient fire
        The Heart that hides thee hardly covers?
What did their weapons but set wide the doores
For thee? Faire purple *Doores* of Loves devising;   215
The Rubie windows which inrich't the East
             Of thy so oft repeated Rising.
Each wound of theirs was thy new Morning
And re-inthron'd thee in thy Rosy Nest,
    With blush of thine owne Blood thy day adorning.   220
It was the wit of Love o'reflowd the bounds
Of *Wrath,* and made thee way through all those wounds.
Welcome deare, All adored *Name!*
             For sure there is no Knee
             That Knowes not thee,   225
        Oh if there be such Sonnes of shame

201 *bare:* bore.
203 *ware:* wore.

Alas what will they doe
When stubborn Rocks shall bow,
And Hills hang down their Heav'n saluting heads
To seeke for humble Beds   230
Of Dust, where in the bashfull shades of night
Next to their own low nothing they may ly,
And couch before the dazeling light of thy dread Majesty?
They that by Love's milde dictate now
Will not adore *Thee*   235
Shall then, with just confusion bow
And breake before thee.

An Hymne of the Nativity, sung as by the Shepheards

Chor. Come we shepheards whose blest sight
   Hath met Loves noone, in Natures night,
  Come lift we up our loftier song,
   And wake the *Sun* that lyes too long.

  To all our world of well-stoln joy,   5
   He slept, and dream't of no such thing;
  While we found out Heav'ns fairer eye,
   And kist the cradle of our *King;*
  Tell him he rises now too late,
  To shew us ought worth looking at.   10

  Tell him we now can shew him more
   Than he e're shewd to mortall sight,
  Than he himself e're saw before,
   Which to be seen needs not his light;
  Tell him *Tityrus* where th'hast been,   15
  Tell him *Thyrsis* what th'hast seen.

AN HYMNE OF THE NATIVITY.
10 *shew:* show.

[256]

Tit.   Gloomy night embrac't the place
           Where the noble Infant lay,
      The *Babe* look't up and shew'd his face,
          In spite of darknesse it was day: 20
      It was thy day, *Sweet!* and did rise,
      Not from the *East,* but from thine eyes.

Chorus.   It was thy day sweet, &c.

Thyrs.   *Winter* chid aloud, and sent
          The angry North to wage his wars,   25
      The North forgot his fierce intent,
          And left perfumes instead of scars,
      By those sweet eyes perswasive powers,
      Where he mean't frost, he scatter'd flowers.

Chorus.   By those sweet Eyes, &c.   30

Both.   We saw thee in thy Balmey Nest,
          Bright *dawn* of our eternall *day!*
      We saw thine eyes break from their *East,*
          And chace the trembling shades away.
      We saw thee, and we blest the sight,   35
      We saw thee by thine owne sweet light.

Tit.   Poore world (said I) what wilt thou doe
          To entertaine this starrie *stranger?*
      Is this the best thou canst bestow,
          A cold, and not too cleanly *manger?*   40
      Contend ye powers of heav'n and earth
      To fit a bed for this huge birth.

Chorus.   Contend ye Powers, &c.

Thyrs.   Proud world (said I) cease your contest,
          And let the mighty *Babe* alone,   45
      The Phænix builds the Phænix' nest.
          Love's Architecture is all one.

[257]

> The Babe whose Birth embraves this *morne*,
>> Made his own Bed ere he was borne.

Chorus.	The Babe, &c.	50

Tit.	I saw the curl'd drops, soft and slow,

> I saw the curl'd drops, soft and slow,
>> Come hovering ore the places head,
> Offering their whitest sheets of snow,
>> To furnish the faire *Infant's* Bed:
> Forbeare (said I) be not too bold,
> Your fleece is white, but 'tis too cold.

Chorus.   Forbeare (said I,) &c.

Thyrs.   I saw the obsequious *Seraphins*
>> Their Rosie *Fleece* of *Fire* bestow,
> For well they now can spare their wings
>> Since Heaven it selfe lyes here below:
> Well done (said I) but are you sure
> Your downe so warme, will passe for pure.

Chorus.   Well done (said we,) &c.

Tyt.   No, no, your *King's* not yet to seeke
>> Where to repose his Royall *Head*,
> See see, how soone his new-bloom'd *cheeke*
>> Twixt's mothers brests is gone to bed.
> Sweet choice (said Il) no way but so
> Not to lye cold, yet sleep in snow.

Chorus.   Sweet choice, &c.

Both.   We saw thee in thy Baulmey nest,
>> Bright *Dawn* of our eternall *Day*,

48 *embraves:* adorns.
58 *obsequious:* prompt to serve.

[258]

We saw thine eyes breake from their *East*,
   And chase the trembling shades away.   75
We saw thee, and we blest the sight,
We saw thee, by thine owne sweet light.

Chorus.   Wee saw thee, &c.

Full   Welcome all *wonders* in one sight!
Chorus.   Eternitie shut in a span,   80
Summer in winter, day in night,
   Heaven in Earth, and God in man;
Great little one! Whose all embracing birth
Lift's earth to heav'n, stoops heav'n to earth.

Welcom though not to gold nor silke,   85
   To more than *Cæsars* birthright is;
Two Sister Seas of Virgin *Milke*,
   With many a rarely temper'd Kisse
That breath's at once both *Maide* & *Mother*,
Warmes in the one, cooles in the other.   90

She sings thy Teares a sleep, and dips
   Her Kisses in thy weeping eye,
She spreads the red leaves of thy lips,
   That in their buds yet blushing lye.
She 'gainst those Mother-Diamonds tries   95
The points of her young Eagles eyes.

Welcome, though not to those gay flyes
   Guilded i'th beames of earthly Kings,
Slippery soules in smiling eyes,
   But to poor Shepheards, home-spun things,   100
Whose wealth's their flock; whose wit to be
Well read in their simplicitie.

80 *span:* a small measure (nine inches).
91–96: see NOTE.

Yet when young *Aprill's* husband showers,
    Shall blesse the fruitfull *Maia's* bed,
Wee'l bring the first borne of her flowers,   105
    To kisse thy feet, and crowne thy head.
To thee dread *Lamb!* whose love must keepe
The shepheards more than they their sheepe.

To thee meeke *Majestie!* soft King
    Of simple *Graces* and sweet *Loves;*   110
Each of us his *Lamb* will bring,
    Each his paire of Silver Doves,
Till burnt at last in fire of thy faire eyes,
Our selves become our owne best sacrifice.

A Hymne for the *Epiphanie*. Sung as by the three Kings

Bright Babe! whose awfull Beauties make
    The morn incurre a sweet mistake,
For whom th'officious Heav'ns devise
    To dis-inherit the Suns rise,
Delicately to displace   5
    The day, and plant it fairer in thy face.
1.   O thou born *King* of Loves,
     2.   Of lights,
     3.   Of joyes!
Chorus.   Looke up sweet *Babe,* looke up and see,   10
        For love of thee,
        Thus farre from home
        The *East* is come,
    To seeke her self in thy sweet Eyes.
1.   We who strangely went astray,   15

A HYMNE FOR THE EPIPHANIE.

  3 *officious:* eager to serve, dutiful.
  15–18 The Magi have been devoted to the Persian cult of sun worship.

Lost in a bright
Meridian Night,

2. A darkenesse made of too much day,

3. Becken'd from farre
By thy faire starre   20

Lo at last have found our way.

Chorus.   To thee thou day of night! thou East of West!

Lo we at last have found the way:

To thee the world's great universall East,

The Generall and indifferent day.   25

1. All-circling Point, All-centring spheare,
   The world's One, Round, Æternall yeare,
2. Whose full, and all-unwrinckled face
   Nor sinkes nor swells with Time, or Place,
3. But every where, and every while,   30
   Is one consistent solid smile;

1. Not vext and tost,
2. Twixt spring and frost,

3. Nor by alternate shreds of light
   Sordidly shifting hands with shades and night.   35

Chorus.   *O Little All!* In thy Embrace

The world lyes warme, and likes his place,
Nor does his full Globe faile to be
Kist on both his cheekes by thee;
Time is too narrow for thy *yeare*   40
Nor makes the whole World thy halfe spheare.

1. To *thee*, to *Thee*
From *Him* we flee,

2. From *Him*, whom by a more Illustrious Lye
   The blindnesse of the world did call the *Eye;*   45
3. To *him*, who by these mortall clouds hast made
   Thy self our *Sun*, though thine owne shade.

1. Farewell the *world's* false light,
Farewell the white
Ægypt, A long farewell to thee   50

25 *indifferent:* impartial.
50 *Ægypt:* region of idolatry, bondage, and darkness.

    Bright Idoll, black *Idolatrie,*
The dire face of inferiour *Darkenesse* kist,
And courted in the pompous mask of a more specious mist.
      2. Farewell, farewell
      The proud and misplac't Gates of Hell,   55
        Pertch't in the mornings way,
      And double-gilded as the doores of *Day;*
The deep *Hypocrisy* of *Death,* and *Night,*
More desperately darke, because more bright.
      3. Welcome the *Worlds* sure way!   60
      Heav'ns wholsome Ray;
Chorus. Welcome to us, and wee
      (*Sweet*) to our selves, in *Thee.*
1. The deathlesse *Heir* of all thy *Fathers* day!
      2. Decently born,   65
Embosom'd in a much more Rosie *Morne,*
The blushes of thy *All*-unblemish't *Mother.*
      3. No more that other
      Aurora shall set ope
Her Rubie casements, or hereafter hope   70
      From mortall eyes
To meet Religious *Welcomes* at her Rise.
Chorus. We (pretious ones!) in you have won
      A gentler *Morn,* a juster *Sun.*
1. His superficiall beames Sun burnt our skin,   75
      2. But left within
3. The night, and Winter still of *Death* and *Sin.*
Chorus. Thy softer, yet more certaine *Darts,*
      Spare our eyes, but pierce our *Hearts.*
1. Therefore with his prowd Persian spoyles   80
2. We court *Thy* more concerning *smiles,*
        3.   Therefore with his disgrace
We guild the humble cheeke of thy chast place,
Chorus. And at thy *feet* powre forth his *face.*
1. The doating Nations now no more   85
      Shall any *Day,* but *Thine* adore;

53 *specious:* attractive in appearance.

2. Nor (much lesse) shall they leave these eyes
   For cheap *Ægyptian* deities,
3. In what so'ere more sacred shape
   Of *Ram, Hee-goat,* or Reverend *Ape,*   90
   Those beauteous Ravishers opprest so sore
   The too-hard-tempted Nations.
         1. Never more
     By wanton *Heyfer* shall be worn
       2. A Garland or a gilded Horn,   95
   The *Altar-stall'd Oxe,* fat *Osyris,* now
         With his faire Sister *Cow*
   Shall Kick the cloudes no more;
        3. But lean and tame,
   See his horn'd face, and dye for shame.   100
Chorus. And *Mithra* now shall be no name;
       1. No longer shall the immodest lust
         Of *Adulterous Godles* dust
      Fly in the face of Heav'n,
           2. As if it were   105
   The poore World's fault, that he is faire,
3. Nor with perverse loves, and Religious *Rapes*
   Revenge thy bounties in their beauteous shapes,
   And punish best things worst; because they stood
   Guiltie of being much for them to good.   110
1. Proud sons of death! that durst compell,
   Heav'n it self to find them Hell;
2. And by strange will of madnesse wrest
   From this World's *East,* the others *West.*
3. All *Idolizing* Wormes! that thus could crowd   115
   And urge their *Sun* into thy cloud;
   Forcing his sometimes Ecclips'd face to bee
   A long *Deliquium* to the light of thee.

96 *Altar-stall'd:* having his stall at the altar: Osiris was identified with the bull Apis.
97 *Sister Cow:* Isis, represented with the horns of a cow.
101 *Mithra:* Persian sun-god.
116 *into thy cloud:* into becoming thy cloud.
118 *Deliquium:* failure, eclipse.

Chorus.   Alas with how much heavier shade
           The shamefac't lamp hung down his head   120
           For that one Ecclipse he made
           Than all those he suffered?
1.   For this he look't so big, and every morn,
    With a red face confest his scorne,
    Or hiding his vex't cheekes in a hir'd mist   125
    Kept them from being so unkindly Kist.
2.   It was for this the day did rise
         So oft with blubber'd eys,
    For this the Evening wept; and we ne're Knew
              But call'd it dew.   130
      3.   This daily wrong
   Silenc't the morning *Suns;* and damp't their song;
Chorus.   Nor was't our deafenes, but our sins, that thus
   Long made th'harmonious Orbes, All mute to us.
      1.   Time has a day in store   135
        When this so proudly poore
   And self-oppressed spark, that has so long
      By the love-sick world bin made
      Not so much their Sun as *Shade,*
      Wearie of this glorious wrong,   140
    From Them and from Himself shall flee
    For shelter to the shadow of thy *Tree.*
Chorus.   Proud to have gain'd this pretious losse,
    And chang'd his false crowne for thy *crosse.*
2.   That darke day's clear doome shall define   145
   Whose is the master *Fire,* which *Sun* should shine?
   That sable Judgement seate shall by new lawes
      Decide and settle the great cause

124 *scorne:* insult (to God).
126 *unkindly Kist:* unnaturally (wickedly) worshiped by man.
128 *blubber'd:* overflowing with tears.
132 See Job 38:7; *damp't:* stifled.
135 f. See Matthew 27:45; Mark 15:33; Luke 23:44–45.
145 *doome:* judgment.
148 *cause:* legal case.

Of controverted light,
Chorus.   And Natures wrongs rejoyce to doe Thee right.   150
3.   That forfeiture of *Noon* to night shall pay
     All the Idolatrous Thefts done by this night of day,
     And the great Penitent presse his owne pale lips
          With an elaborate Love-Ecclipse,
                    To which the low World's lawes   155
                    Shall lend no cause,
Chorus.   Save those domesticks, which he borrowes
     From our Sins, and his owne Sorrowes.
1.   Three sad-houres sackcloath then shall shew to us
His penance, as our fault, conspicuous,   160
2.   And he more needfully and Nobly prove
     The Nations terror now, than 'erst their love.
3.   Their hated love's chang'd into wholsome feares,
Chorus.   The shutting of his eye shall open theirs.
1.   As by a fair-ey'd fallacy of Day   165
     Misled, before they lost their way,
     So shall they, by the seasonable fright,
          Of an unseasonable Night,
     Losing it once againe, stumble on true light.
2.   And as before his too bright Eye   170
     Was their more blind Idolatrie,
     So his officious Blindnesse now shall be,
     Their black, but faithfull perspective of Thee.
3.   His new prodigious Night,
     Their new, and admirable Light,   175
     The supernaturall *Dawn* of thy pure day,
               While wondering they
            (The happy converts now of him
     Whom they compell'd before to be their sin)
                    Shall henceforth see   180
          To Kisse him onely as their Rod,

149 *controverted:* made a subject of controversy.
156 *cause:* used here in general sense.
157 *domesticks:* things pertaining to or produced at home.
162 *erst:* before.

        Whom they so long courted as God.
Chorus.   And the best use of him they worship't be
        To learne of him at least to worship thee.
      1.   It was their weakenes woo'd his beautie,   185
              But it shall bee
         Their wisdome now as well as dutie
        T'enjoy his blot; and as a large black letter
           Use to spell thy beauties better,
        And make the night it self their torch to thee.   190
2. By the oblique ambush of this close night,
           Coucht in the conscious shade,
         The right-ey'd Areopagite
         Shall with a vigorous guesse invade
      And catch thy quick reflex; And sharply see   195
             On this dark ground,
             To descant *Thee.*
3. O prize of the Rich *Spirit!* with what fierce chace,
           Of his strong soule, shall he
          Leape at thy loftie *Face,*   200
      And seize the swift Flash, in Rebound
      From this obsequious cloud;
           Once call'd a Sun,
          Till dearely thus undone,
Chorus. Till thus triumphantly tam'd (ô ye Two   205
        Twin-Suns) and taught now to negotiate you.
1.   Thus shall that Reverend child of light
2.   By being Scholler first of that new night,
3.   Come forth great master of the Mystick day,
        And teach obscure *Mankind* a more close way,   210
          By the frugall Negative light
        Of a most wise and well abused night,

---

193 *Areopagite:* mystical theologian of the fifth century A.D.; see NOTE.
195 *reflex:* reflection.
202 *obsequious:* obedient, dutiful.
206 *Twin-Suns:* the eyes of the infant Christ (see line 14); *negotiate:* deal with.
210 *obscure:* enveloped in darkness.
212 *abused:* in the sense of Latin *abutor:* used, used fully (with effect here of witty paradox).

To read more legible thine originall Ray,
Chorus. And make our darknesse serve *Thy day,*
Maintaining 'twixt thy world and ours   215
A commerce of contrary Powres,
A mutuall trade
'Twixt *Sun,* and *Shade.*
By confederate *Black* and *White,*
Borrowing *day* and lending night.   220
1. Thus we, who when with all the noble Powres
That (at thy cost) are call'd not vainely ours,
We vow to make brave way
Upwards, and presse on for the pure intelligentiall Prey,
2. At least to play   225
The amorous spyes,
And peep and proffer at thy sparkling Throne,
3. Instead of bringing in the Blissefull *Prize*
And fastning on Thine Eyes,
Forfeit our owne,   230
And nothing gaine
But more ambitious losse, at least of Braine;
Chorus. Now by abased lids shall learne to be
Eagles; and shut our Eyes that we may see.

The Close.   235

Therefore to *Thee,* and thine auspicious Ray,
(*Dread sweet*) lo thus
At least by us,
The delegated *Eye* of *Day*
Does first his Scepter, then *Himself,* in solemne Tribute pay;   240
Thus he undresses
His sacred unshorne Tresses;
At thy adored feet, thus, he layes downe
1. His glorious Tire
Of flame and fire,   245
2. His glittering *Robe,* (3.) His sparkling *Crown,*

227 *proffer at:* make a tentative movement toward.
233 *abased:* lowered.
244 *Tire:* attire; specifically, headdress.

1.   His *Gold,* (2.) His *Myrrh,* (3.) His *Frankincense,*
Chorus.   To which he now has no pretence;
For being shew'd by this day's light, how far
He is from *Sun,* enough to make thy *star,*   250
His best ambition now, is but to be
Something a brighter *Shadow* (*Sweet*) of *Thee.*
Or on Heav'ns azure forehead high to stand
Thy Golden Index; with a duteous hand,
Pointing us home to our own *Sun,*   255
The World's and his *Hyperion.*

An ode which was prefixed to a Prayer booke given to a young Gentlewoman

Loe here a little volume but great booke,
   A nest of new-borne sweetes,
      Whose Native fires disdaining
To lye thus folded and complaining
    Of these ignoble sheetes   5
      Affect more comely Bands,
      (Faire one) from thy kind hands,
        And confidently looke
         To find the rest
Of a rich binding in your brest.   10

It is in one choice handfull, heaven and all
   Heavens royall hoast, incampt thus small;
  To prove that true, Schooles use to tell,
Ten thousand Angells in one point can dwell.

252 *Something:* to some extent.
254 *Index:* pointer (forefinger).
AN ODE WHICH WAS PREFIXED TO A PRAYER BOOKE.
  6 *Affect:* aspire to; *Bands:* things that bind together.

It is loves great Artyllery,   15
Which here contracts it self, and comes to ly
Close coucht in your white bosome, and from thence
As from a snowy fortresse of defence
Against the Ghostly foe to take your part:
And fortifie the hold of your chast heart.   20

It is an Armory of light,
Let constant use but keep it bright,
      You'l find it yields,
    To holy hands and humble Hearts,
         More swords and shields,   25
Then sinne hath snares, or Hell hath Darts.

      Onely be sure
      The Hands be pure
That hold these weapons, and the eyes
Those of Turtles, chast, and true,   30
      Wakefull, and wise;
Here is a friend shall fight for you;
Hold but this booke before your heart,
Let Prayer alone to play its part.

But ô the heart   35
That studies this high art,
Must be a sure house Keeper,
  And yet no sleeper.
Deare soule be strong,
Mercy will come ere long,   40
And bring its bosome full of blessings,
Flowers of never fading graces,
To make immortall dressings
For worthy soules, whose wise embraces
Store up themselves for Him, who is alone   45
The Spouse of Virgins, and the Virgins son.

19 *Ghostly:* spiritual.
30 *Turtles:* turtledoves.

[269]

But if the noble *Bridegroome* when he come,
 Shall find the loyt'ring *Heart* from home,
  Leaving its chast aboad,
   To gad abroad,   50
Amongst the gay Mates of the God of flyes;
 To take her pleasure, and to play,
 And keep the devills Holy day;
To dance ith' sunne-shine of some smiling
     But beguiling   55
Spheare of sweet, and sugred lies,
  Some slippery paire,
  Of false perhaps as faire,
Flattering, but forswearing eyes;

Doubtlesse some other heart   60
  Will get the start,
  And stepping in before,
Will take possession of the sacred store
  Of hidden sweets, and holy joyes,
 Words which are not heard with ears, 65
(Those tumultuous shops of noise)
Effectuall *whispers,* whose still voice,
The soul it selfe more feeles than heares.

Amorous Languishments; Luminous Trances,
Sights which are not seen with *Eyes;* 70
Spirituall, and *Soule-piercing* glances,
Whose pure and subtile lightning *Flyes,*
Home to the Heart, and sets the house on fire,
And melts it downe in sweet desire:
   Yet doth not stay   75
To aske the windowes leave to passe that way.

Delicious deaths, soft *exhalations*
Of *Soule;* deare and Divine *annihilations.*
  A thousand unknowne *Rites*
  Of Ioyes and *rarefy'd Delights,* 80

51 *God of flyes:* Beelzebub.

A hundred thousand *Goods, Glories,* and *Graces,*
    And many a mistick thing,
    Which the divine embraces
Of the deare *spouse* of *Spirits,* with them will bring,
      For which it is no shame,   85
That dull mortality must not know a name.

    Of all this store
Of blessings, and ten thousand more;
      (If when he come
      He find the Heart from home)   90
        Doubtlesse he will unload
    Himselfe some other where,
      And powre abroad
      His precious sweets,
On the faire soule whom first he meets.   95

O faire! ô Fortunate! ô rich! ô deare!
    O happy and thrice happy shee
      Selected *Dove,*
      Who e're she bee,
      Whose early love   100
      With winged vowes,
Makes hast to meet her Morning spouse:
And close with his immortall kisses.
    Happie indeed who never misses,
    To improve that precious hower,   105
      And every day,
      Seize her sweet prey;
    All fresh and fragrant as he rises,
    Dropping with a balmy showre
    A delicious dew of spices.   110

O let the blissefull *Heart* hold fast
Her *Heav'nly Arme-full,* she shall tast,
At once ten thousand Paradices;
    She shall have Power,
    To rifle and Deflower,   115

The rich and Roseall spring of those rare sweets,
Which with a swelling bosome there she meets.
Boundlesse and infinite_____
_____Bottomlesse treasures,
           Of pure inebriating pleasures,   120
Happy *proofe!* she shall discover,
      What *Joy* what *Blisse*
   How many *Heav'ns* at once it is,
To have her God become her lover.

On Mr. *George Herberts* booke intitu-
led the Temple of Sacred Poems,
sent to a Gentle-woman

Know you faire on what you looke;
 Divinest love lyes in this booke:
Expecting fier from your eyes,
To kindle this his sacrifice.
When your hands untie these strings,   5
 Think yo'have an Angell by the wings.
One that gladly will be nigh,
To waite upon each morning sigh.
To flutter in the balmy aire,
Of your well-perfumed praier;   10
These white plumes of his hee'l lend you,
Which every day to heaven will send you:
To take acquaintance of the *spheare,*
And all the smooth-fac'd kindred there.
    And though *Herbert's* name doe owe   15
     These devotions, fairest, know
    That while I lay them on the shrine
    Of your white hand, they are mine.

ON MR. GEORGE HERBERTS BOOKE.
  15 *owe:* own.

In memory of the vertuous and Learned Lady *Madre de Teresa* that sought an early Martyrdome

Love thou art absolute sole Lord
Of life and death. ——— To prove the word,
Wee'l now appeale to none of all
Those thy old Souldiers, Great and tall
Ripe men of Martyrdome, that could reach downe,   5
With strong armes their Triumphant crowne:
Such as could with lustie breath,
Speake loud into the face of death,
Their great Lord's glorious name; To none
Of those whose spatious bosomes spread a throne   10
For love at large to fill: spare Blood and sweat,
And see him take a privat seat,
Making his mansion in the mild
And milky soule of a soft child.
Scarce hath she learnt to lisp the name,   15
Of Martyr; yet she thinkes it shame
Life should so long play with that breath,
Which spent can buy so brave a death.
She never undertooke to know,
What death with love should have to doe;   20
Nor hath she e're yet understood
Why to shew love, she should shed blood,
Yet though she can not tell you why,
She can *love*, and she can *dye*.
Scarce hath she blood enough, to make   25
A guilty sword blush for her sake;

IN MEMORY OF . . . TERESA.
  12 *seat:* residence.
  18 *brave:* excellent, splendid.

Yet hath she a heart dares hope to prove,
How much lesse strong is Death then Love.
Be Love but there, let poore six yeares,
Be pos'd with the maturest feares   30
Man trembles at, you streight shall find
Love knowes no nonage, nor the Mind.
'Tis *Love,* not years, nor Limbs, that can
Make the *Martyr* or the *Man.*
Love toucht her *Heart,* and lo it beates   35
High, and burnes with such brave Heates:
Such *Thirsts* to dye, as dares drink up
A thousand cold *Deaths* in one cup.
Good reason; for she breaths all *fire,*
Her weake breast heaves with strong desire,   40
Of what she may with fruitlesse wishes
Seeke for amongst her Mothers Kisses.
    Since 'tis not to be had at home,
Shee'l travell for *A Martyrdome.*
No *Home* for hers confesses she,   45
But where she may a Martyr be.
Shee'l to the *Moores* and trade with them,
For this unvalued *Diadem,*
Shee'l offer them her dearest Breath,
With *Christ's* name in't, in change for death.   50
Shee'l bargain with them, and will give
Them God, and teach them how to live
In him; Or if they this deny,
For him, she'l teach them how to dye.
So shall she leave amongst them sown,   55
Her *Lords* Blood, or at least her *own.*
Farewell then all the world! Adiew,
Teresa is no more for you:
Farewell all pleasures, sports, and joys,

30 *pos'd:* placed in a difficulty.
31 *streight:* at once.
32 *nonage:* the period of being under age.
48 *unvalued:* of extreme (inestimable) value.

(Never till now esteemed *Toyes*)   60
Farewell what ever deare may bee,
Mother's armes or Father's Knee.
Farewell house and farewell home:
She's for the *Moores* and *Martyrdome.*

Sweet not so fast! Lo thy faire *Spouse,*   65
Whom thou seekst with so swift vowes
Calls thee back, and bidds thee come,
T'embrace a milder Martyrdome.
Blest powers forbid thy tender life,
Should bleed upon a barbarous Knife;   70
Or some base hand have power to race,
Thy Brest's chast cabinet, and uncase
A soule kept there so sweet. O no;
Wise Heaven will never have it so.
Thou art *Loves* Victim; and must dye   75
A death more mysticall and *high.*
Into *Loves* armes thou shalt let fall,
A still surviving funerall.
His is the *Dart* must make the *Death,*
Whose stroake shall taste thy hallow'd *breath;*   80
A Dart thrice dipt in that rich *flame,*
Which writes thy spouses radiant *Name,*
Upon the roofe of Heav'n, where ay
It shines, and with a sovereigne Ray
Beates bright upon the burning faces   85
Of soules, which in that Name's sweet graces
Find everlasting smiles; so rare,
So spirituall, pure, and faire,
Must be th'immortall instrument,
Upon whose choice point shall be sent,   90
A life so lov'd; And that there be
Fit executioners for thee,
The fair'st, and first borne sons of fire,

71 *race:* cut, slash.
83 *ay:* ever.

Blest *Seraphims* shall leave their Quire,
And turne *Love's Souldiers,* upon thee, 95
To exercise their *Archerie.*
O how oft shalt thou complaine
Of a sweet and subtile *paine?*
Of intollerable *joyes?*
Of a *death,* in which who *dyes* 100
Loves his *death,* and dyes againe,
And would for ever so be slaine!
And lives, and dyes; and knows not why
To live; But that he thus may never leave to dye.
How kindly will thy gentle *Heart,* 105
Kisse the sweetly-killing *Dart?*
And close in his embraces keepe,
Those *delicious wounds* that *weepe*
Balsome to heale themselves with. Thus
When these thy *Deathes* so numerous, 110
Shall all at last dye into one,
And melt thy soules sweet *mansion;*
Like a soft lump of Incense, hasted
By too hot a fire, and wasted,
Into perfuming clouds, so fast 115
Shalt thou exhale to Heav'n at last,
In a resolving sigh, and then,
O what?—aske not the tongues of men.
Angells cannot tell. Suffice,
Thy self shall feele thine own full joyes, 120
And hold them fast for ever. There,
So soon as thou shalt first *appeare,*
The Moon of maiden stars, thy white
Mistresse attended by such bright
Soules as thy shining-self, shall come, 125
And in her first rankes make thee roome.
Where 'mongst her snowy family,
Immortall welcomes waite for thee.
O what delight when reveal'd life shall stand,
And teach thy lips heav'n with her hand, 130
On which thou now maist to thy wishes,

[276]

Heape up thy *consecrated kisses!*
What joyes shall seize thy soule, when she
Bending her blessed eyes on thee
(Those second smiles of Heav'n) shall dart,   135
Her mild rayes through thy melting Heart?
Angells thy old friends, there shall greet thee,
Glad at their owne home now to meet thee.
All thy good works which went before,
And waited for thee at the doore,   140
Shall owne thee there; and all in one
Weave a *Constellation*
Of crownes with which the King thy spouse,
Shall build up thy triumphant browes.
All thy old woes shall now smile on thee,   145
And thy Paines sit bright upon thee.
All thy sorrows here shall shine,
And thy suff'rings be divine;
Teares shall take comfort, and turne *Gems,*
And *wrongs* repent to *Diadems.*   150
Ev'n thy *Deaths* shall live; and new
Dresse the soule, that erst they slew.
Thy Wounds shall blush to such bright scars,
As keep accompt of the *Lamb's* wars.
Those *rare-workes* where thou shalt leave writ,   155
Loves noble *Historie,* with wit
Taught thee by none but him, while here
They feed our *soules,* shall cloath thine there.
Each heavn'ly word, by whose hid flame
Our hard hearts shall strike fire, the same   160
Shall flourish on thy browes, and be
Both *fire* to us, and *flame* to thee;
Whose light shal live bright, in thy Face
By *glorie,* in our Hearts by *grace.*
Thou shalt looke round about, and see   165
Thousands of crown'd soules throng to bee
Themselves thy *crowne;* sonnes of thy vowes,

154 *accompt:* account.

The virgin-births, with which thy soveraigne spouse
Made fruitfull thy faire soule. Goe now
And with them all about thee, bow   170
To him, Put on (hee'l say) put on
(*My Rosie Love*) That thy rich Zone,
Sparkling with the sacred flames,
Of thousand soules, whose happy names
Heav'n keep's upon thy score (Thy bright   175
Life brought them first to kisse the light
That kindled them to stars) and so
Thou with the *Lamb*, thy Lord, shalt goe;
And where soe're he sets his white
Steps, walk with *Him* those waies of light.   180
Which who in death would live to see,
Must learne in life to dye like Thee.

The flaming Heart. Upon the booke and picture of *Teresa*. As she is usually expressed with a *Seraphim* beside her

Well meaning Readers! you that come as Friends,
And catch the pretious name this piece pretends,
Make not so much hast to admire
That faire cheek't fallacie of fire.
That is a *Seraphim* they say,   5
And this the great *Teresia*.
Readers, be rul'd by me, and make,
Here a well plac't, and wise mistake.
You must transpose the picture quite,
And spell it wrong to reade it right;   10

172 *Zone:* belt.
175 *score:* record.
THE FLAMING HEART: *expressed:* portrayed; see NOTE.
  2 *pretends:* offers, sets forth.

Read *Him* for *Her*, and *Her* for *Him*,
And call the *Saint*, the *Seraphim*.
Painter, what did'st thou understand
To put her dart into his *Hand*?
See, even the yeares, and size of Him,   15
Shew this the Mother *Seraphim*.
This is the Mistrisse *Flame*; and duteous *hee*
Her happier *fire-works*, here, comes down to see.
O most poore spirited of men!
Had thy cold Pencill kist her Pen   20
Thou could'st not so unkindly err
To shew us this faint shade for Her.
Why man, this speakes pure mortall frame,
And mocks with Femall Frost Love's manly flame.
One would suspect thou mean'st to paint,   25
Some weake, inferior, *Woman Saint*.
But had thy pale-fac't purple tooke
Fire from the burning Cheekes of that *bright booke*,
Thou would'st on her have heap't up all
That could be form'd *Seraphicall*.   30
What e're this youth of fire wore faire,
Rosie Fingers, Radiant Haire,
Glowing cheekes, and glistring wings,
All those, faire and flagrant things,
But before All, that fierie Dart,   35
Had fill'd the *Hand* of this great *Heart*.
Do then as equall Right requires,
Since *his* the blushes be, and *hers* the fires,
Resume and rectifie thy rude designe,
Undresse thy *Seraphim* into *mine*.   40
Redeeme this injury of thy art,
Give *him* the *veyle*, give *her* the *Dart*.
Give *him* the *veyle*, that he may cover,
The red cheekes of a rivall'd Lover;
Asham'd that our world now can show   45

33 *glistring:* glittering.
34 *flagrant:* flaming, burning.

[279]

Nests of new *Seraphims* here below.
Give *her* the *dart,* for it is *she*
(Faire youth) shoot's both thy shafts and *thee.*
Say, all ye wise and well pierc't Hearts
That live, and dye amid'st Her darts,   50
What is't your tast-full spirits doe prove
In that rare Life of *her,* and Love?
Say and beare witnesse. Sends she not,
A *Seraphim* at every shot?
What *Magazins* of immortall armes there shine!   55
Heav'ns great *Artillery* in each *Love-spun-line.*
Give then the *Dart* to *Her,* who gives the *Flame;*
Give *Him* the *veyle,* who kindly takes the shame.
    But if it be the frequent *Fate*
     Of worst faults to be *Fortunate;*   60
    If all's *prescription;* and proud wrong,
    Hearkens not to an humble song;
    For all the *Gallantry* of *Him,*
    Give me the suff'ring *Seraphim.*
    His be the bravery of all those Bright things,   65
    The glowing cheekes, the glittering wings,
    The *Rosie* hand, the *Radiant Dart,*
    Leave her alone the *flaming-Heart.*
    Leave her that, and thou shalt leave her,
    Not one loose shaft, but *loves* whole quiver.   70
    For in *Love's* field was never found,
    A nobler *Weapon* than a *wound.*
    Love's Passives, are his *activ'st* part,
    The *wounded* is the *wounding-heart.*
    O Heart! the equall *Poise,* of *Love's* both *Parts,*   75
    Big alike with *wounds* and *Darts,*
Live in these conquering *leaves;* live all the same,
And walke through all tongues one triumphant flame.
Live here *great heart;* and Love, and dye, and kill,
And bleed, and wound, and yield, and conquer still.   80

61 *prescription:* right or title acquired by long possession.
65 *bravery:* splendor.

Let this immortall Life, where e'er it comes,
Walke in a crowd of *Loves*, and *Martyrdomes*.
Let *Mystick Deaths* waite on't; and wise soules bee,
The *love-slaine-witnesses*, of this life of *Thee*.
O sweet incendiary! shew here thy art,   85
Upon this carcasse of a hard, cold, hart,
Let all thy scatter'd shafts of light, that play
Among the leaves of thy larg Books of day,
Combin'd against this *Brest* at once break in
And take away from me my self & sin,   90
This gratious Robbery shall thy bounty be;
And my best fortunes such fair spoiles of me.
O thou undanted daughter of desires!
By all thy dowr of *Lights* & *Fires;*
By all the eagle in thee, all the dove;   95
By all thy lives & deaths of love;
By thy larg draughts of intellectuall day,
And by thy thrists of love more large then they;
By all thy brim-fill'd Bowles of feirce desire
By thy last Morning's draught of liquid fire;   100
By the full kingdome of that finall kisse
That seiz'd thy parting Soul, & seal'd thee his;
By all the heav'ns thou hast in him
(Fair sister of the *Seraphim!*)
By all of *Him* we have in *Thee;*   105
Leave nothing of my *Self* in me.
Let me so read thy life, that I
Unto all life of mine may dy.

85–108. See NOTE.
98 *thrists:* obsolete form of "thirsts".

An Apologie for the precedent Hymnes
on *Teresa*

Thus have I back againe to thy bright name,
(Faire floud of holy fires) transfus'd the Flame
I tooke from reading Thee. 'Tis to thy wrong
I know, that in my weake and worthlesse song
Thou here art set to shine, where thy full day   5
Scarce dawnes. O pardon if I dare to say
Thine owne deere bookes are guilty: for from thence
I learn'd to know that *Love* is *eloquence*.
That hopefull maxime gave me heart to trye,
If, what to other Tongues is tun'd so high,   10
Thy praise might not speake English too. Forbid
(By all thy mysteries that here lye hid)
Forbid it *Mighty Love!* let no fond hate
Of names and words so farre prejudicate;
Soules are not *Spaniards* too. One friendly floud,   15
Of *Baptisme*, blends them all into a Blood.
Christ's faith makes but one Body of all Soules;
And *Love's* that Bodie's Soule. No law comptrolls
Our free traffique for Heav'n, we may maintaine
Peace, sure, with piety, though it come from *Spaine*.   20
What Soule so e're in any language can
Speake Heav'n like hers, is my Soules countrey-man.
O 'tis not *Spanish*, but 'tis Heav'n she speakes!
'Tis heaven that lyes in ambush there, and breakes
From thence into the wondring Reader's brest;   25
Who feeles his warme *Heart* hatch'd into a nest

AN APOLOGIE: defense, justification; see NOTE.
    13 *fond:* foolish.
    14 *prejudicate:* create prejudice.
    18 *comptrolls:* controls.
    19 *traffique:* dealings, business.

Of little *Eagles* and young *Loves,* whose high
Flights scorne the *Lazie* dust, and things that dy.
There are enow whose draughts (as deep as Hell)
Drinke up all *Spaine* in Sack. Let my soule swell   30
With thee, strong *Wine* of *Love!* Let others swim,
In Puddles; we will pledge this *Seraphim*
Boules full of richer Blood than blush of grape
Was ever guilty of. Change we our shape
My soule, Some drinke from men to beasts, ô then,   35
Drinke we till we prove more, not lesse than *men,*
And turne not *beasts* but *Angels.* Let the King,
Me ever into these his *Cellars* bring.
Where flowes such wine, as we can have of none
But *Him* who trod the *Wine-presse* all alone.   40
Wine of youth, life, and the sweet deaths of love,
Wine of immortall mixture; which can prove
Its tincture from the rosy *nectar;* wine,
That can exalt weake earth, and so refine
Our dust, that in one draught, Mortality   45
May drinke it self up, and forget to dy.

On the assumption

Hark! she is call'd, the parting houre is come.
Take thy farewell, poore world! Heav'n must goe home.
A peece of Heav'nly Earth, purer and brighter
Than the chast stars, whose choice lamps come to light her,
While through the Christall orbes, clearer than they,   5
She climbs; and makes a farre more milky way.

29 *enow:* enough.
30 *Sack:* white wine.
40 See Isaiah 63:3.
43 *tincture:* infusion of a particular quality.
ON THE ASSUMPTION.
   5 *orbes:* "the concentric hollow spheres supposed to surround the earth and carry the planets and stars with them in their revolution" (OED).

She's call'd. Harke how the deare immortall *Dove*
Sighes to his silver mate. *Rise up my Love,*
 Rise up my faire, my spotlesse one,
 The winters past, the Rain is gone: 10
 The spring is come, the Flowers appeare,
 No sweets but thou are wanting here.
    Come away my love,
    Come away my dove,
      Cast off delay: 15
   The Court of Heav'n is come,
   To waite upon thee home;
    Come, come away.
   ————— The Flowers appeare,
  Or quickly would, were thou once here. 20
  The spring is come; Or if it stay,
  'Tis to keepe time with thy delay.
The raine is gone, Except as much as wee,
Detain in needfull *Teares,* to weep the want of thee.
    ————— The winters past, 25
   Or if he make lesse haste,
   His answer is, Why, she doth so;
If summer come not, how can winter go?
   Come away, come away,
The shrill winds chide, the waters weep thy stay, 30
The fountaines murmure; and each loftiest Tree,
Bowes lowest his leavy top, to looke for thee.
   Come away my love,
   Come away my dove, &c.
She's call'd again; And will she goe?   35
When Heav'n bids come, who can say No?
Heav'n calls her, and she must away,
Heav'n will not, and she cannot stay.
Goe then, goe (*glorious*) on the golden wings
Of the bright youth of Heav'n that sings 40
Under so sweet a burden, *Goe,*
Since thy dread *Son* will have it so.
And while thou goest, our Song and wee,

8–13 See Song of Solomon 2:10–14.

Will as wee may reach after thee.
   Haile, holy Queen, of humble Hearts! 45
   We in thy praise wil have our parts.
And though thy dearest lookes must now be light
To none but the blest heavens, whose bright
Beholders lost in sweet delight,
Feed for ever their faire sight 50
With those divinest eyes, which wee
And our darke world no more shall see;
Though our poore joyes are parted so,
Yet shall our lips never let goe
Thy gracious name, but to the last 55
Our loving song shall hold it fast.
   Thy precious Name shall bee
   Thy self to us, and wee
   With holy care will keep it by us.
      Wee to the last 60
      Will hold it fast;
   And no Assumption shall deny us.
      All the sweetest showers
      Of our fairest flowers,
Will wee strow upon it; 65
      Though our sweets cannot make
      It sweeter, they can take
   Themselves new sweetnesse from it.
  Maria, Men and Angels sing,
  Maria, Mother of our King. 70
Live, Rosie Princesse, live, and may the bright
Crowne of a most incomparable light
Embrace thy radiant browes: O may the best
Of everlasting joyes bath thy white brest.
   Live our chaste love, the holy mirth 75
   Of heav'n, the Humble pride of Earth.
   Live, crowne of women, Queen of men;
   Live Mistrisse of our Song; And when
   Our weake desires have done their best,
   Sweet Angels come, and sing the Rest. 80

75 *mirth:* joy, happiness.

Charitas nimia, or
the deare bargain

Lord, what is man? why should he cost you
So deare? what had his ruine lost you?
Lord what is man, that thou hast over-bought
   So much a thing of nought?
Love is too kind, I see, and can   5
Make but a simple Merchant man;
'T was for such sorry merchandise
Bold Painters have put out his eyes.
Alas sweet Lord, what wer't to thee
If there were no such wormes as wee?   10
 Heav'n ne're the lesse still Heav'n would bee,
    Should mankind dwell
    In the deep hell,
 What have his woes to doe with thee?
    Let him goe weepe   15
    O're his own wounds;
    Seraphims will not sleep,
Nor *Spheares* let fall their faithfull rounds;
  Still would the youthfull spirits sing,
  And still the spacious Palace ring: 20
Still would those beautious ministers of light
    Burn all as bright,
  And bow their flaming heads before thee;
Still Thrones and Dominations would adore thee;
Still would those wakeful sonnes of fire   25
    Keep warm thy praise
    Both nights and daies,

CHARITAS NIMIA: excessive love.
 7 *sorry merchandise:* poor trading.
 24 *Thrones and Dominations:* the third and fourth ranks in the nine orders
of angels (seraphim and cherubim forming the first two ranks).

And teach thy lov'd name to their noble Lire.
    Let froward dust then doe its kind,
And give it selfe for sport to the proud wind;   30
Why should a piece of peevish clay plead shares
In the Eternitie of thy old cares?
Why should'st thou bow thy awfull brest to see
What mine own madnesses have done with mee?
    Should not the King still keep his Throne   35
    Because some desperate foole's undone?
    Or will the world's illustrious eyes
    Weepe for every worme that dyes?
        Will the gallant Sun
        E're the lesse glorious run?   40
    Will he hang down his Golden head,
Or e're the sooner seeke his western bed,
        Because some foolish flye
        Growes wanton, and will dye?
    If I was lost in miserie,   45
    What was it to thy heav'n and thee?
    What was it to thy pretious bloud
    If My foule heart call'd for a floud?
    What if my faithlesse soule and I
        Would needs fall in   50
        With Guilt and sin?
What did the *Lamb* that he should dy?
What did the *Lamb* that he should need,
When the Woolfe sinnes, himselfe to bleed?
        If my base lust   55
Bargain'd with death, and well-beseeming dust;
        Why should the white
        Lamb's bosome write
        The purple name,
        Of my sins shame?   60
    Why should his unstain'd brest make good
    My blushes with his own Heart-blood?

---

29 *froward:* perverse; *doe its kind:* act in accord with its nature.
56 *well-beseeming:* well-appearing.

O my *Saviour*, make me see,
How dearely thou hast paid for mee,
That *Lost* again, my life may prove,   65
As then in *Death*, so now in *Love*.

ANDREW MARVELL
1621–1678

A Dialogue, between the Resolved Soul, and Created Pleasure

Courage my Soul, now learn to wield
The weight of thine immortal Shield.
Close on thy Head thy Helmet bright.
Ballance thy Sword against the Fight.
See where an Army, strong as fair,   5
With silken Banners spreads the air.
Now, if thou bee'st that thing Divine,
In this day's Combat let it shine:
And shew that Nature wants an Art
To conquer one resolved Heart.   10

Pleasure

Welcome the Creations Guest,
Lord of Earth, and Heavens Heir.
Lay aside that Warlike Crest,
And of Nature's banquet share:
Where the Souls of fruits and flow'rs   15
Stand prepar'd to heighten yours.

Soul

I sup above, and cannot stay
To bait so long upon the way.

A DIALOGUE, BETWEEN THE RESOLVED SOUL, AND CREATED PLEASURE.
   1–4 See Ephesians 6:16–17.
   9 *wants:* lacks.
   18 *bait:* stop for food.

[291]

Pleasure

On these downy Pillows lye,
Whose soft Plumes will thither fly: 20
On these Roses strow'd so plain
Lest one Leaf thy Side should strain.

Soul

My gentler Rest is on a Thought,
Conscious of doing what I ought.

Pleasure

If thou bee'st with Perfumes pleas'd,   25
Such as oft the Gods appeas'd,
Thou in fragrant Clouds shalt show
Like another God below.

Soul

A Soul that knowes not to presume
Is Heaven's and its own perfume.   30

Pleasure

Every thing does seem to vie
Which should first attract thine Eye:
But since none deserves that grace,
In this Crystal view *thy* face.

21 *strow'd:* strewn; *plain:* level.
27 *show:* appear.

[292]

Soul

When the Creator's skill is priz'd,   35
The rest is all but Earth disguis'd.

Pleasure

Heark how Musick then prepares
For thy Stay these charming Aires;
Which the posting Winds recall,
And suspend the Rivers Fall.   40

Soul

Had I but any time to lose,
On this I would it all dispose.
Cease Tempter. None can chain a mind
Whom this sweet Chordage cannot bind.

Chorus

Earth cannot shew so brave a Sight   45
As when a single Soul does fence
The Batteries of alluring Sense,
And Heaven views it with delight.
    Then persevere: for still new Charges sound:
    And if thou overcom'st thou shalt be crown'd.   50

39 "which call back the rushing winds."
45 *brave:* splendid.

Pleasure

All this fair, and soft, and sweet,
   Which scatteringly doth shine,
Shall within one Beauty meet,
   And she be only thine.

Soul

If things of Sight such Heavens be,   55
What Heavens are those we cannot see?

Pleasure

Where so e're thy Foot shall go
   The minted Gold shall lie;
Till thou purchase all below,
   And want new Worlds to buy.   60

Soul

Wer't not a price who'ld value Gold?
And that's worth nought that can be sold.

Pleasure

Wilt thou all the Glory have
   That War or Peace commend?
Half the World shall be thy Slave   65
   The other half thy Friend.

51 *soft:* see NOTE.
61 *a price:* a sum of money.

Soul

What Friends, if to my self untrue?
What Slaves, unless I captive you?

Pleasure

Thou shalt know each hidden Cause;
   And see the future Time: 70
Try what depth the Centre draws;
   And then to Heaven climb.

Soul

None thither mounts by the degree
Of Knowledge, but Humility.

Chorus

Triumph, triumph, victorious Soul;   75
The World has not one Pleasure more:
The rest does lie beyond the Pole,
And is thine everlasting Store.

71 *Centre:* earth.
78 *Store:* stock (of pleasures).

A Dialogue between the Soul and Body

Soul

O who shall, from this Dungeon, raise
A Soul inslav'd so many wayes?
With bolts of Bones, that fetter'd stands
In Feet; and manacled in Hands.
Here blinded with an Eye; and there   5
Deaf with the drumming of an Ear.
A Soul hung up, as 'twere, in Chains
Of Nerves, and Arteries, and Veins.
Tortur'd, besides each other part,
In a vain Head, and double Heart.   10

Body

O who shall me deliver whole,
From bonds of this Tyrannic Soul?
Which, stretcht upright, impales me so,
That mine own Precipice I go;
And warms and moves this needless Frame: 15
(A Fever could but do the same.)
And, wanting where its spight to try,
Has made me live to let me dye.
A Body that could never rest,
Since this ill Spirit it possest.   20

Soul

What Magick could me thus confine
Within anothers Grief to pine?
Where whatsoever it complain,
I feel, that cannot feel, the pain.
And all my Care its self employes,   25
That to preserve, which me destroys:
Constrain'd not only to indure
Diseases, but, whats worse, the Cure:
And ready oft the Port to gain,
Am Shipwrackt into Health again.   30

Body

But Physick yet could never reach
The Maladies Thou me dost teach;
Whom first the Cramp of Hope does Tear:
And then the Palsie Shakes of Fear.
The Pestilence of Love does heat: 35
Or Hatred's hidden Ulcer eat.
Joy's chearful Madness does perplex:
Or Sorrow's other Madness vex.
Which Knowledge forces me to know;
And Memory will not foregoe.   40
What but a Soul could have the wit
To build me up for Sin so fit?
So Architects do square and hew,
Green Trees that in the Forest grew.

A DIALOGUE BETWEEN THE SOUL AND BODY.
  31 *Physick:* medicine.
  41 *wit:* ingenuity.

Clorinda and Damon

C. *Damon* come drive thy flocks this way.
D. No: 'tis too late they went astray.
C. I have a grassy Scutcheon spy'd,
    Where *Flora* blazons all her pride.
    The Grass I aim to feast thy Sheep: 5
    The Flow'rs I for thy Temples keep.
D. Grass withers; and the Flow'rs too fade.
C. Seize the short Joyes then, ere they vade.
    Seest thou that unfrequented Cave?
D. That den? *C.* Loves Shrine. *D.* But Virtue's Grave. 10
C. In whose cool bosome we may lye
    Safe from the Sun. *D.* not Heaven's Eye.
C. Near this, a Fountaines liquid Bell
    Tinkles within the concave Shell.
D. Might a Soul bath there and be clean,   15
    Or slake its Drought? *C.* What is't you mean?
D. These once had been enticing things,
    Clorinda, Pastures, Caves, and Springs.
C. And what late change? *D.* The other day
    Pan met me. *C.* What did great *Pan* say?   20
D. Words that transcend poor Shepherds skill,
    But He ere since my Songs does fill:
    And his Name swells my slender Oate.
C. Sweet must *Pan* sound in *Damons* Note.

CLORINDA AND DAMON.

  2 *late:* lately, recently.

  3 *Scutcheon:* a shield bearing a coat of arms.

  4 *Flora:* goddess of flowers; *blazons:* paints brightly, as in creating a coat of arms.

  8 *vade:* pass away.

  20 *Pan:* since *pan* in Greek means "all", the name was traditionally used to imply Christ, as it does to Damon; but Clorinda may still be thinking of the pagan god of flocks and shepherds.

D. *Clorinda's* voice might make it sweet.   25
C. Who would not in *Pan's* Praises meet?

Chorus

Of Pan *the flowry Pastures sing,*
Caves eccho, and the Fountains ring.
Sing then while he doth us inspire;
For all the World is our Pan's *Quire.*   30

On a Drop of Dew

See how the Orient Dew,
Shed from the Bosom of the Morn
  Into the blowing Roses,
Yet careless of its Mansion new;
For the clear Region where 'twas born   5
  Round in its self incloses:
  And in its little Globes Extent,
Frames as it can its native Element.
  How it the purple flow'r does slight,
    Scarce touching where it lyes,   10
  But gazing back upon the Skies,
    Shines with a mournful Light;
      Like its own Tear,
Because so long divided from the Sphear.
  Restless it roules and unsecure,   15
    Trembling lest it grow impure:
  Till the warm Sun pitty it's Pain,
And to the Skies exhale it back again.
  So the Soul, that Drop, that Ray

ON A DROP OF DEW.
  1 *Orient:* shining, brilliant.
  3 *blowing:* blooming.
  5 *For:* because of.
  6 "closes itself in within its own round shape."
  8 *Frames:* creates.
  14 *Sphear:* the heavens.

[299]

Of the clear Fountain of Eternal Day,   20
Could it within the humane flow'r be seen,
    Remembring still its former height,
    Shuns the sweat leaves and blossoms green;
    And, recollecting its own Light,
Does, in its pure and circling thoughts, express   25
The greater Heaven in an Heaven less.
    In how coy a Figure wound,
    Every way it turns away:
    So the World excluding round,
    Yet receiving in the Day.   30
    Dark beneath, but bright above:
    Here disdaining, there in Love.
  How loose and easie hence to go:
  How girt and ready to ascend.
  Moving but on a point below,   35
  It all about does upwards bend.
Such did the Manna's sacred Dew destil;
White, and intire, though congeal'd and chill.
Congeal'd on Earth: but does, dissolving, run
Into the Glories of th' Almighty Sun.   40

The Coronet

When for the Thorns with which I long, too long,
  With many a piercing wound,
  My Saviours head have crown'd,
I seek with Garlands to redress that Wrong:
  Through every Garden, every Mead,   5
I gather flow'rs (my fruits are only flow'rs)

24 *recollecting*: drawing together, concentrating.
27 *coy*: reserved.
37–40 See Exodus 16:13–31.
THE CORONET.
  5 *Mead*: meadow.

Dismantling all the fragrant Towers
That once adorn'd my Shepherdesses head.
And now when I have summ'd up all my store,
 Thinking (so I my self deceive)   10
 So rich a Chaplet thence to weave
As never yet the king of Glory wore:
 Alas I find the Serpent old
 That, twining in his speckled breast,
 About the flow'rs disguis'd does fold,   15
 With wreaths of Fame and Interest.
Ah, foolish Man, that would'st debase with them,
And mortal Glory, Heavens Diadem!
But thou who only could'st the Serpent tame,
Either his slipp'ry knots at once untie,   20
And disintangle all his winding Snare:
Or shatter too with him my curious frame:
And let these wither, so that he may die,
Though set with Skill and chosen out with Care.
That they, while Thou on both their Spoils dost tread, 25
May crown thy Feet, that could not crown thy Head.

To his Coy Mistress

Had we but World enough, and Time,
This coyness Lady were no crime.
We would sit down, and think which way
To walk, and pass our long Loves Day.
Thou by the *Indian Ganges* side   5
Should'st Rubies find: I by the Tide
Of *Humber* would complain. I would

11 *Chaplet:* wreath.
16 *Interest:* personal advantage.
22 *curious frame:* ingenious construction (of poetry).
TO HIS COY MISTRESS.
 2 *coyness:* shyness, reserve.

Love you ten years before the Flood:
And you should if you please refuse
Till the Conversion of the *Jews*.   10
My vegetable Love should grow
Vaster then Empires, and more slow.
An hundred years should go to praise
Thine Eyes, and on thy Forehead Gaze.
Two hundred to adore each Breast: 15
But thirty thousand to the rest.
An Age at least to every part,
And the last Age should show your Heart.
For Lady you deserve this State;
Nor would I love at lower rate.   20
    But at my back I alwaies hear
Times winged Charriot hurrying near:
And yonder all before us lye
Desarts of vast Eternity.
Thy Beauty shall no more be found;   25
Nor, in thy marble Vault, shall sound
My ecchoing Song: then Worms shall try
That long preserv'd Virginity:
And your quaint Honour turn to dust;
And into ashes all my Lust.   30
The Grave's a fine and private place,
But none I think do there embrace.
    Now therefore, while the youthful hew
Sits on thy skin like morning glew,
And while thy willing Soul transpires   35
At every pore with instant Fires,
Now let us sport us while we may;
And now, like am'rous birds of prey,
Rather at once our Time devour,

19 *State:* pomp, ceremony.
20 *rate:* valuation.
27 *try:* test.
29 *quaint:* fine, elegant, unusual, odd, fastidious, prim.
34 *glew:* glow; see NOTE.
35 *transpires:* passes out as vapor, "breathes through" (Latin *transpiro*).
36 *instant:* urgent (Latin *instans*).

[302]

Than languish in his slow-chapt pow'r.   40
Let us roll all our Strength, and all
Our sweetness, up into one Ball:
And tear our Pleasures with rough strife,
Thorough the Iron gates of Life.
Thus, though we cannot make our Sun   45
Stand still, yet we will make him run.

The Gallery

I.

Clora come view my Soul, and tell
Whether I have contriv'd it well.
Now all its several lodgings lye
Compos'd into one Gallery;
And the great *Arras*-hangings, made   5
Of various Faces, by are laid;
That, for all furniture, you'l find
Only your Picture in my Mind.

II.

Here Thou art painted in the Dress
Of an Inhumane Murtheress;   10
Examining upon our Hearts
Thy fertile Shop of cruel Arts:

40 *slow-chapt:* slow-jawed (slow in eating).

45–46 *make our Sun Stand still:* as Joshua did (Joshua 10:12–13), or as Zeus did, in his seduction of Alcmene.

THE GALLERY.

5 *Arras-hangings:* tapestries, so called from the French town noted for their manufacture.

7 *furniture:* furnishings in general, including tapestries and paintings.

11 *Examining:* testing.

Engines more keen than ever yet
Adorned Tyrants Cabinet;
Of which the most tormenting are   15
Black Eyes, red Lips, and curled Hair.

III.

But, on the other side, th' art drawn
Like to *Aurora* in the Dawn;
When in the East she slumb'ring lyes,
And stretches out her milky Thighs;   20
While all the morning Quire does sing,
And *Manna* falls, and Roses spring;
And, at thy Feet, the wooing Doves
Sit perfecting their harmless Loves.

IV.

Like an Enchantress here thou show'st,   25
Vexing thy restless Lover's Ghost;
And, by a Light obscure, dost rave
Over his Entrails, in the Cave;
Divining thence, with horrid Care,
How long thou shalt continue fair;   30
And (when inform'd) them throw'st away,
To be the greedy Vultur's prey.

V.

But, against that, thou sit'st a float
Like *Venus* in her pearly Boat.

13 *Engines:* contrivances.
14 *Cabinet:* private room (here with ironic ref. to such a room used to display works of art or treasures).

The *Halcyons*, calming all that's nigh,   35
Betwixt the Air and Water fly.
Or, if some rowling Wave appears,
A Mass of Ambergris it bears.
Nor blows more Wind than what may well
Convoy the Perfume to the Smell.   40

VI.

These Pictures and a thousand more,
 Of Thee, my Gallery does store;
In all the Forms thou can'st invent
Either to please me, or torment:
For thou alone to people me,   45
Art grown a num'rous Colony;
And a Collection choicer far
Then or *White-hall's*, or *Mantua's* were.

VII.

But, of these Pictures and the rest,
That at the Entrance likes me best: 50
Where the same Posture, and the Look
Remains, with which I first was took.
A tender Shepherdess, whose Hair
Hangs loosely playing in the Air,
Transplanting Flow'rs from the green Hill,   55
To crown her Head, and Bosome fill.

42 *does:* first ed. reads *dost,* which is ungrammatical; the emendation "do"
(with "Pictures" as subject) is also possible.

48 King Charles I was an art collector of excellent taste, and his palace of
Whitehall was filled with fine paintings, some acquired by the purchase of the
collection of the Duke of Mantua.

The Definition of Love

I.

My Love is of a birth as rare
As 'tis for object strange and high:
It was begotten by despair
Upon Impossibility.

II.

Magnanimous Despair alone   5
Could show me so divine a thing,
Where feeble Hope could ne'r have flown
But vainly flapt its Tinsel Wing.

III.

And yet I quickly might arrive
Where my extended Soul is fixt,   10
But Fate does Iron wedges drive,
And alwaies crouds it self betwixt.

IV.

For Fate with jealous Eye does see
Two perfect Loves; nor lets them close:
Their union would her ruine be,   15
And her Tyrannick pow'r depose.

[306]

V.

And therefore her Decrees of Steel
Us as the distant Poles have plac'd,
 (Though Loves whole World on us doth wheel)
Not by themselves to be embrac'd.   20

VI.

Unless the giddy Heaven fall,
And Earth some new Convulsion tear;
And, us to joyn, the World should all
Be cramp'd into a *Planisphere*.

VII.

As Lines so Loves *oblique* may well   25
Themselves in every Angle greet:
But ours so truly *Paralel*,
Though infinite can never meet.

VIII.

Therefore the Love which us doth bind,
But Fate so enviously debarrs,   30
Is the Conjunction of the Mind,
And Opposition of the Stars.

THE DEFINITION OF LOVE.

24 *Planisphere:* an astronomical instrument in which the circles of the heavens were projected on the two sides of a round plate, with the poles thus brought together (*World* here seems to mean "universe"); but the planisphere could also be a similar flat projection of the earth.

The Nymph complaining for the death of her *Faun*

The wanton Troopers riding by
Have shot my Faun and it will dye.
Ungentle men! They cannot thrive
To kill thee. Thou neer didst alive
Them any harm: alas nor cou'd   5
Thy death yet do them any good.
I'me sure I never wisht them ill;
Nor do I for all this; nor will:
But, if my simple Pray'rs may yet
Prevail with Heaven to forget   10
Thy murder, I will Joyn my Tears
Rather then fail. But, O my fears!
It cannot dye so. Heavens King
Keeps register of every thing:
And nothing may we use in vain.   15
Ev'n Beasts must be with justice slain;
Else Men are made their *Deodands*.
Though they should wash their guilty hands
In this warm life-blood, which doth part
From thine, and wound me to the Heart,   20
Yet could they not be clean: their Stain
Is dy'd in such a Purple Grain.
There is not such another in
The World, to offer for their Sin.
   Unconstant *Sylvio*, when yet   25
I had not found him counterfeit,
One morning (I remember well)

THE NYMPH COMPLAINING.

1 *wanton:* unruly, having no regard for justice or humanity; *Troopers:* cavalrymen.

17 *Deodands:* referring to the law that any animal or object which caused a man's death was to be forfeited to the Crown to be used for charity; from Latin *Deo dandum:* "to be given to God."

Ty'd in this silver Chain and Bell,
Gave it to me: nay and I know
What he said then; I'me sure I do.   30
Said He, look how your Huntsman here
Hath taught a Faun to hunt his *Dear*.
But *Sylvio* soon had me beguil'd.
This waxed tame, while he grew wild,
And quite regardless of my Smart,   35
Left me his Faun, but took his Heart.

Thenceforth I set my self to play
My solitary time away,
With this: and very well content,
Could so mine idle Life have spent.   40
For it was full of sport; and light
Of foot, and heart; and did invite,
Me to its game: it seem'd to bless
Its self in me. How could I less
Than love it? O I cannot be   45
Unkind, t' a Beast that loveth me.

Had it liv'd long, I do not know
Whether it too might have done so
As *Sylvio* did: his Gifts might be
Perhaps as false or more than he.   50
But I am sure, for ought that I
Could in so short a time espie,
Thy Love was far more better then
The love of false and cruel men.

With sweetest milk, and sugar, first   55
I it at mine own fingers nurst.
And as it grew, so every day
It wax'd more white and sweet than they.
It had so sweet a Breath! And oft
I blusht to see its foot more soft,   60
And white, (shall I say then my hand?)

34 *waxed:* grew.
43–44 See Jeremiah 4:3: "the nations shall bless themselves in him" (the Lord).

NAY any Ladies of the Land.
   It is a wond'rous thing, how fleet
'Twas on those little silver feet.
With what a pretty skipping grace,   65
It oft would challenge me the Race:
And when 'thad left me far away,
'Twould stay, and run again, and stay.
For it was nimbler much than Hindes;
And trod, as on the four Winds.   70
   I have a Garden of my own,
But so with Roses over grown,
And Lillies, that you would it guess
To be a little Wilderness.
And all the Spring time of the year   75
It onely loved to be there.
Among the beds of Lillyes, I
Have sought it oft, where it should lye;
Yet could not, till it self would rise,
Find it, although before mine Eyes.   80
For, in the flaxen Lillies shade,
It like a bank of Lillies laid.
Upon the Roses it would feed,
Until its Lips ev'n seem'd to bleed:
And then to me 'twould boldly trip,   85
And print those Roses on my Lip.
But all its chief delight was still
On Roses thus its self to fill:
And its pure virgin Limbs to fold
In whitest sheets of Lillies cold.   90
Had it liv'd long, it would have been
Lillies without, Roses within.
   O help! O help! I see it faint:
And dye as calmely as a Saint.
See how it weeps. The Tears do come   95

71-92 Evoking the imagery of garden, rose, lillies, and "young hart" found in the Song of Solomon 2-6; esp. 2:16: "he feedeth among the lillies"; see also 3:1: "I sought him whom my soul loveth."

Sad, slowly dropping like a Gumme.
So weeps the wounded Balsome: so
The holy Frankincense doth flow.
The brotherless *Heliades*
Melt in such Amber Tears as these.   100
   I in a golden Vial will
Keep these two crystal Tears; and fill
It till it do o'reflow with mine;
Then place it in *Diana's* Shrine.
   Now my Sweet Faun is vanish'd to   105
Whether the Swans and Turtles go:
In fair *Elizium* to endure,
With milk-white Lambs, and Ermins pure.
O do not run too fast: for I
Will but bespeak thy Grave, and dye.   110
   First my unhappy Statue shall
Be cut in Marble; and withal,
Let it be weeping too: but there
Th' Engraver sure his Art may spare;
For I so truly thee bemoane,   115
That I shall weep though I be Stone:
Until my Tears, still dropping, wear
My breast, themselves engraving there.
There at my feet shalt thou be laid,
Of purest Alabaster made: 120
For I would have thine Image be
White as I can, though not as Thee.

---

98 *Frankincense:* gained from the gum of a tree.

99 *Heliades:* the three sisters of Phaeton, daughters of the Sun, who were changed into willow trees, and their tears into amber.

106 *Turtles:* turtle-doves.

110 *bespeak:* order, reserve.

116 Like Niobe, whose grief transformed her into a statue that wept forever.

An *Horatian* Ode upon *Cromwel's* Return from *Ireland*

The forward Youth that would appear
Must now forsake his *Muses* dear,
 Nor in the Shadows sing
 His Numbers languishing.
'Tis time to leave the Books in dust,   5
And oyl th' unused Armours rust:
 Removing from the Wall
 The Corslet of the Hall.
So restless *Cromwel* could not cease
In the inglorious Arts of Peace,   10
 But through adventrous War
 Urged his active Star.
And, like the three-fork'd Lightning, first
Breaking the Clouds where it was nurst,
 Did through his own Side   15
 His fiery way divide.
For 'tis all one to Courage high
The Emulous or Enemy;
 And with such to inclose
 Is more then to oppose.   20
Then burning through the Air he went,
And Pallaces and Temples rent:
 And *Cæsars* head at last

AN HORATIAN ODE: Cromwell returned from Ireland in May 1650 and began his campaign in Scotland in July 1650; the poem was evidently written within this interval of time.

1 *forward:* eager, spirited.

12 *active Star:* the star whose supposed astrological influence affects his life.

15 *Side:* (1) group or party; (2) the side of the cloud.

19–20 "To inclose such a man within the rivals on his own side is worse than to fight him as an enemy."

23 *Caesar* was a generic term for a ruler; here Charles I, who was beheaded by the Parliamentary forces on January 30, 1649.

Did through his Laurels blast.
'Tis Madness to resist or blame   25
The force of angry·Heavens flame:
  And, if we would speak true,
  Much to the Man is due.
Who, from his private Gardens, where
He liv'd reserved and austere,   30
  As if his highest plot
  To plant the Bergamot,
Could by industrious Valour climbe
To ruine the great Work of Time,
  And cast the Kingdome old   35
  Into another Mold.
Though Justice against Fate complain,
And plead the antient Rights in vain:
  But those do hold or break
  As Men are strong or weak.   40
Nature that hateth emptiness,
Allows of penetration less:
  And therefore must make room
  Where greater Spirits come.
What Field of all the Civil Wars,   45
Where his were not the deepest Scars?
  And *Hampton* shows what part
  He had of wiser Art.
Where, twining subtile fears with hope,
He wove a Net of such a scope,   50
  That *Charles* himself might chase
  To *Caresbrooks* narrow case.
That thence the *Royal Actor* born
The *Tragick Scaffold* might adorn:
  While round the armed Bands   55
  Did clap their bloody hands.

32 *Bergamot:* a variety of pear.

42 *penetration:* "occupation of the same space by two bodies at the same time" (OED).

47–52 In November 1647 Charles I fled from his palace at Hampton Court to Carisbrooke Castle on the Isle of Wight, an action that weakened his position.

52 *case:* condition, plight; also a box (prison).

He nothing common did or mean
Upon that memorable Scene:
 But with his keener Eye
 The Axes edge did try: 60
Nor call'd the *Gods* with vulgar spight
To vindicate his helpless Right,
 But bow'd his comely Head,
 Down as upon a Bed.
This was that memorable Hour   65
Which first assur'd the forced Pow'r.
 So when they did design
 The *Capitols* first Line,
A bleeding Head where they begun,
Did fright the Architects to run;   70
 And yet in that the *State*
 Foresaw it's happy Fate.
And now the *Irish* are asham'd
To see themselves in one Year tam'd:
 So much one Man can do,   75
 That does both act and know.
They can affirm his Praises best,
And have, though overcome, confest
 How good he is, how just,
 And fit for highest Trust: 80
Nor yet grown stiffer with Command,
But still in the *Republick's* hand:
 How fit he is to sway
 That can so well obey.
He to the *Common Feet* presents   85
A *Kingdome,* for his first years rents:
 And, what he may, forbears
 His Fame to make it theirs:

60 *try:* test.

68–72 At the building of the Capitol, the temple of Jupiter on the Capitoline Hill in Rome, a human head was allegedly found; this was interpreted as a good omen.

85 *Common:* public, pertaining to the common body of people; (usually emended to "Commons").

And has his Sword and Spoyls ungirt,
To lay them at the *Publick's* skirt.   90
  So when the Falcon high
  Falls heavy from the Sky,
She, having kill'd, no more does search,
But on the next green Bow to pearch;
  Where, when he first does lure,   95
  The Falckner has her sure.
What may not then our *Isle* presume
While Victory his Crest does plume!
  What may not others fear
  If thus he crown each Year!   100
A *Cæsar* he ere long to *Gaul*,
To *Italy* an *Hannibal*,
  And to all States not free
  Shall *Clymacterick* be.
The *Pict* no shelter now shall find   105
Within his party-colour'd Mind;
  But from this Valour sad
  Shrink underneath the Plad:
Happy if in the tufted brake
The *English Hunter* him mistake;   110
  Nor lay his Hounds in near
  The *Caledonian* Deer.
But thou the Wars and Fortunes Son
March indefatigably on;
  And for the last effect   115
  Still keep thy Sword erect:

95 *lure:* a technical term from falconry, meaning to recall the hawk by means of the *lure:* "an apparatus used by falconers . . . constructed of a bunch of feathers, to which is attached a long cord" (OED).

104 *Clymacterick:* "constituting an important epoch or crisis" (OED).

105 *Pict:* Scot; thought to be derived from Latin *pictus,* painted, colored (see next line).

106 *party-colour'd;* multi-colored (as in a Scotch plaid), that is, devious, deceptive; also colored with party-prejudice, partisan.

107 *sad:* steadfast, firm.

109 *brake:* clump of bushes.

Besides the force it has to fright
The Spirits of the shady Night,
  The same *Arts* that did *gain*
  A *Pow'r* must it *maintain*.   120

The Mower against Gardens

Luxurious Man, to bring his Vice in use,
  Did after him the World seduce:
And from the fields the Flow'rs and Plants allure,
  Where Nature was most plain and pure.
He first enclos'd within the Gardens square   5
  A dead and standing pool of Air:
And a more luscious Earth for them did knead,
  Which stupifi'd them while it fed.
The Pink grew then as double as his Mind;
  The nutriment did change the kind.   10
With strange perfumes he did the Roses taint.
  And Flow'rs themselves were taught to paint.
The Tulip, white, did for complexion seek;
  And learn'd to interline its cheek:
Its Onion root they then so high did hold,   15
  That one was for a Meadow sold.
Another World was search'd, through Oceans new,
  To find the *Marvel of Peru.*
And yet these Rarities might be allow'd,
  To Man, that sov'raign thing and proud;   20
Had he not dealt between the Bark and Tree,
  Forbidden mixtures there to see.
No Plant now knew the Stock from which it came;
  He grafts upon the Wild the Tame:
That the uncertain and adult'rate fruit   25
  Might put the Palate in dispute.

117–118 Since the hilt of a sword forms a cross, it was thought to ward off
evil spirits.

His green *Seraglio* has its Eunuchs too;
    Lest any Tyrant him out-doe.
And in the Cherry he does Nature vex,
    To procreate without a Sex.   30
'Tis all enforc'd; the Fountain and the Grot;
    While the sweet Fields do lye forgot:
Where willing Nature does to all dispence
    A wild and fragrant Innocence:
And *Fauns* and *Faryes* do the Meadows till,   35
    More by their presence then their skill.
Their Statues polish'd by some ancient hand,
    May to adorn the Gardens stand:
But howso'ere the Figures do excel,
    The *Gods* themselves with us do dwell.   40

Damon the Mower

I.

Heark how the Mower *Damon* Sung,
With love of *Juliana* stung!
While ev'ry thing did seem to paint
    The Scene more fit for his complaint.
Like her fair Eyes the day was fair;   5
But scorching like his am'rous Care.
Sharp like his Sythe his Sorrow was,
And wither'd like his Hopes the Grass.

II.

Oh what unusual Heats are here,
Which thus our Sun-burn'd Meadows sear!   10
The Grass-hopper its pipe gives ore;
And hamstring'd Frogs can dance no more.

But in the brook the green Frog wades;
And Grass-hoppers seek out the shades.
Only the Snake, that kept within,   15
Now glitters in its second skin.

III.

This heat the Sun could never raise,
Nor Dog-star so inflame's the dayes.
It from an higher Beauty grow'th,
Which burns the Fields and Mower both: 20
Which made the Dog, and makes the Sun
Hotter than his own *Phaeton.*
Not *July* causeth these Extremes,
But *Juliana's* scorching beams.

IV.

Tell me where I may pass the Fires   25
Of the hot day, or hot desires.
To what cool Cave shall I descend,
Or to what gelid Fountain bend?
Alas! I look for Ease in vain,
When Remedies themselves complain.   30
No moisture but my Tears do rest,
Nor Cold but in her Icy Breast.

DAMON THE MOWER.

18 *Dog-star:* the star Sirius, whose rising supposedly influenced the "dog-days," the hottest days of the year.

22 *Phaeton:* son of Apollo, who scorched the earth and was killed by Zeus when he tried to drive the chariot of the Sun.

31 *rest:* remain.

V.

How long wilt Thou, fair Shepheardess,
Esteem me, and my Presents less?
To Thee the harmless Snake I bring,   35
Disarmed of its teeth and sting.
To Thee *Chameleons* changing-hue,
And Oak leaves tipt with hony due.
Yet Thou ungrateful hast not sought
Nor what they are, nor who them brought.   40

VI.

I am the Mower *Damon,* known
Through all the Meadows I have mown.
On me the Morn her dew distills
Before her darling Daffadils.
And, if at Noon my toil me heat,   45
The Sun himself licks off my Sweat.
While, going home, the Ev'ning sweet
In cowslip-water bathes my feet.

VII.

What, though the piping Shepherd stock
The plains with an unnum'red Flock,   50
This Sithe of mine discovers wide
More ground than all his Sheep do hide.
With this the golden fleece I shear
Of all these Closes ev'ry Year.

51 *discovers:* uncovers.
54 *Closes:* enclosed fields.

And though in Wooll more poor then they,   55
Yet am I richer far in Hay.

VIII.

Nor am I so deform'd to sight,
If in my Sithe I looked right;
In which I see my Picture done,
As in a crescent Moon the Sun.   60
The deathless Fairyes take me oft
To lead them in their Danses soft;
And, when I tune my self to sing,
About me they contract their Ring.

IX.

How happy might I still have mow'd,   65
Had not Love here his Thistles sow'd!
But now I all the day complain,
Joyning my Labour to my Pain;
And with my Sythe cut down the Grass,
Yet still my Grief is where it was: 70
But, when the Iron blunter grows,
Sighing I whet my Sythe and Woes.

X.

While thus he threw his Elbow round,
Depopulating all the Ground,
And, with his whistling Sythe, does cut   75
Each stroke between the Earth and Root,
The edged Stele by careless chance
Did into his own Ankle glance;

And there among the Grass fell down,
By his own Sythe, the Mower mown.   80

XI.

Alas! said He, these hurts are slight
To those that dye by Loves despight.
With Shepherds-purse, and Clowns-all-heal,
The Blood I stanch, and Wound I seal.
Only for him no Cure is found,   85
Whom *Julianas* Eyes do wound.
'Tis death alone that this must do:
For Death thou art a Mower too.

The Mower to the Glo-Worms

I.

Ye living Lamps, by whose dear light
The Nightingale does sit so late,
And studying all the Summer-night,
Her matchless Songs does meditate;

II.

Ye Country Comets, that portend   5
No War, nor Princes funeral,
Shining unto no higher end
Then to presage the Grasses fall;

83 Plants thought to have medicinal qualities.

III.

Ye Glo-worms, whose officious Flame
To wandring Mowers shows the way,   10
That in the Night have lost their aim,
And after foolish Fires do stray;

IV.

Your courteous Lights in vain you wast,
Since *Juliana* here is come,
For She my Mind hath so displac'd   15
That I shall never find my home.

The Mower's Song

I.

My Mind was once the true survey
Of all these Medows fresh and gay;
And in the greenness of the Grass
Did see its Hopes as in a Glass;
When *Juliana* came, and She   5
What I do to the Grass, does to my Thoughts and Me.

II.

But these, while I with Sorrow pine,
Grew more luxuriant still and fine;

THE MOWER TO THE GLO-WORMS.
9 *officious:* ready to serve or please.

That not one Blade of Grass you spy'd,
But had a Flower on either side;   10
When *Juliana* came, and She
What I do to the Grass, does to my Thoughts and Me.

III.

Unthankful Medows, could you so
A fellowship so true forego,
And in your gawdy May-games meet,   15
While I lay trodden under feet?
When *Juliana* came, and She
What I do to the Grass, does to my Thoughts and Me.

IV.

But what you in Compassion ought,
Shall now by my Revenge be wrought: 20
And Flow'rs, and Grass, and I and all,
Will in one common Ruine fall.
For *Juliana* comes, and She
What I do to the Grass, does to my Thoughts and Me.

V.

And thus, ye Meadows, which have been   25
Companions of my thoughts more green,
Shall now the Heraldry become
With which I shall adorn my Tomb;
For *Juliana* comes, and She
What I do to the Grass, does to my Thoughts and Me.   30

The Picture of little *T. C.* in a Prospect of Flowers

I.

See with what simplicity
This Nimph begins her golden daies!
In the green Grass she loves to lie,
And there with her fair Aspect tames
The Wilder flow'rs, and gives them names: 5
But only with the Roses playes;
     And them does tell
What Colour best becomes them, and what Smell.

II.

Who can foretel for what high cause
This Darling of the Gods was born!   10
Yet this is She whose chaster Laws
The wanton Love shall one day fear,
And, under her command severe,
See his Bow broke and Ensigns torn.
     Happy, who can   15
Appease this virtuous Enemy of Man!

THE PICTURE OF LITTLE T. C.
  4 *Aspect:* both her gaze and her appearance.
  5 *gives them names:* like Adam, Genesis 2:20.

III.

O then let me in time compound,
And parly with those conquering Eyes;
Ere they have try'd their force to wound,
Ere, with their glancing wheels, they drive   20
In Triumph over Hearts that strive,
And them that yield but more despise.
       Let me be laid,
Where I may see thy Glories from some Shade.

IV.

Mean time, whilst every verdant thing   25
It self does at thy Beauty charm,
Reform the errours of the Spring;
Make that the Tulips may have share
Of sweetness, seeing they are fair;
And Roses of their thorns disarm: 30
      But most procure
That Violets may a longer Age endure.

V.

But O young beauty of the Woods,
Whom Nature courts with fruits and flow'rs,
Gather the Flow'rs, but spare the Buds;   35
Lest *Flora* angry at thy crime,
To kill her Infants in their prime,
Do quickly make th' Example Yours;
      And, ere we see,
Nip in the blossome all our hopes and Thee.   40

17 *compound:* come to terms with.

The Garden

I.

How vainly men themselves amaze
To win the Palm, the Oke, or Bayes;
And their uncessant Labours see
Crown'd from some single Herb or Tree,
Whose short and narrow verged Shade   5
Does prudently their Toyles upbraid;
While all Flow'rs and all Trees do close
To weave the Garlands of repose.

II.

Fair quiet, have I found thee here,
And Innocence thy Sister dear!   10
Mistaken long, I sought you then
In busie Companies of Men.
Your sacred Plants, if here below,
Only among the Plants will grow.
Society is all but rude,   15
To this delicious Solitude.

THE GARDEN.

1 *amaze:* bewilder.

2 *Palm, Oke, Bayes:* wreaths symbolizing military, civic, and poetic achievement.

5 *verged:* brimmed, edged.

16 *To:* compared to.

III.

No white nor red was ever seen
So am'rous as this lovely green.
Fond Lovers, cruel as their Flame,
Cut in these Trees their Mistress name.   20
Little, Alas, they know, or heed,
How far these Beauties Hers exceed!
Fair Trees! where s'eer your barkes I wound,
No Name shall but your own be found.

IV.

When we have run our Passions heat,   25
Love hither makes his best retreat.
The *Gods*, that mortal Beauty chase,
Still in a Tree did end their race.
Apollo hunted *Daphne* so,
Only that She might Laurel grow.   30
And *Pan* did after *Syrinx* speed,
Not as a Nymph, but for a Reed.

V.

What wond'rous Life in this I lead!
Ripe Apples drop about my head;
The Luscious Clusters of the Vine   35
Upon my Mouth do crush their Wine;
The Nectaren, and curious Peach,
Into my hands themselves do reach;
Stumbling on Melons, as I pass,
Insnar'd with Flow'rs, I fall on Grass.   40

37 *curious:* exquisite.

VI.

Mean while the Mind, from pleasure less,
Withdraws into its happiness:
The Mind, that Ocean where each kind
Does streight its own resemblance find;
Yet it creates, transcending these,   45
Far other Worlds, and other Seas;
Annihilating all that's made
To a green Thought in a green Shade.

VII.

Here at the Fountains sliding foot,
Or at some Fruit-trees mossy root,   50
Casting the Bodies Vest aside,
My Soul into the boughs does glide:
There like a Bird it sits, and sings,
Then whets, and combs its silver Wings;
And, till prepar'd for longer flight,   55
Waves in its Plumes the various Light.

VIII.

Such was that happy Garden-state,
While Man there walk'd without a Mate:
After a Place so pure, and sweet,
What other Help could yet be meet!   60
But 'twas beyond a Mortal's share

41 *from pleasure less:* from lesser pleasure.
44 *streight:* confined, packed together; also, straightway, immediately.
47 *Annihilating:* a common term in mystical theology; see NOTE.
51 *Vest:* vesture (the body as clothing for the soul).
60 See Genesis 2:18.

To wander solitary there:
Two Paradises 'twere in one
To live in Paradise alone.

IX.

How well the skilful Gardner drew   65
Of flow'rs and herbes this Dial new;
Where from above the milder Sun
Does through a fragrant Zodiack run;
And, as it works, th' industrious Bee
Computes its time as well as we.   70
How could such sweet and wholsome Hours
Be reckon'd but with herbs and flow'rs!

Bermudas

Where the remote *Bermudas* ride
In th' Oceans bosome unespy'd,
From a small Boat, that row'd along,
The listning Winds receiv'd this Song.
   What should we do but sing his Praise   5
That led us through the watry Maze,
Unto an Isle so long unknown,
And yet far kinder than our own?
Where he the huge Sea-Monsters wracks,
That lift the Deep upon their Backs.   10
He lands us on a grassy Stage;
Safe from the Storms, and Prelat's rage.
He gave us this eternal Spring,
   Which here enamells every thing;

BERMUDAS.
  9 *wracks:* wrecks.
  14 *enamells:* beautifies with varied colors.

And sends the Fowl's to us in care,   15
On daily Visits through the Air.
He hangs in shades the Orange bright,
Like golden Lamps in a green Night.
And does in the Pomgranates close,
Jewels more rich than *Ormus* show's.   20
He makes the Figs our mouths to meet;
And throws the Melons at our feet.
But Apples plants of such a price,
No Tree could ever bear them twice.
With Cedars, chosen by his hand,   25
From *Lebanon,* he stores the Land.
And makes the hollow Seas, that roar,
Proclaime the Ambergris on shoar.
He cast (of which we rather boast)
The Gospels Pearl upon our Coast.   30
And in these Rocks for us did frame
A Temple, where to sound his Name.
Oh let our Voice his Praise exalt,
Till it arrive at Heavens Vault:
Which thence (perhaps) rebounding, may   35
Eccho beyond the *Mexique Bay.*
Thus sung they, in the *English* boat,
An holy and a chearful Note,
And all the way, to guide their Chime,
With falling Oars they kept the time.   40

20 *Ormus:* in the Persian Gulf, noted as a market for pearls and gems.
23 *Apples:* pineapples; *price:* value.
31 *frame:* construct.

HENRY VAUGHAN
1621?–1695

From SILEX SCINTILLANS (1650)
Authoris (de se) Emblema

Tentâsti, fateor, sine vulnere sœpius, & me
  Consultum voluit Vox, *sine voce, frequens;*
Ambivit placido divinior aura meatu,
  Et frustrà sancto murmure præmonuit.
Surdus eram, mutusq; Silex: *Tu, (quanta tuorum*   5
  Cura tibi est!) aliâ das renovare viâ,
Permutas Curam: Jamq; irritatus Amorem
  Posse negas, & vim, Vi, *superare paras,*
Accedis propior, molemq;, & Saxea *rumpis*
  Pectora, fitq; Caro, *quod fuit ante* Lapis.   10
En lacerum! Cœlosq; tuos ardentia tandem
  Fragmenta, & liquidas ex Adamante *genas.*
Sic olim undantes Petras, Scopulosq; *vomentes*
  Curâsti, O populi providus usq; tui!
Quam miranda tibi manus est! Moriendo, revixi;   15
  Et fractas *jam sum* ditior *inter* opes.

[The Author's Emblem (concerning himself)]

You have often touched me, I confess, without a wound, and your *Voice*, without a voice, has often sought to counsel me; your diviner breath has encompassed me with its calm motion, and in vain has cautioned me with its sacred murmur. I was deaf and dumb: a *Flint:* You (how great care you take of your own!) try to revive another way, you change the Remedy; and now angered you say that *Love* has no power, and you prepare to conquer force with *Force,* you come closer, you break through the *Rocky* barrier of my heart, and it is made *Flesh* that was before a *Stone*. Behold me torn asunder!

AUTHORIS (DE SE) EMBLEMA.
  13 See Exodus 17:6.

[333]

and at last the *Fragments* burning toward your skies, and the cheeks streaming with tears out of the *Adamant.* Thus once upon a time you made the *Rocks* flow and the *Crags* gush, oh ever provident of your people! How marvellous toward me is your hand! In *Dying,* I have been born again; and in the midst of my *shattered means* I am now *richer.*]

The Dedication

My God, thou that didst dye for me,
These thy deaths fruits I offer thee.
Death that to me was life, and light
But darke, and deep pangs to thy sight.
Some drops of thy all-quickning bloud
Fell on my heart, these made it bud
And put forth thus, though, Lord, before
The ground was curs'd, and void of store.
   Indeed, I had some here to hire
Which long resisted thy desire,
That ston'd thy Servants, and did move
To have thee murther'd for thy Love,
But, Lord, I have expell'd them, and so bent
Begge thou wouldst take thy Tenants Rent.

Regeneration

A Ward, and still in bonds, one day
      I stole abroad,
It was high-spring, and all the way
      Primros'd, and hung with shade;
    Yet, was it frost within,
        And surly winds
Blasted my infant buds, and sinne
    Like Clouds ecclips'd my mind.

5

2.

Storm'd thus; I straight perceiv'd my spring
    Meere stage, and show,   10
My walke a monstrous, mountain'd thing
   Rough-cast with Rocks, and snow;
   And as a Pilgrims Eye
    Far from reliefe,
Measures the melancholy skye   15
   Then drops, and rains for griefe,

3.

So sigh'd I upwards still, at last
    'Twixt steps, and falls
I reach'd the pinacle, where plac'd
   I found a paire of scales,   20
   I tooke them up and layd
    In th'one late paines,
The other smoake, and pleasures weigh'd
   But prov'd the heavier graines;

4.

With that, some cryed, *Away;* straight I   25
    Obey'd, and led
Full East, a faire, fresh field could spy
   Some call'd it, *Jacobs Bed;*
   A Virgin-soile, which no
    Rude feet ere trod,   30
Where (since he stept there,) only go
   Prophets, and friends of God.

REGENERATION: for stanza-form and journey of stanzas 1–4, see Herbert, "The Pilgrimage."
 27–28 See Genesis 28:10–22.

5.

Here, I repos'd; but scarse well set,
    A grove descryed
Of stately height, whose branches met   35
    And mixt on every side;
   I entred, and once in
     (Amaz'd to see't,)
Found all was chang'd, and a new spring
    Did all my senses greet;   40

6.

The unthrift Sunne shot vitall gold
    A thousand peeces,
And heaven its azure did unfold
    Checqur'd with snowie fleeces,
   The aire was all in spice   45
     And every bush
A garland wore; Thus fed my Eyes
    But all the Eare lay hush.

7.

Only a little Fountain lent
    Some use for Eares,   50
And on the dumbe shades language spent
    The Musick of her teares;
   I drew her neere, and found
     The Cisterne full
Of divers stones, some bright, and round
    Others ill-shap'd, and dull.   55

41 *unthrift:* spendthrift; *vitall:* life-giving.
55 Cf. the "lively stones" (the redeemed) of 1 Peter 2:5.

8.

The first (pray marke,) as quick as light
        Danc'd through the floud,
But, th'last more heavy then the night
        Nail'd to the Center stood;   60
        I wonder'd much, but tyr'd
            At last with thought,
My restless Eye that still desir'd
        As strange an object brought;

9.

It was a banke of flowers, where I descried   65
        (Though 'twas mid-day,)
Some fast asleepe, others broad-eyed
        And taking in the Ray,
        Here musing long, I heard
            A rushing wind   70
Which still increas'd, but whence it stirr'd
        No where I could not find;

10.

I turn'd me round, and to each shade
        Dispatch'd an Eye,
To see, if any leafe had made   75
        Least motion, or Reply,
        But while I listning sought
            My mind to ease

60 *Center:* earth.
70 See Acts 2:2.

By knowing, where 'twas, or where not,
    It whisper'd; *Where I please.*   80

Lord, then said I, *On me one breath,*
    And let me dye before my death!

Cant. Cap. 5. ver. 17.
*Arise O North, and come thou South-wind, and blow upon my
garden, that the spices thereof may flow out.*

Resurrection and Immortality:

Heb. cap. 10. ve: 20.
*By that new, and living way, which he hath prepared for us,
through the veile, which is his flesh.*

Body

1.

Oft have I seen, when that renewing breath
    That binds, and loosens death
Inspir'd a quickning power through the dead
        Creatures a bed,
    Some drowsie silk-worme creepe   5
        From that long sleepe
And in weake, infant hummings chime, and knell
    About her silent Cell
Untill at last full with the vitall Ray
        She wing'd away,   10
    And proud with life, and sence,
        Heav'ns rich Expence,

80 See John 3:8.
81–82 See NOTE.
RESURRECTION AND IMMORTALITY: see NOTE.
3 *Inspir'd:* breathed in.

Esteem'd (vaine things!) of two whole Elements
        As meane, and span-extents.
Shall I then thinke such providence will be   15
        Lesse friend to me?
    Or that he can endure to be unjust
    Who keeps his Covenant even with our dust.

Soule

2.

Poore, querulous handfull! was't for this
        I taught thee all that is?   20
Unbowel'd nature, shew'd thee her recruits,
        And Change of suits
    And how of death we make
        A meere mistake,
For no thing can to *Nothing* fall, but still   25
        Incorporates by skill,
And then returns, and from the wombe of things
        Such treasure brings
    As *Phenix*-like renew'th
        Both life, and youth;   30
For a preserving spirit doth still passe
        Untainted through this Masse,
Which doth resolve, produce, and ripen all
        That to it fall;
        Nor are those births which we   35
        Thus suffering see
Destroy'd at all; But when times restles wave
        Their substance doth deprave

13 *two whole Elements:* earth and water (preferring the air and fire of the heavens).

14 *span-extents:* things extending only the "span" of a hand.

21 *recruits:* fresh supplies, means of renewal.

26 *Incorporates:* takes on a body.

And the more noble *Essence* finds his house
                              Sickly, and loose,   40
               He, ever young, doth wing
                              Unto that spring,
And *source* of spirits, where he takes his lot
               Till time no more shall rot
His passive Cottage; which (though laid aside,)   45
                              Like some spruce Bride,
Shall one day rise, and cloath'd with shining light
                              All pure, and bright
       Re-marry to the soule, for 'tis most plaine
       Thou only fal'st to be refin'd againe.   50

3.

Then I that here saw darkly in a glasse
                              But mists, and shadows passe,
And, by their owne weake *Shine*, did search the springs
                              And Course of things
               Shall with Inlightned Rayes   55
                              Peirce all their wayes;
And as thou saw'st, I in a thought could goe
               To heav'n, or Earth below
To reade some *Starre*, or *Min'rall*, and in State
                              There often sate,   60
               So shalt thou then with me
                              (Both wing'd, and free,)
Rove in that mighty, and eternall light
               Where no rude shade, or night
Shall dare approach us; we shall there no more   65
                              Watch stars, or pore
               Through melancholly clouds, and say
                              Would it were Day!
       One everlasting *Saboth* there shall runne
       Without *Succession,* and without a *Sunne.*   70

51 See 1 Corinthians 13:12.

Dan: Cap: 12. ver: 13.
*But goe thou thy way untill the end be, for thou shalt rest, and
stand up in thy lot, at the end of the dayes.*

Religion

My God, when I walke in those groves,
And leaves thy spirit doth still fan,
I see in each shade that there growes
An Angell talking with a man.

Under a *Juniper*, some house,   5
Or the coole *Mirtles* canopie,
Others beneath an *Oakes* greene boughs,
Or at some *fountaines* bubling Eye;

Here *Jacob* dreames, and wrestles; there
Elias by a Raven is fed,   10
Another time by th' Angell, where
He brings him water with his bread;

In *Abr'hams* Tent the winged guests
(O how familiar then was heaven!)
Eate, drinke, discourse, sit downe, and rest   15
Untill the Coole, and shady *Even;*

Nay thou thy selfe, my God, in *fire*,
Whirle-winds, and *Clouds*, and the *soft voice*
Speak'st there so much, that I admire
We have no Conf'rence in these daies;   20

RELIGION: see Herbert, "Decay."
  2 *leaves:* the leaves of the Bible.
  5–16 See 1 Kings 17:2–6, 19:4–8; Judges 6:11; Genesis 18:1–10, 28:10–22,
32:24; Zechariah 1:8–11.
  17–18 See 1 Kings 19:11–12.

Is the truce broke? or 'cause we have
A mediatour now with thee,
Doest thou therefore old Treaties wave
And by appeales from him decree?

Or is't so, as some green heads say   25
That now all miracles must cease?
Though thou hast promis'd they should stay
The tokens of the Church, and peace;

No, no; Religion is a Spring
That from some secret, golden Mine   30
Derives her birth, and thence doth bring
Cordials in every drop, and Wine;

But in her long, and hidden Course
Passing through the Earths darke veines,
Growes still from better unto worse,   35
And both her taste, and colour staines,

Then drilling on, learnes to encrease
False *Ecchoes*, and Confused sounds,
And unawares doth often seize
On veines of *Sulphur* under ground;   40

So poison'd, breaks forth in some Clime,
And at first sight doth many please,
But drunk, is puddle, or meere slime
And 'stead of Phisick, a disease;

Just such a tainted sink we have   45
Like that *Samaritans* dead *Well*,
Nor must we for the Kernell crave
Because most voices like the *shell*.

37 *drilling*: trickling.
46 See John 4:5–15, where the water of the well is contrasted with the "living water" of Christ.

Heale then these waters, Lord; or bring thy flock,
Since these are troubled, to the springing rock, 50
Looke downe great Master of the feast; O shine,
And turn once more our *Water* into *Wine!*

Cant. cap. 4. ver. 12.
My sister, my spouse is as a garden Inclosed, as a Spring shut up,
and a fountain sealed up.

The Search

'Tis now cleare day: I see a Rose
Bud in the bright East, and disclose
The Pilgrim-Sunne; all night have I
Spent in a roving Extasie
To find my Saviour; I have been 5
As far as *Bethlem,* and have seen
His Inne, and Cradle; Being there
I met the *Wise-men,* askt them where
He might be found, or what starre can
Now point him out, grown up a Man? 10
To *Egypt* hence I fled, ran o're
All her parcht bosome to *Nile's* shore
Her yearly nurse; came back, enquir'd
Amongst the *Doctors,* and desir'd
To see the *Temple,* but was shown 15
A little dust, and for the Town
A heap of ashes, where some sed
A small bright sparkle was a bed,
Which would one day (beneath the pole,)
Awake, and then refine the whole. 20

50 *springing rock:* the rock from which water springs (Exodus 17:6), a sym-
bol of Christ.
THE SEARCH.
4 *Extasie:* withdrawal of soul from body (see Donne's poem by this title).

Tyr'd here, I come to *Sychar;* thence
To *Jacobs wel,* bequeathed since
Unto his sonnes, (where often they
In those calme, golden Evenings lay
Watring their flocks, and having spent   25
Those white dayes, drove home to the Tent
Their *well-fleec'd* traine;) And here (O fate!)
I sit, where once my Saviour sate;
The angry Spring in bubbles swell'd
Which broke in sighes still, as they fill'd,   30
And whisper'd, *Jesus had been there*
But *Jacobs children would not heare.*
Loath hence to part, at last I rise
But with the fountain in my Eyes,
And here a fresh search is decreed   35
He must be found, where he did bleed;
I walke the garden, and there see
Idæa's of his Agonie,
And moving anguishments that set
His blest face in a bloudy sweat;   40
I climb'd the Hill, perus'd the Crosse
Hung with my gaine, and his great losse,
Never did tree beare fruit like this,
Balsam of Soules, the bodyes blisse;
But, O his grave! where I saw lent   45
(For he had none,) a Monument,
An undefil'd, and new-heaw'd one,
But there was not the *Corner-stone;*
Sure (then said I,) my Quest is vaine,
Hee'le not be found, where he was slaine,   50
So mild a Lamb can never be
'Midst so much bloud, and Crueltie;
I'le to the Wilderness, and can
Find beasts more mercifull then man,

21–32 See John 4:5–15.
44 *Balsam:* balm, medicinal oil.
48 *Corner-stone:* Christ; see Acts 4:11; 1 Peter 2:6.

He liv'd there safe, 'twas his retreat   55
From the fierce *Jew*, and *Herods* heat,
And forty dayes withstood the fell,
And high temptations of hell;
With Seraphins there talked he
His fathers flaming ministrie,   60
He heav'nd their *walks*, and with his eyes
Made those wild shades a Paradise,
Thus was the desert sanctified
To be the refuge of his bride;
I'le thither then; see, It is day,   65
The Sun's broke through to guide my way.
   But as I urg'd thus, and writ down
What pleasures should my Journey crown,
What silent paths, what shades, and Cells,
Faire, virgin-flowers, and hallow'd *Wells*   70
I should rove in, and rest my head
Where my deare Lord did often tread,
Sugring all dangers with successe,
Me thought I heard one singing thus;

1.

Leave, leave thy gadding thoughts;   75
Who Pores
and spies
Still out of Doores
descries
Within them nought.   80

2.

The skinne, and shell of things
Though faire,
are not

74 See Herbert, "The Collar," line 35.

Thy wish, nor Pray'r,
        but got   85
By meere Despaire
    of wings.

3.

To rack old Elements,
    or Dust;
        and say   90
Sure here he must
    needs stay
    Is not the way,
        nor Just.

Search well another world; who studies this,   95
Travels in Clouds, seekes *Manna*, where none is.

Acts Cap. 17. ve. 27, 28.
*That they should seeke the Lord, if happily they might feele after
him, and find him, though he be not far off from every one of us, for
in him we live, and move, and have our being.*

The Brittish Church

Ah! he is fled!
And while these here their *mists*, and *shadowes* hatch,
My glorious head
Doth on those hills of Myrrhe, and Incense watch.
    Hast, hast my deare,   5
    The Souldiers here
    Cast in their lotts againe,

95 *another world*: the "little world" of the self: see stanza 1 above.
THE BRITTISH CHURCH: see NOTE.

That seamless coat
The Jewes touch'd not,
These dare divide, and staine.   10

2.

O get thee wings!
Or if as yet (untill these clouds depart,
      And the day springs,)
Thou think'st it good to tarry where thou art,
            Write in thy bookes   15
            My ravish'd looks
      Slain flock, and pillag'd fleeces,
            And haste thee so
            As a young Roe
Upon the mounts of spices.   20

*O Rosa Campi! O lilium Convallium! quomodò nunc
    facta es pabulum Aprorum!*

The Lampe

'Tis dead night round about: Horrour doth creepe
And move on with the shades; stars nod, and sleepe,
And through the dark aire spin a firie thread
Such as doth gild the lazie glow-worms bed.
    Yet, burn'st thou here, a full day; while I spend   5
My rest in Cares, and to the dark world lend
These flames, as thou dost thine to me; I watch
That houre, which must thy life, and mine dispatch;
But still thou doest out-goe me, I can see
Met in thy flames, all acts of piety;   10
Thy light, is *Charity;* Thy heat, is *Zeale;*
And thy aspiring, active fires reveale

Devotion still on wing; Then, thou dost weepe
Still as thou burn'st, and the warme droppings creepe
To measure out thy length, as if thou'dst know 15
What stock, and how much time were left thee now;
Nor dost thou spend one teare in vain, for still
As thou dissolv'st to them, and they distill,
They're stor'd up in the socket, where they lye,
When all is spent, thy last, and sure supply, 20
And such is true repentance, ev'ry breath
Wee spend in sighes, is treasure after death;
Only, one point escapes thee; That thy Oile
Is still out with thy flame, and so both faile;
But whensoe're I'm out, both shalbe in, 25
And where thou mad'st an end, there I'le begin.

Mark Cap. 13. ver. 35.

Watch you therefore, for you know not when the master of the house commeth, at Even, or at mid-night, or at the Cock-crowing, or in the morning.

Mans fall, and Recovery

Farewell you Everlasting hills! I'm Cast
Here under Clouds, where stormes, and tempests blast
    This sully'd flowre
Rob'd of your Calme, nor can I ever make
Transplanted thus, one leafe of his t'awake, 5
    But ev'ry houre
He sleepes, and droops, and in this drowsie state
Leaves me a slave to passions, and my fate;
    Besides I've lost
A traine of lights, which in those Sun-shine dayes 10
Were my sure guides, and only with me stayes
    (Unto my cost,)
One sullen beame, whose charge is to dispense
More punishment, than knowledge to my sence;

Two thousand yeares   15
I sojourn'd thus; at last *Jeshuruns* king
Those famous tables did from *Sinai* bring;
    These swell'd my feares,
Guilts, trespasses, and all this Inward Awe,
For sinne tooke strength, and vigour from the Law.   20
    Yet have I found
A plenteous way, (thanks to that holy one!)
To cancell all that e're was writ in stone,
    His saving wound
Wept bloud, that broke this Adamant, and gave   25
To sinners Confidence, life to the grave;
    This makes me span
My fathers journeys, and in one faire step
O're all their pilgrimage, and labours leap,
    For God (made man,)   30
Reduc'd th'Extent of works of faith; so made
Of their *Red Sea*, a *Spring;* I wash, they wade.

Rom. Cap. 18. ver. 19.

As by the offence of one, the fault came on all men to condemna-
tion; So by the Righteousness of one, the benefit abounded towards
all men to the Justification of life.

The Showre

'Twas so, I saw thy birth: That drowsie Lake
From her faint bosome breath'd thee, the disease
Of her sick waters, and Infectious Ease.
    But, now at Even
      Too grosse for heaven,   5
Thou fall'st in teares, and weep'st for thy mistake.

MANS FALL, AND RECOVERY: see NOTE.
  16 *Jeshuruns king:* Moses: see Deuteronomy 33:4–5.
  16–20 See Romans 7.

2.

Ah! it is so with me; oft have I prest
Heaven with a lazie breath, but fruitles this
Peirc'd not; Love only can with quick accesse
      Unlock the way,   10
      When all else stray
The smoke, and Exhalations of the brest.

3.

Yet, if as thou doest melt, and with thy traine
Of drops make soft the Earth, my eyes could weepe
O're my hard heart, that's bound up, and asleepe,   15
      Perhaps at last
      (Some such showres past,)
My God would give a Sun-shine after raine.

Vanity of Spirit

Quite spent with thoughts I left my Cell, and lay
Where a shrill spring tun'd to the early day.
    I beg'd here long, and gron'd to know
    Who gave the Clouds so brave a bow,
    Who bent the spheres, and circled in   5
    Corruption with this glorious Ring,
    What is his name, and how I might
    Descry some part of his great light.
I summon'd nature: peirc'd through all her store,
Broke up some seales, which none had touch'd before,   10

VANITY OF SPIRIT.
  4 *brave*: splendid.

Her wombe, her bosome, and her head
Where all her secrets lay a bed
I rifled quite, and having past
Through all the Creatures, came at last
To search my selfe, where I did find   15
Traces, and sounds of a strange kind.
Here of this mighty spring, I found some drills,
With Ecchoes beaten from th' eternall hills;
 Weake beames, and fires flash'd to my sight,
 Like a young East, or Moone-shine night, 20
 Wich shew'd me in a nook cast by
 A peece of much antiquity,
 With Hyerogliphicks quite dismembred,
 And broken letters scarce remembred.
I tooke them up, and (much Joy'd,) went about 25
T' unite those peeces, hoping to find out
 The mystery; but this neer done,
 That little light I had was gone:
 It griev'd me much. At last, said I,
 Since in these veyls my Ecclips'd Eye 30
 May not approach thee, (for at night
 Who can have commerce with the light?)
 I'le disapparell, and to buy
 But one half glaunce, most gladly dye.

The Retreate

 Happy those early dayes! when I
 Shin'd in my Angell-infancy.
 Before I understood this place
 Appointed for my second race,
 Or taught my soul to fancy ought 5
 But a white, Celestiall thought,
 When yet I had not walkt above

17 *drills:* trickles, small streams.

A mile, or two, from my first love,
And looking back (at that short space,)
Could see a glimpse of his bright-face; 10
When on some *gilded Cloud*, or *flowre*
My gazing soul would dwell an houre,
And in those weaker glories spy
Some shadows of eternity;
Before I taught my tongue to wound 15
My Conscience with a sinfull sound,
Or had the black art to dispence
A sev'rall sinne to ev'ry sence,
But felt through all this fleshly dresse
Bright *shootes* of everlastingnesse. 20
   O how I long to travell back
And tread again that ancient track!
That I might once more reach that plaine,
Where first I left my glorious traine,
From whence th' Inlightned spirit sees 25
That shady City of Palme trees;
But (ah!) my soul with too much stay
Is drunk, and staggers in the way.
Some men a forward motion love,
But I by backward steps would move, 30
And when this dust falls to the urn
In that state I came return.

¶

    Come, come, what doe I here?
       Since he is gone
    Each day is grown a dozen year,

THE RETREATE: see NOTE.
  18 *sev'rall:* individual.
  24 *traine:* way of life, course of action.
  23–26 See Deuteronomy 34:1–3.
"COME, COME, WHAT DOE I HERE?": see NOTE.

And each houre, one;
    Come, come!   5
Cut off the sum,
    By these soil'd teares!
    (Which only thou
    Know'st to be true,)
    Dayes are my feares.   10

2.

Ther's not a wind can stir,
        Or beam passe by,
But strait I think (though far,)
        Thy hand is nigh;
        Come, come!   15
    Strike these lips dumb:
    This restles breath
    That soiles thy name,
    Will ne'r be tame
    Untill in death.   20

3.

Perhaps some think a tombe
        No house of store,
But a dark, and seal'd up wombe,
        Which ne'r breeds more.
        Come, come!   25
    Such thoughts benum;
    But I would be
    With him I weep
    A bed, and sleep
    To wake in thee.   30

Midnight

When to my Eyes
(Whilst deep sleep others catches,)
Thine hoast of spyes
The starres shine in their watches,
    I doe survey   5
    Each busie Ray,
And how they work, and wind,
    And wish each beame
    My soul doth streame,
With the like ardour shin'd;   10
    What Emanations,
    Quick vibrations
And bright stirs are there?
    What thin Ejections,
    Cold Affections,   15
And slow motions here?

2.

Thy heav'ns (some say,)
Are a firie-liquid light,
    Which mingling aye
Streames, and flames thus to the sight.   20
    Come then, my god!
    Shine on this bloud,
And water in one beame,
    And thou shalt see
    Kindled by thee   25
Both liquors burne, and streame.

MIDNIGHT.
  19 *aye:* always.

O what bright quicknes,
Active brightnes,
And celestiall flowes
Will follow after 30
On that water,
Which thy spirit blowes!

Math. Cap. 3. ver. xi.
*I indeed baptize you with water unto repentance, but he that
commeth after me, is mightier than I, whose shooes I am not worthy
to beare, he shall baptize you with the holy Ghost, and with fire.*

The Storm

I see the use: and know my bloud
Is not a Sea,
But a shallow, bounded floud
Though red as he;
Yet have I flows, as strong as his, 5
And boyling stremes that rave
With the same curling force, and hisse,
As doth the mountain'd wave.

2.

But when his waters billow thus,
Dark storms, and wind 10
Incite them to that fierce discusse,
Else not Inclin'd,
Thus the Enlarg'd, inraged air
Uncalmes these to a floud,
But still the weather that's most fair 15
Breeds tempests in my bloud;

THE STORM.
1 *use:* moral application.
11 *discusse:* debate.

3.

Lord, then round me with weeping Clouds,
   And let my mind
In quick blasts sigh beneath those shrouds
   A spirit-wind,   20
So shall that storme purge this *Recluse*
   Which sinfull ease made foul,
And *wind,* and *water* to thy use
   Both *wash,* and *wing* my soul.

The Morning-watch

O Joyes! Infinite sweetnes! with what flowres,
And shoots of glory, my soul breakes, and buds!
   All the long houres
   Of night, and Rest
   Through the still shrouds   5
   Of sleep, and Clouds,
  This Dew fell on my Breast;
   O how it *Blouds,*
And *Spirits* all my Earth! heark! In what Rings,
And *Hymning Circulations* the quick world 10
   Awakes, and sings;
   The rising winds,
   And falling springs,
   Birds, beasts, all things
  Adore him in their kinds.   15

17 *round me:* surround me.
21–24 See Herbert, "The Storm," esp. lines 1–3, 17–18.
23 *to thy use:* for thy use or purpose.
THE MORNING-WATCH: morning prayer (*watch:* religious service); see NOTE.
1 See Herbert, "The H. Scriptures. I," line 1.

Thus all is hurl'd
In sacred *Hymnes,* and *Order,* The great *Chime*
And *Symphony* of nature. Prayer is
      The world in tune,
      A spirit-voyce,   20
      And vocall joyes
  Whose *Eccho is* heav'ns blisse.
      O let me climbe
When I lye down! The Pious soul by night
Is like a clouded starre, whose beames though sed   25
      To shed their light
      Under some Cloud
      Yet are above,
      And shine, and move
  Beyond that mistie shrowd.   30
      So in my Bed
That Curtain'd grave, though sleep, like ashes, hide
My lamp, and life, both shall in thee abide.

The Evening-watch

A Dialogue

  Farewell! I goe to sleep; but when   *Body.*
  The day-star springs, I'le wake agen.

  Goe, sleep in peace; and when thou lyest   *Soul.*
Unnumber'd in thy dust, when all this frame
Is but one dramme, and what thou now descriest   5
  In sev'rall parts shall want a name,
Then may his peace be with thee, and each dust
Writ in his book, who ne'r betray'd mans trust!

  Amen! but hark, e'r we two stray,   *Body.*
  How many hours do'st think 'till day?   10

18–22 See Herbert's sonnet "Prayer," lines 8–9.

Ah! go; th'art weak, and sleepie. Heav'n   *Soul.*
Is a plain watch, and without figures winds
All ages up; who drew this Circle even
     He fils it; Dayes, and hours are *Blinds.*
Yet, this take with thee; The last gasp of time   15
Is thy first breath, and mans *eternall Prime.*

¶

Silence, and stealth of dayes! 'tis now
     Since thou art gone,
Twelve hundred houres, and not a brow
     But Clouds hang on.
As he that in some Caves thick damp   5
     Lockt from the light,
Fixeth a solitary lamp,
     To brave the night,
And walking from his Sun, when past
     That glim'ring Ray   10
Cuts through the heavy mists in haste
     Back to his day,
So o'r fled minutes I retreat
     Unto that hour
Which shew'd thee last, but did defeat   15
     Thy light, and pow'r,
I search, and rack my soul to see
     Those beams again,
But nothing but the snuff to me
     Appeareth plain;   20
That dark, and dead sleeps in its known,

THE EVENING-WATCH.

16 *Prime:* literally, the first hour of the day; also, the Spring.
"SILENCE, AND STEALTH OF DAYES!": see NOTE.

9 *Sun:* the lamp within the cave.

19 *snuff:* the charred part of the candlewick.

And common urn,
But those fled to their Makers throne,
There shine, and burn;
O could I track them! but souls must   25
Track one the other,
And now the spirit, not the dust
Must be thy brother.
Yet I have one *Pearle* by whose light
All things I see,   30
And in the heart of Earth, and night
Find Heaven, and thee.

Peace

My Soul, there is a Countrie
Far beyond the stars,
Where stands a winged Centrie
All skilfull in the wars,
There above noise, and danger   5
Sweet peace sits crown'd with smiles,
And one born in a Manger
Commands the Beauteous files,
He is thy gracious friend,
And (O my Soul awake!)   10
Did in pure love descend
To die here for thy sake,
If thou canst get but thither,
There growes the flowre of peace,
The Rose that cannot wither,   15
Thy fortresse, and thy ease;
Leave then thy foolish ranges;
For none can thee secure,
But one, who never changes,
Thy God, thy life, thy Cure.   20

29 *Pearle:* the "pearl of great price" (Matthew 13:46); here the presence of Christ, or the Image of God, within his soul.

The Passion

O my chief good!
My dear, dear God!
When thy blest bloud
Did Issue forth forc'd by the Rod,
What pain didst thou   5
Feel in each blow!
How didst thou weep,
And thy self steep
In thy own precious, saving teares!
What cruell smart   10
Did teare thy heart!
How didst thou grone it
In the spirit,
O thou, whom my soul Loves, and feares!

2.

Most blessed Vine!   15
Whose juice so good
I feel as Wine,
But thy faire branches felt as bloud,
How wert thou prest
To be my feast!   20
In what deep anguish
Didst thou languish,
What springs of Sweat, and bloud did drown thee!

THE PASSION.
  1 The same as the opening line of Herbert's "Good Friday."
  17–18 See Herbert, "The Agonie," lines 17–18.
  19–20 See Herbert, "The bunch of grapes," lines 27–28.

How in one path
Did the full wrath   25
Of thy great Father
Crowd, and gather,
Doubling thy griefs, when none would own thee!

3.

How did the weight
Of all our sinnes,   30
And death unite
To wrench, and Rack thy blessed limbes!
How pale, and bloudie
Lookt thy Body!
How bruis'd, and broke   35
With every stroke!
How meek, and patient was thy spirit!
How didst thou cry,
And grone on high
Father forgive,   40
And let them live,
I dye to make my foes inherit!

4.

O blessed Lamb!
That took'st my sinne,
That took'st my shame   45
How shall thy dust thy praises sing!
I would I were
One hearty tear!
One constant spring!
Then would I bring   50
Thee two small mites, and be at strife
Which should most vie,

My heart, or eye,
Teaching my years
In smiles, and tears
To weep, to sing, thy *Death,* my *Life.*   55

Rom. Cap. 8. ver. 19.

Etenim res Creatæ exerto Capite observantes expectant revelationem Filiorum Dei.

And do they so? have they a Sense
Of ought but Influence?
Can they their heads lift, and expect,
And grone too? why th'Elect
Can do no more: my volumes sed   5
They were all dull, and dead,
They judg'd them senslesse, and their state
Wholly Inanimate.
Go, go; Seal up thy looks,
And burn thy books.   10

2.

I would I were a stone, or tree,
Or flowre by pedigree,
Or some poor high-way herb, or Spring
To flow, or bird to sing!
Then should I (tyed to one sure state,)   15
All day expect my date;

"AND DO THEY SO?" *Etenim . . . Dei:* "For created things watching with lifted head wait for the revelation of the Sons of God."

2 *Influence:* the supposed influence of the stars upon the growth of things on earth.

3–4 See Romans 8:19–22.

9–14 See Herbert, "Affliction (I)," lines 55–60.

16 *expect:* await.

PLATE III   Engraved title page of the second edition of Crashaw's *Steps to the Temple*, 1648.

But I am sadly loose, and stray
    A giddy blast each way;
    O let me not thus range!
        Thou canst not change.   20

3.

Sometimes I sit with thee, and tarry
    An hour, or so, then vary.
Thy other Creatures in this Scene
    Thee only aym, and mean;
Some rise to seek thee, and with heads   25
    Erect peep from their beds;
Others, whose birth is in the tomb,
    And cannot quit the womb,
    Sigh there, and grone for thee,
        Their liberty.   30

4.

O let not me do lesse! shall they
    Watch, while I sleep, or play?
Shall I thy mercies still abuse
    With fancies, friends, or newes?
O brook it not! thy bloud is mine,   35
    And my soul should be thine;
O brook it not! why wilt thou stop
    After whole showres one drop?
    Sure, thou wilt joy to see
        Thy sheep with thee.   40

39 See Herbert, "The Starre," line 29.

The Relapse

My God, how gracious art thou! I had slipt
      Almost to hell,
And on the verge of that dark, dreadful pit
      Did hear them yell,
But O thy love! thy rich, almighty love   5
      That sav'd my soul,
And checkt their furie, when I saw them move,
      And heard them howl;
O my sole Comfort, take no more these wayes,
      This hideous path,   10
And I wil mend my own without delayes,
      Cease thou thy wrath!
I have deserv'd a thick, Egyptian damp,
      Dark as my deeds,
Should *mist* within me, and put out that lamp   15
      Thy spirit feeds;
A darting Conscience full of stabs, and fears;
      No shade but *Yewgh,*
Sullen, and sad Ecclipses, Cloudie spheres,
      These are my due.   20
But he that with his bloud, (a price too deere,)
      My scores did pay,
Bid me, by vertue from him, chalenge here
      The brightest day;
Sweet, downie thoughts; soft *Lilly*-shades; Calm streams;
      Joyes full, and true;
Fresh, spicie mornings; and eternal beams
      These are his due.

THE RELAPSE.

11 See Herbert, "The Thanksgiving," line 34.

13 See Exodus 10:22; and Herbert, "Sighs and Grones": "I have deserv'd
that an Egyptian night / Should thicken all my powers."

The Resolve

I have consider'd it; and find
        A longer stay
Is but excus'd neglect. To mind
        One path, and stray
Into another, or to none,   5
        Cannot be love;
When shal that traveller come home,
        That will not move?
If thou wouldst thither, linger not,
        Catch at the place,   10
Tell youth, and beauty they must rot,
        They'r but a *Case;*
Loose, parcell'd hearts wil freeze: The Sun
        With scatter'd locks
Scarce warms, but by contraction   15
        Can heat rocks;
Call in thy *Powers;* run, and reach
        Home with the light,
Be there, before the shadows stretch,
        And *Span* up night;   20
Follow the *Cry* no more: there is
        An ancient way
All strewed with flowres, and happiness
        And fresh as *May;*

THE RESOLVE.

  1 See Herbert, "The Reprisall," line 1.

  10 See Herbert, "Affliction (I)," line 17.

  13 *parcell'd:* divided into parts.

  20 *Span up:* make tight.

  21 *Cry:* general opinion; perhaps also with ref. to the "cry" of a pack of hounds.

  23–24 See Herbert, "Affliction (I)," lines 21–22.

There turn, and turn no more; Let wits,   25
        Smile at fair eies,
Or lips; But who there weeping sits,
        Hath got the *Prize*.

The Match

Dear friend! whose holy, ever-living lines
        Have done much good
    To many, and have checkt my blood,
My fierce, wild blood that still heaves, and inclines,
        But is still tam'd   5
    By those bright fires which thee inflam'd;
Here I joyn hands, and thrust my stubborn heart
        Into thy *Deed*,
    There from no *Duties* to be freed,
And if hereafter *youth*, or *folly* thwart   10
        And claim their share,
    Here I renounce the pois'nous ware.

ii

Accept, dread Lord, the poor Oblation,
        It is but poore,
    Yet through thy Mercies may be more.   15
O thou! that canst not wish my souls damnation,
        Afford me life,
    And save me from all inward strife!
Two *Lifes* I hold from thee, my gracious Lord,
        Both cost thee deer,   20

THE MATCH.

1 *friend:* George Herbert, as lines 7–8 make clear by their explicit reference
to the last two stanzas of Herbert's "Obedience."

19–23 *Two Lifes:* with ref. to the legal tenure known as a "lifehold"; see
Herbert's "Love unknown": "A Lord I had, / And have, of whom some grounds,
which may improve, / I hold for two lives, and both lives in me."

For one, I am thy Tenant here;
The other, the true life, in the next world
      And endless is,
  O let me still mind *that* in *this!*
To thee therefore my *Thoughts, Words, Actions*   25
      I do resign,
  Thy will in all be done, not mine.
Settle my *house,* and shut out all distractions
      That may unknit
  My heart, and thee planted in it;   30
Lord *Jesu!* thou didst bow thy blessed head
      Upon a tree,
  O do as much, now unto me!
O hear, and heal thy servant! Lord, strike dead
      All lusts in me,   35
  Who onely wish life to serve thee!
Suffer no more this dust to overflow
      And drown my eies,
  But seal, or pin them to thy skies.
And let this *grain* which here in tears I sow   40
      Though *dead,* and *sick,*
  Through thy *Increase* grow *new,* and *quick.*

Rules and Lessons

When first thy Eies unveil, give thy Soul leave
To do the like; our Bodies but forerun
The spirits duty; True hearts spread, and heave
Unto their God, as flow'rs do to the Sun.
    Give him thy first thoughts then; so shalt thou keep   5
    Him company all day, and in him sleep.

Yet, never sleep the Sun up; Prayer shou'd
Dawn.with the day; There are set, awful hours

31–32 See Herbert, "Longing," lines 31–32.

'Twixt heaven, and us; The *Manna* was not good
After Sun-rising, far-day sullies flowres.   10
  Rise to prevent the Sun; sleep doth sins glut,
  And heav'ns gate opens, when this world's is shut.

Walk with thy fellow-creatures: note the *hush*
And *whispers* amongst them. There's not a *Spring*,
Or *Leafe* but hath his *Morning-hymn;* Each *Bush*   15
And *Oak* doth know *I AM;* canst thou not sing?
  O leave thy Cares, and follies! go this way
  And thou art sure to prosper all the day.

Serve God before the world; let him not go
Until thou hast a blessing, then resigne   20
The whole unto him; and remember who
Prevail'd by *wrestling* ere the *Sun* did *shine.*
  Poure *Oyle* upon the *stones,* weep for thy sin,
  Then journey on, and have an eie to heav'n.

Mornings are *Mysteries;* the first worlds *Youth,*   25
Mans *Resurrection,* and the futures *Bud*
Shrowd in their births: The Crown of life, light, truth
Is stil'd their *starre,* the *stone,* and *hidden food.*
  Three *blessings* wait upon them, two of which
  Should move; They make us *holy, happy,* rich.   30

When the world's up, and ev'ry swarm abroad,
Keep thou thy temper, mix not with each Clay;
Dispatch necessities, life hath a load

RULES AND LESSONS: for the stanza and epigrammatic manner see Herbert, "The Church-porch."
 9–10 See Exodus 16:19–21.
 11 *prevent:* anticipate.
 15–16 See Exodus 3:2–14.
 19–24 See Genesis 32:24–30, 28:18–22, 29:1.
 27 *Shrowd in:* are concealed in.
 27–28 See Revelation 2:10, 17, 28; 22:16.
 32 *temper:* mental balance, proper disposition.

Which must be carri'd on, and safely may.
    Yet keep those cares without thee, let the heart   35
    Be Gods alone, and choose the better part.

Through all thy *Actions, Counsels,* and *Discourse,*
Let *Mildness,* and *Religion* guide thee out,
If truth be thine, what needs a brutish force?
But what's not *good,* and *just* ne'r go about.   40
    Wrong not thy Conscience for a rotten stick,
    That gain is dreadful, which makes spirits sick.

To God, thy Countrie, and thy friend be true,
If *Priest,* and *People* change, keep thou thy ground.
Who sels Religion, is a *Judas Jew,*   45
And, oathes once broke, the soul cannot be sound.
    The perjurer's a devil let loose: what can
    Tie up his hands, that dares mock God, and man?

Seek not the same steps with the *Crowd;* stick thou
To thy sure trot; a Constant, humble mind   50
Is both his own Joy, and his Makers too;
Let folly dust it on, or lag behind.
    A sweet *self-privacy* in a right soul
    Out-runs the Earth, and lines the utmost pole.

To all that seek thee, bear an open heart;   55
Make not thy breast a *Labyrinth,* or *Trap;*
If tryals come, this wil make good thy part,
For honesty is safe, come what can hap;
    It is the good mans *feast;* The prince of flowres
    Which thrives in *storms,* and smels best after *showres.*   60

Seal not thy Eyes up from the poor, but give
Proportion to their *Merits,* and thy *Purse;*

54 *lines:* reaches, "as with a measuring-line" (OED).
58 *hap:* occur.

Thou mai'st in Rags a mighty Prince relieve
Who, when thy sins call for't, can fence a Curse.
    Thou shalt not lose one *mite*. Though waters stray,   65
    The Bread we cast returns in fraughts one day.

Spend not an hour so, as to weep another,
For tears are not thine own; If thou giv'st words
Dash not thy *friend*, nor *Heav'n*; O smother
A vip'rous thought; some *Syllables* are *Swords*.   70
    Unbitted tongues are in their penance double,
    They shame their *owners*, and the *hearers* trouble.

Injure not modest bloud, whose *spirits* rise
In judgement against *Lewdness;* that's base wit
That voyds but *filth*, and *stench*. Hast thou no prize   75
But *sickness*, or *Infection?* stifle it.
    Who makes his jests of sins, must be at least
    If not a very *devill*, worse than a *Beast*.

Yet, fly no friend, if he be such indeed,
But meet to quench his *Longings*, and thy *Thirst;*   80
Allow your Joyes *Religion;* That done, speed
And bring the same man back, thou wert all first.
    Who so returns not, cannot pray aright,
    But shuts his door, and leaves God out all night.

To highten thy *Devotions*, and keep low   85
All mutinous thoughts, what busines e'r thou hast
Observe God in his works; here *fountains* flow,
Birds sing, *Beasts* feed, *Fish* leap, and th'*Earth* stands fast;
    Above are restles *motions*, running *Lights*,
    Vast Circling *Azure*, giddy *Clouds*, days, nights.   90

63–64 See Matthew 25:31–46.
64 *fence:* ward off.
66 *fraughts:* shiploads (see Ecclesiastes 11:1).
71 *unbitted:* uncontrolled.
75 *voyds:* empties out.

When *Seasons* change, then lay before thine Eys
His wondrous *Method;* mark the various *Scenes*
In heav'n; *Hail, Thunder, Rain-bows, Snow,* and *Ice,*
Calmes, Tempests, Light, and *darknes* by his means;
    Thou canst not misse his Praise; Each *tree, herb, flowre*   95
    Are shadows of his *wisedome,* and his Pow'r.

To *meales* when thou doest come, give him the praise
Whose *Arm* supply'd thee; Take what may suffice,
And then be thankful; O admire his ways
Who fils the worlds unempty'd granaries!   100
    A thankles feeder is a *Theif,* his feast
    A very *Robbery,* and himself no *guest.*

High-noon thus past, thy time decays; provide
Thee other thoughts; Away with friends, and mirth;
The Sun now stoops, and hasts his beams to hide   105
Under the dark, and melancholy Earth.
    All but preludes thy End. Thou art the man
    Whose *Rise, hight,* and *Descent* is but a span.

Yet, set as he doth, and 'tis well. Have all
Thy Beams home with thee: trim thy *Lamp,* buy *Oyl,*   110
And then set forth; who is thus drest, The *Fall*
Furthers his glory, and gives death the foyl.
    Man is a *Summers day;* whose *youth,* and *fire*
    Cool to a glorious *Evening,* and Expire.

When night comes, list thy deeds; make plain the way   115
'Twixt Heaven, and thee; block it not with delays,
But perfect all before thou sleep'st; Then say
Ther's one Sun more strung on my Bead of days.
    What's good score up for Joy; The bad wel scann'd
    Wash off with tears, and get thy *Masters* hand.   120

108 *span:* the extent of a hand: nine inches.

Thy Accounts thus made, spend in the grave one houre
Before thy time; Be not a stranger there
Where thou may'st sleep whole ages; Lifes poor flowr
Lasts not a night sometimes. Bad spirits fear
    This Conversation; But the good man lyes   125
    Intombed many days before he dyes.

Being laid, and drest for sleep, Close not thy Eys
Up with thy Curtains; Give thy soul the wing
In some good thoughts; So when the day shall rise
And thou *unrak'st* thy *fire,* those *sparks* will bring   130
    New *flames;* Besides where these lodge vain *heats* mourn
    And die; That *Bush* where God is, shall not burn.

When thy *Nap's* over, stir thy fire, unrake
In that *dead age;* one beam i'th' dark outvies
Two in the day; Then from the *Damps,* and *Ake*   135
Of night shut up thy *leaves,* be Chast; God prys
    Through thickest nights; Though then the Sun be far
    Do thou the works of *Day,* and rise a *Star.*

Briefly, *Doe as thou would'st be done unto,*
Love God, and Love thy Neighbour; Watch, and Pray.   140
These are the *Words,* and *Works* of life; This do,
And live; who doth not thus, hath lost *Heav'ns* way.
    O lose it not! look up, wilt Change those *Lights*
    For *Chains* of *Darknes,* and *Eternal Nights?*

Corruption

Sure, It was so. Man in those early days
    Was not all stone, and Earth,
He shin'd a little, and by those weak Rays
    Had some glimpse of his birth.

125 *Conversation:* company.
132 See Exodus 3:2.

He saw Heaven o'r his head, and knew from whence 5
    He came (condemned,) hither,
And, as first Love draws strongest, so from hence
    His mind sure progress'd thither.
Things here were strange unto him: Swet, and till
    All was a thorn, or weed, 10
Nor did those last, but (like himself,) dyed still
    As soon as they did *Seed,*
They seem'd to quarrel with him; for that Act
    That fel him, foyl'd them all,
He drew the Curse upon the world, and Crackt 15
    The whole frame with his fall.
This made him long for *home,* as loath to stay
    With murmurers, and foes;
He sigh'd for *Eden,* and would often say
    Ah! what bright days were those? 20
Nor was Heav'n cold unto him; for each day
    The vally, or the Mountain
Afforded visits, and still *Paradise* lay
    In some green shade, or fountain.
Angels lay *Leiger* here; Each Bush, and Cel, 25
    Each Oke, and high-way knew them,
Walk but the fields, or sit down at some *wel,*
    And he was sure to view them.
Almighty *Love!* where art thou now? mad man
    Sits down, and freezeth on, 30
He raves, and swears to stir nor fire, nor fan,
    But bids the thread be spun.
I see, thy Curtains are Close-drawn; Thy bow
    Looks dim too in the Cloud,
Sin triumphs still, and man is sunk below 35
    The Center, and his shrowd;

CORRUPTION.
  9 *till:* tillage, plowing the ground.
  14 *fel:* a misprint for *feld* (felled)? or perhaps equivalent to *befell?*
  21–28 See Herbert, "Decay," lines 6–10.
  25 *Leiger:* resident as ambassadors.

All's in deep sleep, and night; Thick darknes lyes
  And hatcheth o'r thy people;
   But hark! what trumpets that? what Angel cries
    Arise! Thrust in thy sickle.   40

H. Scriptures

Welcome dear book, souls Joy, and food! The feast
  Of Spirits, Heav'n extracted lyes in thee;
   Thou art lifes Charter, The Doves spotless neast
Where souls are hatch'd unto Eternitie.

In thee the hidden stone, the *Manna* lies,   5
  Thou art the great *Elixir*, rare, and Choice;
   The Key that opens to all Mysteries,
The *Word* in Characters, God in the *Voice*.

O that I had deep Cut in my hard heart
  Each line in thee! Then would I plead in groans 10
   Of my Lords penning, and by sweetest Art
Return upon himself the *Law*, and *Stones*.
   Read here, my faults are thine. This Book, and I
    Will tell thee so; *Sweet Saviour thou didst dye!*

---

38 *hatcheth:* broods.
39–40 See Revelation 14:14–19.
H. SCRIPTURES.
 5 See Revelation 2:17.
 8 *Characters:* letters of the alphabet.
 9–10 See Herbert, "The Altar," lines 5–12.
 13 See Herbert, "Judgement," line 15.

Unprofitablenes

How rich, O Lord! how fresh thy visits are!
'Twas but Just now my bleak leaves hopeles hung
    Sullyed with dust and mud;
Each snarling blast shot through me, and did share
Their Youth, and beauty, Cold showres nipt, and wrung   5
    Their spiciness, and bloud;
But since thou didst in one sweet glance survey
Their sad decays, I flourish, and once more
    Breath all perfumes, and spice;
I smell a dew like *Myrrh,* and all the day   10
Wear in my bosome a full Sun; such store
    Hath one beame from thy Eys.
But, ah, my God! what fruit hast thou of this?
What one poor leaf did ever I yet fall
    To wait upon thy wreath?   15
Thus thou all day a thankless weed doest dress,
And when th' hast done, a stench, or fog is all
    The odour I bequeath.

Christs Nativity

    Awake, glad heart! get up, and Sing,
    It is the Birth-day of thy King,
        Awake! awake!
        The Sun doth shake
    Light from his locks, and all the way   5
    Breathing Perfumes, doth spice the day.

UNPROFITABLENES: for many echoes see Herbert, "The Flower," "The Glance,"
"The Odour."
    4 *share:* shear.

2.

Awak, awak! heark, how th' *wood* rings,
Winds whisper, and the busie *springs*
    A Consort make;
    Awake, awake!
Man is their high-priest, and should rise
To offer up the sacrifice.

10

3.

I would I were some *Bird*, or Star,
Flutt'ring in woods, or lifted far
    Above this *Inne*
    And Rode of sin!
Then either Star, or *Bird*, should be
Shining, or singing still to thee.

15

4.

I would I had in my best part
Fit Roomes for thee! or that my heart
    Were so clean as
    Thy manger was!
But I am all filth, and obscene,
Yet, if thou wilt, thou canst make clean.

20

CHRISTS NATIVITY.

9 *Consort:* harmonious music.

11–12 See Herbert, "Providence": "Man is the worlds high Priest: he doth present / The sacrifice for all."

5.

Sweet *Jesu!* will then; Let no more   25
This Leper haunt, and soyl thy door,
    Cure him, Ease him
    O release him!
And let once more by mystick birth
The Lord of life be borne in Earth.   30

II

How kind is heav'n to man! If here
    One sinner doth amend
Strait there is Joy, and ev'ry sphere
    In musick doth Contend;
And shall we then no voices lift?   35
    Are mercy, and salvation
Not worth our thanks? Is life a gift
    Of no more acceptation?
Shal he that did come down from thence,
    And here for us was slain,   40
Shal he be now cast off? no sense
    Of all his woes remain?
Can neither Love, nor suff'rings bind?
    Are we all stone, and Earth?
Neither his bloudy passions mind,   45
    Nor one day blesse his birth?
Alas, my God! Thy birth now here
Must not be numbred in the year.

29–30 *mystick birth:* the mysterious birth of the Spirit of Christ within the
redeemed man.

45 *passions:* sufferings; *mind:* remember.

47–48 The Puritans had abolished the celebration of Christmas.

Admission

How shril are silent tears? when sin got head
    And all my Bowels turn'd
To brasse, and iron; when my stock lay dead,
    And all my powers mourn'd;
    Then did these drops (for Marble sweats,   5
       And Rocks have tears,)
  As rain here at our windows beats,
    Chide in thine Ears;

2.

No quiet couldst thou have: nor didst thou wink,
    And let thy Begger lie,   10
But e'r my eies could overflow their brink
    Didst to each drop reply;
  Bowels of Love! at what low rate,
    And slight a price
  Dost thou relieve us at thy gate,   15
    And stil our Cries?

3.

Wee are thy Infants, and suck thee; If thou
    But hide, or turn thy face,
Because where thou art, yet, we cannot go,
    We send tears to the place,   20

ADMISSION: this poem and the following five, given in this order in 1650, may
be regarded as a sequence.

1 See Herbert, "The Familie," line 20; *got head:* gained power.

2 *Bowels:* feelings: the interior of the body "considered as the seat of the
tender and sympathetic emotions" (OED).

9 *wink:* close the eyes, sleep.

13–14 See Herbert, "The Pearl," line 35.

17 See Herbert, "Longing," line 17.

These find thee out, and though our sins
    Drove thee away,
Yet with thy love that absence wins
    Us double pay.

4.

O give me then a thankful heart! a heart   25
    After thy own, not mine;
So after thine, that all, and ev'ry part
    Of mine, may wait on thine;
O hear! yet not my tears alone,
    Hear now a floud,   30
A floud that drowns both tears, and grones,
    My Saviours bloud.

Praise

King of Comforts! King of life!
    Thou hast cheer'd me,
And when fears, and doubts were rife,
    Thou hast cleer'd me!

Not a nook in all my Breast   5
    But thou fill'st it,
Not a thought, that breaks my rest,
    But thou kill'st it;

Wherefore with my utmost strength
    I wil praise thee,   10
And as thou giv'st line, and length,
    I wil raise thee;

29–32 See Herbert, "Church-lock and key," lines 9–12.
PRAISE: see NOTE.

Day, and night, not once a day
    I will blesse thee,
And my soul in new array   15
    I will dresse thee;

Not one minute in the year
    But I'l mind thee,
As my seal, and bracelet here
    I wil bind thee;   20

In thy word, as if in heaven
    I wil rest me,
And thy promise 'til made even
    There shall feast me.

Then, thy sayings all my life   25
    They shal please me,
And thy bloudy wounds, and strife
    They wil ease me;

With thy grones my daily breath
    I will measure,   30
And my life hid in thy death
    I will treasure.

    Though then thou art
    Past thought of heart
All perfect fulness,   35
    And canst no whit
    Accesse admit
From dust and dulness;

    Yet to thy name
    (as not the same   40
With thy bright Essence,)

Our foul, Clay hands
At thy Commands
Bring praise, and Incense;

If then, dread Lord, 45
When to thy board
Thy wretch comes begging,
He hath a flowre
Or (to his pow'r,)
Some such poor Off'ring; 50

When thou hast made
Thy begger glad,
And fill'd his bosome,
Let him (though poor,)
Strow at thy door 55
That one poor Blossome.

Dressing

O thou that lovest a pure, and whitend soul!
That feedst among the Lillies, 'till the day
Break, and the shadows flee; touch with one Coal
My frozen heart; and with thy secret key

Open my desolate rooms; my gloomie Brest 5
With thy cleer fire refine, burning to dust
These dark Confusions, that within me nest,
And soyl thy Temple with a sinful rust.

46 *board:* Communion table.
DRESSING: preparing to partake of the Lord's Supper.
2–3 See Song of Solomon 2:16–17.
4–5 See Herbert, "The H. Communion," lines 21–22.

Thou holy, harmless, undefil'd high-priest!
The perfect, ful oblation for all sin,   10
Whose glorious conquest nothing can resist,
But even in babes doest triumph still and win;

    Give to thy wretched one
   Thy mysticall *Communion*,
      That, absent, he may see,   15
      Live, die, and rise with thee;
Let him so follow here, that in the end
He may take thee, as thou doest him intend.

    Give him thy private seal,
  Earnest, and sign; Thy gifts so deal   20
     That these forerunners here
     May make the future cleer;
Whatever thou dost bid, let faith make good,
Bread for thy body, and Wine for thy blood.

    Give him (with pitty) love,   25
  Two flowres that grew with thee above;
     Love that shal not admit
     Anger for one short fit,
And pitty of such a divine extent
That may thy members, more than mine, resent.   30

    Give me, my God! thy grace,
  The beams, and brightnes of thy face,
     That never like a beast
     I take thy sacred feast,
Or the dread mysteries of thy blest bloud   35
Use, with like Custome, as my Kitchin food.
     Some sit to thee, and eat
    Thy body as their Common meat,

30 *resent*: feel as a cause of sorrow, feel deeply.
35–42 The Puritans refused to follow the tradition of kneeling at the service.
38 *meat*: food.

O let not me do so!
Poor dust should ly still low, 40
Then kneel my soul, and body; kneel, and bow;
If *Saints,* and *Angels* fal down, much more thou.

Easter-day

Thou, whose sad heart, and weeping head lyes low,
Whose Cloudy brest cold damps invade,
Who never feel'st the Sun, nor smooth'st thy brow,
But sitt'st oppressed in the shade,
Awake, awake, 5
And in his Resurrection partake,
Who on this day (that thou might'st rise as he,)
Rose up, and cancell'd two deaths due to thee.

Awake, awake; and, like the Sun, disperse
All mists that would usurp this day; 10
Where are thy Palmes, thy branches, and thy verse?
Hosanna! heark; why doest thou stay?
Arise, arise,
And with his healing bloud anoint thine Eys,
Thy inward Eys; his bloud will cure thy mind, 15
Whose spittle only could restore the blind.

EASTER-DAY: a remarkably close imitation of Herbert's "The Dawning."
8 *two deaths:* death of the body and condemnation of the soul at the Last
Judgment.
16 See John 9:1–7.

Easter Hymn

Death, and darkness get you packing,
Nothing now to man is lacking,
All your triumphs now are ended,
And what *Adam* marr'd, is mended;
Graves are beds now for the weary,   5
Death a nap, to wake more merry;
Youth now, full of pious duty,
Seeks in thee for perfect beauty,
The weak, and aged tir'd, with length
Of daies, from thee look for new strength,   10
And Infants with thy pangs Contest
As pleasant, as if with the brest;
   Then, unto him, who thus hath thrown
Even to Contempt thy kingdome down,
And by his blood did us advance   15
Unto his own Inheritance,
To him be glory, power, praise,
From this, unto the last of daies.

The Holy Communion

Welcome sweet, and sacred feast; welcome life!
    Dead I was, and deep in trouble;
But grace, and blessings came with thee so rife,
    That they have quicken'd even drie stubble;
    Thus soules their bodies animate,   5

THE HOLY COMMUNION.
  1 See Herbert, "The Banquet," lines 1–2.
  4 *quicken'd:* given life to.

And thus, at first, when things were rude,
    Dark, void, and Crude
They, by thy Word, their beauty had, and date;
    All were by thee,
    And stil must be,   10
    Nothing that is, or lives,
But hath his Quicknings, and reprieves
    As thy hand opes, or shuts;
    Healings, and Cuts,
Darkness, and day-light, life, and death   15
Are but meer leaves turn'd by thy breath.
    Spirits without thee die,
    And blackness sits
    On the divinest wits,
As on the Sun Ecclipses lie.   20
But that great darkness at thy death
When the veyl broke with thy last breath,
    Did make us see
    The way to thee;
And now by these sure, sacred ties,   25
    After thy blood
    (Our sov'rain good,)
    Had clear'd our eies,
    And given us sight;
Thou dost unto thy self betroth   30
    Our souls, and bodies both
    In everlasting light.

Was't not enough that thou hadst payd the price
    And given us eies
When we had none, but thou must also take   35
    Us by the hand
    And keep us still awake,
    When we would sleep,
    Or from thee creep,
Who without thee cannot stand?   40

21–22 See Matthew 27:45, 51.

Was't not enough to lose thy breath
And blood by an accursed death,
    But thou must also leave
    To us that did bereave
Thee of them both, these seals the means   45
     That should both cleanse
      And keep us so,
      Who wrought thy wo?
O rose of *Sharon!* O the Lilly
     Of the valley!   50
How art thou now, thy flock to keep,
Become both *food,* and *Shepheard* to thy sheep!

The Tempest

How is man parcell'd out? how ev'ry hour
    Shews him himself, or somthing he should see?
    This late, long heat may his Instruction be,
And tempests have more in them than a showr.

    When nature on her bosome saw   5
      Her Infants die,
    And all her flowres wither'd to straw,
      Her brests grown dry;
    She made the Earth their nurse, & tomb,
      Sigh to the sky,   10
    'Til to those sighes fetch'd from her womb
      Rain did reply,
    So in the midst of all her fears
      And faint requests
    Her Earnest sighes procur'd her tears   15
      And fill'd her brests.

O that man could do so! that he would hear
    The world read to him! all the vast expence
    In the Creation shed, and slav'd to sence
Makes up but lectures for his eie, and ear.   20

[386]

Sure, mighty love foreseeing the discent
    Of this poor Creature, by a gracious art
    Hid in these low things snares to gain his heart,
And layd surprizes in each Element.

All things here shew him heaven; *Waters* that fall   25
    Chide, and fly up; *Mists* of corruptest fome
    Quit their first beds & mount; trees, herbs, flowres, all
Strive upwards stil, and point him the way home.

How do they cast off grossness? only *Earth*,
    And *Man* (like *Issachar*) in lodes delight,   30
    Water's refin'd to *Motion,* Aire to *Light,*
Fire to all three, but man hath no such mirth.

Plants in the *root* with Earth do most Comply,
    Their *Leafs* with water, and humiditie,
    The *Flowres* to air draw neer, and subtiltie,   35
And *seeds* a kinred fire have with the sky.

All have their *keyes,* and set *ascents;* but man
    Though he knows these, and hath more of his own,
    Sleeps at the ladders foot; alas! what can
These new discoveries do, except they drown?   40

Thus groveling in the shade, and darkness, he
    Sinks to a dead oblivion; and though all
    He sees, (like *Pyramids,*) shoot from this ball
And less'ning still grow up invisibly,

Yet hugs he stil his durt; The *stuffe* he wears   45
    And painted trimming takes down both his eies,
    Heaven hath less beauty than the dust he spies,
And money better musick than the *Spheres.*

THE TEMPEST.
  30 See Genesis 49:14.
  32 *three:* marginal gloss: *Light, Motion, heat.*
  35 *Subtiltie:* thinness of composition.

Life's but a blast, he knows it; what? shal straw,
    And bul-rush-fetters temper his short hour? 50
    Must he nor sip, nor sing? grows ne'r a flowr
To crown his temples? shal dreams be his law?

O foolish man! how hast thou lost thy sight?
    How is it that the Sun to thee alone
    Is grown thick darkness, and thy bread, a stone? 55
Hath flesh no softness now? mid-day no light?

Lord! thou didst put a soul here; If I must
    Be broke again, for flints will give no fire
    Without a steel, O let thy power cleer
Thy gift once more, and grind this flint to dust! 60

The Pilgrimage

    As travellours when the twilight's come,
    And in the sky the stars appear,
    The past daies accidents do summe
    With, *Thus wee saw there, and thus here.*

    Then *Jacob*-like lodge in a place 5
    (A place, and no more, is set down,)
    Where till the day restore the race
    They rest and dream homes of their own.

    So for this night I linger here,
    And full of tossings too and fro, 10
    Expect stil when thou wilt appear
    That I may get me up, and go.

THE PILGRIMAGE.
  3 *accidents:* incidents.
  4–5 See Genesis 28:11.

I long, and grone, and grieve for thee,
For thee my words, my tears do gush,
O that I were but where I see!   15
Is all the note within my Bush.

As Birds rob'd of their native wood,
Although their Diet may be fine,
Yet neither sing, nor like their food,
But with the thought of home do pine;   20

So do I mourn, and hang my head,
And though thou dost me fullnes give,
Yet look I for far better bread
Because by this man cannot live.

O feed me then! and since I may   25
Have yet more days, more nights to Count,
So strengthen me, Lord, all the way,
That I may travel to thy Mount.

Heb. Cap. xi. ver. 13.
And they Confessed, that they were strangers, and Pilgrims on the earth.

The World

I saw Eternity the other night
Like a great *Ring* of pure and endless light,
    All calm, as it was bright,
And round beneath it, Time in hours, days, years
     Driv'n by the spheres   5
Like a vast shadow mov'd, In which the world
    And all her train were hurl'd;

The doting Lover in his queintest strain
    Did their Complain,
Neer him, his Lute, his fancy, and his flights,   10
    Wits sour delights,
With gloves, and knots the silly snares of pleasure
    Yet his dear Treasure
All scatter'd lay, while he his eys did pour
    Upon a flowr.   15

2.

The darksome States-man hung with weights and woe
Like a thick midnight-fog mov'd there so slow
    He did nor stay, nor go;
Condemning thoughts (like sad Ecclipses) scowl
    Upon his soul,   20
And Clouds of crying witnesses without
    Pursued him with one shout.
Yet dig'd the Mole, and lest his ways be found
    Workt under ground,
Where he did Clutch his prey, but one did see   25
    That policie,
Churches and altars fed him, Perjuries
    Were gnats and flies,
It rain'd about him bloud and tears, but he
    Drank them as free.   30

3.

The fearfull miser on a heap of rust
Sate pining all his life there, did scarce trust
    His own hands with the dust,
Yet would not place one peece above, but lives
    In feare of theeves.   35

THE WORLD.
  8 *queintest:* most ingenious or clever.
  26 *policie:* clever statecraft, political cunning.

Thousands there were as frantick as himself
    And hug'd each one his pelf,
The down-right Epicure plac'd heav'n in sense
    And scornd pretence
While others slipt into a wide Excesse   40
    Said little lesse;
The weaker sort slight, triviall wares Inslave
    Who think them brave,
And poor, despised truth sate Counting by
    Their victory.   45

4.

Yet some, who all this while did weep and sing,
And sing, and weep, soar'd up into the *Ring*,
    But most would use no wing.
O fools (said I,) thus to prefer dark night
    Before true light,   50
To live in grots, and caves, and hate the day
    Because it shews the way,
The way which from this dead and dark abode
    Leads up to God,
A way where you might tread the Sun, and be   55
    More bright than he.
But as I did their madnes so discusse
    One whisper'd thus,
This Ring the Bride-groome did for none provide
    But for his bride.   60

[1] John Cap. 2. ver. 16, 17.
All that is in the world, the lust of the flesh, the lust of the Eys,
and the pride of life, is not of the father, but is of the world.
    And the world passeth away, and the lusts thereof, but he that
doth the will of God abideth for ever.

43 *brave:* splendid.

The Shepheards

Sweet, harmles lives! (on whose holy leisure
    Waits Innocence and pleasure,)
Whose leaders to those pastures, and cleer springs,
    Were *Patriarchs*, Saints, and Kings,
How happend it that in the dead of night   5
    You only saw true light,
While *Palestine* was fast a sleep, and lay
    Without one thought of Day?
Was it because those first and blessed swains
    Were pilgrims on those plains   10
When they receiv'd the promise, for which now
    'Twas there first shown to you?
'Tis true, he loves that Dust whereon they go
    That serve him here below,
And therefore might for memory of those   15
    His love there first disclose;
But wretched *Salem* once his love, must now
    No voice, nor vision know,
Her stately Piles with all their height and pride
    Now languished and died,   20
And *Bethlems* humble Cotts above them stept
    While all her Seers slept;
Her Cedar, firr, hew'd stones and gold were all
    Polluted through their fall,
And those once sacred mansions were now   25
    Meer emptiness and show,
This made the Angel call at reeds and thatch,
    Yet where the shepheards watch,

THE SHEPHEARDS.
  17 *Salem:* Jerusalem.
  21 *Cotts:* cottages.

And Gods own lodging (though he could not lack,)
    To be a common *Rack;*   30
No costly pride, no soft-cloath'd luxurie
    In those thin Cels could lie,
Each stirring wind and storm blew through their Cots
    Which never harbour'd plots,
Only Content, and love, and humble joys   35
    Lived there without all noise,
Perhaps some harmless Cares for the next day
    Did in their bosomes play,
As where to lead their sheep, what silent nook,
    What springs or shades to look,   40
But that was all; And now with gladsome care
    They for the town prepare,
They leave their flock, and in a busie talk
    All towards *Bethlem* walk
To see their souls great shepheard, who was come   45
    To bring all straglers home,
Where now they find him out, and taught before
    That Lamb of God adore,
That Lamb whose daies great Kings and Prophets wish'd
    And long'd to see, but miss'd.   50
The first light they beheld was bright and gay
    And turn'd their night to day,
But to this later light they saw in him,
    Their day was dark, and dim.

The Sap

    Come sapless Blossom, creep not stil on Earth
        Forgetting thy first birth;
    'Tis not from dust, or if so, why dost thou
        Thus cal and thirst for dew?

30 *Rack:* the manger.
51 The rainbow of the Covenant: see Genesis 9:8–17.

It tends not thither, if it doth, why then 5
    This growth and stretch for heav'n?
Thy root sucks but diseases, worms there seat
    And claim it for their meat.
Who plac'd thee here, did something then Infuse
    Which now can tel thee news. 10
There is beyond the Stars an hil of myrrh
    From which some drops fal here,
On it the Prince of *Salem* sits, who deals
    To thee thy secret meals,
There is thy Country, and he is the way 15
    And hath withal the key.
Yet liv'd he here sometimes, and bore for thee
    A world of miserie,
For thee, who in the first mans loyns didst fal
    From that hil to this vale, 20
And had not he so done, it is most true
    Two deaths had bin thy due;
But going hence, and knowing wel what woes
    Might his friends discompose,
To shew what strange love he had to our good 25
    He gave his sacred bloud
By wil our sap, and Cordial; now in this
    Lies such a heav'n of bliss,
That, who but truly tasts it, no decay
    Can touch him any way, 30
Such secret life, and vertue in it lies
    It wil exalt and rise
And actuate such spirits as are shed
    Or ready to be dead,
And bring new too. Get then this sap, and get 35
    Good store of it, but let
The vessel where you put it be for sure
    To all your pow'r most pure;

THE SAP.

13 *Prince of Salem:* see Herbert, "Peace," lines 22–23 and fn.
29–36 See Herbert, "Peace," lines 33–37.
31 *vertue:* beneficial power.

There is at all times (though shut up) in you
    A powerful, rare dew,   40
Which only grief and love extract; with this
    Be sure, and never miss,
To wash your vessel wel: Then humbly take
    This balm for souls that ake,
And one who drank it thus, assures that you   45
    Shal find a Joy so true,
Such perfect Ease, and such a lively sense
    Of grace against all sins,
That you'l Confess the Comfort such, as even
    Brings to, and comes from Heaven.   50

Mount of Olives

When first I saw true beauty, and thy Joys
Active as light, and calm without all noise
Shin'd on my soul, I felt through all my powr's
Such a rich air of sweets, as Evening showrs
Fand by a gentle gale Convey and breath   5
On some parch'd bank, crown'd with a flowrie wreath;
Odors, and Myrrh, and balm in one rich floud
O'r-ran my heart, and spirited my bloud,
My thoughts did swim in Comforts, and mine eie
Confest, *The world did only paint and lie.*   10
And where before I did no safe Course steer
But wander'd under tempests all the year,
Went bleak and bare in body as in mind,
And was blow'n through by ev'ry storm and wind,

45–50 See Herbert, "The H. Communion," "The Invitation," "The Banquet."
MOUNT OF OLIVES: the place of Christ's abode (Luke 21:37), and his place of
retirement for prayer (Luke 22:39–46); see NOTE.

1 See the opening lines of Herbert's "Jordan," "Affliction (I)," and esp. "The
Glance." Vaughan's poem throughout echoes "The Flower" as well as "The
Glance."

4 *sweets:* perfumes.

14 See Herbert, "Affliction (I)," line 36.

I am so warm'd now by this glance on me,   15
That, midst all storms I feel a Ray of thee;
So have I known some beauteous *Paisage* rise
In suddain flowres and arbours to my Eies,
And in the depth and dead of winter bring
To my Cold thoughts a lively sense of spring.   20
   Thus fed by thee, who dost all beings nourish,
My wither'd leafs again look green and flourish,
I shine and shelter underneath thy wing
Where sick with love I strive thy name to sing,
Thy glorious name! which grant I may so do   25
That these may be thy *Praise,* and my *Joy* too.

Man

   Weighing the stedfastness and state
Of some mean things which here below reside,
Where birds like watchful Clocks the noiseless date
    And Intercourse of times divide,
Where Bees at night get home and hive, and flowrs   5
      Early, aswel as late,
Rise with the Sun, and set in the same bowrs;

2.

   I would (said I) my God would give
The staidness of these things to man! for these
To his divine appointments ever cleave,   10
    And no new business breaks their peace;
The birds nor sow, nor reap, yet sup and dine,
    The flowres without clothes live,
Yet *Solomon* was never drest so fine.

17 *Paisage:* landscape.
MAN.
   3 *date:* duration.
   9 *staidness:* stability, constancy.
   12–14 See Matthew 6:26–29.

3.

Man hath stil either toyes, or Care,   15
He hath no root, nor to one place is ty'd,
But ever restless and Irregular
    About this Earth doth run and ride,
He knows he hath a home, but scarce knows where,
       He sayes it is so far   20
That he hath quite forgot how to go there.

4.

He knocks at all doors, strays and roams,
Nay hath not so much wit as some stones have
Which in the darkest nights point to their homes,
    By some hid sense their Maker gave;   25
Man is the shuttle, to whose winding quest
       And passage through these looms
God order'd motion, but ordain'd no rest.

¶

I walkt the other day (to spend my hour,)
       Into a field
Where I sometimes had seen the soil to yield
       A gallant flowre,
But Winter now had ruffled all the bowre   5
       And curious store
       I knew there heretofore.

    23 *wit:* intelligence.
"I WALKT THE OTHER DAY."
    4 See Herbert, "Peace," line 14.
    6 *curious store:* exquisite abundance.

2.

Yet I whose search lov'd not to peep and peer
      I'th' face of things
Thought with my self, there might be other springs   10
      Besides this here
Which, like cold friends, sees us but once a year,
      And so the flowre
    Might have some other bowre.

3.

Then taking up what I could neerest spie   15
      I digg'd about
That place where I had seen him to grow out,
      And by and by
I saw the warm Recluse alone to lie
      Where fresh and green   20
    He lived of us unseen.

4.

Many a question Intricate and rare
      Did I there strow,
But all I could extort was, that he now
      Did there repair   25
Such losses as befel him in this air
      And would e'r long
    Come forth most fair and young.

15–21 See Herbert, "The Flower," lines 8–14.

5.

This past, I threw the Clothes quite o'r his head,
    And stung with fear   30
Of my own frailty dropt down many a tear
    Upon his bed,
Then sighing whisper'd, *Happy are the dead!*
    What peace doth now
    Rock him asleep below?   35

6.

And yet, how few believe such doctrine springs
    From a poor root
Which all the Winter sleeps here under foot
    And hath no wings
To raise it to the truth and light of things,   40
    But is stil trod
    By ev'ry wandring clod.

7.

O thou! whose spirit did at first inflame
    And warm the dead,
And by a sacred Incubation fed   45
    With life this frame
Which once had neither being, forme, nor name,
    Grant I may so
    Thy steps track here below,

46 *frame:* structure (referring both to human body and to universe).

8.

That in these Masques and shadows I may see 50
        Thy sacred way,
And by those hid ascents climb to that day
        Which breaks from thee
Who art in all things, though invisibly;
        Shew me thy peace, 55
    Thy mercy, love, and ease,

9.

And from this Care, where dreams and sorrows raign
        Lead me above
Where Light, Joy, Leisure, and true Comforts move
        Without all pain, 60
There, hid in thee, shew me his life again
        At whose dumbe urn
    Thus all the year I mourn.

Begging

    King of Mercy, King of Love,
    In whom I live, in whom I move,
    Perfect what thou hast begun,
    Let no night put out this Sun;
    Grant I may, my chief desire! 5
    Long for thee, to thee aspire,
    Let my youth, my bloom of dayes
    Be my Comfort, and thy praise,

59 See Herbert, "Heaven," line 19.
BEGGING: for the meter and for the phrasing of line 1, see Herbert, "L'Envoy."

That hereafter, when I look
O'r the sullyed, sinful book,   10
I may find thy hand therein
Wiping out my shame, and sin.
O it is thy only Art
To reduce a stubborn heart,
And since thine is victorie,   15
Strong holds should belong to thee;
Lord then take it, leave it not
Unto my dispose or lot,
But since I would not have it mine,
O my God, let it be thine!   20

Jude ver. 24, 25.

Now unto him that is able to keep us from falling, and to present
us faultless before the presence of his glory with exceeding joy,
To the only wise God, our Saviour, be glory, and majesty, Dominion
and power, now and ever, Amen.

From SILEX SCINTILLANS (*Book 2: 1655*)

Ascension-day

Lord Jesus! with what sweetness and delights,
Sure, holy hopes, high joys and quickning flights
Dost thou feed thine! O thou! the hand that lifts
To him, who gives all good and perfect gifts.
Thy glorious, bright Ascension (though remov'd   5
So many Ages from me) is so prov'd
And by thy Spirit seal'd to me, that I
Feel me a sharer in thy victory.
        I soar and rise
        Up to the skies,   10

     Leaving the world their day,
     And in my flight,
     For the true light
     Go seeking all the way;
I greet thy Sepulchre, salute thy Grave,   15
That blest inclosure, where the Angels gave
The first glad tidings of thy early light,
And resurrection from the earth and night.
I see that morning in thy* Converts tears,
Fresh as the dew, which but this dawning wears!   20
I smell her spices, and her ointment yields,
As rich a scent as the now Primros'd-fields:
The Day-star smiles, and light with thee deceast,
Now shines in all the Chambers of the East.
What stirs, what posting intercourse and mirth   25
Of Saints and Angels glorifie the earth?
What sighs, what whispers, busie stops and stays;
Private and holy talk fill all the ways?
They pass as at the last great day, and run
In their white robes to seek the risen Sun;   30
I see them, hear them, mark their haste, and move
Amongst them, with them, wing'd with faith and love.
Thy forty days more secret commerce here,
After thy death and Funeral, so clear
And indisputable, shews to my sight   35
As the Sun doth, which to those days gave light.
I walk the fields of *Bethani* which shine
All now as fresh as *Eden,* and as fine.
Such was the bright world, on the first seventh day,
Before man brought forth sin, and sin decay;   40
When like a Virgin clad in *Flowers* and *green*
The pure earth sat, and the fair woods had seen

ASCENSION-DAY.
  19 * *St. Mary Magdalene.* [Vaughan's footnote—Ed.]
  25 *posting:* swift.
  33 *commerce:* dealings, interchange.

No frost, but flourish'd in that youthful vest,
With which their great Creator had them drest:
When Heav'n above them shin'd like molten glass,   45
While all the Planets did unclouded pass;
And Springs, like dissolv'd Pearls their Streams did pour
Ne'r marr'd with floods, nor anger'd with a showre.
With these fair thoughts I move in this fair place,
And the last steps of my milde Master trace;   50
I see him leading out his chosen Train,
All sad with tears, which like warm Summer-rain
In silent drops steal from their holy eyes,
Fix'd lately on the Cross, now on the skies.
And now (eternal Jesus!) thou dost heave   55
Thy blessed hands to bless, these thou dost leave;
The cloud doth now receive thee, and their sight
Having lost thee, behold two men in white!
Two and no more: *what two attest, is true,*
Was thine own answer to the stubborn Jew.   60
Come then thou faithful witness! come dear Lord
Upon the Clouds again to judge this world!

Ascension-Hymn

Dust and clay
Mans antient wear!
Here you must stay,
But I elsewhere;
Souls sojourn here, but may not rest;   5
Who will ascend, must be undrest.

43 *vest:* vesture, garb.
51 *Train:* group of followers.
57–58 See Acts 1:9–10.
59–60 See John 8:17.
ASCENSION-HYMN: this poem immediately follows "Ascension-day" in 1655, as a companion-poem, or conclusion.

And yet some
That know to die
Before death come,
Walk to the skie   10
Even in this life; but all such can
Leave behinde them the old Man.

If a star
Should leave the Sphære,
She must first mar   15
Her flaming wear,
And after fall, for in her dress
Of glory, she cannot transgress.

Man of old
Within the line   20
Of *Eden* could
Like the Sun shine
All naked, innocent and bright,
And intimate with Heav'n, as light;

But since he   25
That brightness soil'd,
His garments be
All dark and spoil'd,
And here are left as nothing worth,
Till the Refiners fire breaks forth.   30

Then comes he!
Whose mighty light
Made his cloathes be
Like Heav'n, all bright;
The Fuller, whose pure blood did flow   35
To make stain'd man more white then snow.

35 *Fuller:* one who *fulls* (cleanses) cloth. See Mark 9:3.

            Hee alone
      And none else can
      Bring bone to bone
      And rebuild man,   40
    And by his all subduing might
    Make clay ascend more quick then light.

                        ¶

They are all gone into the world of light!
      And I alone sit lingring here;
Their very memory is fair and bright,
      And my sad thoughts doth clear.

It glows and glitters in my cloudy brest   5
      Like stars upon some gloomy grove,
Or those faint beams in which this hill is drest,
      After the Sun's remove.

I see them walking in an Air of glory,
      Whose light doth trample on my days: 10
My days, which are at best but dull and hoary,
      Meer glimering and decays.

O holy hope! and high humility,
      High as the Heavens above!
These are your walks, and you have shew'd them me   15
      To kindle my cold love,

Dear, beauteous death! the Jewel of the Just,
      Shining no where, but in the dark;
What mysteries do lie beyond thy dust;
      Could man outlook that mark!   20

"THEY ARE ALL GONE INTO THE WORLD OF LIGHT!": see NOTE.

He that hath found some fledg'd birds nest, may know
    At first sight, if the bird be flown;
But what fair Well, or Grove he sings in now,
    That is to him unknown.

And yet, as Angels in some brighter dreams   25
    Call to the soul, when man doth sleep:
So some strange thoughts transcend our wonted theams,
    And into glory peep.

If a star were confin'd into a Tomb
    Her captive flames must needs burn there;   30
But when the hand that lockt her up, gives room,
    She'l shine through all the sphære.

O Father of eternal life, and all
    Created glories under thee!
Resume thy spirit from this world of thrall   35
    Into true liberty.

Either disperse these mists, which blot and fill
    My perspective (still) as they pass,
Or else remove me hence unto that hill,
    Where I shall need no glass.   40

Cock-crowing

Father of lights! what Sunnie seed,
What glance of day hast thou confin'd
Into this bird? To all the breed
This busie Ray thou hast assign'd;
    Their magnetisme works all night,   5
    And dreams of Paradise and light.

35 *Resume:* take back.
38 *perspective:* telescope, spyglass.
COCK-CROWING: see NOTE.
 1 See James 1:17.

Their eyes watch for the morning-hue,
Their little grain expelling night
So shines and sings, as if it knew
The path unto the house of light.   10
      It seems their candle, howe'r done,
      Was tinn'd and lighted at the sunne.

If such a tincture, such a touch,
So firm a longing can impowre
Shall thy own image think it much   15
To watch for thy appearing hour?
      If a meer blast so fill the sail,
      Shall not the breath of God prevail?

O thou immortall light and heat!
Whose hand so shines through all this frame,   20
That by the beauty of the seat,
We plainly see, who made the same.
      Seeing thy seed abides in me,
      Dwell thou in it, and I in thee.

To sleep without thee, is to die;   25
Yea, 'tis a death partakes of hell:
For where thou dost not close the eye
It never opens, I can tell.
      In such a dark, Ægyptian border,
      The shades of death dwell and disorder.   30

If joyes, and hopes, and earnest throws,
And hearts, whose Pulse beats still for light
Are given to birds; who, but thee, knows
A love-sick souls exalted flight?
      Can souls be track'd by any eye   35
      But his, who gave them wings to flie?

12 *tinn'd:* kindled.
13 *tincture:* infused quality.
21 *seat:* residence.
31 *throws:* throes.

Onely this Veyle which thou hast broke,
And must be broken yet in me,
This veyle, I say, is all the cloke
And cloud which shadows thee from me.   40
   This veyle thy full-ey'd love denies,
    And onely gleams and fractions spies.

O take it off! make no delay,
But brush me with thy light, that I
May shine unto a perfect day,   45
And warme me at thy glorious Eye!
   O take it off! or till it flee,
    Though with no Lilie, stay with me!

The Starre

What ever 'tis, whose beauty here below
Attracts thee thus & makes thee stream & flow,
   And wind and curle, and wink and smile,
    Shifting thy gate and guile:

Though thy close commerce nought at all imbarrs   5
My present search, for Eagles eye not starrs,
   And still the lesser by the best
    And highest good is blest:

Yet, seeing all things that subsist and be,
Have their Commissions from Divinitie,   10
   And teach us duty, I will see
    What man may learn from thee.

37–40 See 2 Corinthians 3:12–16.
41 See Herbert, "The Glance," line 20.
THE STARRE.
 3 See Herbert, "The Starre," line 26.
 5 *close:* secret; *imbarrs:* embars, stops.

First, I am sure, the Subject so respected
Is well disposed, for bodies once infected,
    Deprav'd or dead, can have with thee   15
        No hold, nor sympathie.

Next, there's in it a restless, pure desire
And longing for thy bright and vitall fire,
    Desire that never will be quench'd,
        Nor can be writh'd, nor wrench'd.   20

These are the Magnets which so strongly move
And work all night upon thy light and love,
    As beauteous shapes, we know not why,
        Command and guide the eye.

For where desire, celestiall, pure desire   25
Hath taken root, and grows, and doth not tire,
    There God a Commerce states, and sheds
        His Secret on their heads.

This is the Heart he craves; and who so will
But give it him, and grudge not; he shall feel   30
    That God is true, as herbs unseen
        Put on their youth and green.

The Palm-tree

Deare friend sit down, and bear awhile this shade
As I have yours long since; This Plant, you see
So prest and bow'd, before sin did degrade
Both you and it, had equall liberty

13 *respected:* regarded, esteemed.
14 *well disposed:* in good health.
27 *a Commerce states:* sets up a relationship or communication.
THE PALM-TREE: see NOTE for interpretation.
 1 *Deare friend sit down:* the opening words of Herbert's "Love unknown."

With other trees: but now shut from the breath   5
And air of *Eden,* like a male-content
It thrives no where. This makes these weights (like death
And sin) hang at him; for the more he's bent

The more he grows. Celestial natures still
Aspire for home; This *Solomon* of old   10
By flowers and carvings and mysterious skill
Of Wings, and Cherubims, and Palms foretold.

This is the life which hid above with Christ
In God, doth always (hidden) multiply,
And spring, and grow, a tree ne'r to be pric'd,   15
A Tree, whose fruit is immortality.

Here Spirits that have run their race and fought
And won the fight, and have not fear'd the frowns
Nor lov'd the smiles of greatness, but have wrought
Their masters will, meet to receive their Crowns.   20

Here is the patience of the Saints: this Tree
Is water'd by their tears, as flowers are fed
With dew by night; but One you cannot see
Sits here and numbers all the tears they shed.

Here is their faith too, which if you will keep   25
When we two part, I will a journey make
To pluck a Garland hence, while you do sleep
And weave it for your head against you wake.

10–12 For these details of Solomon's Temple see 1 Kings 6:23–35.
13–14 See Colossians 3:3.
17–20 See 2 Timothy 4:7–8; 1 Corinthians 9:24–26; Hebrews 12:1.
21, 25 See Revelation 13:10, 14:12.
28 *against you wake:* in preparation for the time when you awake.

Silex Scintillans:
or
SACRED POEMS
and
Private Eiaculations
By
Henry Vaughan Silurist

LONDON Printed by T:W. for H. Blunden
at ye Castle in Cornehill. 1650

PLATE IV   Title page of the first edition of Vaughan's *Silex Scintillans,*
1650.

The Bird

Hither thou com'st: the busie wind all night
Blew through thy lodging, where thy own warm wing
Thy pillow was. Many a sullen storm
(For which course man seems much the fitter born,)
     Rain'd on thy bed   5
     And harmless head.

And now as fresh and chearful as the light
Thy little heart in early hymns doth sing
Unto that *Providence,* whose unseen arm
Curb'd them, and cloath'd thee well and warm.   10
     All things that be, praise him; and had
     Their lesson taught them, when first made.

So hills and valleys into singing break,
And though poor stones have neither speech nor tongue,
While active winds and streams both run and speak,   15
Yet stones are deep in admiration.
Thus Praise and Prayer here beneath the Sun
Make lesser mornings, when the great are done.
For each inclosed Spirit is a star
     Inlightning his own little sphære,   20
Whose light, though fetcht and borrowed from far,
     Both mornings makes, and evenings there.

But as these Birds of light make a land glad,
Chirping their solemn Matins on each tree:
So in the shades of night some dark fowls be,   25
Whose heavy notes make all that hear them, sad.

THE BIRD.
    26 *heavy:* melancholy.

> The Turtle then in Palm-trees mourns,
>   While Owls and Satyrs howl;
> The pleasant Land to brimstone turns
>   And all her streams grow foul.   30

> Brightness and mirth, and love and faith, all flye,
> Till the Day-spring breaks forth again from high.

The Seed growing secretly

S. Mark 4. 26.

> If this worlds friends might see but once
> What some poor man may often feel,
> Glory, and gold, and Crowns and Thrones
> They would soon quit and learn to kneel.

> My dew, my dew! my early love,   5
> My souls bright food, thy absence kills!
> Hover not long, eternal Dove!
> Life without thee is loose and spills.

> Somthing I had, which long ago
> Did learn to suck, and sip, and taste,   10
> But now grown sickly, sad and slow,
> Doth fret and wrangle, pine and waste.

> O spred thy sacred wings and shake
> One living drop! one drop life keeps!
> If pious griefs Heavens joys awake,   15
> O fill his bottle! thy childe weeps!

27 *Turtle*: turtledove.
28 *Satyrs:* biblical monsters: see Isaiah 34:14.
29–30 See Isaiah 34:9.
THE SEED GROWING SECRETLY.
  16 See Genesis 21:14–19.

Slowly and sadly doth he grow,
And soon as left, shrinks back to ill;
O feed that life, which makes him blow
And spred and open to thy will!   20

For thy eternal, living wells
None stain'd or wither'd shall come near:
A fresh, immortal *green* there dwells,
And spotless *white* is all the wear.

Dear, secret *Greenness!* nurst below   25
Tempests and windes, and winter-nights,
Vex not, that but one sees thee grow,
That *One* made all these lesser lights.

If those bright joys he singly sheds
On thee, were all met in one Crown,   30
Both Sun and Stars would hide their heads;
And Moons, though full, would get them down.

Let glory be their bait, whose mindes
Are all too high for a low Cell:
Though Hawks can prey through storms and winds,   35
The poor Bee in her hive must dwel.

Glory, the Crouds cheap tinsel still
To what most takes them, is a drudge;
And they too oft take good for ill,
And thriving vice for vertue judge.   40

What needs a Conscience calm and bright
Within it self an outward test?
Who breaks his glass to take more light,
Makes way for storms into his rest.

19 *blow:* bloom.
27 *Vex not:* be not vexed.
33 *bait:* food.

Then bless thy secret growth, nor catch   45
At noise, but thrive unseen and dumb;
Keep clean, bear fruit, earn life and watch,
Till the white winged Reapers come!

¶

As time one day by me did pass
    Through a large dusky glasse
    He held, I chanc'd to look
    And spyed his curious book
Of past days, where sad Heav'n did shed   5
A mourning light upon the dead.

Many disordered lives I saw
    And foul records which thaw
    My kinde eyes still, but in
    A fair, white page of thin   10
And ev'n, smooth lines, like the Suns rays,
Thy name was writ, and all thy days.

O bright and happy Kalendar!
    Where youth shines like a star
    All pearl'd with tears, and may   15
    Teach age, *The Holy way;*
Where through thick pangs, high agonies
Faith into life breaks, and death dies.

As some meek *night-piece* which day quails,
    To candle-light unveils: 20
    So by one beamy line
    From thy bright lamp did shine,
In the same page thy humble grave
Set with green herbs, glad hopes and brave.

"AS TIME ONE DAY BY ME DID PASS."
    4 *curious:* carefully compiled.
    9 *kinde:* sympathetic.
    19 *night-piece:* a picture of a night scene; *quails:* spoils.

Here slept my thoughts dear mark! which dust   25
    Seem'd to devour, like rust;
    But dust (I did observe)
    By hiding doth preserve,
As we for long and sure recruits,
Candy with sugar our choice fruits.   30

O calm and sacred bed where lies
    In deaths dark mysteries
    A beauty far more bright
    Then the noons cloudless light;
For whose dry dust green branches bud   35
And robes are bleach'd in the *Lambs* blood.

Sleep happy ashes! (blessed sleep!)
    While haplesse I still weep;
    Weep that I have out-liv'd
    My life, and unreliev'd   40
Must (soul-lesse shadow!) so live on,
Though life be dead, and my joys gone.

The Night

John 3. 2.

Through that pure *Virgin-shrine,*
That sacred vail drawn o'r thy glorious noon
That men might look and live as Glo-worms shine,
    And face the Moon:
    Wise *Nicodemus* saw such light   5
    As made him know his God by night.

25 *mark:* goal, target.
29 *recruits:* supplies.
36 See Revelation 7:13–14.

Most blest believer he!
Who in that land of darkness and blinde eyes
Thy long expected healing wings could see,
    When thou didst rise,   10
    And what can never more be done,
    Did at mid-night speak with the Sun!

    O who will tell me, where
He found thee at that dead and silent hour!
What hallow'd solitary ground did bear   15
        So rare a flower,
    Within whose sacred leafs did lie
    The fulness of the Deity.

    No mercy-seat of gold,
No dead and dusty *Cherub*, nor carv'd stone,   20
But his own living works did my Lord hold
        And lodge alone;
    Where *trees* and *herbs* did watch and peep
    And wonder, while the *Jews* did sleep.

    Dear night! this worlds defeat;   25
The stop to busie fools; cares check and curb;
The day of Spirits; my souls calm retreat
        Which none disturb!
    *Christs** progress, and his prayer time;
    The hours to which high Heaven doth chime.   30

    Gods silent, searching flight:
When my Lords head is fill'd with dew, and all
His locks are wet with the clear drops of night;
        His still, soft call;
    His knocking time; The souls dumb watch,   35
    When Spirits their fair kinred catch.

THE NIGHT: see NOTE.
  19–20 See Exodus 25:17–22.
  29 * *Mark, chap.* 1. 35. S. *Luke, chap.* 21. 37. [Vaughan's footnote]
  32–33 See Song of Solomon 5:2.

Were all my loud, evil days
Calm and unhaunted as is thy dark Tent,
Whose peace but by some *Angels* wing or voice
      Is seldom rent;   40
    Then I in Heaven all the long year
    Would keep, and never wander here.

    But living where the Sun
Doth all things wake, and where all mix and tyre
Themselves and others, I consent and run   45
      To ev'ry myre,
    And by this worlds ill-guiding light,
    Erre more then I can do by night.

    There is in God (some say)
A deep, but dazling darkness; As men here   50
Say it is late and dusky, because they
      See not all clear;
    O for that night! where I in him
    Might live invisible and dim.

The Water-fall

With what deep murmurs through times silent stealth
Doth thy transparent, cool and watry wealth
      Here flowing fall,
      And chide, and call,
As if his liquid, loose Retinue staid   5
Lingring, and were of this steep place afraid,
      The common pass
      Where, clear as glass,
      All must descend
      Not to an end: 10

49–54 With ref. to the mystical theology of such writers as "Dionysius the Areopagite"; see Crashaw's poem on the Epiphany, lines 190 ff., and NOTE.

But quickned by this deep and rocky grave,
Rise to a longer course more bright and brave.

Dear stream! dear bank, where often I
Have sate, and pleas'd my pensive eye,
Why, since each drop of thy quick store   15
Runs thither, whence it flow'd before,
Should poor souls fear a shade or night,
Who came (sure) from a sea of light?
Or since those drops are all sent back
So sure to thee, that none doth lack,   20
Why should frail flesh doubt any more
That what God takes, hee'l not restore?

O useful Element and clear!
My sacred wash and cleanser here,
My first consigner unto those   25
Fountains of life, where the Lamb goes?
What sublime truths, and wholesome themes,
Lodge in thy mystical, deep streams!
Such as dull man can never finde
Unless that Spirit lead his minde,   30
Which first upon thy face did move,
And hatch'd all with his quickning love.
As this loud brooks incessant fall
In streaming rings restagnates all,
Which reach by course the bank, and then   35
Are no more seen, just so pass men.
O my invisible estate,
My glorious liberty, still late!
Thou art the Channel my soul seeks,
Not this with Cataracts and Creeks.   40

THOMAS TRAHERNE
1637–1674

The Salutation

1

These little Limmes,
These Eys and Hands which here I find,
These rosie Cheeks wherwith my Life begins,
        Where have ye been,? Behind
What Curtain were ye from me hid so long!   5
Where was? in what Abyss, my Speaking Tongue?

2

When silent I,
So many thousand thousand yeers,
Beneath the Dust did in a Chaos lie,
        How could I Smiles or Tears,   10
Or Lips or Hands or Eys or Ears perceiv?
Welcom ye Treasures which I now receiv.

3

I that so long
Was Nothing from Eternitie,
Did little think such Joys as Ear or Tongue,   15
        To Celebrat or See:
Such Sounds to hear, such Hands to feel, such Feet,
Beneath the Skies, on such a Ground to meet.

4

New Burnisht Joys!
Which yellow Gold and Pearl excell!   20
Such Sacred Treasures are the Lims in Boys,
        In which a soul doth Dwell;
Their Organized Joynts, and Azure Veins
More Wealth include, then all the World contains.

5

From Dust I rise,   25
And out of Nothing now awake,
These Brighter Regions which salute mine Eys,
        A Gift from GOD I take.
The Earth, the Seas, the Light, the Day, the Skies,
The Sun and Stars are mine; if those I prize.   30

6

Long time before
I in my Mothers Womb was born,
A GOD preparing did this Glorious Store,
        The World for me adorne.
Into this Eden so Divine and fair,   35
So Wide and Bright, I com his Son and Heir.

7

A Stranger here
Strange Things doth meet, Strange Glories See;
Strange Treasures lodg'd in this fair World appear,
        Strange all, and New to me.   40
But that they mine should be, who nothing was,
That Strangest is of all, yet brought to pass.

[422]

Wonder

1

How like an Angel came I down!
    How Bright are all Things here!
When first among his Works I did appear
    O how their GLORY me did Crown?
The World resembled his *Eternitie*,   5
    In which my Soul did Walk;
    And evry Thing that I did see,
        Did with me talk.

2

The Skies in their Magnificence,
    The Lively, Lovely Air;   10
Oh how Divine, how soft, how Sweet, how fair!
    The Stars did entertain my Sence,
And all the Works of GOD so Bright and pure,
    So Rich and Great did seem,
    As if they ever must endure,   15
        In my Esteem.

3

A Native Health and Innocence
    Within my Bones did grow,
And while my GOD did all his Glories shew,
    I felt a Vigour in my Sence   20

WONDER.
  12 *Sence:* the power of sensory apprehension, chiefly sight.

That was all SPIRIT. I within did flow
    With Seas of Life, like Wine;
I nothing in the World did know,
    But 'twas Divine.

4

Harsh ragged Objects were conceald,   25
    Oppressions Tears and Cries,
Sins, Griefs, Complaints, Dissentions, Weeping Eys,
    Were hid: and only Things reveald,
Which Heav'nly Spirits, and the Angels prize.
      The State of Innocence   30
    And Bliss, not Trades and Poverties,
      Did fill my Sence.

5

The Streets were pavd with Golden Stones,
    The Boys and Girles were mine,
Oh how did all their Lovly faces shine!   35
    The Sons of Men were Holy Ones.
Joy, Beauty, Welfare did appear to me,
      And evry Thing which here I found,
    While like an Angel I did see,
      Adornd the Ground.   40

6

Rich Diamond and Pearl and Gold
    In evry Place was seen;
Rare Splendors, Yellow, Blew, Red, White and Green,
    Mine Eys did evrywhere behold,

Great Wonders clothd with Glory did appear,   45
    Amazement was my Bliss.
That and my Wealth was evry where:
    No Joy to this!

7

Cursd and Devisd Proprieties,
    With Envy, Avarice   50
And. Fraud, those Feinds that Spoyl even Paradice,
    Fled from the Splendor of mine Eys.
And so did Hedges, Ditches, Limits, Bounds,
    I dreamd not ought of those,
But wanderd over all mens Grounds,   55
    And found Repose.

8

Proprieties themselvs were mine,
    And Hedges Ornaments;
Walls, Boxes, Coffers, and their rich Contents
    Did not Divide my Joys, but shine.   60
Clothes, Ribbans, Jewels, Laces, I esteemd
    My Joys by others worn;
For me they all to wear them seemd
    When I was born.

49 *Devisd:* legally willed; also, contrived; *Proprieties:* private possessions.

Eden

1

A learned and a Happy Ignorance
        Divided me,
      From all the Vanitie,
From all the Sloth Care Pain and Sorrow that advance,
    The madness and the Miserie   5
Of Men. No Error, no Distraction I
Saw soil the Earth, or overcloud the Skie.

2

I knew not that there was a Serpents Sting,
        Whose Poyson shed
      On Men, did overspread   10
The World: nor did I Dream of such a Thing
    As Sin; in which Mankind lay Dead.
They all were Brisk and Living Weights to me,
Yea Pure, and full of Immortalitie.

3

Joy, Pleasure, Beauty, Kindness, Glory, Lov,   15
      Sleep, Day, Life, Light,
      Peace, Melody, my Sight,
My Ears and Heart did fill, and freely mov.
    All that I saw did me Delight.

EDEN.
  13 *Weights:* wights, persons.

The *Universe* was then a World of Treasure,   20
To me an Universal World of Pleasure.

4

Unwelcom Penitence was then unknown,
   Vain Costly Toys,
   Swearing and Roaring Boys,
Shops, Markets, Taverns, Coaches were unshewn; 25
   So all things were that Drownd my Joys.
No Thorns choakt up my Path, nor hid the face
Of Bliss and Beauty, nor Ecclypst the Place.

5

Only what Adam in his first Estate,
   Did I behold;   30
   Hard Silver and Drie Gold
As yet lay under Ground; my Blessed Fate
   Was more acquainted with the Old
And Innocent Delights, which he did see
In his Original Simplicitie.   35

6

Those Things which first his Eden did adorn,
   My Infancy
   Did crown. Simplicitie
Was my Protection when I first was born.
   Mine Eys those Treasures first did see, 40
Which God first made. The first Effects of Lov
My first Enjoyments upon Earth did prov;

35 *Simplicitie:* naturalness, freedom from artifice or pretence.

7

And were so Great, and so Divine, so Pure,
    So fair and Sweet,
      So True; when I did meet   45
Them here at first, they did my Soul allure,
    And drew away my Infant feet
Quite from the Works of Men; that I might see
The Glorious Wonders of the DEITIE.

Innocence

1

But that which most I Wonder at, which most
I did esteem my Bliss, which most I Boast,
And ever shall Enjoy, is that within
    I felt no Stain, nor Spot of Sin.

    No Darkness then did overshade,   5
    But all within was Pure and Bright,
    No Guilt did Crush, nor fear invade
    But all my Soul was full of Light.

    A Joyfull Sence and Puritie
      Is all I can remember.   10
    The very Night to me was Bright,
    Twas Summer in December.

2

A Serious Meditation did employ
My Soul within, which taken up with Joy
Did seem no Outward thing to note, but flie   15
    All Objects that do feed the Eye.

    While it those very Objects did
    Admire, and prize, and prais, and love,
    Which in their Glory most are hid,
    Which Presence only doth remove.   20

    Their Constant Daily Presence I
        Rejoycing at, did see;
    And that which takes them from the Ey
    Of others, offerd them to me.

3

No inward Inclination did I feel   25
To Avarice or Pride: My Soul did kneel
In Admiration all the Day. No Lust, nor Strife,
    Polluted then my Infant Life.

    No Fraud nor Anger in me movd
    No Malice Jealousie or Spite;   30
    All that I saw I truly lovd.
    Contentment only and Delight

    Were in my Soul. O Heav'n! what Bliss
        Did I enjoy and feel!
    What Powerfull Delight did this   35
    Inspire! for this I daily Kneel.

4

Whether it be that Nature is so pure,
And Custom only vicious; or that sure
God did by Miracle the Guilt remov,
    And make my Soul to feel his Lov,   40

    So Early: Or that 'twas one Day,
    Wher in this Happiness I found;
    Whose Strength and Brightness so do Ray,
    That still it seemeth to Surround.

    What ere it is, it is a Light   45
        So Endless unto me
    That I a World of true Delight
    Did then and to this Day do see.

5

That Prospect was the Gate of Heav'n, that Day
The anchient Light of Eden did convey   50
Into my Soul: I was an Adam there,
    A little Adam in a Sphere

    Of Joys! O there my Ravisht Sence
    Was entertaind in Paradice,
    And had a Sight of Innocence.   55
    All was beyond all Bound and Price.

    An Antepast of Heaven sure!
        I on the Earth did reign.
    Within, without me, all was pure.
    I must becom a Child again.   60

INNOCENCE.
  57 *Antepast:* appetizer, foretaste.
  60 See Matthew 18:3.

The Preparative

1

My Body being Dead, my Lims unknown;
    Before I skild to prize
    Those living Stars mine Eys,
Before my Tongue or Cheeks were to me shewn,
    Before I knew my Hands were mine,   5
Or that my Sinews did my Members joyn,
    When neither Nostril, Foot, nor Ear,
As yet was seen, or felt, or did appear;
        I was within
A House I knew not, newly clothd with Skin.   10

2

Then was my Soul my only All to me,
    A Living Endless Ey,
    Far wider then the Skie
Whose Power, whose Act, whose Essence was to see.
    I was an Inward *Sphere of Light,*   15
Or an Interminable Orb of *Sight,*
    An Endless and a Living Day,
A *vital Sun* that round about did *ray*
        All Life and Sence,
A Naked Simple Pure *Intelligence.*   20

THE PREPARATIVE: preparation.
  2 *skild:* knew how to.
  18 *vital:* life-giving.

3

I then no Thirst nor Hunger did conceiv,
    No dull Necessity,
    No Want was Known to me;
Without Disturbance then I did receiv
    The fair Ideas of all Things,   25
And had the Hony even without the Stings.
    A Meditating Inward Ey
Gazing at Quiet did within me lie,
    And evry Thing
Delighted me that was their Heavnly King.   30

4

For *Sight* inherits Beauty, *Hearing* Sounds,
    The *Nostril* Sweet Perfumes,
    All *Tastes* have hidden Rooms
Within the *Tongue;* and *Feeling Feeling* Wounds
    With Pleasure and Delight: but I   35
Forgot the rest, and was all Sight, or Ey.
    Unbodied and Devoid of Care,
Just as in Heavn the Holy Angels are.
    For Simple Sence
Is Lord of all Created Excellence.   40

5

Be'ing thus prepard for all Felicity,
    Not prepossest with Dross,
    Nor stifly glued to gross
And dull Materials that might ruine me,
    Not fetterd by an Iron Fate   45

With vain Affections in my Earthy State
    To any thing that might Seduce
My Sence, or misemploy it from its use
        I was as free
As if there were nor Sin, nor Miserie.   50

6

Pure Empty Powers that did nothing loath,
    Did like the fairest Glass,
    Or Spotless polisht Brass,
Themselvs soon in their Objects Image cloath.
    Divine Impressions when they came,   55
Did quickly enter and my Soul inflame.
    Tis not the Object, but the Light
That maketh Heaven; Tis a Purer Sight.
       Felicitie
Appears to none but them that purely see.   60

7

A Disentangled and a Naked Sence
    A Mind thats unpossest,
    A Disengaged Brest,
An Empty and a Quick Intelligence
    Acquainted with the Golden Mean,   65
An Even Spirit Pure and Serene,
    Is that where Beauty, Excellence,
And Pleasure keep their Court of Residence.
      My Soul retire,
Get free, and so thou shalt even all Admire.   70

From THE THIRD CENTURY

1

Will you see the Infancy of this sublime and celestial Greatness? Those Pure and Virgin Apprehensions[1] I had from the Womb, and that Divine Light wherewith I was born, are the Best unto this Day, wherin I can see the Universe. By the Gift of GOD they attended me into the World, and by his Special favor I remember them till now. Verily they seem the Greatest Gifts His Wisdom could bestow. for without them all other Gifts had been Dead and Vain. They are unattainable by Book, and therfore I will teach them by Experience. Pray for them earnestly: for they will make you Angelical, and wholy Celestial. Certainly Adam in Paradice had not more sweet and Curious[2] Apprehensions of the World, then I when I was a child.

2

All appeared New, and Strange at the first, inexpressibly rare, and Delightfull, and Beautifull. I was a little Stranger which at my Enterance into the World was Saluted[3] and Surrounded with innumerable Joys. My Knowledg was Divine. I knew by Intuition those things which since my Apostasie, I Collected again, by the Highest Reason. My very Ignorance was Advantageous. I seemed as one Brought into the Estate of Innocence. All Things were Spotles and Pure and Glorious: yea, and infinitly mine, and Joyfull and Precious.

THE THIRD CENTURY.
  [1] perceptions, conceptions.
  [2] exquisite.
  [3] greeted.

I Knew not that there were any Sins, or Complaints, or Laws. I Dreamed not of Poverties Contentions or Vices. All Tears and Quarrels, were hidden from mine Eys. Evry Thing was at Rest, Free, and Immortal. I Knew Nothing of Sickness or Death, or Exaction, in the Absence of these I was Entertained like an Angel with the Works of GOD in their Splendor and Glory; I saw all in the Peace of Eden; Heaven and Earth did sing my Creators Praises and could not make more Melody to Adam, then to me. All Time was Eternity, and a Perpetual Sabbath. Is it not Strange, that an Infant should be Heir of the World, and see those Mysteries which the Books of the Learned never unfold?

3

The Corn was Orient[4] and Immortal Wheat, which never should be reaped, nor was ever sown. I thought it had stood from everlasting to everlasting. The Dust and Stones of the Street were as Precious as GOLD. The Gates were at first the End of the World, The Green Trees when I saw them first through one of the Gates Transported and Ravished me; their Sweetnes and unusual Beauty made my Heart to leap, and almost mad with Extasie, they were such strange and Wonderfull Thing: The Men! O what Venerable and Reverend Creatures did the Aged seem! Immortal Cherubims! And yong Men Glittering and Sparkling Angels and Maids strange Seraphick Pieces of Life and Beauty! Boys and Girles Tumbling in the Street, and Playing, were moving Jewels. I knew not that they were Born or should Die. But all things abided Eternaly as they were in their Proper Places. Eternity was Manifest in the Light of the Day, and som thing infinit Behind evry thing appeared: which talked with my Expectation and moved my Desire. The Citie seemed to stand in Eden, or to be Built in Heaven. The Streets were mine, the Temple was mine, the People were mine, their Clothes and Gold and Silver was mine, as much as their Sparkling Eys Fair Skins and ruddy faces.

4 *Corn:* grain; *Orient:* shining, brilliant.

The Skies were mine, and so were the Sun and Moon and Stars, and all the World was mine, and I the only Spectator and Enjoyer of it. I knew no Churlish Proprieties, nor Bounds nor Divisions: but all Proprieties and Divisions were mine: all Treasures and the Possessors of them. So that with much adoe I was corrupted; and made to learn the Dirty Devices of this World. Which now I unlearn, and becom as it were a little Child again, that I may enter into the Kingdom of GOD.

4

Upon those Pure and Virgin Apprehensions which I had in my Infancy, I made this Poem.

1

That Childish Thoughts such Joys Inspire,
Doth make my Wonder, and His Glory higher;
His Bounty, and my Wealth more Great:
It shews His Kingdom, and His Work Compleat.
In which there is not any Thing,   5
Not meet to be the Joy of Cherubim.

2

He in our Childhood with us Walks,
And with our Thoughts Mysteriously He talks;
He often Visiteth our Minds,
But cold Acceptance in us ever finds.
We send Him often grievd away,   10
Who els would shew us all His Kingdoms Joy.

3

O Lord I Wonder at Thy Lov,
Which did my Infancy so Early mov:
   But more at that which did forbear   15
And mov so long, though sleighted many a yeer:
   But most of all, at last that Thou
Thy self shouldst me convert, I scarce Know how.

4

Thy Gracious Motions[5] oft in vain
Assaulted me: My Heart did hard remain   20
   Long time! I sent my God away
Grievd much, that He could not giv me His Joy.
   I careless was, nor did regard
The End for which He all those Thoughts prepard.

5

But now, with New and Open Eys,   25
I see beneath, as if I were abov the Skies:
   And as I backward look again
See all His Thoughts and mine most Clear and Plain.
   He did approach, He me did Woe.[6]
I Wonder that my GOD this thing would doe.   30

[5] promptings, stirrings.
[6] woo.

6

From Nothing taken first I was;
What Wondrous things His Glory brought to pass!
   Now in the World I Him behold,
And Me, Inveloped in Precious Gold;
   In deep Abysses of Delights,   35
In present Hidden Glorious Benefits.

7

Those Thoughts His Goodness long before
Prepard as Precious and Celestial Store:
   With Curious Art in me inlaid,
That Childhood might it self alone be said   40
   My Tutor Teacher Guid to be,
Instructed then even by the Dietie.

5

Our Saviors Meaning, when He said, He must be Born again and
becom a little Child that will enter into the Kingdom of Heaven:[7]
is Deeper far then is generaly believed. It is not only in a Careless
Reliance upon Divine Providence, that we are to becom Little
Children, or in the feebleness and shortness of our Anger and
Simplicity of our Passions: but in the Peace and Purity of all our
Soul. Which Purity also is a Deeper Thing then is commonly ap-
prehended. for we must disrobe our selvs of all fals Colors, and un-
clothe our Souls of evil Habits; all our Thoughts must be Infant-like
and Clear: the Powers of our Soul free from the Leven of this World,

---

[7] See John 3:3; Mark 10:15; Matthew 18:3.

and disentangled from mens conceits[8] and customs. Grit in the Ey or the yellow Jandice will not let a Man see those Objects truly that are before it. And therfore it is requisit that we should be as very Strangers to the Thoughts Customs and Opinions of men in this World as if we were but little Children. So those Things would appear to us only which do to Children when they are first Born. Ambitions, Trades, Luxuries, inordinat Affections,[9] Casual and Accidental[10] Riches invented since the fall would be gone, and only those Things appear, which did to Adam in Paradice, in the same Light, and in the same Colors. GOD in His Works, Glory in the Light, Lov in our Parents, Men, our selvs, and the Face of Heaven. Evry Man naturaly seeing those Things, to the Enjoyment of which He is Naturaly Born.

6

Evry one provideth Objects, but few prepare Senses wherby, and Light wherin to see them. Since therfore we are Born to be a Burning and Shining Light, and whatever men learn of others, they see in the Light of others Souls: I will in the Light of my Soul shew you the Univers. Perhaps it is Celestial, and will teach you how Beneficial we may be to each other. I am sure it is a Sweet and Curious Light to me: which had I wanted:[11] I would hav given all the Gold and Silver in all Worlds to hav Purchased. But it was the Gift of GOD and could not be bought with Mony. And by what Steps and Degrees I proceeded to that Enjoyment of all Eternity which now I possess I will likewise shew you. A Clear, and familiar Light it may prove unto you.

[8] conceptions, opinions.
[9] immoderate emotions (see Colossians 3:5).
[10] non-essential.
[11] lacked.

7

The first Light which shined in my Infancy in its Primitive and Innocent Clarity was totaly ecclypsed: insomuch that I was fain[12] to learn all again. If you ask me how it was ecclypsed? Truly by the Customs and maners of Men, which like Contrary Winds blew it out: by an innumerable company of other Objects, rude vulgar and Worthless Things that like so many loads of Earth and Dung did over whelm and Bury it: by the Impetuous Torrent of Wrong Desires in all others whom I saw or knew that carried me away and alienated me from it: by a Whole Sea of other Matters and Concernments that Covered and Drowned it: finaly by the Evil Influence of a Bad Education that did not foster and cherish it. All Mens thoughts and Words were about other Matters; They all prized New Things which I did not dream of. I was a stranger and unacquainted with them; I was little and reverenced their Authority; I was weak, and easily guided by their Example: Ambitious also, and Desirous to approve my self[13] unto them. And finding no one Syllable in any mans Mouth of those Things, by Degrees they vanishd, My Thoughts, (as indeed what is more fleeting then a Thought) were blotted out. And at last all the Celestial Great and Stable Treasures to which I was born, as wholy forgotten, as if they had never been.

8

Had any man spoken of it, it had been the most easy Thing in the World, to hav taught me, and to hav made me believ, that Heaven and Earth was GODs Hous, and that He gav it me. That the Sun was mine and that Men were mine, and that Cities and Kingdoms were mine also: that Earth was better then Gold, and that Water

12 obliged.
13 show myself worthy of approval.

was, every Drop of it, a Precious Jewel. And that these were Great and Living Treasures: and that all Riches whatsoever els was Dross in Comparison. From whence I clearly find how Docible[14] our Nature is in natural Things, were it rightly entreated.[15] And that our Misery proceedeth ten thousand times more from the outward Bondage of Opinion and Custom, then from any inward corruption or Depravation of Nature: And that it is not our Parents Loyns, so much as our Parents lives, that Enthrals and Blinds us. Yet is all our Corruption Derived from Adam: inasmuch as all the Evil Examples and inclinations of the World arise from His Sin. But I speak it in the presence of GOD and of our Lord Jesus Christ, in my Pure Primitive Virgin Light, while my Apprehensions were natural, and unmixed, I can not remember, but that I was ten thousand times more prone to Good and Excellent Things, then evil. But I was quickly tainted and fell by others.

9

It was a Difficult matter to persuade me that the Tinsild Ware upon a Hobby hors was a fine thing. They did impose upon me, and Obtrude[16] their Gifts that made me believ a Ribban or a Feather Curious. I could not see where the Curiousness or fineness: And to Teach me that A Purs of Gold was of any valu seemed impossible, the Art by which it becomes so, and the reasons for which it is accounted so were so Deep and Hidden to my Inexperience. So that Nature is still nearest to Natural Things. and farthest off from preternatural,[17] and to esteem that the Reproach of Nature, is an Error in them only who are unacquainted with it. Natural Things are Glorious, and to know them Glorious: But to call things preternatural Natural, Monstrous. Yet all they do it, who esteem Gold Silver Houses Lands Clothes &c. the Riches of Nature, which are indeed the Riches of Invention. Nature Knows no such Riches. but Art and

[14] teachable.
[15] treated.
[16] thrust forward.
[17] unnatural.

Error makes them. Not the God of Nature, but Sin only was the Parent of them. The Riches of Nature are our Souls and Bodies, with all their Faculties Sences and Endowments. And it had been the Easiest thing in the whole World, that all felicity consisted in the Enjoyment of all the World, that it was prepared for me before I was born, and that Nothing was more Divine and Beautifull.

10

Thoughts are the most Present things to Thoughts, and of the most Powerfull Influence. My Soul was only Apt and Disposed to Great Things; But Souls to Souls are like Apples to Apples, one being rotten rots another. When I began to speak and goe,[18] Nothing began to be present to me, but what was present in their Thoughts. Nor was any thing present to me any other way, then it was so to them. The Glass of Imagination was the only Mirror, wherin any thing was represented or appeared to me. All Things were Absent which they talkt not of. So I began among my Play fellows to prize a Drum, a fine Coat, a Peny, a Gilded Book &c. who before never Dreamd of any such Wealth. Goodly Objects to drown all the Knowledg of Heaven and Earth: As for the Heavens and the Sun and Stars they disappeared, and were no more unto me than the bare Walls. So that the Strange Riches of Mans Invention quite overcame the Riches of Nature. Being learned more laboriously and in the second Place.

11

By this let Nurses, and those Parents that desire Holy Children learn to make them Possessors of Heaven and Earth betimes.[19] to remove silly Objects from before them, to Magnify nothing but what is Great

[18] walk.
[19] early in life.

indeed, and to talk of God to them and of His Works and Ways before they can either Speak or go. For Nothing is so Easy as to teach the Truth becaus the Nature of the Thing confirms the Doctrine. As when we say The Sun is Glorious, A Man is a Beautifull Creature, Soveraign over Beasts and Fowls and Fishes, The Stars Minister unto us, The World was made for you, &c. But to say This Hous is yours, and these Lands are another Mans and this Bauble is a Jewel and this Gugaw a fine Thing, this Rattle makes Musick &c. is deadly Barbarous and uncouth to a little Child; and makes him suspect all you say, becaus the Nature of the Thing contradicts your Words. Yet doth that Blot out all Noble and Divine Ideas, Dissettle his foundation, render him uncertain in all Things, and Divide him from GOD. To teach him those Objects are little vanities, and that tho GOD made them, by the Ministery of Man, yet Better and more Glorious Things are more to be Esteemed, is Natural and Easy.

12

By this you may see who are the Rude and Barbarous Indians For verily there is no Salvage[20] Nation under the Cope[21] of Heaven, that is more absurdly Barbarous than the Christian World. They that go Naked and Drink Water and liv upon Roots are like Adam, or Angels in Comparison of us. But they indeed that call Beads and Glass Buttons Jewels, and Dress them selvs with feather, and buy pieces of Brass and broken hafts of Knives of our Merchants are som what like us. But We Pass them in Barbarous Opinions, and Monstrous Apprehensions: which we Nick Name Civility, and the Mode, amongst us. I am sure those Barbarous People that go naked, com nearer to Adam God, and Angels in the Simplicity of their Wealth, tho not in Knowledg.

[20] savage.
[21] canopy, vault.

13

You would not think how these Barbarous Inventions spoyle your Knowledg. They put Grubs and Worms in Mens Heads: that are Enemies to all Pure and True Apprehensions, and eat out all their Happines. They make it impossible for them, in whom they reign, to believ there is any Excellency in the Works of GOD, or to taste any Sweetness in the Nobility of Nature, or to Prize any Common, tho never so Great a Blessing. They alienat men from the Life of GOD, and at last make them to live without GOD in the World. To liv the Life of GOD is to live to all the Works of GOD, and to enjoy them in His Image. from which they are wholy Diverted that follow fashions. Their fancies are corrupted with other Gingles.

14

Being Swallowed up therfore in the Miserable Gulph of idle talk and worthless vanities, thenceforth I lived among Shadows, like a Prodigal Son feeding upon Husks with Swine. A Comfortless Wilderness full of Thorns and Troubles the World was, or wors: a Waste Place covered with Idleness and Play, and Shops and Markets and Taverns. As for Churches they were things I did not understand. And Scholes were a Burden: so that there was nothing in the World worth the having, or Enjoying, but my Game and Sport, which also was a Dream and being passed wholy forgotten. So that I had utterly forgotten all Goodness Bounty Comfort and Glory: which things are the very Brightness of the Glory of GOD: for lack of which therfore He was unknown.

15

Yet somtimes in the midst of these Dreams, I should com a litle to my self. so far as to feel I wanted som thing, secretly to Expostulate with GOD for not giving me Riches, to long after an unknown Happiness, to griev that the World was so empty, and to be dissatisfied with my present State becaus it was vain and forlorn. I had heard of Angels, and much admired that here upon earth nothing should be but Dirt and Streets and Gutters. for as for the Pleasures that were in Great Mens Houses I had not seen them: and it was my real Happiness they were unknown. for becaus Nothing Deluded me, I was the more Inquisitive.

16

Once I remember (I think I was about 4 yeer old, when) I thus reasoned with my self. sitting in a little Obscure Room in my Fathers poor House. If there be a God, certainly He must be infinit in Goodness. And that I was prompted to, by a real Whispering Instinct of Nature. And if He be infinit in Goodness, and a Perfect Being in Wisdom and Love, certainly He must do most Glorious Things: and giv us infinit Riches; how comes it to pass therfore that I am so poor? of so Scanty and Narrow a fortune, enjoying few and Obscure Comforts? I thought I could not believ Him a GOD to me, unless all His Power were Employed to Glorify me. I knew not then my Soul, or Body: nor did I think of the Heavens and the Earth, the Rivers and the Stars, the Sun or the Seas: all those were lost, and Absent from me. But when I found them made out of Nothing for me, then I had a GOD indeed, whom I could Prais, and rejoyce in.

17

Som times I should be alone, and without Employment, when suddainly my Soul would return to it self, and forgetting all Things in the whole World which mine Eys had seen, would be carried away to the Ends of the Earth: and my Thoughts would be deeply Engaged with Enquiries, How the Earth did End? Whether Walls did Bound it, or Suddain Precipices. or Whether the Heavens by Degrees did com to touch it; so that the face of the Earth and Heaven were so neer, that a Man with Difficulty could Creep under? Whatever I could imagin was inconvenient,[22] and my Reason being Posed[23] was Quickly Wearied. What also upheld the Earth (becaus it was Heavy) and kept it from falling; Whether Pillars, or Dark Waters? And if any of these, What then upheld those, and what again those, of which I saw there would be no End? Little did I think that the Earth was Round, and the World so full of Beauty, Light, and Wisdom. When I saw that, I knew by the Perfection of the Work there was a GOD, and was satisfied, and Rejoyced. People underneath and feilds and flowers with another Sun and another Day Pleased me mightily: but more when I knew it was the same Sun that served them by night, that served us by Day.

23

Another time, in a Lowering and sad Evening, being alone in the field, when all things were dead and quiet, a certain Want and Horror fell upon me, beyond imagination. The unprofitableness and Silence of the Place dissatisfied me, its Wideness terrified me, from the utmost Ends of the Earth fears surrounded me. How did I know but Dangers might suddainly arise from the East, and invade me

[22] unsuitable, incongruous.
[23] puzzled.

from the unknown Regions beyond the Seas? I was a Weak and little child, and had forgotten there was a man alive in the Earth. Yet som thing also of Hope and Expectation comforted me from every Border. This taught me that I was concerned in all the World: and that in the remotest Borders the Causes of Peace delight me, and the Beauties of the Earth when seen were made to entertain me: that I was made to hold a Communion with the Secrets of Divine Providence in all the World: that a Remembrance of all the Joys I had from my Birth ought always to be with me: that the Presence of Cities Temples and Kingdoms ought to Sustain me, and that to be alone in the World was to be Desolate and Miserable. The Comfort of Houses and friends, and the clear Assurance of Treasures evry where, Gods Care and Lov, His Goodnes Wisdom, and Power, His presence and Watchfulness in all the Ends of the Earth, were my Strength and Assurance for ever: and that these things being Absent to my Ey, were my Joys and consolations: as present to my Understanding as the Wideness and Emptiness of the Universe which I saw before me.

24

When I heard of any New Kingdom beyond the seas, the Light and Glory of it pleased me immediatly, enterd into me, it rose up within me and I was Enlarged Wonderfully. I entered into it, I saw its Commodities,[24] Rarities, Springs, Meadows Riches, Inhabitan[t]s, and became Possessor of that New Room, as if it had been prepared for me, so much was I Magnified and Delighted in it. When the Bible was read my Spirit was present in other Ages. I saw the Light and Splendor of them: the Land of Canaan, the Israelites entering into it, the ancient Glory of the Amorites, their Peace and Riches, their Cities Houses Vines and Fig trees, the long Prosperity of their Kings, their Milk and Honie, their slaughter and Destruction, with the Joys and Triumphs of GODs People all which

[24] advantages, useful products.

Entered into me, and GOD among them. I saw all and felt all in such a lively maner, as if there had been no other Way to those Places, but in Spirit only. This shewd me the Liveliness of interior presence, and that all Ages were for most Glorious Ends, Accessible to my Understanding, yea with it, yea within it. for without changing Place in my self I could behold and Enjoy all those. Any thing when it was proposed, tho it was 10000 Ages agoe, being always before me.

25

When I heard any News I received it with Greediness and Delight, becaus my Expectation was awakend with som Hope that My Happiness and the Thing I wanted was concealed in it. Glad Tidings[25] you know from a far Country brings us our Salvation: And I was not deceived. In Jury was Jesus Killed, and from Jerusalem the Gospel came. Which when I once knew I was very Confident that evry Kingdom contained like Wonders and Causes of Joy, tho that was the fountain of them. As it was the First fruits so was it the Pledg of what I shall receiv in other Countries. Thus also when any curious Cabinet, or secret in Chymistrie, Geometry or Physick[26] was offered to me, I diligently looked in it, but when I saw it to the Bottom and not my Happiness I despised it. These Imaginations and this Thirst of News occasioned these Reflexions.

[25] an allusion to the literal meaning of the word *gospel,* derived from the Old English word *godspel:* good tidings.

[26] medicine.

26

On News

1

News from a forrein Country came,
As if my Treasure and my Wealth lay there:
   So much it did my Heart Enflame!
Twas wont to call my Soul into mine Ear.
     Which thither went to Meet   5
      The Approaching Sweet:
    And on the Threshhold stood,
   To entertain the Unknown Good.
      It Hoverd there,
     As if twould leav mine Ear.   10
And was so Eager to Embrace
The Joyfull Tidings as they came,
Twould almost leav its Dwelling Place,
    To Entertain the Same.

2

   As if the Tidings were the Things,   15
My very Joys themselvs, my forrein Treasure,
   Or els did bear them on their Wings;
With so much Joy they came, with so much Pleasure.
     My Soul stood at the Gate
      To recreat   20
    It self with Bliss: And to
   Be pleasd with Speed. A fuller View

26.8 *entertain:* receive.
  20 *recreat:* refresh.

It fain would take
Yet Journeys back would make
Unto my Heart: as if twould fain   25
Go out to meet, yet stay within
To fit a place, to Entertain,
    And bring the Tidings in.

3

What Sacred Instinct did inspire
My Soul in Childhood with a Hope so Strong?   30
What Secret Force movd my Desire,
To Expect my Joys beyond the Seas, so Yong?
    Felicity I knew
      Was out of View:
    And being here alone,   35
I saw that Happiness was gone,
    From Me! for this,
    I Thirsted Absent Bliss,
And thought that sure beyond the Seas,
Or els in som thing near at hand   40
I knew not yet, (since nought did pleas
    I knew.) my Bliss did stand.

4

But little did the Infant Dream
That all the Treasures of the World were by:
    And that Himself was so the Cream   45
And Crown of all, which round about did lie.
    Yet thus it was. The Gem,
      The Diadem,
    The Ring Enclosing all
That Stood upon this Earthy Ball;   50
    The Heavenly Ey,
    Much Wider then the Skie,

23 *fain:* gladly.

Wher in they all included were
The Glorious Soul that was the King
Made to possess them, did appear   55
    A Small and little thing!

46

When I came into the Country, and being seated among silent Trees, had all my Time in mine own Hands, I resolved to Spend it all, whatever it cost me, in Search of Happiness, and to Satiat that burning Thirst which Nature had Enkindled, in me from my Youth. In which I was so resolut, that I chose rather to liv upon 10 pounds a yeer, and to go in Lether Clothes, and feed upon Bread and Water, so that I might hav all my time clearly to my self: then to keep many thousands per Annums in an Estate of Life where my Time would be Devoured in Care and Labor. And GOD was so pleased to accept of that Desire, that from that time to this I hav had all things plentifully provided for me, without any Care at all, my very Study of Felicity making me more to Prosper, then all the Care in the Whole World. So that through His Blessing I liv a free and a Kingly Life, as if the World were turned again into Eden, or much more, as it is at this Day.

47

1

A life of Sabbaths here beneath!
Continual Jubilees and Joys!
The Days of Heaven, while we breath
On Earth! Where Sin all Bliss Destroys.
This is a Triumph of Delights!   5
That doth exceed all Appetites.
 No Joy can be Compard to this,
 It is a Life of Perfect Bliss.

[451]

2

Of perfect Bliss! How can it be?
To Conquer Satan, and to Reign   10
In such a Vale of Miserie,
Where Vipers, Stings and Tears remain;
Is to be Crownd with Victorie.
To be Content, Divine and free,
Even here beneath is Great Delight   15
And next the Beatifick Sight.

3

But inward lusts do oft assail,
Temptations Work us much Annoy.
Weel therfore Weep, and to prevail
Shall be a more Celestial Joy.   20
To hav no other Enemie,
But one; and to that one to Die:
To fight with that and Conquer it,
Is better then in Peace to sit.

4

Tis Better for a little time: 25
For he that all His Lusts doth quell,
Shall find this Life to be His Prime,
And Vanquish Sin and Conquer Hell.
The Next shall be His Double Joy:
And that which here seemed to Destroy,   30
Shall in the Other Life appear
A Root of Bliss; a Pearl each Tear.

16 "And next to the Beatific Vision" (of God).

48

Thus you see I can make Merry with Calamities, and while I griev at Sins, and War against them, abhorring the World, and my self more: Descend into the Abysses of Humilitie, and there Admire a New Offspring and Torrent of Joys, GODs Mercies. Which accepteth of our fidelity in Bloody Battails, tho every Wound defile and Poyson; and when we slip or fall, turneth our true Penitent Tears into Solid Pearl, that shall abide with Him for evermore. But Oh let us take heed that we never Willingly commit a Sin against so Gracious a Redeemer, and so Great a Father.

49

Sin!
O only fatal Woe,
That makst me Sad and Mourning go!
That all my Joys dost Spoil,
His Kingdom and my Soul Defile!   5
I never can Agree
With Thee!

2

Thou!
Only Thou! O Thou alone,
(And my Obdurat Heart of Stone,)   10
The Poyson and the Foes
Of my Enjoyments and Repose,
The only Bitter Ill:
Dost Kill!

3

Oh!   15
I cannot meet with Thee,
Nor once approach thy Memory,
But all my Joys are Dead,
And all my Sacred Treasures fled;
As if I now did Dwell   20
In Hell.

4

Lord!
O hear how short I Breath!
See how I Tremble here beneath!
A Sin! Its Ugly face   25
More Terror, then its Dwelling Place,
Contains, (O Dreadfull Sin!)
Within!

50

The Recovery

Sin! wilt Thou vanquish me!
And shall I yeeld the victory?
Shall all my Joys be Spoild,
And Pleasures soild
By Thee!   5
Shall I remain
As one thats Slain
And never more lift up the Head?

26 *its Dwelling Place:* i.e., Hell.

Is not my Savior Dead!
His Blood, thy Bane; my Balsam, Bliss, Joy, Wine;   10
Shall Thee Destroy; Heal, Feed, make me Divine.

51

I cannot meet with Sin, but it Kils me, and tis only by Jesus Christ
that I can Kill it, and Escape. Would you blame me to be con-
founded, when I have offended my Eternal Father, who gav me all
the Things in Heaven and Earth? One Sin is a Dreadfull Stumbling
Block in the Way to Heaven. It breeds a long Parenthesis in the
fruition of our Joys. Do you not see my Friend, how it Disorders
and Disturbs my Proceeding? There is no Calamity but Sin alone.

52

When I came into the Country, and saw that I had all time in my
own hands, having devoted it wholy to the study of Felicitie, I knew
not where to begin or End; nor what Objects to chuse, upon which
most Profitably I might fix my Contemplation. I saw my self like som
Traveller, that had Destined his Life to journeys, and was resolved
to spend his Days in visiting Strange Places: who might wander in
vain, unless his Undertakings were guided by som certain Rule; and
that innumerable Millions of Objects were presented before me,
unto any of which I might take my journey. fain I would hav visited
them all, but that was impossible. What then I should do? Even
imitat a Traveller, who becaus He cannot visit all Coasts, Wilder-
nesses, Sandy Deserts, Seas, Hills, Springs and Mountains, chuseth
the most Populous and flourishing Cities, where he might see the
fairest Prospects, Wonders, and Rarities, and be entertained with
greatest Courtesie: and where indeed he might most Benefit himself
with Knowledg Profit and Delight: leaving the rest, even the naked

50.10 *Bane:* poison; *Balsam:* medicinal oil.

and Empty Places unseen. For which caus I made it my Prayer to
GOD Almighty, that He, whose Eys are open upon all Things, would
guid me to the fairest and Divinest.

53

And what Rule do you think I walked by? Truly a Strange one, but
the Best in the Whole World. I was Guided by an Implicit Faith in
Gods Goodness: and therfore led to the Study of the most Obvious[27]
and Common Things. For thus I thought within my self: GOD be-
ing, as we generaly believ, infinit in Goodness, it is most Consonant[28]
and Agreeable with His nature, that the Best Things should be most
Common. for nothing is more Naturall to infinit Goodness, then to
make the Best Things most frequent; and only Things Worthless,
Scarce. Then I began to Enquire what Things were most Common:
Air, Light, Heaven and Earth, Water, the Sun, Trees, Men and
Women, Cities Temples &c. These I found Common and Obvious
to all: Rubies Pearls Diamonds Gold and Silver, these I found scarce,
and to the most Denied. Then began I to consider and compare the
value of them, which I measured by their Serviceableness, and by
the Excellencies which would be found in them, should they be
taken away. And in Conclusion I saw clearly, that there was a Real
Valuableness in all the Common things; in the Scarce, a feigned.

54

Besides these Common things I hav named, there were others as
Common, but Invisible. The Laws of God, the Soul of Man, Jesus
Christ and His Passion on the Crosse, with the Ways of GOD in all
Ages. And these by the General Credit they had Obtained in the
World confirmed me more. For the Ways of God were transeunt
Things, they were past and gon; our Saviors Sufferings were in one

[27] commonly occurring.
[28] agreeable.

particular Obscure Place, the Laws of God were no Object of the Ey, but only found in the Minds of Men; these therfore which were so Secret in their own Nature, and made common only by the Esteem Men had of them, must of Necessity include unspeakable Worth for which they were celebrated, of all, and so generaly remembered. As yet I did not see the Wisdom and Depths of Knowledg, the Clear Principles, and Certain Evidences wherby the Wise and Holy, the Ancients and the Learned that were abroad in the World knew these Things, but was led to them only by the fame which they had vulgarly[29] received. Howbeit I believed that there were unspeakable Mysteries contained in them, and tho they were Generaly talkt of their valu was unknown. These therfore I resolved to Study, and no other. But to my unspeakable Wonder, they brought me to all the Things in Heaven and in Earth, in Time and Eternity, Possible and Impossible, Great and Little, Common and Scarce, and Discovered them all to be infinit Treasures.

55

That any thing may be found to be an infinit Treasure, its Place must be found in Eternity, and in Gods Esteem. For as there is a Time, so there is a Place for all Things. Evry thing in its Place is Admirable Deep and Glorious: out of its Place like a Wandering Bird, is Desolat and Good for Nothing. How therfore it relateth to God and all Creatures must be seen before it can be Enjoyed. And this I found by many Instances. The Sun is Good, only as it relateth to the Stars, to the Seas, to your Ey, to the feilds, &c. As it relateth to the Stars it raiseth their Influences; as to the Seas it melteth them and maketh the Waters flow; as to your Ey, it bringeth in the Beauty of the World; as to the feilds; it clotheth them with Fruits and flowers: Did it not relate to others it would not be Good. Divest it of these Operations, and Divide it from these Objects it is Useless and Good for nothing. And therfore Worthless, because Worthles and Useless go together. A Piece of Gold cannot be Valued, unless we Know how it relates to Clothes, to Wine, to Victuals, to the Esteem

[29] commonly.

of Men, and to the Owner. Som little Piece in a Kingly Monument severd from the rest hath no Beauty at all. It enjoys its valu in its Place, by the Ornament it gives to, and receivs from all the Parts. By this I discerned, that even a little Knowledg could not be had in the Mysterie of Felicity, without a great deal. And that that was the reason why so many were ignorant of its nature, and why so few did attain it. for by the Labor required to much Knowledg they were discouraged, and for lack of much did not see any Glorious motives to allure them.

56

Therfore of Necessity they must at first believ that Felicity is a Glorious tho an unknown Thing. And certainly it was the infinit Wisdom of God, that did implant by Instinct so strong a Desire of felicity in the Soul, that we might be excited to labor after it, tho we know it not, the very force wherwith we covet it supplying the place of Understanding. That there is a Felicity we all know by the Desires after, that there is a most Glorious felicity we know by the Strength and vehemence of those Desires: And that nothing but Felicity is worthy of our Labor, becaus all other things are the Means only which conduce unto it. I was very much animated by the Desires of Philosophers, which I saw in Heathen Books aspiring after it. But the misery is *It was unknown.* An altar was erected to it like that in Athens with this inscription TO THE UNKNOWN GOD.[30]

57

Two things in Perfect Felicity I saw to be requisite: and that Felicity must be perfect, or not Felicity. The first was the Perfection of its Objects, in Nature Serviceableness Number and Excellency. The second was the Perfection of the Maner wherin they are Enjoyed,

[30] See Acts 17:23.

for Sweetness Measure and Duration. And unless in these I could be satisfied I should never be contented. Especialy about the later. for the Maner is always more Excellent the Thing. And it far more concerneth us that the Maner wherin we enjoy be compleat and Perfect: then that the Matter which we Enjoy be compleat and Perfect. For the Maner as we contemplat its Excellency is it self a great Part of the Matter of our Enjoyment.

58

In Discovering the Matter or Objects to be Enjoyed, I was greatly aided by remembering that we were made in Gods Image. For thereupon it must of Necessity follow that GODs Treasures be our Treasures, and His Joys our Joys. So that by enquiring what were GODs, I found the Objects of our felicity Gods Treasures being ours. for we were made in his Image that we might liv in His similitud. And herin I was mightily confirmed by the Apostles Blaming the Gentiles, and charging it upon them as a very great Fault that they were alienated from the life of God, for herby I perceived that we were to liv the Life of God: when we lived the tru life of Nature according to Knowledg: and that by Blindness and Corruption we had Strayed from it.[31] Now GODs Treasures are his own Perfections, and all His Creatures.

59

The Image of God implanted in us, guided me to the maner wherin we were to Enjoy. for since we were made in the similitud of God, we were made to Enjoy after his Similitude. Now to Enjoy the Treasures of God in the Similitud of God, is the most perfect Blessedness God could Devise. For the Treasures of GOD are the most Perfect Treasures and the Manėr of God is the most perfect Maner. To En-

[31] See Ephesians 4:17–18.

joy therfore the Treasures of God after the similitud of God is to Enjoy the most perfect Treasures in the most Perfect Maner. Upon which I was infinitly satisfied in God, and knew there was a Dietie, becaus I was satisfied. For Exerting Himself wholy in atchieving thus an infinit felicity He was infinitly Delightfull Great and Glorious, and my Desires so August and Insatiable that nothing less then a Deity could satisfy them.

60

This Spectacle once seen, will never be forgotten. It is a Great Part of the Beatifick Vision. A Sight of Happiness is Happiness. It transforms the Soul and makes it Heavenly, it powerfully calls us to Communion with God, and weans us from the Customs of this World. It puts a Lustre upon GOD and all his Creatures and makes us to see them in a Divine and Eternal Light. I no sooner discerned this but I was (as Plato saith, In summâ Rationis Arce Quies habitat[32]) seated in a Throne of Repose and Perfect Rest. All Things were well in their Proper Places, I alone was out of frame[33] and had need to be Mended. for all things were Gods Treasures in their Proper places, and I was to be restored to Gods Image. Wherupon you will not believ how I was withdrawn from all Endeavors of altering and Mending Outward Things. They lay so well methoughts, they could not be Mended: but I must be Mended to Enjoy them.

66

Little did I imagine that, while I was thinking these Things, I was Conversing with GOD. I was so Ignorant that I did not think any Man in the World had had such thoughts before. seeing them therfore so Amiable, I Wonderd not a little, that nothing was Spoken of

[32] "Peace lives in the highest citadel of Reason" (apparently not a direct citation from Plato).
[33] order.

them in former Ages. but as I read the Bible I was here and there Surprized with such Thoughts and found by Degrees that these Things had been written of before, not only in the Scriptures but in many of the fathers and that this was the Way of Communion with God in all Saints, as I saw Clearly in the Person of David. Me thoughts a New Light Darted in into all his Psalmes, and finaly spread abroad over the whole Bible. So that things which for their Obscurity I thought not in being were there contained: Things which for their Greatness were incredible, were made Evident and Things Obscure, Plain. GOD by this means bringing me into the very Heart of His Kingdom.

67

There I saw Moses blessing the Lord for the Precious Things of Heaven, for the Dew and for the Deep that coucheth beneath: and for the Precious fruits brought forth by the Sun, and for the Precious things put forth by the Moon: and for the chief things of the ancient Mountains and for the Precious things of the lasting Hills: and for the Precious things of the Earth, and fulness therof.[34] There I saw Jacob, with Awfull Apprehensions Admiring the Glory of the World, when awaking out of His Dream he said, How dreadfull is this Place? This is none other then the Hous of GOD, and the Gate of Heaven.[35] There I saw GOD leading forth Abraham, and shewing him the Stars of Heaven; and all the Countries round about him, and saying All these will I give Thee, and thy Seed after thee.[36] There I saw Adam in Paradice, surrounded with the Beauty of Heaven and Earth, void of all Earthly Comforts to wit such as were devised, Gorgeous Apparel, Palaces, Gold and Silver, Coaches, Musical Instruments &c, And entertained only with Celestial Joys. The sun and moon and stars, Beasts and fowles and fishes, Trees and fruits and flowers, with the other Naked and simple Delights of Nature.

[34] See Deuteronomy 33:13–16.
[35] See Genesis 28:16–17.
[36] See Genesis 13:14–17, 15:5.

By which I evidently saw, that the Way to becom Rich and Blessed, was not by heaping Accidental and Devised Riches to make ourselvs great in the vulgar maner, but to approach more near, and to see more Clearly with the Ey of our understanding, the Beauties and Glories of the whole world: and to hav communion with the Diety in the Riches of GOD and Nature.

68

I saw moreover that it did not so much concern us what Objects were before us, as with what Eys we beheld them; with what Affections we esteemed them, and what Apprehensions we had about them. All men see the same Objects, but do not equaly understand them. Intelligence is the Tongue that discerns and Tastes them, Knowledg is the Light of Heaven. Lov is the Wisdom and Glory of GOD. Life Extended to all Objects, is the Sence that enjoys them. So that Knowledg Life and Lov, are the very means of all Enjoyment. which abov all Things we must seek for and Labor after. All Objects are in God Eternal: which we by perfecting our faculties are made to Enjoy. Which then are turned into Act when they are exercised about their Objects. but without them are Desolat and Idle; or Discontented and forlorn. Wherby I perceived the Meaning of the Definition wherin Aristotle Describeth Felicity. when he saith Felicity is the Perfect Exercise of Perfect Virtu in a Perfect Life.[37] for Life is perfect when it is perfectly Extended to all Objects, and perfectly sees them and perfectly loves them: which is don by a perfect Exercise of Virtu about them.

[37] See *Nicomachean Ethics* 1:7–10.

COMMENTARY

The following books, concerned with the whole group of poets in this volume, should be consulted:

ANTHOLOGIES *The Metaphysical Poets*, ed. Helen Gardner, Penguin, rev. ed., 1966.
Metaphysical Lyrics and Poems of the Seventeenth Century, Donne to Butler, ed. H. J. C. Grierson, Oxford University Press, 1921.
European Metaphysical Poetry, ed. and tr. Frank J. Warnke, Yale University Press, 1961.

STUDIES Joan Bennett, *Five Metaphysical Poets: Donne, Herbert, Vaughan, Crashaw, Marvell*, Cambridge University Press, 1964.
Lloyd E. Berry, *A Bibliography of Studies in Metaphysical Poetry, 1939–1960*, University of Wisconsin Press, 1964.
Douglas Bush, *English Literature in the Earlier Seventeenth Century, 1600–1660*, Oxford University Press, 2nd ed. rev., 1962.
Rosalie L. Colie, *Paradoxia Epidemica: The Renaissance Tradition of Paradox*, Princeton University Press, 1966.
Joseph E. Duncan, *The Revival of Metaphysical Poetry: The History of a Style, 1800 to the Present*, University of Minnesota Press, 1959.
Robert Ellrodt, *Les Poètes Métaphysiques Anglais*, 3 vols., Paris, Corti, 1960.
William R. Keast, ed., *Seventeenth-Century English Poetry: Modern Essays in Criticism*, Galaxy Books, 1962.
J. B. Leishman, *The Metaphysical Poets: Donne, Herbert, Vaughan, Traherne*, Oxford University Press, 1934.
Theodore Spencer and Mark Van Doren, *Studies in Metaphysical Poetry: Two Essays and a Bibliography*, Columbia University Press, 1939.
Helen C. White, *The Metaphysical Poets: A Study in Religious Experience*, New York, Macmillan, 1936.
George Williamson, *The Donne Tradition: A Study in English Poetry from Donne to the death of Cowley*, Harvard University Press, 1930.

[465]

ROBERT SOUTHWELL

LIFE   Southwell was born near Norwich in 1561. From 1576 until
1586 he studied at Douai, Paris, and Rome, entering the novitiate of
the Jesuit order in 1578. He returned to England as a missionary priest
in 1586, and lived chiefly in London, in secret residences, until his
capture and imprisonment in 1592. He was executed on a charge of
treason in 1595. His poems were published immediately after his death.

EDITION   *The Poems of Robert Southwell, S.J.*, ed. James H. McDon-
ald and Nancy Pollard Brown, Oxford, Clarendon Press, 1967. (With
excellent Introduction and Commentary.)

STUDIES   Pierre Janelle, *Robert Southwell the Writer: A Study in Re-
ligious Inspiration*, New York, Sheed & Ward, 1935.
Christopher Devlin, *The Life of Robert Southwell, Poet and Martyr*, New
York, Farrar, Straus, 1956.

TEXT   The texts of Southwell's poems here were provided by Mrs.
Nancy Pollard Brown for *The Meditative Poem* (1963); I am grateful
to Mrs. Brown for permitting this preliminary use of her texts; see her
edition above for full details concerning textual problems.

WILLIAM ALABASTER

LIFE   Alabaster was born at Hadleigh, Suffolk, in 1568 and educated
at Westminster School and Trinity College, Cambridge. In his early
years he won Spenser's attention as a Latin poet. In 1596 he became
chaplain to the Earl of Essex and sailed with him on the Cadiz ex-
pedition. In 1597 his dramatic conversion to Catholicism caused deep
reverberations in Anglican circles. He performed the Spiritual Exer-
cises of Ignatius Loyola, in 1598, under the direction of the under-
ground Jesuit, John Gerard, with the aim of joining the Jesuit order—
an aim never carried out. His sonnets appear to have been composed
during this period of his conversion, in 1597–98. After years of moving
back and forth between the Continent and England, and after shifting
his religious allegiance at least twice, he seems to have settled down

in the Anglican Church in 1614. He died in 1640. Only one of Alabaster's sonnets was printed in his lifetime.

EDITION *The Sonnets of William Alabaster,* ed. G. M. Story and Helen Gardner, Oxford University Press, 1959 (contains a biography and detailed commentary).

TEXT The numbering at the head of each sonnet here is that of the Oxford edition, where the poems are given in modernized form, and arranged in an order different from that of the manuscripts. The texts of the sonnets in this selection are based upon the manuscripts, as follows: Sonnets 1, 2, 15, 16, and 19 are taken from the only manuscript in which they occur, that in the library of St. John's College, Cambridge, pressmark T.9.30; I am grateful to the Master and the College for permission to print these sonnets and to use a few variant readings from this manuscript in the remaining sonnets of this selection, which are based upon the manuscript in the Bodleian Library (MS. Eng. Poet. e. 57). I am grateful to the Keeper of Western Manuscripts at the Bodleian and to that Library for permission to print the last ten sonnets here from this manuscript. For Sonnets 70 and 71 I have also consulted the version of these poems in the manuscript compiled by Peter Mowle, now in the library of Oscott College (MS. E. 3. 11). I am grateful to the Rector of Oscott College for permission to cite some of the readings and titles of this manuscript. The numbering of each sonnet in the basic manuscript is given here at the end of each sonnet (J: St. John's; B: Bodleian). Punctuation has been added and altered in places where difficulty in reading might occur, and the erratic use of capital letters has been modified. Only the most important of the textual problems are noted below. I am throughout deeply indebted to the Oxford edition.

NOTES SONNET 15. An extensive paraphrase is perhaps the best way of clarifying the intricate, but exact, account of the process of meditation presented in this sonnet: "My soul is a little world (universe), a microcosm, in which the heavens (the Ptolemaic spheres) are comprised of my internal sense (in the old collective meaning of the whole perceptive faculty of the mind or soul). This faculty is activated by the human will, as the Ptolemaic spheres were said to have been moved or guided by Intelligences (Spirits or Angels). Now in this little universe my heart is the sky (Element), in which, as the sun moves about the earth, my love moves about its own proper center: the sphere (area) of heavenly or divine matters. And just as the sun draws vapors from the earth into the sky, where they condense and return to earth as rain, so in my heart love draws from divine matters the purest argument or topic that human wit (understanding, intellect) can desire. When these conceits (thoughts, conceptions) have been digested by thought's retirement from distractions, then they turn into the tears of Christian devotion." See Miss Gardner's very helpful note in the Oxford ed., p. 49.

SONNET 24.

6 *place:* from J; B reads *Cross;* but the place where he was cured must be the speaker's own soul: see Miss Gardner's note, p. 51.

SONNET 32. B has heading: "uppon the Crucifix," omitted here. For the "cluster of grapes," traditionally interpreted as a symbol of Christ on the Cross, see Numbers 13, and Herbert, "The bunch of grapes."

SONNET 33. B has heading: "Ego sum vitis" ("I am the vine"), omitted here: see John 15:1.

SONNET 34. B has heading: "uppon the Crucifix," omitted here.
8 *upp in his:* J reads *uppon this,* which may be right.

SONNET 44.

1 *unvalted:* from J; B reads *unwonted.*
12 *due breath'd:* J reads *dulced.*
14 B reads *with interest of ever;* J reads *with interest of.* Miss Gardner suggests (p. 56) that Alabaster may have "intended to break off dramatically as he hears the song of heaven."

SONNET 46.

3 *leward:* from J; B reads *backward;* the line seems to use a nautical image of "coming about" or "coming round": i.e., changing from the course of tacking into the wind to the easier course of sailing before the wind.
10 *smothering:* J reads *smoldren:* smouldering.

SONNET 70. Oscott ms. has title: "A Morninge Meditation."
7 *yellow:* Oscott ms. reads *tawnie.*
14 *all end in Actione:* the reading of B and J; cf. Traherne, *Centuries,* 3.68: "All Objects are in God Eternal: which we by perfecting our faculties are made to Enjoy. Which then are turned into Act when they are exercised about their Objects." Oscott ms. reads *yet actinge all in one,* an attractive possibility.

SONNET 71. Oscott ms. has heading: "The diference twixt compunction and colde Devotion in beholdinge the Passion of our Saviour."
2 *passion:* I have adopted the reading of J and Oscott, in preference to the *Passione* of B, which seems to spoil the general reference of the word in this context.

JOHN DONNE

LIFE   Donne was born in London in 1572 and reared in a devout Catholic family. Two of his uncles were Jesuit priests: one, Jasper Heywood, headed a Jesuit mission to England in the early 1580s. Donne attended Oxford, and possibly Cambridge as well, and then went on to study law in London in the early 1590s. He sailed on the expeditions to Cadiz and to the Azores in 1596 and 1597. In 1598 he became secretary to Sir Thomas Egerton, Lord Keeper, by which time he had clearly given up his allegiance to the Roman Church. He was dismissed from this promising post after his secret marriage in 1601 and lived a meager existence for the next fourteen years, subsisting on the generosity of friends and relatives, along with occasional employment in religious controversy on the Anglican side. He was at last ordained in the English Church in 1615, appointed Reader in Divinity at Lincoln's Inn in 1616, and Dean of St. Paul's in 1621, a post which he held until his death in 1631. His collected poems were first published in 1633.

EDITIONS   *Poems,* ed. H. J. C. Grierson, 2 vols., Oxford University Press, 1912.
Divine Poems, ed. Helen Gardner, Oxford, Clarendon Press, 1952.
The Elegies, and The Songs and Sonnets, ed. Helen Gardner, Oxford, Clarendon Press, 1965.
The Satires, Epigrams and Verse Letters, ed. W. Milgate, Oxford, Clarendon Press, 1967.
Complete Poetry, ed. John T. Shawcross, Anchor Books, 1967.
Songs and Sonets, ed. Theodore Redpath, London, Methuen, 1956.
The Anniversaries, ed. Frank Manley, Johns Hopkins Press, 1963.
Sermons, ed. George R. Potter and Evelyn M. Simpson, 10 vols., University of California Press, 1953–62.

(All these editions contain detailed and very helpful commentary.)

STUDIES   N. J. C. Andreasen, *John Donne: Conservative Revolutionary,* Princeton University Press, 1967.

C. M. Coffin, *John Donne and the New Philosophy*, Columbia University Press, 1937.

J. Clay Hunt, *Donne's Poetry*, Yale University Press, 1954.

Geoffrey L. Keynes, *A Bibliography of Dr. John Donne*, 3rd ed., Cambridge University Press, 1958 (contains a listing of biographical and critical studies of Donne).

J. B. Leishman, *The Monarch of Wit*, 7th ed., London, Hutchinson, 1965.

William R. Mueller, *John Donne: Preacher*, Princeton University Press, 1962.

Douglas L. Peterson, *The English Lyric from Wyatt to Donne*, Princeton University Press, 1967.

Evelyn M. Simpson, *A Study of the Prose Works of John Donne*, 2nd ed., Oxford, Clarendon Press, 1948.

Arnold Stein, *John Donne's Lyrics*, University of Minnesota Press, 1962.

Isaak Walton, *Life*, 1640 (revised 1658, 1670, 1675); available in World's Classics ed. of Walton's *Lives*.

Joan Webber. *Contrary Music: The Prose Style of John Donne*, University of Wisconsin Press, 1963.

See also the useful collections of essays by various authors, selected by Frank Kermode, *Discussions of John Donne*, Boston, Heath, 1962, and by Helen Gardner, Prentice-Hall Series of "Twentieth Century Views," 1962.

TEXT   For the present selections the text of the poems has been taken from, or based upon, Grierson's edition of Donne's *Poems* as published in the Oxford Standard Authors series in 1933; Grierson's text here is derived from his edition of 1912, but contains some corrections and prints the poems with the modern form of the letter "s"; I am grateful to the Clarendon Press for permission to use the texts of these poems. Dr. Frank Manley has very generously supplied me with approximately forty alterations in the text of the *Anniversaries*, before the appearance of his edition of these poems, listed above. Manley's readings, some concerning important words, others concerning punctuation and italics, are based on the first editions of the *Anniversaries*. I am grateful to him for permission to include some of his discoveries here.

ARRANGEMENT   The arrangement of this selection from Donne has been made in accordance with the few facts and reasonable conjectures that we may apply to the dating of Donne's poetry. Such an arrangement, while far from definitive, has the advantage of suggesting the inseparable interrelationship that exists among Donne's writings in all genres. The love-elegies here included appear to be among the earliest of Donne's poems; Miss Gardner suggests convincingly that they were probably written during the years 1593–96 (see her edition of 1965, pp. xxxii–xxxiii). With regard to Satire 3, no precise dating is possible, although Milgate's date of 1594 or 1595 seems very likely (see his edition of the *Satires*, pp. 139–40).

The poems in the following group of Donne's love-songs cannot be given very reliable dates, although the references to the King in "The Canonization" and "The Sunne Rising" may suggest that they were written after 1603. One may tend to feel, with Miss Gardner, that the simpler poems here belong to the earlier part of Donne's career, and that the more complex and "philosophic" of these poems tend to belong to Donne's middle years (see her edition of 1965, pp. l–lxii). But the whole matter is extremely problematical, and therefore I have given the love-songs in their relative positions as they appear in Grierson's edition. For these poems Grierson follows, with one exception, the order of the second (1635) edition of Donne's poetry, where these love-songs appeared under the general title "Songs and Sonets" (*sonets*: meaning here "short lyrics"). The one exception is "The Flea", which was placed first in 1635; but Grierson has given this poem the less prominent position that it occupied in the first edition of 1633. It seems best to say only that these love-songs appear to have been written at various times, ranging from the early 1590s up to 1610 or even later.

The dating of the three verse-letters that follow here is equally uncertain, although the mention in the second poem to Rowland Woodward of "love-song weeds, and Satyrique thornes" indicates that this poem was written toward the end of the 1590s, at the very earliest (Milgate suggests a possible date of 1597: see his edition, p. 223).

With "La Corona" we are on safer ground, for this sequence can be dated, with strong probability, in 1607 (see Grierson, II, 228–29; Gardner, *Divine Poems*, pp. 55–56). The following sixteen Holy Sonnets appear to belong to the period in or near 1609, as Miss Gardner has shown in her very important and skillfully marshaled argument for bringing these sonnets into the middle period of Donne's career (see her edition of *Divine Poems*, pp. xxxvii–l). I have placed the famous "Valediction: forbidding mourning" after these sonnets, on the basis of Isaak Walton's statement that this poem was given by Donne to his wife when he left for France with Sir Robert Drury in 1611. One should note, however, that Walton's dates are highly unreliable. With the two long *Anniversaries* we are on completely solid ground, for the

Anatomie was published in 1611, and the *Progres,* early in 1612; both poems being clearly composed very shortly before the times of publication. "Goodfriday, 1613" dates itself. I have placed the "Nocturnall" next, before the sonnet on the death of Donne's wife, and close to the final Hymns, because this placing serves to suggest the possibility that the "Nocturnall" is a meditation based on the death of Donne's wife (1617). The "Nocturnall" seems to express a religious renunciation of the world, and there is nothing improper in the thought that Donne, as an ordained priest, should have written such a poem in memory of his wife. The conclusion of the "Nocturnall," indeed, seems to lead the way toward the following sonnet and the Hymns. For Sonnets 18 and 19, I accept Miss Gardner's arguments for their late composition, especially her definitive interpretation of Sonnet 18 (see her edition, pp. 77–78, 121–27). The "Hymn to Christ" was composed before Donne visited Germany in 1619, and the last two Hymns may both have been composed in 1623, although the "Hymne to God my God" is placed by Walton on the occasion of Donne's final illness, in 1631 (see Miss Gardner's discussion, pp. 132–35). For an interesting summary of the evidence concerning the dating of Donne's poems, see the "Chronological Schedule" in Shawcross's edition, pp. 411–17.

NOTES   THE EXTASIE. The title alludes to the mystical experience of *extasis,* in which the soul divests itself of bodily experience, and gains a direct apprehension of divine truth. For excellent interpretations showing the dependence of this poem on Renaissance doctrines of love, see the article by Miss Helen Gardner, "The Argument about 'The Ecstacy,'" in *Elizabethan and Jacobean Studies Presented to Frank Percy Wilson,* Oxford, Clarendon Press, 1959, pp. 279–306; and the article by A. J. Smith, "The Metaphysic of Love," *Review of English Studies,* new series, 9 (1958), 362–75.

LA CORONA.   The title suggests the Italian tradition of the series of linked sonnets called the *corona di sonnetti,* along with the sevenfold meditations associated with an old form of the rosary known as the Corona (see Martz, *The Poetry of Meditation,* pp. 107–12).

HOLY SONNETS, 1–16.   Grierson (I, 322) and Miss Gardner (*Divine Poems,* p. xxxix) note that several manuscripts entitle these sonnets "Divine Meditations." Miss Gardner has convincingly argued that the group of twelve sonnets appearing together in some manuscripts and in the first edition of 1633 form "a consecutive set of twelve, made up of two contrasted sets of six," the first six dealing with the Last Things, and the second six dealing with Love (see her Introduction, pp. xl–xli). The twelve sonnets concerned, which Miss Gardner prints in the order of 1633, run as follows, in Grierson's numbering: 2, 4, 6, 7, 9, 10, 11, 12, 13, 14, 15, 16. The remaining four sonnets, first printed in 1635, are grouped together by Miss Gardner as a set of "penitential sonnets," in the following order: 1, 5, 3, 8 (see her Introduction, p. l). These groupings are effective, especially for the twelve sonnets of 1633, although the sonnets, with their individual integrity, create the effect of separate compositions.

THE FIRST ANNIVERSARY. The title, "The First Anniversarie," was not given in the first edition of the "Anatomie" in 1611: it was added when this poem was republished as a companion to the "Progres" in 1612. Neither poem was composed for the "anniversary" of Elizabeth Drury's death, in the usual sense of that word. Elizabeth, the daughter of Sir Robert Drury, who became Donne's generous patron, died in the early part of December 1610, in her fifteenth year. The "Anatomie," as the poem says in line 39, was composed "some moneths" afterward; and the "Progres" begins by saying that "a yeare is runne" since the girl's death; both poems, then, are paying a year's commemorative tribute in advance. The word "anniversary" could mean "enduring for or completed in a year"; and it also holds here some echoes of the old term "anniversary days," referring to the days on which the martyrdoms or deathdays of saints were celebrated annually by the Roman Church. For a full account of Donne's relation with the Drury family see R. C. Bald, *Donne & the Drurys*, Cambridge University Press, 1959.

The two *Anniversaries* are carefully constructed in ways that the following outlines may help to make clear. The *First Anniversary* is divided into an Introduction, five sections that form the body of the work, and a Conclusion. Each of the five main sections is subdivided into three parts, with the last part beginning with the refrain:

> Shee, shee is dead; shee's dead: when thou knowest this,
> Thou knowest how poore a trifling thing man is.
> And learn'st thus much by our Anatomie . . . .

In the following outline part of the second line of each refrain is used as the heading for each section:

Introduction, 1–90. The world is sick, "yea, dead, yea putrified," since she, its "intrinsique balme" and "preservative," its prime example of Virtue, is dead.

Section I, 91–190: "how poore a trifling thing man is."

1. Meditation, 91–170. Because of Original Sin man has decayed in length of life, in physical size, in mental capacity.
2. Eulogy, 171–82. The girl was perfect virtue; she purified herself and had a purifying power over all.
3. Refrain and Moral, 183–90. Our only hope is in religion.

Section II, 191–246: "how lame a cripple this world is."

1. Meditation, 191–218. The "universall frame" has received injury from the sin of the Angels, and now in universe, in state, in family, " 'Tis all in peeces, all cohaerence gone."
2. Eulogy, 219–36. Only this girl possessed the power which might have unified the world.
3. Refrain and Moral, 237–46. Contemn and avoid this sick world.

Section III, 247–338: "how ugly a monster this world is."

1. Meditation, 247–304. Proportion, the prime ingredient of beauty, no longer exists in the universe.
2. Eulogy, 305–24. The girl was the "measure of all Symmetree" and harmony.
3. Refrain and Moral, 325–38. Human acts must be "done fitly and in proportion."

Section IV, 339–76: "how wan a Ghost this our world is."

1. Meditation, 339–58. "Beauties other second Element, Colour, and lustre now, is as neere spent."
2. Eulogy, 359–68. The girl had the perfection of color and gave color to the world.
3. Refrain and Moral, 369–76. There is no pleasure in an ugly world; it is wicked to use false colors.

Section V, 377–434: "how drie a Cinder this world is."

1. Meditation, 377–98. Physical "influence" of the heavens upon the earth has been weakened.
2. Eulogy, 399–426. The girl's virtue has little effect on us now because of this weakened "correspondence" between heavens and earth; in fact the world's corruption weakened her effect while she lived.

3. Refrain and Moral, 427–34. Nothing "Is worth our travaile, griefe, or perishing," except the joys of religious virtue.

Conclusion, 435–74.

The *Second Anniversary* shows a closely related, but significantly modified construction, which may be clarified by the following outline (descriptive quotations are taken from the marginal notes in the first edition):

Introduction, 1–44.

Section I, 45–84.

    1. Meditation, 45–64: "A just disestimation of this world."

    2. Eulogy, 65–80.

    3. Refrain and Moral, 81–84.

Section II, 85–156.

    1. Meditation, 85–120: "Contemplation of our state in our death-bed."

    2. Eulogy, 121–46.

    3. Moral, 147–56.

Section III, 157–250.

    1. Meditation.

        a. 157–78: "Incommodities of the Soule in the Body."

        b. 179–219: the soul's "liberty by death."

    2. Eulogy (with brief moral), 220–50.

Section IV, 251–320.

    1. Meditation.

        a. 251–89: the soul's "ignorance in this life."

        b. 290–300: the soul's "knowledge in the next" life.

    2. Eulogy (with brief moral), 301–20.

Section V, 321–82.

    1. Meditation.

        a. 321–38: "Of our company in this life."

        b. 339–55: of our company "in the next" life.

    2. Eulogy (with brief moral), 356–82.

Section VI, 383–470.

    1. Meditation.
        a. 383–434: "Of essentiall joy in this life."
        b. 435–46: of essential joy "in the next" life.
    2. Eulogy, 447–70.

Section VII, 471–510.

    1. Meditation.
        a. 471–86: of "accidentall joyes" in this life.
        b. 487–96: of "accidentall joyes" in the next life.
    2. Eulogy, 497–510.

Conclusion, 511–28.

    The outline of the *First Anniversary* is taken from Martz, *The Poetry of Meditation* (© 1954 by Yale University Press), pp. 222–23; the second outline is based on the outline and discussion in that book, pp. 236–38, with a more precise set of subdivisions for Sections III–VII, prompted by Frank Manley's suggestion that the three-part subdivisions in the *First Anniversary* bear a relation to the usual division of the faculties of the soul: Memory, Understanding, and Will (see his edition of the *Anniversaries*, pp. 41–44). The last five sections (III–VII) of the *Second Anniversary* seem to accord especially well with this traditional threefold action.

A NOCTURNALL UPON S. LUCIES DAY. The word *nocturnall* holds an allusion to the *nocturn*, one of the divisions of the nocturnal office of Matins in the Roman Catholic Church: the office of Matins is, in strict usage, performed at midnight. St. Lucy's Day was December 13 in the old calendar, according to which the winter solstice occurred on December 12. The strong religious allusions, the depth of feeling expressed, and the references to a long period of devoted, yet turbulent, love—these qualities combine to suggest that this poem is related to the death of Donne's wife: see the following sonnet.

TO CHRIST. Grierson prints two versions of this poem, one based on the printed text of 1633, another on the manuscripts. I choose the second as the better version, although the poem is better known under its 1633 title: "A Hymne to God the Father." Contractions for "which" and "that" have here been expanded.

GEORGE HERBERT

LIFE   Herbert was born in 1593, of a prominent and influential family. His remarkable mother, Magdalen Herbert, was a friend of John Donne, and thus her son had the opportunity to become well acquainted with the older poet. Herbert was educated at Westminster School and Trinity College, Cambridge. In 1614 he became Fellow of Trinity, in 1618 Reader in Rhetoric at Cambridge, and in 1620 Orator for the University, a post that opened the avenues toward a secular career, which Herbert almost certainly considered for a time. He was, however, ordained deacon by 1626, and ordained priest in 1630, the year in which he took up his post at Bemerton, near Salisbury, where he remained until his death in 1633. His English poems were first published in 1633, a few months after his death. It is important for Herbert's poetry to note that he was a skillful musician and is reported to have set some of his own poems to music, though none of these settings have survived.

EDITIONS   *Works,* ed. F. E. Hutchinson, Oxford, Clarendon Press, 1941 (with very important Introduction and Commentary).
The Latin Poetry of George Herbert, A Bilingual Edition, trans. by Mark McCloskey and Paul R. Murphy, Ohio University Press, 1965.

STUDIES   Margaret Bottrall, *George Herbert,* London, Murray, 1954.
Marchette G. Chute, Life of Herbert, in *Two Gentle Men,* New York, Dutton, 1959.
Mary Ellen Rickey, *Utmost Art: Complexity in the Verse of George Herbert,* University of Kentucky Press, 1966.
Arnold Stein, *George Herbert's Lyrics,* Johns Hopkins Press, 1968.
Joseph H. Summers, *George Herbert, His Religion and Art,* Harvard University Press, 1954.
Rosemond Tuve, *A Reading of George Herbert,* University of Chicago Press, 1952.
Isaak Walton, *Life,* 1670 (revised, 1674, 1675); available in World's Classics ed. of Walton's *Lives.*

TEXT   The text of the present selection is based upon the first edition of *The Temple,* 1633, with a few alterations suggested by F. E. Hutchinson's edition. I have also consulted the manuscript of the *Temple* in the

Bodleian Library (Ms. Tanner 307), and the manuscript of the early version owned by Dr. Williams's Library, London (Ms. Jones B 62); I am grateful to the authorities of both these libraries for permission to study these manuscripts.

ARRANGEMENT   The following selection attempts to retain something of the essential "architecture" of the whole *Temple*, which is divided into "The Church-porch," "The Church," and "The Church Militant," with the major body of poetry being contained within the middle section. "The Church" creates a flexible, organic unity, with frequent linkages between poems, and with a total, gradual movement from a sacramental introduction, through a long series of conflicts, and finally into a state of serene assurance.

NOTES   EASTER.

15 *vied:* OED ("vie," *v.* 6) explains this use of *vie* as meaning "to increase in number by addition or repetition"; but the usage here seems primarily to indicate something "placed in competition," the parts *vying* with each other. See "The Banquet," line 54: "Strive in this, and love the strife"; and the use of *vies* in "The Pearl," line 13.

EASTER WINGS.   The manuscripts present these emblematic verses horizontally, but the first edition prints them vertically.

19 *imp:* a term from falconry; "to engraft feathers in the wing of a bird, so as to make good losses or deficiencies" (OED, "imp," *v.* 4).

AFFLICTION (I).

47 *neare:* see Hutchinson's edition, p. 491. The Williams ms. reads *where*, while the Bodleian ms. reads *neere*, with *where* written above. 65–66 "Though I have been, as it seems, completely forgotten by you (or, perhaps: though I have completely forgotten my obligations to you), I do love you, and if I should not, I deserve the punishment of being cut off from loving you." See the detailed discussion of this ending by William Empson, *Seven Types of Ambiguity*, 2nd ed. rev., Norfolk, Conn., New Directions, 1947, pp. 183–84.

THE H. COMMUNION.   The first poem under this title (not contained in the early Williams ms.) represents Herbert's mature position on the bitter controversies regarding the doctrine of transubstantiation and the Real Presence of Christ in the elements of the Eucharist. He accepts a direct action by the physical elements upon the physical parts of man; and thus in a carefully guarded way he preserves a measure of the old doctrine; but in the last two stanzas he makes it plain that the more important presence is spiritual, working through grace. Thus, in the Anglican way, he preserves a "mean" between strict Catholic doctrine and strict Protestant doctrine.

3 *from:* Bodleian ms. reads *for,* which may be preferable.

SONNETS FROM WALTON'S LIFE. These two early compositions are given here because they provide an opportunity to compare Herbert's early style of "metaphysical wit" with the more mature manner of the two sonnets in the *Temple,* which also deal with the problem of converting poetry from the service of earthly love toward the service of the love of God. Walton tells us that these two sonnets were sent by Herbert to his mother as a New Year's gift during his first year at Cambridge: that is, during 1609–10, when Herbert was nearly seventeen.

THE TEMPER. Basically the word *temper* is used here to indicate a state of mind in which all qualities are properly proportioned (OED, "temper," *sb.* 1); at the same time the poem holds connotations of *tempering* steel by expansion and contraction through extremes of heat and cold; and it also alludes in lines 21–22 to the *tempering,* or tuning, of a stringed instrument (see OED, "temper," *v.* 14, 15).

AFFLICTION (IV). There are five poems by this title in the *Temple.*
12 *prick:* both mss. read *pink,* meaning "pierce."

MAN.
8 *more fruit:* the reading of the Williams ms. The first edition and the Bodleian ms. read *no fruit.* See Hutchinson's excellent note on this difficult choice of readings (p. 508).

JORDAN. The title places the river of baptism in contrast with Helicon, from which flowed the fountains of the pagan Muses. The "baptism" of Herbert's muse is indicated here by the way in which the poem echoes the opening sonnet in Sidney's *Astrophil and Stella:* "Foole, said my Muse to me, looke in thy heart and write."

THE BUNCH OF GRAPES. For detailed interpretation see Tuve, *A Reading of George Herbert,* pp. 112–17.

A PARODIE. The neutral, or positive, use of this term has a basis in musical tradition: see the article by Rosemond Tuve in *Studies in the Renaissance,* 8 (1961), 249–90. An excellent brief account of the musical meaning of *parody* is given by Frederick W. Sternfeld, *Goethe and*

Music, New York Public Library, 1954, p. 8. In explaining the roots of the word he says, "The prefix *para* means 'beside' in two senses: outside of, and therefore distorting the original, as in *paradox;* and alongside of, and therefore in sympathy with the original, as in *paraphrase.* Parody in musical terms means 'alongside a song,' 'to a song,' using the prefix *para* in the second sense." He points out that the practice was applied in the Parody Masses of Palestrina, Lassus, and Victoria. "Goethe and his contemporaries as well as his forebears wrote parodies by creating new texts to older tunes and rhythms, without any implication of irony." Thus Herbert has created a "sacred parody" by imitating the rhythms, the stanza-form, and some of the words in the love-song attributed to William Herbert, 3rd Earl of Pembroke, which is here reproduced for convenience of comparison from Grierson's OSA edition of the *Poems of Donne;* the love-song was included in early editions of Donne's poetry, but it is almost certainly by Pembroke.

LOVE (III). This poem, immediately preceded by "Judgement" and "Heaven," forms the last piece in "The Church"; after this comes the long didactic poem, "The Church Militant"; and "L'Envoy" then forms the conclusion of the whole volume.

FRANCIS QUARLES

LIFE   Quarles was born in 1592 at Romford, Essex, and educated at Christ's College, Cambridge. After receiving his degree he studied law at Lincoln's Inn. The first of his numerous books of religious verse appeared in 1620. Sometime before 1629 he became private secretary to Ussher, Archbishop of Armagh, Ireland, and went to live in Dublin. Before 1633 he appears to have returned to his native Essex. In 1639 he was appointed chronologer for the city of London, where he resided until his death in 1644. He was a staunch royalist and supporter of the established church.

STUDIES   Gordon S. Haight, "The Sources of Quarles's *Emblems," The Library,* 16 (1935–36), 188–209. (Demonstrates the indebtedness of Quarles's volume of 1635 to Jesuit emblem-books.)

Mario Praz, *Studies in Seventeenth-Century Imagery,* 2nd ed., Rome, Edizioni di Storia, 1964. (Deals with the whole range of emblem-books in this era.)

Rosemary Freeman, *English Emblem Books,* London, Chatto, 1948.

TEXT   The text of the poems here and the accompanying emblems are taken from the first edition of Quarles's *Emblemes*, 1635. The engravings have been re-rendered to make suitable linecuts.

RICHARD CRASHAW

LIFE   Crashaw was born in London in 1612 or early in 1613, his father being a prominent preacher, with Puritan tendencies. He was educated at the Charterhouse and at Pembroke College, Cambridge. About 1635 he was elected Fellow of Peterhouse, Cambridge, an institution then associated with strong High Church tendencies. He had been ordained by 1639, when he was curate of Little St. Mary's Church in Cambridge. His Royalist and High Church position led to his formal eviction from his posts at Cambridge in 1644, although he seems to have left the university some months earlier. He was certainly living as an exile in Holland in February 1644. It is uncertain whether or not he returned to England after this, although it is quite possible that he did so. In September 1646, he was in Paris at the court of the exiled Queen, and had been converted to Roman Catholicism, perhaps a year or more before this date. In the next year he held a minor clerical post at Rome, and in 1649 received a post at Loreto, where he died in the same year. The first edition of his English poems, religious as well as secular, appeared in London in 1646.

EDITION   *Poems*, ed. L. C. Martin, 2nd ed., Oxford, Clarendon Press, 1957 (with valuable Introduction and Commentary).

STUDIES   James V. Mirollo, *The Poet of the Marvelous: Giambattista Marino*, Columbia University Press, 1963. (Important for an understanding of the Italian background of Crashaw's poetry).

Lowry Nelson, Jr., *Baroque Lyric Poetry*, Yale University Press, 1961. (Contains important background for Crashaw.)

Mario Praz, "The Flaming Heart: Richard Crashaw and the Baroque," in *The Flaming Heart*, Anchor Books, 1958.

Mary Ellen Rickey, *Rhyme and Meaning in Richard Crashaw*, University of Kentucky Press, 1961.

Ruth Wallerstein, *Richard Crashaw: A Study in Style and Poetic Development*, University of Wisconsin Press, 1935.

Austin Warren, *Richard Crashaw: A Study in Baroque Sensibility*, Louisiana State University Press, 1939.

George Walton Williams, *Image and Symbol in the Sacred Poetry of Richard Crashaw,* University of South Carolina Press, 1963.

TEXT   The text of the poems in the present selection is based upon the second edition of *Steps to the Temple,* 1648, the last edition of Crashaw's poems published during his lifetime, and one that represents the first publication of several of his most important poems, along with revised versions of several other poems, such as "The Weeper." Crashaw was of course not in England at the time of publication, but it is clear that the volume was put together by someone with direct access to Crashaw's recent compositions and revisions. The posthumous volume, *Carmen Deo Nostro,* published at Paris in 1652 under the supervision of Crashaw's friend, Thomas Car, is usually regarded as having higher authority than the 1648, since it contains some additional passages not hitherto published, notably the last twenty-four lines of "The flaming Heart." Yet the 1652 omits some passages given in the 1648, and although we may assume that Car had manuscript authority for these omissions, there is no certainty on this matter. A weighing of the many small variants between the two editions produces no clear decision in favor of either. I incline to believe, that, on the whole, the edition of 1648 has far higher authority than it has usually been allowed, and I have therefore based the text here upon it, making changes and additions where the text of 1652 shows a clear superiority. Only the most important variants are noted below.

NOTES   THE WEEPER.

2 *Silver-forded:* this is the reading in the editions of 1646 and 1648; 1652 reads *sylver-footed,* giving an easier meaning, but not necessarily a better one. The thought of rills with silver fords (quiet, shallow places) makes an effective image.

65 *Blossom:* 1648 reads *Balsome.*

92 *and tears, and smiles disputing,:* 1652 reads *of teares with smiles disputing!*

98 *bosom:* 1648 reads *balsome.*

116 *large:* 1652 reads *rare.*

118 *wealth:* 1648 reads *wrath.*

ON THE NAME OF JESUS.   This poem falls into distinctly articulated movements, as follows:

I.   1–12.   Proposal of subject and preparatory prayer.
II.   13–44.   Preparatory self-address of humility.

III.	45–86.	Address to the other creatures, asking their help.
IV.	87–113.	Return to self-address, with greater confidence.
V.	114–149.	Invocation of the Name.
VI.	150–194.	Celebration of the Name.
VII.	195–237.	Conclusion: a contrast between present-day conditions and the faith of the ancient martyrs of the Church.

For further details concerning the meditative background of this poem see Martz, *The Poetry of Meditation*, pp. 331–52.

49 1648 reads *habit fit of self tun'd Harmonie;* 1652 reads *hasty Fitt-tun'd Harmony. habit* seems clearly a misprint for *hasty;* but the musical meaning of *fit* and the conception of a *self tun'd Harmonie* seem thoroughly in accord with the context.

72 *Provinces:* 1648 reads *powers.*

AN HYMNE OF THE NATIVITY.

32 *Bright:* 1652 reads *Young.*

47 *all one:* 1652 reads *his own.*

91–96 Omitted in 1652.

A HYMNE FOR THE EPIPHANIE.

113 *will:* 1652 reads *witt.*

145 *clear:* 1648 reads *deere.*

157 *domesticks:* 1652 reads *domestick.*

193 f. *Areopagite:* an allusion to the mystical theology set forth by "Dionysius the Areopagite," a writer of the fifth century A.D. who took the name of the Dionysius converted by Paul (Acts 17:34). He set forth the "negative way" of mystical ascent, under strong neo-platonic influence. The following passage from the opening chapter of his brief treatise, *The Mystical Theology* (tr. C. E. Rolt, New York, Macmillan, 1920), will illustrate the views upon which Crashaw has based the conclusion of his poem:

"Guide us to that topmost height of mystic lore which exceedeth light and more than exceedeth knowledge, where the simple, absolute, and unchangeable mysteries of heavenly Truth lie hidden in the dazzling obscurity of the secret Silence, outshining all brilliance with the intensity of their darkness, and surcharging our blinded intellects with the utterly impalpable and invisible fairness of glories which exceed all beauty! Such be my prayer; and thee, dear Timothy, I counsel that, in the earnest exercise of mystic contemplation, thou leave the senses and the activities of the intellect and all things that the senses or the intellect can perceive, and all things in this world of nothingness, or in that world of being, and that, thine understanding being laid to rest, thou strain (so far as thou mayest) towards an union with Him whom neither being nor understanding can contain. For, by the unceasing and absolute renunciation of thyself and all things, thou shalt in pureness cast all things aside, and be released from all, and so shalt be led upwards to the Ray of that divine Darkness which exceedeth all existence."

IN MEMORY OF . . . TERESA.

47 *trade:* from 1646 and 1652; 1648 reads *try.*
72 *chast:* from 1646 and 1652; 1648 reads *soft.*
107 *his:* from 1646 and 1652; 1648 reads *thine.*

THE FLAMING HEART. The title is the same as that given to the English translation of Teresa's autobiography attributed to Sir Toby Matthew: *The Flaming Hart or the Life of the Glorious S. Teresa,* Antwerp, 1642. The following passage of this book (pp. 419–20) is important for both of Crashaw's poems on Teresa:

"It pleased our Blessed Lord, that I should haue sometimes, this following Vision. I saw an Angell very neer me, towards my left side, and he appeared to me, in a Corporeall forme; though yet I am not wont to see anie thing of that kind, but very rarely. For, though Angells be represented often to me, it is yet, without my seeing them, but only according to that other kind of Vision, whereof I spake before. But, in this Vision, our Lord was pleased, that I should see this Angell, after this other manner. He was not great; but rather little; yet withall, he was of very much beautie. His face was so inflamed, that he appeared to be of those most Superiour Angells, who seem to be, all in a fire; and he well might be of them, whome we call *Seraphins;* but as for me, they neuer tell me their names, or rankes; yet howsoeuer, I see thereby, that there is so great a difference in Heauen, between one Angell, and another, as I am no way able to expresse. I saw, that he had a long Dart of gold in his hand; and at the end of the iron below, me thought, there was a little fire; and I conceaued, that he thrust it, some seuerall times, through my verie Hart, after such a manner, as that it passed the verie inwards, of my Bowells; and when he drew it back, me thought, it carried away, as much, as it had touched within me; and left all that, which remained, wholy inflamed with a great loue of Almightie God. The paine of it, was so excessiue, that it forced me to vtter those groanes;

and the suauitie, which that extremitie of paine gaue, was also so very excessiue, that there was no desiring at all, to be ridd of it; nor can the Soule then, receaue anie contentment at all, in lesse, then God Almightie himself."

85–108 These lines are not contained in 1648; they are here printed from 1652, with *u* and *v* normalized and words in capitals changed to italics (in accordance with the usage of 1648). The poem has a sense of completeness without these lines, which may have been a later addition by Crashaw; on the other hand, as colloquy and application to the self, the lines bring the poem to an appropriate and a richer conclusion. They may have been omitted in error or because of some theological objection to the strong adulation of the saint.

AN APOLOGIE FOR THE PRECEDENT HYMNES ON TERESA. This poem was originally published in 1646 as a companion piece to the first poem on Teresa, with the heading, "An Apologie for the precedent Hymne." In 1648 it was printed, with the present title, in a position immediately after the two poems on Teresa. In 1652 it was again placed after the first poem, with the following title: "An Apologie. For the Fore-going Hymne as having been writt when the author was yet among the protestantes." The added explanation of 1652 sounds like an editorial addition.

ON THE ASSUMPTION.
32 *leavy:* 1652 reads *heavy*.
41 *sweet:* 1648 reads *great*.
47–56 Omitted in 1652.

ANDREW MARVELL

LIFE   Marvell was born in 1621 in Holderness, Yorkshire, the son of an Anglican clergyman. He was educated at the Hull Grammar School and Trinity College, Cambridge. After receiving his degree he traveled widely for four years on the Continent. In 1651 he became tutor to the daughter of Lord Fairfax, the retired general of the Parliamentary army; he lived for two years at Nunappleton House, the Fairfax estate in Yorkshire. After this he became tutor to a ward of Cromwell. It is clear that he gradually became a firm supporter of the Cromwellian regime; in 1657 he took the post of Assistant in the Foreign Secretary's office, a post for which John Milton had recommended him in 1653. In

1658 he became a Member of Parliament for Hull, a position which he
held until his death in 1678. During the last twenty years of his life
Marvell was deeply engaged in political activities, including missions
to Holland and Russia, along with widespread writing of political pam-
phlets and satires. The poems included in the present selection may
date from his earlier years, perhaps from the early 1650s; but there is
no assurance about their dating. His *Miscellaneous Poems* first ap-
peared in 1681.

EDITIONS   *Poems and Letters,* ed. H. M. Margoliouth, 2 vols., 2nd ed.,
   Oxford, Clarendon Press, 1952 (with valuable Commentary).
Complete Poetry, ed. George deF. Lord, New York, Modern Library,
   1968. (An important new edition with excellent introduction and notes,
   a significant emphasis on Marvell's political poetry, and translations of
   his poems in Latin and Greek.)

STUDIES   Muriel C. Bradbrook and M. G. Lloyd Thomas, *Andrew
   Marvell,* Cambridge University Press, 1940.
Lawrence W. Hyman, *Andrew Marvell,* New York, Twayne, 1964.
Pierre Legouis, *Andrew Marvell, Poet, Puritan, Patriot,* Oxford, Claren-
   don Press, 1965.
J. B. Leishman, *The Art of Marvell's Poetry,* London, Hutchinson, 1966.
George deF. Lord, ed., *Twentieth-Century Views: Andrew Marvell,*
   Englewood Cliffs, N.J., Prentice-Hall, 1968 (a collection of essays by
   various hands).
Stanley Stewart, *The Enclosed Garden: The Tradition and the Image in
   Seventeenth-Century Poetry,* University of Wisconsin Press, 1966.
Harold E. Toliver, *Marvell's Ironic Vision,* Yale University Press, 1965.
John M. Wallace, *Destiny his Choice: The Loyalism of Andrew Marvell,*
   Cambridge University Press, 1968.

TEXT   Based on the *Miscellaneous Poems,* 1681. I have also examined
   the revisions made by an unknown hand in a copy of the 1681 *Poems*
   in the Bodleian Library (MS Eng. poet d.49). From these variants and
   from those listed in Margoliouth's edition, I have been led to make a
   few changes in the 1681 text.

NOTES   A DIALOGUE, BETWEEN THE RESOLVED SOUL, AND CREATED
   PLEASURE.
   51 *soft:* 1681 reads *cost,* which is emended to *soft* by Margoliouth
   and by the annotator of the above-mentioned Bodleian copy.

TO HIS COY MISTRESS.

34 *glew:* this reading of 1681 has caused great discussion and has resulted in general acceptance of the emendation *dew.* Yet no emendation seems to be needed, if we regard *glew* as simply a variant spelling of *glow* (on the analogy of *shew: show*). OED records the spelling *glewe* for the verb *glow* in the fifteenth century only. But it is interesting to note that the annotator of the Bodleian copy, writing evidently in the eighteenth century (see Margoliouth's second ed., p. xv), corrects the couplet here as follows: "Now therefore, while the youthful *glew* / Sits on thy skin like morning *dew.*" Here *glew* seems to mean *glow* in the sense for which OED cites a Shakespearean example: "Brightness and warmth of colour; a state of glowing brightness, a flush" (OED "glow," *sb. 2*). Most important, *glew: glow* makes better sense in the context than *dew.* The speaker is talking about a *hue,* a color; and what could be more appropriate than to compare his lady's hue with the morning-glow of sunrise? The next couplet may contain a suggestion of moisture; and yet even here it is the *Fires* that transpire through the pores: *Fires* and *glow* fit well together.

THE GARDEN.

47 *Annihilating:* in mystical writings of the era the conception of *annihilation* had a positive, creative value. It referred to the soul's withdrawal from self-interest and from the attraction of created things, as it moved toward a mystical intuition of the Divine. Thus, in his *Spiritual Canticle,* St. John of the Cross says: "It seems to the soul that its former knowledge, and even the knowledge of the whole world, is pure ignorance by comparison with that knowledge [of God]; . . . and the exaltation of the mind in God wherein it is as if enraptured, immersed in love, and become wholly absorbed in God, allows it not to take notice of any thing soever in the world; . . . For it is withdrawn not only from all other things, but even from itself, and is *annihilated,* as though it were dissolved in love. . . ." (*Complete Works of Saint John of the Cross,* tr. and ed. by E. Allison Peers, new ed. rev., 3 vols., Westminster, Md., Newman Press, 1953, II, 100.) Marvell, of course, is using the conception for his own particular purposes here.

HENRY VAUGHAN

LIFE   Vaughan was born in 1621 or early in 1622, of Welsh ancestry, and spent most of his life at Newton, on the Usk River, in Breconshire,

Wales. He was educated at Jesus College, Oxford, along with his twin-brother Thomas, who became an ardent scholar of the Hermetic philosophy. He went on to study law in London, apparently in 1640–42. His secular volume of 1646, *Poems, with the tenth Satyre of Juvenal Englished*, shows the strong influence of Ben Jonson and the "Sons of Ben," along with traces of Donneian influence. He appears to have undergone an experience of religious conversion sometime around 1648. He was devoted to the Royalist cause and to the Church of England. Sometime near 1655 he seems to have begun the practice of medicine, which he pursued successfully as a country doctor until his death in 1695. He wrote very little poetry during the last forty years of his life.

EDITIONS   *Works*, ed. L. C. Martin, 2nd ed., Oxford, Clarendon Press, 1957 (with helpful notes).

Poetry and Selected Prose, ed. L. C. Martin, Oxford University Press, 1963.

Complete Poetry, ed. French Fogle, Anchor Books, 1964.

Secular Poems, ed. E. L. Marilla, Uppsala, Lundequistska, 1958 (with very extensive commentary).

STUDIES   R. A. Durr, *On the Mystical Poetry of Henry Vaughan*, Harvard University Press, 1962.

Ross Garner, *Henry Vaughan: Experience and the Tradition*, University of Chicago Press, 1959.

F. E. Hutchinson, *Henry Vaughan: A Life and Interpretation*, Oxford, Clarendon Press, 1947.

E. L. Marilla, *A Comprehensive Bibliography of Henry Vaughan*, University of Alabama Press, 1948.

E. L. Marilla and James D. Simmonds, *Henry Vaughan: A Bibliographical Supplement, 1946–1960*, University of Alabama Press, 1963. (Contains a full listing of studies of Henry Vaughan.)

Louis L. Martz, *The Paradise Within*, Yale University Press, 1964 (chapter 1).

Ernest C. Pettet, *Of Paradise and Light: A Study of Vaughan's Silex Scintillans*, Cambridge University Press, 1960.

TEXT   For the poems contained in *Silex Scintillans*, 1650, the text is derived from that edition; for the poems of the second part, from the edition of 1655, which consists of the unsold sheets of 1650 (with two cancelled leaves), bound up with new introductory matter and a second "book" of poems. The present selection retains, complete, the brief introductory matter of 1650: Latin poem, engraved title page, and short "Dedication." The volume of 1655 omits both the Latin poem and the engraved title page, while the "Dedication" is expanded in the direction of conventional piety. At the same time the 1655 volume opens with a long and crabbed prose preface out of tune with the devotional quality of the 1650 poems. The motto from Job on the 1655 title page, "Where is God my Maker, who giveth Songs in the night?" suggests an attitude considerably different from that found in the intimate Latin poem of 1650. The second book of 1655, while containing a few of Vaughan's best poems, shows a notable falling-off in poetic power and a tendency to turn toward the topics of conventional piety.

ARRANGEMENT   The poems from 1650 are here given in the order of their appearance in that volume; the selection has been made with the aim of retaining this volume's effect of total integrity: an effect that arises, first, from the persistent mode of Augustinian meditation, probing the memory; and second, from what appears to be a deliberate effort to evoke a comparison with Herbert's *Temple:* a tribute by imitation. The notes point out many significant echoes of Herbert; for others, see the notes to Martin's edition and the study by Pettet.

NOTES   TITLE PAGE. *Silurist:* Vaughan liked to place this title after his name, with reference to the local British tribe of Vaughan's region, called by Tacitus the *Silures.* Note that the subtitle of Vaughan's volume is identical with the subtitle of Herbert's *Temple.*

THE AUTHOR'S EMBLEM.   The editor is indebted to the Reverend Marcus Haworth for suggesting some of the phrases in this translation.

REGENERATION.   The biblical motto at the end has a wrong verse-reference and does not accord in phrasing with the King James version (as is frequently the case with Vaughan's citations). The verse here comes from Song of Solomon 4:16; verses 12–15 of this chapter are highly important for the imagery of this poem from Stanza 5 to the end. See the detailed interpretation of this poem by Pettet, pp. 104–17.

RESURRECTION AND IMMORTALITY.   The last two stanzas show Vaughan's acquaintance with the Hermetic philosophy; that is, the occult science attributed to the mythical Hermes Trismegistus and cultivated by the alchemists (see Martin's notes, pp. 729–30). But, equally important, the poem shows how carefully Vaughan qualified the Hermetic terms by drawing them into the orbit of traditional Christian conceptions. Note particularly how the poem is enclosed within two biblical quotations.

THE BRITTISH CHURCH. A striking contrast with Herbert's poem under the same title. Here the Church, the "Bride of Christ," is speaking to Christ, as in the Song of Solomon (Chapter 2), under the conditions of the English civil wars in the 1640s. The Latin motto at the end may be translated as follows: "O rose of the field! O lily of the valleys! how have you now become the food of wild boars!" (With allusion to Song of Solomon 2:1 and Psalm 80:13.)

MANS FALL, AND RECOVERY. The biblical reference at the end is wrong: see Romans 5:18.

THE RETREATE. For Vaughan's cautious use of the metaphor of pre-existence see Martin's notes, *Works*, pp. 732–33.

"COME, COME, WHAT DOE I HERE?" There are six untitled poems in the 1650 volume headed by the symbol ¶; all of these appear to refer to the death of his brother William in 1648, which seems to have had a profound effect upon Vaughan's religious outlook.

THE MORNING-WATCH. For detailed interpretation see Pettet, pp. 119–37; Pettet here notes the many echoes of Herbert in this poem (pp. 128–29).

"SILENCE, AND STEALTH OF DAYES!" Vaughan's brother William died about July 14, 1648; thus the poem appears to date from sometime near September 1, 1648 (see line 3).

PRAISE. For the verse-form, the rhyme, and the phrasing of lines 1, 9, and 13, see Herbert's poem here under the same title. In the *Temple* this poem, "Praise," is immediately followed by a double poem under the title, "An Offering" (note "Off'ring" in line 50 of Vaughan's second part here). The second part of Herbert's "Offering" is written in a stanza-form resembling that of Vaughan's second part.

MOUNT OF OLIVES. *Silex Scintillans*, 1650, has another poem under this title, which makes it clear that this Mount is for Vaughan a symbol of poetic inspiration, contrasting with the pagan Mount Helicon:

> Yet, if Poets mind thee well
> They shall find thou art their hill,
>   And fountaine too,
> Their Lord with thee had most to doe;
> He wept once, walkt whole nights on thee,
> And from thence (his suff'rings ended,)
>   Unto glorie
>   Was attended;

Compare Herbert's similar use of "Jordan": the *Temple* has two poems entitled "Jordan," both dealing with problems of poetry; the present selection prints only the second of these.

"THEY ARE ALL GONE INTO THE WORLD OF LIGHT!" For detailed interpretation see Pettet, pp. 156–65.

COCK-CROWING. This poem, like the following one, is strongly pervaded by technical terms from the Hermetic philosophy: see Martin's notes, *Works*, pp. 746–47.

THE PALM-TREE. Here the soul is speaking to the body, as in "The Evening-watch." The poem may be clarified by recalling that the palm tree is a traditional symbol of the Church: see Song of Solomon 7:7–8: "This thy stature is like to a palm tree . . . I said, I will go up to the palm tree, I will take hold of the boughs thereof"—a passage described in the chapter heading of the King James version as part of a "description of the church's graces." The poem seems first to allude to the physical church, as a place where the body will be buried or entombed; but the spiritual church is of course the dominant reference throughout.

THE NIGHT. Heading: 1655 reads *John 2.3*. For detailed interpretation of this poem see Pettet, pp. 140–54.

THOMAS TRAHERNE

LIFE Traherne was born in 1637, the son of a Hereford shoemaker, and appears to have been reared by a prosperous relative. He was educated at Brasenose College, Oxford, ordained in the English Church in 1660, and lived as rector at Credenhill, near Hereford, from 1661 until 1669. In that year he became chaplain to Sir Orlando Bridgeman and lived in London and Teddington until his death in 1674. His poems were first published in 1903, and his *Centuries,* in 1908.

EDITIONS   *Centuries, Poems, and Thanksgivings,* ed. H. M. Margoliouth, 2 vols., Oxford, Clarendon Press, 1958 (with important Introduction and Commentary).
Poems, Centuries, and Three Thanksgivings, ed. Anne Ridler, Oxford University Press, 1966.

STUDIES   Louis L. Martz, *The Paradise Within,* Yale University Press, 1964 (chapter 2).
Keith W. Salter, *Thomas Traherne, Mystic and Poet,* London, Arnold, 1964.
Gladys I. Wade, *Thomas Traherne,* Princeton University Press, 1944.

TEXT   The text of the poems and prose here is reproduced from Margoliouth's edition listed above, with the permission of the Clarendon Press.

APPENDIX

EDWARD DAWSON

THE PRACTICAL METHODE
OF MEDITATION
1614

The Practical Methode of Meditation
(1614)

Meditation which we treate of, is nothing els but a diligent and forcible application of the understanding, to seeke, and knowe, and as it were to tast some divine matter; from whence doth arise in our affectionate[1] powers good motions,[2] inclinations, and purposes which stirre us up to the love and exercise of vertue, and the hatred and avoiding of sinne: it is the shortest and almost the only way to attaine to Christian perfection: it is the path which all holy men (of what estate soever) have troden. Wherfore let those, who desire to enjoy there company, follow their example.

2. And surely it seemes a thing, even impossible, to arrive unto any notable degree of perfection without this so necessary a meanes. For perfection beeing nothing els, but the rooting out, of vices, and planting of vertues in our soules: unles we withdraw our affections[3] from earthly objects, and settle them on heavenly, we shall never performe the one, nor attaine to the other. And seeing that our affectionate part imbraceth nothing, unlesse our understanding both know it, and judge of it, neither can it find out fit objects of heavenly affections unles it discourse[4] on them, nor move therwith the will, except it consider the goodnes which often lieth hidden in them; it followeth evidently, that without meditation no man can attaine to any height of Perfection.

3. Besides, it is the most excellent manner of praising God, employing every power of our soule, in shewing forth the excellencies of their Creator, which is the chiefest end of our creation: neither doth it rest heere, but bringeth a man to heaven (that so I may say) before his tyme, making him enjoy (after a sort) even in this life the blessednes of the life to come: which being nothing els but the see-

[1] pertaining to the affections, the emotions.
[2] inward promptings, emotions.
[3] emotions, inclinations.
[4] reason.

ing, loving, and enjoying of Gods divine Majesty, we giving our selves by meditation to the most perfect knowledge, to the straitest bande[5] of love, and the sweetest fruition of God which this wretched life affoards, we participate in the best manner which our estate will permit us, of the happines of the Blessed in heaven.

4. True it is, that through the unhappy estate of this troublesome world, man beeing distracted by other thoughts, and surprised by other affections, cannot continually, nor without some little violence, especially at the first, enjoy this so great a happines: yet may he, joyning his owne diligence to Gods help, so unite himselfe to his Creator by this exercise, that at least for some determinate[6] time, he may enjoy him with some familiarity.

5. It will therfore be good for those, who intende to reape the fruit of this heavenly emploiment, to appointe unto themselves, by the counsell of some one skilfull in matters of spirit, the tyme they meane to spend every day therin, and that with so stedfast a resolution, that they make conscience [not] to omit it without urgent occasion; which omission (although necessary) let them supply at some other tyme of the day, if it be possible. And let them be but diligent and constant at the beginning, and it will prove an excercise most full of spirituall profit and delight, which will aboundantly countervaile the paines bestowed therin.

6. And let those who thinke Meditation to belong only to Religious persons,[7] and that secular ought not or need not busy themselves therwith, be fully persuaded, that they ar in an errour very pernicious. For as secular men have more distractions by reason of their divers worldly employments, then Religious, more temptations by the continuall presence of many alluring objects, more imperfections, sinnes, and ill habits to conquer: so have they more need to retire themselves by this holy recollection,[8] to propose unto themselves the highest objects most worthy of love, affection, and prosecution, to exercise themselves in the acts of the noblest vertues; all which is performed by meditation. And if religious persons being

---

[5] tightest bond.

[6] limited.

[7] those who have taken formal religious vows.

[8] deliberate withdrawal from distractions; concentration of thought.

Gods sworne souldiars, use these weapons, as thinges belonging to their estate and dignity, secular people must put them on also, at least for their necessary defence; and of these many do make great change of life and happy progresse in vertue by this exercise, even in this cold age of ours. And although they are more frequent in other Countreys, which enjoy the happy freedome of the service of God, without feares or contradictions: yet there want not such (and that of both sexes) even amongest us, who overcomming the tumults of the world, and the terrors of persecution, do bestow daily a good part of their tyme in this important busines, and continually reap the plentifull fruit of their happy labours; which number if it may be increased by this my poore endeavour, I shall thinke it happily bestowed.

7. And although the holy Ghost be the chiefe Maister of this doctrine, yet it shall not be amisse to set downe some briefe method of practise, taken out of approved[9] Authors and experience, that so those who have a will to imploy themselves therein, bee not deprived (at least of a great part) of the profit, for want of instructions.

8. We shall heere omit divers divisions which might be made of meditation, and devide it only into Spirituall and Historicall, which distinction is taken from the diversitie of the matter wheron we meditate. Spirituall meditation is that, wherin the matter is spirituall, in that sense, as we oppose spirituall to corporall, for that it containes for the most part no corporall actions: such are the Meditations of the end of man, of sinnes, death, judgment, hell, heaven, the benefits of God, his infinite perfections, and the like. Historicall Meditation is that, where the matter is some Historie, as the meditations of the life and passion of our Blessed Saviour, of the vertuous actions of his Blessed Mother, or some other Saint. Of both which kinds of matter, many spirituall bookes are full, so that we may easily take our choice, with the counsell of our spirituall Father: and the fittest of all, will be the holy Gospell, especially having helped our selves at the beginning with some larger discourses.

9. For the better order, and more profit, we must begin with the end wherfore man was created, with the judgments of God exercised on sinners, with the multitude and greatnes of our owne sinns,

[9] proved by experience, tested.

with death, judgment, hell, and the like: which will help much to
the rooting out of vices. Then may we meditate on the life, and pas-
sion of Christ, from whose vertues we shall receive glorious light,
to frame the like, with his grace, in our selves. And lastly we may
contemplate the glorious mysteries[10] of our Saviours Resurrection,
Apparitions, Ascension, and the comming of the Holy Ghost, his
excessive love towardes us, his manifould benefits, and the aboun-
dant reward prepared for his friends in heaven.

The preparation for Meditation §1

For the more fruitfull meditating on the divine mysteries, there is
required such puritie of Conscience, that we feele not remorse of
any great sinne; and finding our selves guilty, we must seeke to
cleare our soules, by those remedies which God hath appointed for
that purpose.

2. We must endeavour so to compose our passions, and affections
in a meane, that they be neither too weake, nor too strong.

3. We must so recollect[11] our powers and senses, that willingly
we neither thinke on, see, heare, nor admit any thing, which may
breed distraction. Briefly we must so dispose our selves before our
meditation, as we wish to be, when we shall meditate.

4. The fittest time for Meditation (according to the example of
the Prophet David) is the morning, when the powers of our soule
are free from other objects. To be therfore better prepared, we must
the night before read over that part of the booke, or writing twice,
or thrice, whence we take our matter: then devide it into three
partes or pointes, more or fewer as wee please: after that propose
unto our selves that which we meane to make the especiall end of
our Meditation. As if we meditate on the sinnes of others, our end
may be shame, and confusion, beholding Gods judgments excer-
cised on them for fewer, and lesser offences then we find in our
selves: yf we meditate upon our owne sins, we may propose for our
end Sorrow and Amendment: if on the paines of hell, feare and

[10] events in the life of Christ or a saint.
[11] draw together, concentrate.

horrour: if on the joyes of heaven, joyfull hope and consolation: yf on the life of Christ, imitation of his vertues: yf on his Passion, sorrow, and compassion: yf on his Resurrection, joy and congratulation:[12] and thus according unto the diversitie of the matter, the end or scope[13] of our meditation must be different, which with a litle diligence we may easily find out: and upon this end must our intention be especially fixed at the time of meditation.

5. We must also determine with our selves what *Preludiums*, as they are termed, or preambles we must make (of which we shall speake in their due place.) And lastly we must marke well what persons, wordes, and workes are contained in ech point, yf our matter be historicall. But yf it be spirituall we must call to minde the chiefe things occurring therin. All which must be done by a sleight passage[14] only, to open the way for our meditation; and we may find out all the persons, wordes, and workes, which are expressed, as also all those, which the decencie[15] of the history doth shew unto us; especially the persons, wordes, and workes of God, the angels, and divells, which we may finde in every history fit for meditation, with no small spirituall profit: God, and the holy Angels moving and furthering all good things, and the wicked spirits provoking to evil, and hindering in what they can all good.

6. Being in bed, before we betake our selves to sleepe, we must thinke on the houre we meane to rise at, and call to mind briefly the pointes of our meditation: and the same we may doe so often as we chance to awake.

7. When we awake in the morning, castinge off all other thoughts, we must breifly, but with great affection, give God due thankes for all his benefits, and for those in particuler received that night, and offer up our selves, and all our actions of the day following, to his honour and glory, proposing effectually, with helpe of his holy Grace, to avoid sinne, and imperfection that day, and especially that which wee endeavour most to overcome, by particuler exam-

[12] rejoicing.
[13] aim.
[14] a brief passing-over or survey.
[15] appropriateness to the circumstances.

ine[16] and care. After this we may begin to take some tast of our meditation, and stirre up in our soules somtimes griefe, shame, confusion, or feare, otherwhiles desire to know with some clearenes the mysteries of the life and passion of our Saviour, so to imitate him diligently, and love him fervently; sometimes sorrow and heavines, so to be compartners with Christ, suffering so many paines for us; somtimes also joy and comfort, to congratulate[17] our Lords glorie, and felicitie; and at other times other affections agreable unto ech meditation: Which we may performe more easily, yf we keep in our mind some similitude[18] answering to the affection we would have; or yf we repeate some verse of the psalmes, or other Scripture, or Father, which may be to that purpose, so we do it with attention and affection. And if we meditate more then once in one day, in that quarter of an houre going before our tyme appointed, we must read over diligently the matter of our meditation, devide it, and settle it in our mind, thinking what we are to do, before whome to appeare, and with whome to talke, and making such preparation, as we appointed for our mornings meditation.

The performance of Meditation ∫2

The houre of meditation being come, we may imagine our selves to be invited by our good Angell, or by some other Saint to whome we are particulerly devoted, to appeare in the presence of God: wherefore having made the signe of the holy Crosse, and sprinkled our selves with holy water, we may go presently,[19] with a kinde of spirituall hunger, to the place where we meane to make our meditation, and standing from thence a pace or two, briefly lift up our minde to Almighty God, imagining him to be so present with us (as truly he is) that he behouldeth what we are to do, and doth

---

[16] an examination of the self directed toward the extirpation of some one particular fault.

[17] rejoice in.

[18] comparison, simile, likeness, parable, allegory: any concrete representation of a spiritual matter.

[19] immediately.

shew unto us in that very place his most venerable and glorious countenance.

2. The presence of God is best framed of[20] our Understanding, by making an act of faith, wherby we beleeve Almighty God to be so present there, that he compasseth us round on every side, as the water compasseth the fish, and yet is also within us, and the things before us (as he is in all things) somwhat like the water which is entred into a sponge, and this by his divine essence, presence, and power, which penetrate the nature of every creature, and give them needfull helpe for their operations.

3. It helpeth much our attention to conceive the presence of God after the liveliest manner wee can, and to fix our meditation as much as humaine frailtie will permit, continually in the sight of God, perswading our selves, that he is much pleased to see us proceede with diligence in this spirituall affaire, and much dislikes yf wee performe it negligently, and in this point we must force our selves a little at the first, untill exercise produce facilitie.

4. Having conceived God thus present, we must next looke upon our owne unworthines, and with great reverence say, with the Patriarke Abraham, *Loquar ad Dominum meum, cum sum pulvis et cinis.* I will speake to my Lord, beeing dust and ashes,[21] and with internall adoration, bending the knees of our hart, kneele downe before our Lord, professing the presence of the Blessed Trinity with some wordes fitting that purpose, as *Benedicta sit Sancta et Individua Trinitas:* Blessed be the holy, and undevided Trinity, or, *Gloria Patri, et Filio, et Spiritui Sancto:* Glorie to the Father, to the Sonne, and to the holy Ghost, or, *Sanctus, Sanctus, Sanctus, Dominus Deus omnipotens, qui erat, qui est, et qui venturus est:* Holy, holy, holy, Lord God omnipotent, who was, who is, and who is to come, or the like. But yf through indisposition or weaknes of body we find our selves unapt to kneele, we may, having entred into our meditation, either stand, sit or walke, or use such situation of body as we shall finde fittest for our infirmitie. And although we should have our body well disposed to kneele, yet if we find not in our meditation the comfort we expect, we may change somtime the

---

[20] conceived by.
[21] See Genesis 18:27.

position we were in, as from kneeling to sitting, standing, walking, prostrating our selves upon our face at our Saviours feete etc. and in travaile either on foote, or otherwise, we may meditate as we goe on our journey, but ordinarily, yf wee be not otherwaies hindred, kneling is the fittest position to procure reverence, and devotion.

6. Being on our knees, or otherwaies ready to begin our meditation, let us acknowledge our selves sinners with as much inward feeling of heart as we can, asking humbly pardon of Gods divine Majesty, saying with divotion the foure first verses of the *Miserere* Psalme, the *Confiteor*, or some other prayer to that purpose.

7. Then encouraging our selves with hope of pardon, we may behould the majesty of God there present, and acknowleging the great bande we have to imploy our selves wholy in his service, make with feeling devotion the preparative Praier; which is nothing els but a short petition, wherein we aske helpe of God, that all our powers and actions, and that in particuler we now goe about, may be sincerely directed, and performed to the honour of God, and the benefit of our owne soule.

8. Then must we proceed to the preambles or *Preludiums*, which are three if the matter be historicall, but if it be not of some history, they are only two.

9. The first *Preludium* or Preamble (which is proper onely to the meditation, made upon some historie) is a breife calling to mind of the mystery we are to meditate, no otherwaies then if we should tell it to another, without any discourse[22] theron at all.

10. The seconde is common to all Meditations, and is an imagination of seeing the places where the thinges we meditate on were wrought, by imagining our selves to be really present at those places; which we must endeavour to represent so lively, as though we saw them indeed, with our corporall eyes; which to performe well, it will help us much to behould before-hande some Image wherein that mistery is well represented, and to have read or heard what good Authors write of those places, and to have noted well the distance from one place to another, the height of the hills, and the situation of the townes and villages. And the diligence we employ

---

[22] reasoning, thought.

heerein is not lost; for on the well making of this *Preludium* depends both the understanding of the mystery, and attention in our meditation.

11. Yf our meditation be of some spirituall matter of which we spake before which affordes no historie, we must frame our second *Preludium* according thereunto: as if wee meditate on sinnes, we may imagine our soule to be cast out of Paradise, and to be held prisoner in this body of ours, fettered with the chaines of disordinate[23] Passions, and affections, and clogged with the burden of our owne flesh. If on Hell, we may behould with our imagination the length, breadth, and depth of that horrible place. Yf on Heaven, the spatious plesantnes of that celestiall Countrie, the glorious companie of Angels and Saintes. Yf on Gods judgment which must passe upon us, our Saviour sitting on his Judgment Seate, and we before him expecting the finall Sentence: if on death, our selves laied on our bed, forsaken of the Physitians, compassed about with our weeping friends, and expecting our last agony. Thus our second *Preludium* in these Meditations which are spirituall (as we call them) must be some similitude, answerable to the matter.

12. The third *Preludium* in all Meditations is a short, but earnest prayer to God for that thing which we have proposed, as the scope, and ende of our Meditation, of which we have already spoken. Having finished these *Preludiums,* we must begin the first pointe of our Meditation, exercising thereon the three powers of our Soule, Memorie, Understanding, and Will. With our memorie we must (as it were) rehearse unto our selves in order, that which is conteined in the first point of the matter we prepared, calling to mind also such things as we have read in the holy Scripture, and other good Authors, or heard of discreet and devout persons, yf it make for the matter we have in hand; and lay open to the view of our understanding the persons, wordes, and workes contained in the first point, if it containe any, if none, at least the most notable matters therin.

13. Then we must exercise our understanding upon that which the memory hath proposed, and search out diligently, what may be considered about that present object, inferring one thing from an-

23 transgressing against moral order, immoderate.

other, framing from thence true, pious, and spirituall conceipts,[24] fit to move our Will to vertuous affections. Lastly for that the will is naturally inclined and moved to affect[25] those things which the understanding proposeth, we must procure with all diligence to stir up in our selves those affections which the operations of our understanding going before, incline us unto.

14. And having thus exercised the three powers of our soule upon the first point, we must passe on to the next. But finding our selves imploied with spirituall profit about that we have in hand, we must not be sollicitous to passe on further, although by our long stay in one point, we should not have leasure to goe over them all, within our determined tyme. But it wilbe best to satisfy our selves fully where we find spirituall comfort, and reserve the rest for an other time of Meditation. We must also know, that the exercise of our Memory and Understanding in Meditation, is ordained to the motion of our will, and must therfore be used with such moderation as may serve for the moving therof, and no more, that so our Meditation may be full of pious and good affections, not vaine and filled with curiosities.

15. We may frame[26] our conceites upon divers heades, which our matter will yielde us: as if it be historicall, we may consider in the persons there represented, who they be, their thoughts, and affections, their inwarde vertues, and outward carriage, with other circumstances. In the words we may consider their first and proper sense, as also the figurative and translated[27] signification, if there be any, and the ende wherfore they are spoken. In the workes are to be considered their nature, what they are, with their circumstances, comprehended in this verse usuall amongst those who treate of morall actions, *Quis, Quid, Ubi, Quibus auxiliis, Cur, Quomodo, Quando,* wayghing well what person that is, by whome the action is done, examining what he speaketh, and doth, where, with what helpe, or assistance, for what end, in what manner, and at what tyme.

---

[24] conceptions, thoughts.
[25] be fond of, tend toward, aspire to.
[26] construct, organize.
[27] metaphorical.

16. But if our matter be spirituall and affoard no persons, with their wordes and workes, we must endeavour to conceive the matter throughly[28] in our understanding, and to find out the true sense and meaning of the wordes, which represent the matter unto us, and the right nature of the things therin represented, and we may help our selves much to the framing of spirituall conceites, if we apply unto our matter familiar similitudes, drawne from our ordinary actions, and this as well in historicall, as spirituall meditations.

17. The affections which we ought to procure by these conceipts are many, and diverse; nor can it be assigned, which we should alwaies procure, they chiefly depending on the guift of the holy Ghost. Yet whilst we attended especially to the rooting out of vices, which is termed by the Maisters of spirit *via purgativa*, the purgative way, we ought to labour first for great griefe, with shame and confusion for our sinnes, for our negligence, and couldnes in Gods service, for carelesnes and sloth in seeking perfection. Secondly a feare of offending God, of loosing his grace, of not fulfilling our obligation in answering to his heavenly voice and inspirations, and of severe punishment for our sinnes. Thirdly, a perfect hatred of all sinne, coldnes, and negligence in spirit, of all earthly things which with-hould us from God, and of our owne pleasures and contentments.

18. Fourthly, a desire of mortification of our body, our senses, passions, and inclinations to honour and estimation, submitting our selves to the lowest persons, accompting[29] our selves the basest of all others, and desiring that others should esteeme us so. Likewise when we principally endeavour to plant vertues in our soules, which is termed *via illuminativa*, the illuminative way, we must stir up first a love and desire of all vertues, as also a desire to know the person and actions of our Blessed Saviour, so to imitate him the better. Secondly a hope to please God with the help of his holy grace to persevere in his service, to free our selves from coldnes, and defects, to attaine perfection in this life, and eternal happines in the life to come.

[28] thoroughly.
[29] accounting.

19. Thirdly, sorrow and compassion, for the suffering of our Saviour, for the blindnes and ingratitude of those who offend him so often, and greivously. And whilst we cheifly seeke to unite our soules to God, which is called *via unitiva,* the unitive way, we must stir up in our selves, first an exceeding love of God: Secondly a spirituall rejoycing in his infinite riches and perfections, as also in the glorie and happines of our Saviour risen from death, and received into heaven with triumph and majesty. Thirdly, a gratefull joy for the charity he hath shewed to mankind, and our selves in particuler, and for so many and great benefits bestowed upon his friends. Fourthly, a vehement desire, that Gods name be knowne and sanctified, that he may reigne over all soules without resistance, and that his holy will may be fulfilled in all places: and many more such like affections as we have heere set downe, the Holy Ghost will teach us, in all these waies, if we dispose our selves with a great desire of them, and humility, (altogeather necessary for the receiving of this divine influence) yet not omitting our owne diligence.

20. We may move and strengthen these affections, by earnest demaunding them of God, either with wordes of the holy Scripture or some devout saying of our owne. By obsecration, instantly[30] asking them of God for his infinite love, Goodnes, and mercies sake; for the most gratefull merits of his beloved sonne, for the sanctitie and puritie of his Blessed Mother. By gratitude, giving thankes to God for so many benefits, so many bountifull and assured promises (descending into particulers.) By oblation, offering our selves to God, prepared and ready to do whatsoever he hath taught us, to imitate our Saviour so neere as we can, to suffer whatsoever for his sake, and to seeke all meanes to please his divine majestie. By good purposes, intending most firmly in the sight of the whole Court of heaven to do all that we know, or shall know to appertaine to the glory of God, to make good use of his grace, and heavenly succours, to observe perfectly his Commandements, and fulfill his holy inspirations. By praises, extolling to the highest degree of our power Gods mercy, bounty, patience, charity etc. celebrating his divine greatnes, his infinite wisdome, his unmesurable goodnes, his un-

[30] urgently.

speakable power. By reprehending our selves, as slothfull, undevout, harde, ungratefull, and that after so many benefits and helpes, so many illuminations and incitations to goodnes. By admiration, wondering at the goodnes, patience, and charity of God, at our owne negligence, and coldnes in spirit, at the contempt shewed by us, of so many favours, and graces, so many and cleare inspirations. By framing unto our selves some person, imagining sometymes that God complaines and reprehendes them, that he exhorts and promises us helpe, sometymes imagining that some Saynt, most notable in some one vertue, laments that he is no more imitated, and sometyme that the Divell rejoyceth and triumpheth, that he is more followed then God, and knowes so well the meanes, to bring us to sinne, coldnes, and carelesnesse of our perfection and salvation, sometymes also fayning[31] the very vertues in some venerable shape bewayling their neglect, and contempt: and many more wayes may we find by the help of the holy spirit, the chiefest Maister of this heavenly doctrine of Prayer. Of these wayes we may use more, or lesse, answerable unto the affections we meane to procure, and according unto our owne necessity. And in the exercise of them we may very profitably repeate in our understanding, some affectionate words of the holy Scripture, or Fathers, or some other that are full of devotion.

21. In exercising that which we have hitherto set downe, we must use such moderation, that we hurte not our head, or breast, with overmuch force: for besides those corporall harmes that arise from thence, no small spirituall evills follow, as a certaine languishing and slacknes in meditation, for feare of hurting our selves, a new coldnes and weakenes in our affections, small disposition to receive the seedes of divine inspirations, and influences, facility in leaving of our meditations either of our owne accord, or by the counsell of our Ghostly[32] Father, which evils may be easily avoyded, if we use no violence unto our selves in the acts of meditation. As if we straine not our breast, if we seeke not to wringe out teares, if we be not too intentive[33] in the actions of our soule, but use so much diligence in our meditation, as we would use in talking with some person of

31 feigning, imagining.
32 spiritual.
33 intent.

much respect, which will be sufficient if God, who disposeth all thinges sweetly, do not call us extraordinarily to a more forcible application.

22. At the end of our meditation we must make with our understanding some affectionate speach or Colloquium to God, and somtimes also to some Saints which may be either one or more, according to our devotion, being the conclusion of our whole meditation, and a reverent departure from the great Lord of whome we have had so gracious audience, giving him thankes, offering our selves and ours to him, and demanding grace and succour for our selves, our friendes, and benefactors, and for whom soever we have obligation to pray, which three thinges we may ordinarily use at the end of every meditation. We may somtimes also accuse our selves, and aske pardon, as also impart unto him our affaires, and those of our freinds intreating counsaile and help for their good performance, extolling his infinite mercy and love, still following the affection we shall then feele.

23. In these speaches wee may talke with God as a servant with his Maister, as a sonne with his Father, as one friend with another, as a spouse with her beloved bridgrome, or as a guilty prisoner with his Judge, or in any other manner which the holy Ghost shall teach us.

24. Having ended this our speach, we may adde some vocall prayer, if we will, as the *Pater noster,* if we speake to God the Father, the praier *Anima Christi,* if to the Sonne, the Hymne *Veni Creator,* if to the holy Ghost, *Ave Maria,* or *Ave maris stella,* if to the Blessed Virgin, or some other devout praier, in which we find devotion and comfort.

25. We may make such manner of speaches in other places of our meditation, and it will be best, and almost needfull so to do, but at the end we must never omit them, and then only use the vocall praier to conclude them with all.

26. Departing from the place of Meditation, we may make an internall and externall reverence to God, whose conversation[34] we shall then leave of, with an intent to renew often in the day the remembrance of that which passed in our Meditation.

---

[34] company, social relations.

What is to be done after Meditation §3

Having ended our Prayer, we may either sitting, standing, or walking examine the preparation to our Meditation, the conceyving the presence of God, the making our Preparative praier, and *Preludiums*, the exercise of our memory, understanding, will, imagination, and appetits,[35] and the whole progresse of our meditation, with our speach at the end, that so finding our meditation to have succeeded well, we may proceed in like manner afterwardes, if ill, we may seeke out the faultes and amend them.

2. We may examine the distractions we have suffered, and the remedies we have used to reclaime our selves, which is best done, by settling our attention a new to the matter we have in hand, so soone as we perceive the distraction, or by humbling our selves before God, with reprehension of our negligence, or by calling for help against the violence we endure.

3. We may examine the consolations we have felt, seeking the occasions of them, and thanking God for them. These consolations consist in internall light of Gods grace, wherby we know somthing a new belonging to our salvation, or perfections, or els apprehend more clearly and fully such things already knowen. They consist also in certaine inward motions, which incline us to love nothing but for the love of God. In teares also springing from love, or griefe, or any other cause belonging to the honour and glorie of God. In the increase of faith, hope, and charitie, and in joyfull comfort which kindles in us the desire of perfection.

4. We may examine the desolations if we have had any, searching out their causes, beeing sorrowfull for the fault which we may have committed with purpose of amendment. Under the name of desolations are comprehended that which spreades it selfe like a veile before the eies of our soule, hindring us from the thinges appertayning to the glory of God, and our owne perfections; That which troubles and provokes as to seeke for earthly and externall thinges: That which breedes in us distrust of obtaining perfection, of praying well,

[35] here, spiritual appetites, desires, "affections."

knowing the will of God, and of perseverance in any good course begon: That which weakens hope, obscures fayth, and cooles charity. That, which bringes our soule to spirituall coldnes, slacknes, heavines, and wearines.

5. We may consider whether we have had aboundance of matter for our discourse or scarcity, endeavoring to find the causes of both, proposing amendment of the faultes therin committed. We may examine what affections we have felt, considering how they have beene stirred up, how longe, and in what manner they have endured, that we may use the like good meanes another tyme, and avoid all defects we may have fallen into. We may also examine what, and how many good purposes we have made, from whence they have proceeded, how stedfast and effectuall they have byn, renewing them againe with new fervour.

6. We may note in some little booke those thinges which have passed in our Meditation, or some part of them, if we think them worth the paynes, and thanke Almighty God for the performance thereof, procuring so to live, as we have learned them of his divine Wisdome.

THE
PRACTICAL
Methode of Application of our five Senses, by way of imagination to the divine Mysteries

Having finished the practise of Meditation, which is principally performed by the operations of our Memory, Understanding, and Will, it shall be good to joyne unto it the manner of Application of our senses, by way of imagination to the same objects, which we make matter for meditation; and this the rather, for that it is a branch of meditation, and an exercise also of no small profit, and will yield us more variety to avoid tediousnes, as being a thing more easy to performe then meditation, serving for those who either want skill or ability to performe the other.

The preparation to the application of our Senses §1

Besides the things set downe in the former practice, which after their manner must be used also in this, if we have ability and knowledge, the best preparation will be to meditate according unto the directions given upon the same matter that we meane to apply our senses unto; but for defect of either, we must read or heare attentively once, or oftener the matter, observing the number and quality of persons, wordes, and workes, and other objects of our senses, that so we may be fully possessed of them all.

2. It will be expedient also to recollect our selves, for the space of a quarter of an houre, or not much lesse before we begin, in such sort, that our senses be not distracted, nor imployed (but upon necessity) in any other object, so to be more ready and prepared to admit the matter that shall be proposed unto them.

3. In this same tyme also we may procure to stirre up in our soules some affections answerable unto our matter, as we advised in our former practice, as desire, love, joy, sorrow, and the like, considering also whither we are to go, what to do, and with whom to speake.

The actuall application of our Senses §2

Those thinges set downe in our former practise, to be done before the consideration of the points, are heere also to be used; where we must note, that being to apply our senses to two or more mysteries at once (which is often used) it will be best to joyne the *Preludiums* togeather, as to make of two histories one continued, so likewise of two compositions of places we must make one by imagining our selves successively present to them both, accompayning the persons from one place to another, as also to put two petitions into one, and ask both things in one praier.

[511]

2. The exercise of this application is, to propose the object of some one sense, as of the sight (which is commonly first begon withall[36]) as though we truly saw it: then to make theron a briefe discourse, collecting thence some spirituall conceipts, with the motion of our wills; as beholding our Blessed Saviour on the Crosse, having seene him with our imagination fastned with nailes, crowned with thornes, and clothed with woundes, we may say thus with our understanding: It was in my Saviours hands to suffer this for my sake or not, and none indures paine for another but he loves him excessively; he therfore induring these grievous paines for me, hath testifyed his aboundant charity, with the most certaine proofe of suffering for my sake. What do I then? how do I repay this infinit love of my deare Lord? Why love I not him above all? why serve I not him faythfully, by fulfilling his commandements? why indure I not patiently the Crosses he sends me etc.? we may then strengthen our affections with good purposes and resolutions, in this manner: I will therefore seeke by all meanes possible to love so loving a Lord: I will imploy my selfe wholly in his service, and undertake the hardest difficulties for his sake, and most willingly be nayled with him to the crosse, nor will I by offending him againe make his paynes more grievous: so descending to more particuler affections and purposes, as we shall find our conscience to have need. And having thus viewed one object, we may imbrace another, until we have passed over them all, making thereon the like discourses, with the motion of our affection, to which end we may make use of the wayes set downe in our former practice.

3. To have sufficiency of mater in this application of Senses, it will be needfull to know the principall objects of ech Sense.

4. The sight behoulds colour, light, figure, quantitie, number, motion, rest, distance, situation or position, and such other qualities.

5. The hearing perceives the voice, sighes, grones, laughter, noise, sound, number, motion and the rest.

6. Objects of the tast are meates, and drinkes, and the diversity therof.

7. The Sense of smelling is imployed about smells, and distinguisheth their quantity, quality, number and diversity.

[36] with.

8. The touching is exercised upon bodies, perceiving their quantity, quality, waight, figure, number, motion, rest, distance, situation.

9. Some of these material objects of our senses are sometimes not to be found in mysteries we meditate upon, especially the object of tasting and smelling; we may then apply our senses figuratively upon spirituall objects, with a certaine proportion and relation to corporall. As if we would exercise our Senses upon the speach of our Saviour, we may imagine our selves to see the words of Christ proceeding out of his divine mouth, like a beame of light, reaching unto the eares and very harts of the auditors, to heare their heavenly sound, which no sooner toucheth the hearers harts, but finding them stony or harde, doth mollify and devide them.

10. We need not in this application bind our selves to so strict an order as to begin with the sight, or any other of the senses, and so to apply that first to al the objects therof, but we may begin where we please, and where the objects are most apparent: and if one object may be apprehended by divers senses, it shall be well to apply it to them all, and then afterward make one short discourse theron, for so shall we find our understanding better satisfied, and our affection more forceably moved.

11. We may also apprehend not only those things which are expressed in the mystery we have in hand, but also those which may occur, according to the fit decency of the history.

12. Having ended this exercise, we may make one or more *Coloquiums,* according to the disposition of our affection, even as we make them at the end of our meditation, which we shall doe the better if we maintaine or renew some of those lively imaginations, in which we found most spirituall comfort.

What we ought to do after the application of our Senses §3

We must do all those things which are set downe in our former practice, to be done after meditation, so far forth as they appertaine to this exercise.

2. We may examine in particuler how we have apprehended the objects of the senses with our imagination, whether with ease or

difficulty, with right, or wrong, cleare or doubtfull apprehensions, as we said before of Meditation, purposing to avoid afterwardes that which hath proved ill, and to continue that which hath succeeded well.

NOTE

EDWARD DAWSON was born in London in 1576 or 1578. After a period of study in Spain, he returned to England as a missionary priest, but was exiled from the country in 1606. He entered the Jesuit order at Louvain in 1606 or 1609, returned to England, but was recalled after some years to the Low Countries, where he died about 1624.

Dawson's treatise on meditation was prefixed to a translation made by the Jesuit Richard Gibbons: *An Abridgment of Meditations of the Life, Passion, Death, and Resurrection of our Lord and Saviour Iesus Christ. Written in Italian by the R. Father Vincentius Bruno of the Society of Iesus,* St. Omer, 1614. The treatise is reproduced from this, which appears to have been its only publication.

INDEX

Authors' names are printed in small capitals, titles of poems in italics, and first lines of poems in Roman.